THE WORK, WEALTH
AND HAPPINESS OF MANKIND

THE CONQUEST OF TOIL

THIS single colossal unit machines all the castings for an automobile frame. Its solitary attendant is no Robot: he is its watchful, intelligent controller. But with it he does work that would formerly have demanded the toil and attention of a great multitude of skilled men.

THE WORK,
WEALTH AND HAPPINESS
OF MANKIND

BY
H. G. WELLS

VOLUME I

ILLUSTRATED

GREENWOOD PRESS, PUBLISHERS
NEW YORK   1968

First Greenwood reprinting, 1968

LIBRARY OF CONGRESS catalogue card number: 69-10170

Printed in the United States of America

CONTENTS

VOLUME I

VOLUME II

CHAPTER THE TENTH. The Rich, the Poor,
and Their Traditional Antagonism

HALFTONE ILLUSTRATIONS

VOLUME I

Halftone Illustrations

LIST OF CHARTS

A NOTE ON THE ILLUSTRATIONS. Pictorial diagrams have been added at certain places in this book where the presence of some sort of visualized statistics seemed desirable. For the most part they have been based on data supplied by United States government bureaus; in certain cases they have come from other sources.

To the Bibliographische Institut of Leipzig thanks are due for permission to borrow a number of symbols used in their published charts.

INTRODUCTION

THE OBJECT OF THIS WORK AND THE WAY IN WHICH IT HAS BEEN WRITTEN

INTRODUCTION

THE OBJECT OF THIS WORK AND THE WAY IN WHICH IT HAS BEEN WRITTEN

§ 1. *An Account of Human Activities throughout the World and of the Reasons for These Activities*

THIS book is intended to be a picture of all mankind to-day, a picture of living mankind active, working, spending, making and destroying. There are, we are told, one thousand nine hundred million human beings more or less. They all breathe, eat and sleep, and they are otherwise engaged in the most various activities. They coöperate with one another, and they are in conflict with one another. They die, but continually more are born to take up and extend the activities the dead have relinquished. We seek here to give all the activities in one crowded picture. And further, as our show goes on, we shall put and seek an answer to certain questions that arise naturally out of this spectacle. What sustains all this world-wide activity? Why do these millions live as they do? What are the various manners of living, and what are the motives that lie beneath these various manners of living? That is what we have to display and attempt to elucidate. The "How" is first to be shown and then the "Why?" has to be answered.

Such a general picture of all mankind about its business has not been attempted before. It would have been impossible before the present time, and had it been possible it would have been of doubtful utility. Now it has become possible, and it has been attempted because it is needed. Never before has there been this need and desire to "get the hang" of the world as one whole. Quite suddenly it has come upon us.

3

There have been some very great changes in the circumstances of human life during the past hundred years or so. If in the past anyone had made a survey of all human activities, he would certainly have treated his subject as a huge work upon Geography. He would have described human life country by country, and illustrated and explained their differences and the differences of race and custom. But to-day that is not at all the best method. It is not the best method because of the increased and increasing ease with which communications can now be made between man and man, so that, while in the past men lived in a mosaic of little communities, each almost completely independent of the others, each with its own little but sufficient histories and its general ideas and its moralities, now we are in more and more effective relationship with all the other people in the world, and such mosaic pictures of thought and knowledge suffice no more.

Geography has become something different from what it was. Now we get news of those once inaccessible peoples hourly, and we trade with them, we cannot now dispense with that trade, we can serve and injure them to an extent that would have seemed fantastic in the days of King George the Third. Goldsmith once wrote of the remoteness of China and said that if a Chinaman was killed every time a gun was fired in France or England no one would hear of it nor care in the least if he did. Nowadays we should hear quite a lot about it. And as a consequence of this "abolition of distance" almost all our political and administrative boundaries, the "layout" of the human population, have become, we begin to realize, misfits. Our ways of doing business, dealing with property, employing other people, and working ourselves have undergone all sorts of deformation because of this "change of scale" in human affairs. They are being altered under our eyes, and it behoves us to the very best of our ability to understand the alterations in progress.

Suppose, to borrow an idea from Mr. Bernard Shaw, some young man or young woman, instead of being born in the usual fashion, were to be hatched out of an egg at the age of twenty, alertly intelligent but unformed and uninformed. He or she would blink at our busy world and demand, "What are they all up to? Why are some so active and some so inactive? Why are some toiling so industriously to produce things and some, it seems, doing nothing but consume? Why is this? What is going on?"

This book would be our answer.

§ 2. *The New Education*

The new revolution in human affairs, this modern "Change of Scale" has happened very swiftly, and it has crept upon us one day after another so insensibly that it is only now we are beginning to realize the nature of the thing that has happened to us. The World War of 1914–18 was for great numbers of people the first revelation of how closely states and empires were being pressed together, and how impossible it was now to prevent the concussions of a conflict from affecting every state and person in the world. Indians starved in Labrador because the Paris fur trade was disorganized; they could sell nothing, so that they could not buy sufficient ammunition to kill their food.

It is only now after the World War that people have begun any serious and sustained attempts to grasp the new state of affairs and to break away from the old traditions that had, under modern conditions, brought them so close to disaster and which still keep them in manifest danger of perhaps even greater catastrophe. It has taken a dozen years for the full necessity for such a break-away to be realized by any considerable number of people. But under the continuance of international stresses and social discomfort that number is growing. There is an increasing desire to part from the old limited interpretations that once were serviceable and that now guide us more and more unsatisfactorily, and to look at life plainly in the new, more formidable aspects it now presents.

First here and then there the idea was repeated that for a new time there was needed a new education. You could not run a world reborn, it was suggested, with the senescent ideas of a world that had passed away. This new education was to be not so much a resort to new methods as the continuation of the old methods with a new content. The educational progress of the pre-war period, so far as ways of teaching went, had been very considerable, and it might well be trusted to continue. But there was a growing dissatisfaction with what was taught, with the "educand,"* with the system of ideas about life in general, the *ideology* (to use the word as it is now used by thinkers of the Left) built up in our schools. That no longer corresponded with realities. Reform was attempted in the schools, but schools, it was soon realized, can be reformed only very slowly and only with the assent and stimulus of outside opinion. So that it was inevitable that at first this world-wide movement towards a new ideology, a new way, that is, of looking at ourselves and the world about us, should be most evident and vigorous among those who had left school, among intelligent adolescents and adults, consciously anxious to adjust themselves to the alterations in the world about them.

The first distinctive movement for a new education took the form of the New History movement. History was the subject most obviously in need of revision. The New History was a revolt against local, national, and "period" history. It was an assertion that the history of mankind is a single whole and can only be comprehended as a whole, that we must have a just conception of human origins and the general development of human life before we can form any proper picture of the place of our own nation or city or village in the world, or make any proper plans for our political conduct.

It is for the specialist student to say how this New History movement originated and who were its pioneer exponents. Long ago Lord Acton was saying such things to historians as, for example: "It is our function to keep in view and to command the movement of ideas, which are not the effect but the cause of public events." That is precisely where we stand. The advocates of the New History tell the story of man as a whole, because they want to see political institutions advancing towards world unity, and because that advance is only possible upon a

*Maxwell Garnett: *Education and Citizenship.*

ground of minds prepared for it, expectant of it, and understanding its necessity.

But the conception of a new education has proved to be an expanding one. It involves, we discover, something more than the understanding of history as one process. History reaches back to pre-history, and that passes insensibly into palæontology. The new education also involves, therefore, the assimilation of certain broad biological ideas that have been making their way slowly but surely from the laboratory and specialized biological course, towards the general instruction of the young and the guidance of mankind. And biology also illuminates the nature and working of mind, out of which spring the guiding ideas of History. We live in a world very badly informed of the many pregnant things biology has made manifest. A second factor in the new education is Modern Biology.

The content of a third portion of the new education is still in a far less developed state than either its history or its biology. It is far less developed and far more urgently necessary amidst the perplexities, pressures and conflicts of our time. That is a general conception of economic life, of industrial processes, trade and finance. It is to assist in bringing out this most underdeveloped side of a modern ideology, that this present work is produced. It is intended to sketch out the missing third side, the economic side, of the ideological triangle.

We have remarked that this attempt to build up a modern ideology is going on at present chiefly in the minds of adolescents and adults outside the ordinary educational organizations. No doubt there are many teachers and schools already astir with the new ideas, but they are exceptional teachers and schools. The present state of affairs is a queer and paradoxical one. People leave school and then for the first time hear properly of the new history and of the leading ideas of modern biology which are essential to a modern ideology. They learn for the first time of socialism and of communism, of monetary and financial questions, of tariff issues, and of all the vast tangle of property and business. All this has been kept from them. They have had hardly an inkling of these things at school. And yet such things are the very substance of the lives these people must live. They do what they can to supply the deficiencies they discover in their school teaching and to correct its manifestly antiquated and reactionary influence upon them. Meanwhile the schools are taking the children of these people as they come along and very actively *putting them back among the old ideas.*

For example, while the adult world is learning painfully but steadily that aggressive nationalism is a disastrous obsession, a vast majority of our children are still being made into just as ardent little patriots as we were made before the war. They are even drilled, put under military discipline, made to wave flags and sing militant songs, and are given history teaching of a combative, romantic and narrowing type. This is no doubt a temporary state of affairs. As the modern ideology of the intelligent adult becomes more lucid, assured and complete, he will discriminate with increasing confidence and effect against the traditional teacher in favour of the enlightened one who certainly exists beside his reactionary confrère. One may easily become unjustly impatient with the school teacher. The school teacher cannot outrun public opinion. If he does so, he loses his job, and there is an end to the matter. The first battles for the New Education of our new world must be fought in the adult mind.

§ 3. *Apropos of Roger Bacon*

This present revolt against established teaching and traditional ways of living and managing human affairs is not unprecedented. Again and again individuals or clear-minded groups have set themselves to change the *ideology* of the world about them. The first and perhaps the supremely important effort for a new view of life and a new way of thinking came in the great days of the Academy of Athens, and there was another struggle for a new method at the end of the scholastic controversies in the period of the Renascence and the New Learning, when experimental science dawned upon the world. A third phase was the organization of modern ideas by the French Encyclopédistes.

Upon these major movements of the human mind, these real new phases of human thought, we shall have more to say in our second and fifteenth chapters. But there is one isolated figure in history which must always be very sympathetic to those who are working on the reconstruction of contemporary ideology, the figure of Roger Bacon in the thirteenth century. He, however, does not mark a turning point in human ideas. He failed. The turning was to come later. But he was a pioneer who foretold the modern world, and he gave very clear indications of how mankind could achieve most of the things that have since been achieved. He was the first of the moderns, seven centuries ahead of his time.

He met with great opposition. He spent his declining years in prison, deprived of writing material. To the end, in spite of his suppression, he remained an obedient son of the Church. His dominant idea was to liberalize the teaching of the Church, and he imagined a Pope leading Christendom to exploration and research, power and abundance. He foresaw the modern world in substance even if he saw it still papal in form, but he did not see the centuries of waste and bickering, the endless petty wars, the schisms in the Church and the intricate mischief of princes, the great pestilences, the social disorder, that intervened. He had not taken the measure of mankind.

He was by no means a serene and superior person. He scribbled, he scolded, he was tiresome and almost entirely futile. Everybody about him was too brisk, active, able, and preoccupied with immediate things even to attend properly to a vision that to him was as plain as day. They found no sense in it. Two centuries of the liveliest history followed his death; it was the age of codpiece and crucifix, torture chambers and oubliettes, Plantagenet ambitions and the Wars of the Roses, peasant revolts and frequent famines, a romantic rather than a happy age, until at last successive epidemics of filth disease swept away half the population of Europe, and skulls became a leading theme in decorative art. When at the close of the sixteenth century Francis Bacon revived the vision of science, the Catholic Church was already entering upon its present defensive phase, and crabbed and scattered manuscripts that nearly everyone had forgotten were all that remained of the hopes of Roger Bacon.

His name remained indeed, but it remained as the name of a legendary magician.

Industrious biographers, loyal to their subject, have sought to trace a certain continuity between his ideas and those of Gilbert, the friend and instructor of Francis Bacon, and it has been shown that Columbus, unaware of his existence, quotes him at second hand as one of his inspirations. But if Roger Bacon started anything at all, he started very little. It is doubtful if Clement IV, who asked him to write, ever found time to read him. He had interested Clement before the latter became Pope. Then came his one gleam of opportunity. Would he set out his ideas for his friend to consider? In great haste Bacon poured them out in an *Opus Majus* and sent that with an *Opus Minus,* already done, and some other works. Perhaps Clement never saw these manuscripts. Probably nobody ever read more than scraps of them until the tenacious modern student came hardened to the job. There is no hint in Bacon's story of ally, colleague, or disciple. No band gathered about him. He passed, and the stream of events closed over him.

Yet what he had to say seems to us now the plainest common sense in the world. He wanted the frowsty, pretentious Latin teachers of his time to burn their atrocious translations, abandon their narrow and tedious methods, learn Greek and try to understand what Aristotle really had to say, explore the scientific treasures available in Arabic, turn from books to observation, and make experiments to check their dogmas. Vision and power would reward them. Steamship, aëroplane, and automobile: he saw them all, and many other things.

He could not say it plainly and loudly enough. He had none of that quality which lays hold of wilful men and marshals them to coöperation. He saw opportunity passing, within arm's length, as it seemed, and he lacked the power or the subtlety,—or was it the luck?—to rouse any living contemporary to the quality of that opportunity. Not for two more centuries was mankind even to finger the magic skirts of scientific knowledge—that most indifferent of benefactors, that most bountiful of givers.

It is perhaps because of his bickering uphill struggle, his desperate impatience, and his endearing weaknesses that Roger Bacon appeals now so strongly to those who are battling and toiling to-day in the same old struggle against the conservatism of educational institutions and the lag in progressive development that ensues. At first all educational reform is uphill. That is unavoidable. And all reformers are disposed to self-pity and moods of despair. They know no better. We still fight the enemies that he fought, but with a better hope. We still fight as he put it, "Undue Regard for Authority, Routine, Popular Prejudice and a False Conceit of our own Wisdom." A False Conceit, that is, when we should still be learning. The old tradition necessarily has all the prestige in such conflicts; it has the advantages of the defensive; it sits fortified in the high places and in the habitual assent of men. The reformers are often men no better than, or even of inferior quality to, the established men they attack. To be inspired by an intensive realization of a need does not make one the all-round superior of one's uninspired antagonist. And by the standards of the old education, anyhow, by the accepted standards, that is, it is inevitable that the reformers should appear to be defective, uneducated, minor and presumptuous men. Roger Bacon had the appearance and many of the defects of a presumptuous man. And no doubt to-day many of us who work for the new education have an air of presumptuous arrogance that is far from our real measure of ourselves. David and Jack the Giant Killer must have been in a sense presumptuous men. Even Adam displayed a certain arrogance when he accepted the task of replenishing the earth and inaugurating a world new-made.

The analogy between Roger Bacon and those who are working to-day for a new education must not be carried too far. For Roger Bacon there was no supporter in the world except one short-lived Pope. For the new educationist now an immense support is possible, for he can appeal over the heads of established authority to the Sane Man throughout the wide world.

Roger Bacon was living in an age of authority, and we are living in a democratic age.

We who are concerned with the development of the new education have had to learn many things, and particularly we have had to realize that we possess this power of appeal from the scholastic authority to the general public. At first we were too much disposed to follow Roger Bacon and make a direct attack upon the school and university curricula. We were disposed to harass overworked and hampered teachers because they did not instantly turn their faces towards the new dawn. We waited upon education ministers and education departments and were officially rebuffed. When we could see a thing so plainly, it was difficult for us to realize that it might not be at all apparent yet to these other busier and more closely occupied people. And because of the resistances we encountered some of us were inclined to find ourselves new Roger Bacons, crying prematurely and ineffectively of the possibilities of a better world against an obdurate obscurantism, and so lapse into a self-righteous indolence. We did not realize that now it is through adult education by means of the book that the final definitive revolution of the educational organization must be brought about.

§ 4. *The Outline of History and the Science of Life*

The writer's *Outline of History* affords an excellent instance of the way in which the intelligent adult reader can be brought in now to correct the bias of scholastic usage. Although it has had an immense popular sale, that book was not planned nor written for a popular sale. It was conceived as a school book.

It was the outcome of the writer's experiences in his war propaganda work and in the foundation of the British League of Nations Union. These experiences convinced him that the idea of the League of Nations might be anything or nothing, according to the historical prepossessions of the particular person concerned, and that there could be no effective reorganization of human political affairs until the conception of human solidarity was far more firmly established in men's minds than it is at the present time. He came to apprehend the entire dependence of the political reactions of men upon the picture of history that existed in their minds. He realized that these pictures varied extraordinarily from class to class and still more so from country to country. Nearly all history teaching hitherto had been partial and partisan, and consequently men came to the peace discussions of the time with the best natural intentions and (all unawares of their state) with the most perverted ideas. For the new time there was needed a new teaching of history, the history of man's rise and achievement as one story; history could be treated no longer as a national rather than a universal subject, and it was necessary, if the efforts to reorganize the world at the end of the war were to have any permanent effect, that they should be erected on a common foundation of universal history.

In this belief the writer was not alone. Nor was he in any sense a pioneer. He takes his own experience because it is the handiest experience, because he knows it best, because indolence and egotism dispose him to do so. But in America, even before the war, under the influence of such writers as Breasted and Robinson the teaching of history as one whole was already under way. There has been now for some years an increasingly important New History movement in America. There was no particular originality therefore in the writer's insistence upon the urgent need of this important educational adjustment, and it was only after he had made various appeals to other historians and teachers that he set about writing the *Outline of History* as a proof that the subject could be brought within the compass of a college course, and as a demonstration of the method of treatment which would make it most valuable as an ideological basis for the new time.

No one could have been more astonished than he was at the great popular success of the *Outline*. He went to bed, so to speak, educational reformer and he woke up best seller. He discovered —and it was as great a discovery for his publishers as for himself—that there existed an immense reading public in the world which was profoundly dissatisfied with the history it had learnt at school, and which was eager for just what the *Outline* promised to be, a readable, explicit summary of the human adventure. The book sold and continues to sell enormously—on that promise. Not only does it sell, but several other excellent popular general histories, Van Loon's, for example, have appeared beside it. It has been translated into most civilized languages. Altogether, in all its editions and translations it has found more than two million purchasers, and its sale is still going on. In 1930, for instance, a dollar reprint of an old edition ran to a sale of 450,000 copies in the United States. The writer has at least an average share of egotism and vanity, but nothing will convince him that this immense success is due to any extraordinary merit in the writing of the book. It is a book done in a humdrum fashion, which derives any largeness and splendour it has entirely from its subjects. But it was for a while the only thing that even promised to satisfy the urgent need of intelligent people everywhere for a new and wider view of the human adventure, for a new and wider view made sufficiently clear and accessible for the time and attention they could afford to give it.

Now the discovery of the vast new public by the *Outline of History* was a very astonishing and important thing for all of us who were feeling our way towards a new education and the establishment of a new ideology. Throughout the world there existed this immense multitude of alert and hungry minds, ready for and seeking a wider and more serviceable vision of the past that has made the present, than the schools had given them. Instead of boring away in an uphill struggle for the schools, we could appeal directly to this great adolescent and adult stratum of ordinary intelligent people, and afterwards, with that immense support, turn to the reformation of the schools.

A vision of history as one whole is, as we have already remarked, only one part of a modern system of ideas, and it was natural, therefore, after the encouragement of this first success, to think of supplying the two other main factors for a complete modern ideology. These two other factors, as we have already put it, are biology and economics. The *Outline of History* gives the story of man's origin, his races, his tribes, communities, cities, states and empires, his wars and migrations, the development of his arts and implements, and the series of events that have brought him to his present situation. But on the one hand some account of what is known of the nature and possibilities of life,—what this thing Life is and how it works,—and on the other, some explanation of the toil and motives that bind mankind together in an uneasy unity, are needed to round off the view of existence to which a modern man must adjust himself.

The success of the *Outline of History* had given the writer a peculiar advantage for the launching of these two other needed Outlines, and so he set himself to the problem of their production. Circumstances had given him the opportunity to get this work done in a fashion, and once it has been done in any fashion, it is made easier for abler men with ampler organization and resources to do it over again more lucidly and thoroughly. The reader must not suppose that the producers of the pioneer modern ideology of which this is the third part, have any illusions about the quality and permanence of their work. The *Outline of History* must serve until a better outline replaces it, and so must the outline of Biology and the outline of Economics we are now introducing. As soon as they can be replaced by fuller and more lucid versions of what they have to tell, their usefulness will cease.

The first of these two to be made was the outline of Biology. For reasons we need not dwell upon here it was thought better to call this second work the *Science of Life*. The writer's early training had been biological, and he has always retained a lively interest in biological thought, but the mass of knowledge that has been accumulated since his student days rendered it necessary to call in competent assistance. He found it close at hand in the persons of his friend Professor Julian Huxley, grandson of his own biological teacher, and his own son, G. P. Wells. They produced a résumé of contemporary knowledge in this field, which gives the general reader the sum of what is known about his body and his mind, discusses the origin and evolution of life, surveys all the multifarious spectacle of living things on land and in the sea, brings together all the main trends of psychological thought and culminates in a special study of the very peculiar and exceptional biology of mankind. The publication of the *Science of Life* crowned the labours of two years and more of hard collaboration, and then it was possible to take up the last and most difficult enterprise of all, this outline of Economics, this popular account of the business and toil, the give and take of our strange and unprecedented species.

It has been so perplexing and heavy a task that it is necessary to make clear to the reader the broad facts about the difficulties encountered and give the reason for the form in which, after several false starts, abandonments, and renewed attacks, the work has now been cast. The reader has to be taken into the writer's confidence to that extent. Two convenient conventions, namely an imaginary encyclopædia and a museum of reference, have been adopted, and without them it is difficult to say how this outline of human activities could be exhibited at all. Behind the *Science of Life* there existed actual museums, textbooks, encyclopædias and the like, for the collaborators to summarize. Behind the present outline of economic science there exist indeed certain museums of which we shall tell more fully later, dealing very interestingly with one or other aspect of our many-sided subject, and a vast undigested mass of fact and material, not yet gathered into any ordered arrangement available for summarization. These things are coming into existence, but they are not yet fully here, and so we have had, as it were, to anticipate them and manage as well as possible as if they were already in being.

§ 5. *The Urgent Need for Sound Common Ideas about Work and Wealth*

Of these three systems of knowledge and realization which must make up a modern ideology, the third, in order as we have taken them, is not only the most elusive and difficult to assemble, but the most urgently necessary at the present time. Since the Great War the economic stresses of the world have become more and more painful and distressing. By comparison preceding ages are beginning to assume an air of the most idyllic tranquillity. We are coming to believe that before our time the ordinary human life passed in a peaceful, unchanging security from the cradle to the grave. It might be limited, it might be oppressed, but it was sure. The peasant child learnt to scare crows and plough and so forth, and grew up and ploughed and ploughed his patch to the end of his days. The townsman had his trade or his little shop, and it kept him, and he left it in due course to his son. The lawyer, the doctor went about his business; the woman of the gentler sort was loved and married and lived happily ever afterwards in a round of household duties. The seasons brought the harvest and the hunting, Yuletide, May Day, and the happy summer weather.

In truth things were never like that, but multitudes of people thought they were. The wheel of life seemed to them to be turning in orderly fashion from age to age, they did as their fathers had done before them, life was an even flow of small but sufficient events. Over the hills and far away was adventure, perhaps, but it did not threaten them. Young men went off and returned no longer young, with parrots and lacquer boxes and suchlike objects to witness to other worlds of taste and work, unlike but as stable, it seemed, as our own.

And that life was understandable. The way in which its few and simple parts joined together was plain. It was at hand. One saw every stage from the sowing of the seed to the baking of the bread, from the gathering of the wool to the making of the garment. One saw master and man, and if there arose any doubts about the explanation of the world, the priest at the altar had a wonderful way of dispelling them.

But now we all begin to realize we are living in the break-up of whatever system existed before our time, and that in a great disorder a new system may be coming into being. All sorts of forces are at work disorganizing us now but with a tantalizing air of producing some larger strange organization to which we must adapt our lives. We work, and the things we make are taken away and we see no more of them. Our streets are full of strangers who pass and give way to other strangers. Great factories arise in our familiar landscape, and we do not understand why they have arisen or what they produce. We buy and consume exotic foods. We are employed, we are thrown out of employment, things become dear, or cheap, or inaccessible and we cannot trace the causes of these fluctuations.

It seems all beyond our control. We cannot find out who controls it. Is anyone controlling it? The newspapers tell us this or that about it. They are disturbing and alarming. Vast multitudes, we learn, millions are being thrust out of employment. There is plenty, locked up. There are dire want and misery. Then we find ourselves called upon to decide between politicians who demand that this shall be done and politicians who demand that that shall be done. It appears that we in our muddled multitudinousness are being called upon to make decisions. This immense tangled affair, we gather, is our affair. In various rather obscure ways we have been made responsible for it. We have to vote.

But how can we vote when we do not get the hang of it? Has anyone got the hang of it? Are there any people anywhere in our world to-day who have a really comprehensive vision of the economic world process as one whole? Apparently not. And yet we ordinary people have it thrust upon us, that whatever control can be exercised over this immense complex tumult of world change, must be exercised through our voting and our assent.

When the present author wrote his *Outline of History* he was writing down and doing as exactly as he could for other people what in any case he had to do for himself, to get all the phases of history into one story and in their proper relation to one another, so that he could understand the international problems that unfolded after the war. And now again in this work he is making a practically parallel effort. He is doing it not only for the sake of the reader, but for his own sake. He is trying to assemble and select out of the infinitude of facts in the world about him the cardinal and significant facts that will make the whole mass of working, producing and consuming, one understandable spectacle. He is attempting a book, a survey of the world, a scheme and map of *doing,* which will enable him to say to anyone whatever: "This is the whole world of work and wealth, of making and getting and spending, and here at this point is your place, and this is where you come in. The map is not a very large-scale map, and consequently you and your sphere of activity may not loom very large, but here and not elsewhere is where you are. And so far as can be ascertained the reason why you are at this point and why you do this or that and want to do so and so is as follows. . . . And further there are reasons here given why you should act in a certain fashion and what certain things are justifiable for you and what certain others are not. This world of making and fetching and carrying and buying and selling to which you give the greater part of your waking life is ruled by certain laws, obsessed by certain defects (which perhaps you may help to cure) and threatened by certain dangers you may help to avert. In fact, I am attempting to make for myself and you a complete chart of economic life, not simply to help you to steer yourself through the confusion, but also to supply a common ground upon which we two can coöperate in this great experiment of life; this adventure of mankind.

"Just so far as this attempt is successful, then so far, instead of our present feeling of helplessness against the waves of want and loss and of elation and prosperity that sweep over our lives and the lives of those about us, we may presently find ourselves with ideas in common, with convictions in common, and with a workable plan of campaign for the stabilization and betterment of this strange eventful world."

§ 6. Some Difficulties and Problems in the Writing of This Book. Museums of Industrial Progress. The Device of an Imaginary Encyclopædia

And now let us give the reader some account of the very great difficulties that have been discovered and circumvented in getting this work into shape.

The *Outline of History* was written by a single author who took his work to specialists for verification or correction; it was largely a summary of predigested material. But the *Science of Life* was done in a different fashion; there was an immense body of very technical science in existence, and the work was best done in collaboration with two able experts. The writer's first conception of this third book was as a collaboration also. He thought he would call it the *Conquest of Power*. It seemed to him that it would be possible to treat all the spectacle of to-day as being, in its essence, mankind escaping from toil through the development of power machinery. The work was to tell of the development of invention and science, and then it was to trace the transformation of everyday life, the spreading change in the forms and fashions and methods of everyday life, through this change in the economic basis. Two well informed collaborators were to gather the bulk of the material and assist in the synthesis.

It seemed laborious but possible in these terms. It was only after the project was launched and the first instalment of "material" came to hand that the profound difference in conditions of this enterprise from its predecessor became apparent. It was only then that the author realized how purely customary our productive, manufacturing, credit, monetary and trading systems are. The mass of fact to be dealt with was not only far larger, but it had undergone nothing like the same sifting, scrutiny and classification as the biological material. It had hardly been approached scientifically. We know far more exactly about foraminifera and tadpoles than we do about many business operations, and we are far more in agreement how that sub-human life is to be thought about and told about. The author found himself urging his collaborators towards a dark jungle of fact in which there were no textbooks and only very incidental and limited museums. That sort of clearing, exploratory, synthetic effort was demanded, in which collaborators, advancing in triumvirate formation, might easily become an intolerable drag on the work. It would be all too easy to collect enough material to overwhelm us while leaving the larger part of the jungle unexplored. And nothing annoys a collaborator who aspires to be a colleague more than to tell him to scrap his material and either begin again or resign. Yet there was no way to avoid such masterful repression. Experiments in statement would have to be made, chapters written and torn up, methods of treatment tried out and abandoned, before the right way of doing it was discovered.

As it was surveyed in this collaboration stage the *Conquest of Power* presented itself as a continually swelling mass of fact. The job was to digest it. Because of the ease of aggregation compared with the difficulties of synthesis, any group of collaborators would be committed slowly but surely to the writing of an encyclopædia. That would take years of toil and might never reach completion.

Presently, as it became more and more plain to me that the development of the world's current economic life has much more in it than merely the introduction and consequences of power machinery, the projected title of the enterprise was altered to the *Science of Work and Wealth*. An ever growing series of industrial developments was sketched out. We should have, we thought, to tell the history of steam from Hero's engine to the latest turbine. We should have to trace the development of the metallurgy of every sort of metal. We should have to tell the full story of electrical development. There would have to be lengthy explicit accounts of the utilization of coal, plans, diagrams, photographs of old-fashioned and modern gas works, a pursuit of coal-tar products to their ultimate ramifications, a history of wild and of cultivated rubber, and—in the fullest sense of the phrase—so on and so on. Interminably. When that much was done we should have got at least a technical encyclopædia. We should have accomplished in a book what the Science Museum at South Kensington and—more explicitly and fully —its daughter the Deutsches Museum at Munich—set out to do. And it is a journey of nine miles to walk once round the galleries of the Deutsches Museum! Our enterprise was already becoming colossal and interminable.

But all that would only be the first portion of the design of the *Science of Work and Wealth* as it was opening out. For this account of materials, mines, foundries, factories, engines, machines, was only the framework of what we had to do. So far as that part went we might have sat down in the Deutsches

Museum with notebooks and cameras to turn it into a book. But there would still remain great fields of activity untouched, for which we should have to go elsewhere. The technical museum could, for example, take us as far as the "textile fabric," but to trace the textile fabric to the stylish dress via the costume designer, the milliner and the shop, opened a new and practically unexplored field. The immense activities of distribution, selling, advertisement, the fluctuations of fashion, all fell within the boundaries of our project, but for these as yet no Deutsches Museum exists. That department of anthropology has still to assemble such partial collections as have been made so far. And when it came to catering, to modern food distribution, to the new ideas that are being embodied in contemporary housing, to the hotel industry, to tourism, the material was still more hopelessly scattered, and, in any completeness, unobtainable. And still other vast areas of interest stretched beyond, the pay envelope and the counting house, the farmer's loan and the bank, the financier and the douane. At the douane were national flags and soldiers in uniform. . . . And after all that came the enquiry why all this vast multitude did what they did.

In the face of this unordered multitudinousness the projected collaboration had definitely to be broken up. Some other way had to be found to synthesize this complex spectacle. It was by no means easy to find that other way. I will not weary the reader with the details of this search, the hesitations, the ponderings and goings to and fro. The problem was to reduce this colossal project to manageable dimensions. It had grown until it had become the scheme for an encyclopædia, a whole technical literature, and there still remained vast hinterlands to explore. It had outgrown itself beyond realization. Yet nevertheless, I perceived, it retained a shape. It had not become a mere chaos of material.

Might it not be possible therefore to give merely the gist of it, the idea of it? For example, a scheme for it might be prepared, a rather detailed synopsis. This could be printed and circulated—more or less restrictedly. It would at least give the framework of essential ideas soundly and clearly. Then perhaps it would be possible to reorganize the task on the lines of a multiple collaboration. My mind still harped for a time on comprehensiveness, organization, a concentrated encyclopædism. I would not indeed produce the *Science of Work and Wealth* itself, but an infant, prepared, if the gods willed it, to grow up into the *Science of Work and Wealth*. It could be issued as, let us says, *"Work and Wealth*—A Project for a Review of the World's Economic Life."

That I may call the first phase of the reorientation of the project. Perhaps such a synopsis, I thought, would be as much as I could actually do towards the enterprise. It would be a sort of interim report upon a work in hand done in such a way that presently other hands might take it over. It would be the pencil outline for a fresco which would have all the colour, substance and detail the sketch could merely indicate. It would be possible to broach all the leading ideas and anticipate the main discussions of that contemplated work—that was the main point. It was to be a forecast—but a substantial forecast, much more than a mere agenda—of the whole thing. . . .

On that I went to work, but as the work got done, I saw more and more clearly that I was not writing a synopsis but a book. I was doing what I had been wanting to do, in a fresh, compacter and altogether more convenient fashion. What I was writing was not indeed that encyclopædic, all too vast and detailed *Science of Work and Wealth* that I had found at first so alluring and then so oppressive. But it was its essential form and ideas made all the clearer because they were not embedded in hundreds of illustrations and collaborators' detail. I changed the title. I gave it another title, the title of *The How and the Why of Work and Wealth,* to make it plain to myself that I was doing something starker and less massive than the original project. We were to deal with industry but not technology, with finance but not accounts and statistics. Motives and direction were to be the primary substance; detail was to be secondary and by way of illustration. That title was good in so far as it kept the bare aim in view, but gradually, as the work approaches completion, as it has broadened and opened out and its spectacular quality becomes plainer, this title also was felt insufficient, and it has been rechristened finally, *The Work, Wealth and Happiness of Mankind*.

The discovery of that final title was extremely difficult. It had to be descriptive, expressive, and attractive. It had to tell the reader what he was getting. It had not to promise too much or to terrify unduly. It had to present a candid attractive brow to the world, broad rather than high. Various suggestions were tried over. The footnote below is a sort of vault in which some of the condemned lie in state.* They all help to show the objective of this work. It is now neither a synopsis nor the complete encyclopædia once contemplated, but a real summary, and I hope a serviceable summary, a world display, of the present mental and material poise of our species. It can be read right through. But that projected encyclopædia would never have been read through, because it is only the broad issues that interest us all in these questions, and the technical details of engines, researches, industrial processes, mining, agriculture and so forth, except in so far as they illustrate general principles, are speedily tiresome to those not immediately concerned with them. We all find a certain pleasure in watching work in process but nearly all of us are bored if it is explained to us too fully.

That need for the limitation of detail was brought home to me very vividly by a shrewd friend I had taken to the South Kensington Science Museum. We spent an hour or so over the development of the steam engine; we went on to the story of the ship. Then we went up to the evolution of optical science. My friend began to show signs of brain fag. We went to that central place on the top floor which gives a glimpse of all the floors and galleries. "This is fascinating," said my friend, "but it isn't like reading a history or a novel. It doesn't take you on from a beginning to an end. It's a multitude of strands woven

---

*A Survey of Civilization, What Mankind Is Doing, The Human Complex, The Fabric of Society, The Fabric of Human Society, The Panorama of Mankind, The World of Work and Wealth, The World at Work, The Work and Play of Mankind, Work, Wealth and Play, The Activities of Mankind, The Human Ant-Hill, Homo Sapiens, Man in His World, Homo Contra Mundum, How Man Exists, Man Conquering and to Conquer.

together. Each one is different, but they all go the same way. I would like you to tell me now what it is all about; to take me to this exhibit or that to illustrate this point or that, but I have no use for it all. I like to know it is here. I like to know what the main divisions are. But nobody sane would want to explore all these galleries, just as nobody sane would dream of reading through an encyclopædia from beginning to end. This stuff is for reference. You tell me what it is all about—if you can."

I felt the wisdom of these remarks still more profoundly at Munich as I made my nine-mile pilgrimage through the Deutsches Museum. I would spend a profitable hour or so upon a hundred feet of exhibit and then walk on, taking the bright objects about me for granted and blessing the wisdom and industry that have assembled them. These things have to be done and made accessible, but it is no part of the new education to inflict them in mass upon everyone. What the new education has to give to everyone is a conception of the broad stream of mental growth and purpose upon which all these things are carried along. Then let everyone specialize in the section that attracts him most.

This remains an experimental book. It has all and more than the faults of the *Outline of History* because it is less of a compilation. It is slighter and even more provisional. It has little of the scientific assurances of the *Science of Life*. But its claims are enormous; let there be no mistake about that. It represents all current human activities and motives—all and nothing less. It is a first comprehensive summary of the whole of mankind working or playing or unemployed; it seeks to show the jockey on the race course in relation to the miner in the pit, the baby in the cradle, the savage in the jungle, the city clerk, the fishwife, the lord-in-waiting, the Speaker on the Woolsack, the Soviet envoy, the professional cricketer, the shopwalker, the streetwalker, the dealer in second-hand microscopes, the policeman, the newsvendor, the motor-car "bandit," the political gangster and the university professor. It will have failed of its object so far as any particular reader goes if that reader does not find his own niche clearly indicated in this descriptive fabric.

He must be able to say, "Here I am, and this is how I stand to the rest." Or at the worst he must be able to say, "Here in this lot I should find myself, if the scale were bigger." It has to establish the reader's economic citizenship, *place* his economic rights and duties. It has, among other things, to supersede the vague generalizations on which Marxism rests and concentrate and synthesize all those confused socialist and individualist theorizings of the nineteenth century which still remain as the unstable basis of our economic experiments. It has to be that much sound and thorough, or it would not have been worth doing.

In other words, this is a sincere and strenuous attempt to make economic and social science come alive and be personal. It is a book within the compass of my writing and your reading, but behind it still looms the original, the vaster conception of a huge modern encyclopædia of human skill, knowledge and relationship, the whole *Science of Work and Wealth.* That phrase I use repeatedly in what follows—to suggest a conspectus of modernized economics, the entire literature of the subject and all such studies now in progress. And radiating from our work stretch out the galleries of the South Kensington Museum and the Deutsches Museum, and beyond these, other museums and the anticipatory phantoms of galleries that do not yet exist, a museum that Henry Ford is trying to assemble under von Miller's inspiration, and other museums that as yet no one is trying to assemble; museums of advertisement, of selling and the like, museums of educational methods and apparatus. At one point I raid towards art museums, music libraries and libraries of gramophone records. For all human achievement falls into our prospectus. . . . The reader, after this explanation, will not, I hope, resent my frequent allusions to these collections assembled or still to be assembled. It is a device of very great convenience. It makes a picture that could be made in no other way.

The abandonment of the idea of a triumvirate of collaborators for this work has left the writer wholly responsible for its tone, content and general arrangement, but it has not meant an abandonment of assistance. In fact, it has rather released him to get special help from a great number of people, instead of restricting his channels of supply to two helpers. The first start had already produced a sketchy framework of the undertaking and a certain amount of more or less useful material had been assembled. Moreover, one of the original triumvirate, Mr. Edward Cressy, the well-known writer and popularizer of industrial technology, although he had felt unequal to the labour of collaboration throughout, retained a keen interest in the enterprise; his experienced hand is evident in the earlier chapters, and his advice has been helpful at a number of points. Mrs. G. R. Blanco White, who was originally consulted about certain passages connected with money and banking, upon which subjects she had written various articles and memoranda, took up the matter with so lively and understanding a response, that finally the whole plan was put in her hands and discussed with her, and she became a real collaborator upon the entire work. The special chapter on Women, though it does not by any means present her particular views, was inserted at her suggestion and has been closely argued with her; a considerable part of the material on actual labour conditions comes from her; she assembled the Congo and Putumayo histories; she collected the substance of the summaries of wealth-getting careers, the diagnosis of the current world slump is mainly hers and she has read and prepared proofs for press. Another friend who has contributed material to this book, subject of course to the freest editorial handling, is Mr. J. F. Horrabin, M. P., my collaborator-illustrator in the *Outline of History*, to whom I am indebted for particulars of legislative work as it is done in the House of Commons. It is very pleasant to have his hand in the third as well as the first part of this trilogy. To Madame Odette Keun, the novelist and descriptive writer, I am also greatly indebted. She has assembled material for me, contributed to the discussion of colonial conditions, read and re-read the entire typescript and all the proofs, and throughout she has insisted on the utmost clearness and explicitness in everything she read. Where so much matter has to be condensed there are great possibilities of fogging, and her sharp, critical mind has been of the utmost value. I do not know whether thanks are most due to her from the reader or from myself.

Outside this inner circle of people who have had, so to speak, a finger—or several fingers—in making the original manuscript, I have to thank a number of others who have, in the measure of the demands made upon them, helped me or my collaborators very generously and freely. I went to Munich to see what the Deutsches Museum could do for me, and I had some very stimulating talk with Dr. Oskar von Miller, the virtual creator of that wonderful display, and afterwards I visited Sir Henry Lyons at the South Kensington Museum and followed out the broad lines of his scheme of development. The important share these great collections have had in suggesting my method of dealing with otherwise unmanageable masses of detail, has already been explained in this Introduction, and it will be obvious throughout the entire work.

I have to thank Dr. C. S. Myers, who allowed me to see the working and intentions of his National Institute of Industrial Psychology and who put me on to the admirable Home Office Museum in Horseferry Road. I am also very grateful to Mr. E. W. Murray, who showed me over that museum and made its meaning plain to me.

Some years ago Professor Carr-Saunders visited me and discussed this project at its very beginning, and subsequently I had a very profitable talk about the general scheme with Professor Henry Clay. His *Economics for the General Reader* has been a steadying handbook in the writing of several chapters. Professor Carr-Saunders has since read the proofs of the entire work for me. His care, criticism and knowledge have been of great value. But he is not to be held responsible for the opinions expressed or the tendencies displayed. I am the only whipping-boy for this work.

Another adviser has been Mr. Graham Wallas. Years ago among the Swiss mountains we discussed Ostrogorski's fruitful studies of modern democracy, then newly published, and it has been very pleasant to link up this present work with those earlier trains of interest. Outside an all too limited circle of special workers on both sides of the Atlantic, few people realize how much contemporary thought about political and administrative matters owes to the obstinately critical and enterprising mind of Graham Wallas. To Dr. Finer of the London School of Economics my thanks are also due for helpful counsel. Dr. Finer has taken the civil services of the world as his particular field of study, and I am very fortunate to have had his aid. Mr. Eric Simons of Edgar Allen & Co. has "vetted" Mr. Cressy and myself so far as the account of the steels goes in Chapter II, and Sir Frederick Keeble and Mr. A. P. Allan have played the same generous rôle for Chapter III. Mr. R. A. Duncan has read Chapter V to its great benefit, and so has Mr. Clough Williams Ellis. My son Frank Wells has also made some useful suggestions upon this architectural section. Lord d'Abernon, Mr. Maynard Keynes and Mr. Thomas Lamont have read the typescript of Chapter IX and discussed it with me. Mr. Lamont does not in any way endorse that chapter, which he regards as Utopian, but he has made some very friendly and helpful comments on its statements. My friend Mr. Leif Jones, an "old parliamentary hand," read and discussed the account of Parliament with me. Lord Olivier read over the population and race chapter (XIII) and advised upon it, giving me in particular a very useful note on the state of affairs in Jamaica, and Lady Rhondda has read the chapter on Women and commented thereon. My daughter-in-law Mrs. G. P. Wells has looked up and checked much indispensable material and helped ably with the proofreading. And my friends Professor Harold Laski and Mr. Kingsley Martin have read the entire proofs from beginning to end, to my marked profit.

Mrs. Blanco White has received very useful help from Mr. Robert R. Hyde (of the Industrial Welfare Society), Mr. R. G. Hawtrey of the Treasury, Mr. John Hilton of the Ministry of Labour and Mr. J. F. Darling, Mr. W. Crick and Mr. Parfett of the Midland Bank. Mr. R. G. Hawtrey has read through and discussed the typescript of Chapter IX and saved me from several errors of fact and presentation. Mrs. Blanco White con-

sulted Mr. H. W. Nevinson and Mr. J. H. Harris of the Abori-
gines' Protection Society for material about Putumayo. Among
others to whom I am indebted for ideas, material, answers to
questions and permission to quote, are Sir Robert Hadfield, Sir
Josiah Stamp, Professor T. E. Gregory, Sir R. A. Gregory, Mr.
Percy Redfern, Professor Miles Walker, Mr. Cloudesley Brere-
ton, Mr. W. Clarke Hall, Professor Soddy, Mr. E. M. H.
Lloyd, M. André Gide, Mr. Raymond Fosdyck, Professor Mali-
nowsky, Sir Basil Thompson and Mrs. W. H. Thompson (Joan
Beauchamp). My debt to the new Encyclopædia Britannica is
manifest and is acknowledged at a score of points. But it is almost impossible to recall and name all the friendly and interested
people on whom I have upon occasion inflicted lengthy descriptions of this project during the various stages of its growth, and
who have given me hints, criticism, counsel and ideas. M. Henri
Barbusse, Mr. Maurice Hindus and Mr. Michael Farbman,
for example, have brought me their personal impressions of
Russia. I have found the excellent talk and published views of
Mr. Edward A. Filene particularly illuminating upon modern
distribution and the relations of the manufacturer to the retailer,
and I cannot say how much I owe in the correction and steadying
of my ideas, to the conversation of my friend Sir Arthur Salter.

In a number of footnotes the reader will find the names of
numerous books that have served me. For a couple of years I
have read very little that had not some bearing upon this task
and I have met no one with something to tell, whom I did not
try to turn to account for this work. But in view of the breadth
of the field to be covered, it is impossible not to realize that
there must be many good books I have missed and many authorities I might have consulted with advantage and did not do so.
These authors and writers must forgive my ignorance and not
suppose themselves wilfully ignored. This outline was altogether
too vast to do exhaustively at the first onset. The alternative to
doing it as it has been done was not to do it at all. And it had
to be done.

It remains a sketch, an adventure. It is, I recognize, the least
finished work of a trilogy, because it is the most novel. In the

long run a better work of the same substance must replace it. Or it may share one destiny with its two companions and be fused with them for a common purpose. A further fusion, concentration, stripping down and simplification may be ultimately attempted. At present the *Science of Life* overlaps the opening chapters of the *Outline of History;* our first chapter of this present work does the same, and the concluding sections of the *Outline of History* merge insensibly into the economic and political problems we deal with here. They are all contributory sketches to that complete but clear and concentrated Account of Life, which it behoves us to give to our children, that summary of fundamentals on which the collective energies of a new generation must be based.

Mankind is living too ignorantly and casually, and such education as exists is limited, incoherent and confused in its statement of reality. That is the chief cause of unhappiness in the world to-day, and that is the evil against which the triple effort of these books is directed.

CHAPTER THE FIRST

HOW MAN BECAME AN ECONOMIC ANIMAL

CHAPTER THE FIRST

HOW MAN BECAME AN ECONOMIC ANIMAL

§ 1. *Economics Is a Branch of Biology*

THE first thing to ask of this vast intricacy of human activities in which we live is, What as a whole is it? What is its nature? How did it arise? What do we know of its history? When and how did this world of work and wealth begin?

We must go back first to historical biology, the prelude to history. In the *Science of Life* there is a careful account of the beginnings and ascent of living things, of the dawn and primary nature of human psychological processes, of the development of man as a social animal and as a reasoning creature,—an account which culminates in a special book devoted to Human Biology. At that point this present work takes up its task. Economics, which is neither more nor less than the academic name for the science of work and wealth, is spoken of in the *Science of Life* as a branch of ecology; it is the ecology of the human species. Ecology deals with the welfare of species generally: how they hold their own in their environment, and how they depend upon and serve other species of plants and animals; how they prosper and increase or suffer and decline. It is the science of the balance of life. Economics is the science of the balance of human life and how it prospers or decays. We have to deal here, in this survey of work and wealth and happiness, with the position and prospects in space and time of practically the only economic mammal, *Homo sapiens*. That is the wide framework of our undertaking.

By economic animal we mean an animal that prepares and

stores food socially. Ants and bees are economic animals. Almost immediately we will explain how it is that man differs from all other vertebrates in being economic.

Until recently economic science and discussion have ignored biology and outraged psychology; they have dealt with a sort of standard and inalterable man; it is only now that it becomes possible to bring economic realities into line with these more fundamental sciences and treat them as evolved and evolving facts. But in no field of knowledge has there been such vigorous advance during the last quarter of a century as in the study of social origins. A vast, rapidly organizing mass of fact becomes available for educational use and for application to the economic life of mankind.

The way in which the knowledge of social origins has grown upon the minds of the intelligently curious during these past five and twenty years is a process as fascinating as the development of some long desired picture upon the plate in a photographer's dark room. There was a steady and at first almost unconscious convergence of originally very remote researches. Psychoanalysis, coming from the mental clinic by way of the study of mental stresses, dreams and childish thought, has illuminated mythology and primitive mentality very vividly; archæological discovery, the science of comparative religions, anthropological speculation and mental physiology have all been approaching the interpretation of the rapid and marvellous conversion during the brief space, astronomically speaking, of less than a million years, of a rare and rather solitary and self-centred species of primate into an economic animal with a continually developing social range and a continually increasing biological interdependence. For that is what has happened in and since the Pleistocene period. Man ceased almost suddenly to be an ordinary animal, eating its food where it found it, and he became very rapidly indeed an unprecedented species, leading an economic life resembling only quite superficially the social economic life of the ants, bees and termites. He achieved this social economic life, not as the insects did, by the development of organizing instincts, but by the interplay of motives in his cerebrum. The nature of this transition lies at the root of any sound economic study. A review of human work and wealth and happiness cannot be either sound or helpful unless it rests firmly on this fundamental biological fact.

The *Science of Life* tells the story of the evolution of the cerebral cortex in the mammals, and the way in which hand, eye and brain have educated one another, shows how a new power of abstraction and planning crept into existence with the appearance of the primates and, with a resort to vocal and visual symbols, imposed itself upon the wasteful trial-and-error methods employed by mentalities of a lower grade. And further, biology demonstrates how these symbols of sound and gesture, which appeared at first as a mere means of communication, rendered possible the immense and rapid mental organization of *Home sapiens:* immense in relation to the intelligence of any other living creatures. Man's rapid yet insensible transition from the casual feeding of all other sorts of vertebrates, to economic foresight, was the direct outcome of this mental organization. All this is explained quite clearly in the *Science of Life* or any equivalent biological summary that may exist. And thereby the way is cleared for a sound psychological approach to human economics.

Up to the beginning of the present century such an approach was impossible. Historical and economic speculation was profoundly vitiated by the tacit assumption that man in the opening phases of his social life saw things as definitely, apprehended consequences as clearly, and generally thought as we do now. Historians had still to realize that either geography, climate, or human nature could change. And among other fundamental failures of imagination in their thought, the economics of the last century carried back into the remote past the distinctions we make to-day between the religious and material interests of man. Primitive man was supposed to be mentally already a business man, driving bargains and reaping the "rewards of abstinence." Abstract thought was ascribed to him. Popular writers upon pre-history, anxious to make their subject sympathetic, have always been disposed to exaggerate the resemblances between the life of a man or woman in the late palæolithic age and the life of to-day. They made out the early savage to be a sort of city clerk camping out; they presented the men of Ur and early Egypt as if they had been the population of Pittsburgh or Paris in fancy dress. They minimized or ignored the fact that these people were not only living under widely different stimuli, but reacting to them in ways almost as much beyond our immediate understanding as the mental reactions of a cat or a bird. "Human nature," they said, "never changes." In truth, it never ceases to change.

Anyone who will spend a little time in looking over the carvings on a Maya stele or the representations of Indian gods, and who will reflect that these strange and intricate forms were made with intense effort and regarded with the utmost gravity, that evidently they conveyed meanings that were felt to be otherwise inexpressible, may get some intimations of the width and depth of the mental gulf across which we moderns, with our abstract terms, our logical processes and our prompt rejection of irrelevances and unorthodox associations, must strain to conceive the earlier thoughts of man. Dreamlike and childish is what we call these images now, and dreamlike and childish they are, but such was the quality of the mental atmosphere in which the enlarging social life of humanity began. Man began his social life dreamingly, amidst fear and fantasies, before he could talk very much. Speech and social organization grew complicated together. His fantasies still haunt our social institutions.

The exponent of the science of work and wealth has to bring out all this. The task before the workers in the field of modern economics is to use all this new work to fertilize their barren abstractions. The ideas of Frazer, of Jung, of Atkinson play upon and enrich each other. The last haunting suggestions of a "social contract," of the idea that human society was a deliberate arrangement between intelligent people like ourselves, is being cleared out of our minds by this play of thought between the mythologist and the psychologist, and the way is being opened to a proper understanding of the social mechanism.

§ 2. *Primitive Man Haphazard as an Animal*

Let us recapitulate the broad facts about human origins that have been assembled during the last half century. They are the necessary foundation for all our subsequent generalizations about social interaction.

Man was already a tool-using and fire-making creature before he became man as we know him to-day. Several species of *Homo* have existed on the earth, of which *Homo sapiens,* all mankind now living, is the sole surviving kind. And not only do we know now of other species of man, but we now know also of other genera of primates, Hominidæ also, nearer to us than any ape, and yet not men in any sense of the word: such types as *Pithecanthropus,* the man-ape of Java, and *Sinanthropus,* the ape-man of Pekin, manlike creatures below the tool-using level. There is a rapidly growing body of knowledge now about these sub-men and early men whose lives preceded humanity. One year gives us Rhodesian man; a little later comes this *Sinanthropus*—the sort of Missing Link our grandfathers demanded before they would believe in the animal origins of man. While I write someone may be actually excavating another important fragment to fit into the jig-saw picture of man's origin. Some two or three million years ago or so, there was, it is manifest, a considerable number of species of these quasi-human creatures, "ground apes," perhaps, rather than arboreal creatures, similar in many respects to their cousins, the clambering or climbing great apes, of which the gibbon, orang-outang, chimpanzee and gorilla still linger in the dwindling tropical forests of our planet. Before very long we shall be able to picture their manner of life.

Apes, these early sub-men, and man, constituting together the class of Primates, had and have certain distinctive advantages over most other great mammals. One of these advantages is the possession of exceptionally good eyes. The primates see far more clearly and exactly than the run of mammals. If they do not see so swiftly as a cat or dog, nor are so quick to detect movement, they have a far better apprehension of the form and relations of things. There is a distinctive area of precise vision on their retinas. No other mammals except the monkeys possess this area of distinct vision. And the fore limbs of all the primates had been developed by a phase of arboreal life into more and more competently prehensile organs. Hand and eye therefore worked together with the brain in a rapid mental development. All the early primates were exceptionally wary and ingenious animals, and all very ready and able to use sticks and stones for their immediate ends. A chimpanzee, as the *Science of Life* describes very clearly, will display contrivance quite beyond the range of any other mammalian type. Several of the early species of *Homo,* perhaps all the genus, seem not merely to have caught up sticks and stones for use, but to have shaped and adapted them to particular ends. The sticks have perished; the stones endure.

Many of the more recent geological deposits abound in stone, and particularly in flints, which have certainly been chipped deliberately to point and shape them. It was once supposed that these eoliths, as they are called, were the work of real human beings like ourselves, but it is more probable that they were made by one or more kindred species now extinct. The ancestry of modern man is still difficult to trace precisely. Finds will have to multiply very greatly before we can fill in our genealogy with complete assurance.

The most near and interesting of these extinct human kindred is the species of *Homo* known as the Neanderthal Man (*Homo neanderthalensis*). He differed from our own species (*Homo sapiens*) in his teeth (which were flatter and more complex, without our rather larger, and so more beastlike, canines), in his want of a chin, in his inability to turn his head back and up to the sky, in the fact that his thumb was not so exactly opposable to his forefinger, and in minor differences in his limb bones. Features of his jaw bone make it doubtful if he could use articulate speech of the human kind. The movements of his tongue may have been restricted, but then he may have resorted to gesture or other methods of symbolism. *Homo neanderthalensis* had a fairly big brain, but it was bigger behind and narrower in front than that of *Homo sapiens*. We do not know if he met and interbred with *Homo sapiens* (as dog, jackal and wolf will interbreed with each other), but we do know that he made quite well-shaped implements, buried some of his dead with their tools and ornaments beside them in caves, and used fire. His later implements show more skill than the earlier ones and come nearer to the *Homo sapiens* type of manufacture. So we conclude that the capacity for these things was common to the ancestor of both this species and *Homo sapiens*, and that man was already a fire-using, tool-using animal before he was completely man. And his tool-using must have involved primitive feelings about personal property. Even our ancestral sub-man, the common ancestor of these two species or races, must have trailed an increasing amount of gear about with him. His economic pilgrimage had begun.

Early man of our own line, *Homo sapiens,* was too intelligent to be easily drowned and fossilized, and were it not for this habit of interment he shared with the Neanderthaler, we should know very little indeed about him. We should know as little of him as we do of the other quasi-men who did not bury their dead. But so far as our present records go, the indisputable *Homo sapiens* came upon the scene some forty thousand years ago or more, a distinct race if not a distinct species, and he was then a hunter, wandering in small family groups from pitch to pitch, living like all the rest of the great mammals on the food he found from day to day, fruits and roots, small game, and sometimes a larger kill, using fire for cooking and to keep off hostile beasts, and extending his natural powers by means of stakes, clubs and shaped and sharpened stones. He was certainly not a very numerous race at that time. He had still to develop extensive social habits. He probably wandered in small family groups as the great apes do to-day, and he may have been as rare as they are.

§ 3. *The Dawn of Social and Economic Life*

From this wandering and hunting condition man, true man, that is to say, the species of *Homo* to which we belong, presently made a very extraordinary stride forward. He seems to have made this stride very rapidly from the biological point of view in something between five thousand and ten thousand generations. To geologists and astronomers that will seem a mere instant of time. We have as yet few material traces of this transition. It is possible that this stride forward was taken in regions now submerged and so far inaccessible to scientific exploration. But the most subtle and ingenious probings into human habits, traditions and mental reactions have pieced together the probable outline of the processes by which this stride was achieved. They constitute a complex and fascinating speculative literature, rather too ample and fascinating for intense treatment here. The drift of it, and especially its mental aspect, is given in the *Science of Life*.

The gist of the change was that while hitherto man had subsisted upon the natural food supply of the country in which he lived, he now began to cultivate and store food, keep other animals to be a source of supply to him, live in larger communities than heretofore and establish definite permanent settlements. He had become an economic animal. From the point of view of biology this was a quite extraordinary new departure. Except for a few rodents of which the beaver is the most remarkable, no other mammal, no other vertebrate, has even begun to develop in this direction. Rabbits and gophers associate but do not store; squirrels store but do not form coöperative communities. Dogs and wolves hunt in packs but take no thought for the morrow. Even with the beaver, it is questionable if there is a deliberate storage of food. No mammals cultivate. We have to go to the insect world, to the ants, termites and bees, to find any parallel to human societies. They too are economic animals which are settled in communities and do not live from hand to mouth.

Yet, though the change meant a transition from one sort of life to a sort of life so fundamentally different that scarcely any other vertebrated species displays it, and though it was fraught with the most astounding possibilities for this planet and it may be for the whole universe of matter, it yet went on in all probability generation after generation, age after age, without any very sudden and violent revolutions in human usage. The herdsman, the builder, the cultivator, were already latent in the watchful, ingenious early human wanderer. Already, before his economic life developed, he was talking, he was imitating, he was in his manner experimenting. One thing led to another, and the unforeseen of yesterday became the familiar of to-day. *Tradition* appeared and grew and changed, unaware that it ever changed. Man's increasing ingenuity and curiosity increased the number of his implements and possessions. He had to keep these impedimenta somewhere, and perhaps a store place was the first thing to tie the developing varieties of *Homo* to a definite settling place. Moreover, it was convenient to have a hearth where a fire could be kept alight, for early fire-making had its difficulties. So agriculture found man already disposed to root himself to place. He must have passed through this great transition from animal wandering to economic settlement almost unawares. The story of human work and wealth does not begin, therefore, like something suddenly begotten or hatched out; it does not open as a play does with a curtain suddenly rising on Act One: it dawns.

§ 4. *The Domestication of Animals*

The interest of *Homo sapiens* in other animals was the lively interest of a hungry hunter who was sometimes hunted. He lay in watch and puzzled his brains about what these other animals might do and what might influence their comings and goings. Spears, arrows, traps, fish-hooks are among his earliest productions.

He imitated these beasts, and in his quickening brain, which must have been very like the brain of a bright child of to-day, he suspected his imitations affected the behaviour of his enemies and his quarries. Dances to influence game seem to have begun quite early in his history; they may have been among his first rituals. He shaped the form and movement of his fellow animals in gestures. His opposable thumb and finger made it easy for him to record these gestures and scratch and smear likenesses of beasts on rocks and wood: feats, it would seem, beyond the abilities of *Homo neanderthalensis*. He drew and painted beasts on rocks and in caves, and we discover them now with vast appreciation. He recorded his hunting for us to see, and even made pictures of his camp and dances.

It is a pretty question whether man picked up the dog as an associate, or whether the dog picked up man. The relationship may have begun like the relationship of the lion and jackal, when the latter merely follows the former about to pick up the remains of its kills. Early dog may have hovered about early man, and the superior sociability of the dog may have begun the first rap- ·prochement.

Nature is a great friend of coöperation; it is a gross libel upon her to say she is always "red in tooth and claw." On the contrary, she has something like a passion for making living things interdependent. She elaborates and confirms every disposition to associate. One of the commonest utilizations of the hovering cadger is as a watcher and warner. The rhinoceros and crocodile, for example, have their attendant birds which are vermin pickers and scouts. And for the dog which hunts naturally with other dogs it would be easy to help round up deer, or cattle, or horses, in association with man. At any rate, the dog opens the list of domesticated animals. He was sleeping and barking about the human group while it was still a group of wandering, tool-making beasts.

And man with his dog, though he consumed the herds of reindeer, wild horse, wild ass, wild cattle and sheep that drifted in search of grazing grounds as the age of forests gave way to the age of open plains in Europe and Central Asia, did not pursue them with an inveterate hatred. He protected them as far as he could from the competition of other beasts, wolves and so forth, which wasted them; he sought to restrain their wandering beyond his reach and protection. The possible gradations between hunter and herdsman and between truly wild beasts and beasts that have come to tolerate the approach of men are insensible.

At the end of his great stride from the palæolithic wandering life to the neolithic territorial life, we find man has domesticated dogs, oxen, sheep, pigs, probably goats, the ass, and possibly also in Central Asia the horse. The distinction between domestication and farming is not clearly marked, and we cannot say when or where man attained the latter stage. Breeding in captivity is the characteristic of this phase of control. Oxen came to be used as draught animals, and with them man probably took over the major agricultural operations from woman. For the management of flocks and herds the dog was essential and was well qualified for this both by natural intelligence and by his hunting instinct.

Now, all these creatures brought with them various very convenient by-products—teeth, horns, bones, hides, and hoofs—for the use of man. We find the list of man's material and impedimenta growing longer. He could not change his dwelling place so frequently. Property limited his movements, tied him down to one spot, at any rate, for considerable periods of the year; and as his surroundings grew more familiar, as danger passed from an unknown to a known and calculable element in his environment, as the necessity for constant alertness diminished, came the opportunity for reflection and experiment.

And now commences another development. Man was struck by strange imaginations about these beasts who were becoming his intimates. He began Experimental Zoölogy; he tried to breed the unlike together and to interfere in normal breeding. Mythology is full of fantastic hybrids, from the cockatrice to the minotaur. These legends are the fossils of experimental dispositions that once filled his mind. They show what he was after. At some stage man added the sturdier mule to the tale of his servants and helpers. And also he discovered the changes produced in the temper and texture of animals by castration. There was a curious phase of mutilation in human development which still appears transitorily in boyhood and girlhood. Man chopped himself about, he circumcized, he lopped off limbs, he tattooed, he trepanned, he knocked his teeth out. Evolution had given him the flint knife, and he used it—as a boy will still use a knife—on himself and others.

Moreover, he made certain experiments that must have seemed at first very queer things to do. He tried the milk of these domesticated beasts. We are so accustomed to rely on milk and milk products that it is hard for us to imagine a time when a resort to such nourishment must have seemed unnatural and even monstrous, yet there may have been such a time. There must have been mental phases in these early experiments like the fantastic dreams and imaginings of a little child. Before Freud few people dared to confess what things had passed through their heads during their years of innocence. The ideal child was supposed to have a mind of the genteelest whiteness; it was held that we were born in a state of perfect self-suppression instead of having to learn it for long, painful years. . . . All these opening phases of human life still remain to be worked out. The earliest of the agricultural communities we can trace, had milk, butter and cheese, as well as meat.

§ 5. *The Beginnings of Settlement and Sustained Work*

And while man was thus becoming an experimental zoölogist, he was at the same time acquiring a very considerable practical knowledge of plants. As a wandering hunter he must already have had an extensive acquaintance with edible fruits and herbs, nuts, roots and the like, and it is hardly to be imagined that his concern for the movements of the beasts he tracked and the herds he followed left him regardless of woodland and grass.

But he probably knew of grass and grain without much regard to their phases and processes. One may doubt if in his primordial hunting stage he recognized the relation of seed to tree or of season to fruit and flower. We cannot say with any precision yet at what stage in his development man realized that there was an annual cycle, a year.

We contemporary human beings are taught so much from our earliest years, we are told that this is so and that is so with such reiterated conviction, that a multitude of ideas seem to us to be in the very nature of things, whereas it is merely that at a very early stage they have been built into the fabric of our minds. Children of three or four will say quite confidently that the world is round and that the year goes from summer to winter and from winter to summer; and it is hard to purge these ideas from one's consciousness and imagine an adult mind without these particular assumptions. But the world of the early men was flat and went on forever, and the weather changed, grew hotter and colder, snowy or rainy, sere or green, and it was only the very oldest and most observant who could have had a chance of noting any established rhythm in these phases. When the year had been discovered, it had still to be measured and mapped out. An accurate calendar is a thing of the last two thousand years. Before then man was still struggling to catch the sun and stars and failing to get them. They slipped away through his reckoning of years and centuries, and put him wrong with his sowing.

Just as it is hard to conceive a mind to which extracting and drinking the milk of cows must have seemed a marvel, so also it is hard to conceive a mind with no idea of sowing a seed. But such must have been the intellectual state of the early wandering *Homo sapiens*. He no more looked forward from seedtime to harvest than a cat or a gorilla. It helps us to realize a little that age of primitive ignorance when we learn that several savage peoples remained ignorant of the connection between sexual love and offspring right up to the nineteenth century A. D.

The men of twenty thousand years ago (or thereabouts), who have left us the rock paintings, the carvings and implements of the late Palæolithic Age, had already got to a much higher level of intelligence than that. They probably had an annual migration following the reindeer and horses they ate, and a clear idea of the annual round. It is possible they had even found out the directional value of the stars, and in what seems like the representation of a bridle on one palæolithic carving of a horse head, there is reason to suppose that they employed the horse for draught purposes in their migrations. But to pass from that life to the life of the settled agriculturist must have involved certain steps of which we have at present only very perplexing and incomplete intimations. They were difficult steps to make, and there is plain evidence that they were made in a roundabout way and with much confusion of thought.

To the modern mind, ploughing, manuring, sowing, weeding, harrowing, reaping, seem all such plain, common-sense proceedings that it is difficult to realize that none of them was in the least an obvious thing to do to our remote ancestors. They had to feel their way, generation by generation and age by age, to clear ideas about these proceedings. They did all sorts of things, and the harvest resulted; they had no method of determining what was essential or what was inessential among the things they did.

One of their misconceptions lies at the root of a vast complex of religious and ceremonial practices which still survive. Somehow the first crops were associated in the human mind with the killing of a human being. That is a very strange association from our current point of view, but it is an indisputable fact. For some reason that is now extraordinarily incomprehensible to us that killing seemed to our forefathers to be as necessary as the seed scattering.

Moreover, with no calendar in existence, and no proper measure of the year, it was extremely hard for primitive man to hit on quite the right time for this conjoint sowing of blood and grain. The stars, man had come to know, went through an annual change of position in the sky; the altitude of the sun at midday increased and diminished as the year passed. His clumsy and bloody sowing had to be mixed up therefore with a clumsy, toilsome, and superstitious astronomy. As he emerges to our vision from the archæological obscurity of his first essays on agriculture, we find his settled communities everywhere dominated by a temple and by a priesthood associated with the observation of the sun and stars and devoted to periodic human sacrifice. He did not dream it was possible to sow or reap without them. He did not dream it was possible to live without them.

The temple and the sacrificial priest were of primary importance therefore to the economic scheme of the first settled communities. They embodied a primitive science, however loaded it may have been with guesswork and error, and a primitive religion, full, perhaps, of needless terrors and cruelty, without which mankind might never have passed over from the earlier phase of lonely savagery and casual subsistence to its present condition of economic interdependence. The first religions were as practical in their purpose and as closely interwoven into the texture of life as a hoe or a cooking pot. They were as necessary and inseparable a part of early social life. There was no nonsense about religion being too "spiritual" for business use in that stage of human development.

Biologically this change from a wandering to an economic life was a great success. Very rapidly *Homo sapiens* became a numerous animal instead of a rare one, first perhaps in some region now beneath or round about the Mediterranean, and then spreading slowly and multitudinously over more and more of the available land surface of the globe. He became more numerous than any other species of the primates had ever been. His habitat grew wider and wider. He varied his agriculture considerably to adapt it to a variety of favourable conditions.

With the beginnings of settlement, regular work came into the life of mankind. Work we may define here as exertion when there is no immediate bodily urgency. It is exertion for a remote end. It is undertaken when one is neither hungry nor thirsty, lustful nor frightened nor sportive, in order that later on one may not suffer want. Man, the wandering savage, was probably very much on a level with his fellow beasts; he led his life in obedience to continual urgencies and made his first inventions in a kind of play. His first work was implement-making and fire-feeding. He worked like a gipsy tinker. Hunger and fear and other bodily cravings kept him on the move.

The primitive human communities were certainly very small family groups. The things *Homo sapiens* ate were few and far between and hard to find; quite a wide area, therefore, was needed to sustain a single family. The same is the case with the great apes to-day. They cannot live thickly. A tribe of hundreds in the Early Stone Age would have meant starvation.

Primitive organization was probably not very rigid; there were no records to *fix* things; there could have been little pedantry or exactitude about relationship in truly primitive man. There are sound reasons for believing that the typical primitive social group of man, as of the present-day gorilla, consisted of an old male, a female or so and one or two young. The old man generally drove off the young males as they grew up and became obnoxious to him. But though that was the typical it was not the only sort of group. Young males might keep together for a time after they were driven off; the old man might be killed and his group coalesce with some other group. But the patriarchal family was the dominant type. The only division of labour was the natural difference of masculine and feminine function. The male did more of the fighting, and the female bore, fed and slapped the young. Most of the minor chores were probably put upon the women. They wanted them done more than the men wanted them done.

That was the scale and type of the first human communities. But with growing intelligence and the development of the huntsman-herdsman life, as the forests of a moister age gave place to grass plains, there was a great biological advantage in a larger community with numerous men in it who could hunt in agreement and fight if necessary to retain their hunting ground.

The human community grew social exactly as other animals have grown social, as the African lions seem to be growing social to-day, by an increasing toleration of the young by the old, especially on the part of the males, and by a retardation of full maturity. The basis of all human society is the taboo, restraint, the prohibition of certain impulses. A system of taboos grew up to bar the women of the tribe from the young men and mitigate the disruptive violence of sexual jealousy. There is a world-wide taboo among savages between a man and his sisters and his step-mothers and his half-sisters. There are at least traces of such a taboo in all human societies. A young man who wanted a woman of his own had to steal her from some other group (exogamy). All over the world linger the vestiges of exogamy and marriage by capture. The idea of incest as a sin is an almost universal tradition among human beings, and it finds no equivalent among apes or other animals. There is no instinctive bar to incest in any animal. This taboo of incest may have been the foundation of real human society. It made it possible for father and sons and sons-in-law to endure each other. It made it possible for the group to grow larger and safer.

The psychoanalysts trace the moral conflict in our minds back to its roots in these primordial prohibitions and suppressions, without which social life could not have existed. They do it very convincingly. Through the taboo system humanity underwent an immense training in self-restraint. Diffidence and a respect for taboos were woven into the normal human soul. The sexual side of the moral conflict developed.

Imperceptibly a gradation of duties arose. The old man's headship and prestige were enhanced. The men specialized as hunters and fighters, and the women kept camp. There was probably much individuality about these early communities; there is no reason to suppose they were all of one pattern. Anthropologists are exact-minded men; they forget at times that primitive men are not so. Usually the headman was the depository of wisdom, but often the rôle of medicine man, who drew pictures and did incantations, may have fallen to someone else. And the older women must have done a lot of talking and telling. There must have been endless conflicts and alliances of mind and brain. The prestige of some old men outlived them; they haunted the dreams of the tribe; their strength and their influence were invoked; medicine men saw them in visions, undertook to speak for them, and the first tribal gods were evolved.

From the gradual development of the mysteries of agriculture and the adoption of a mainly vegetarian dietary by such taboo-respecting tribes, the first settled and numerous human communities arose. As these developed, security increased, and with it the need for work. But man has no passion for work; he has to be broken in to work, and social history is largely the record of the attempt to break men in. Or, to be more exact, of men to break other men in. The dawn of economic history shows us humanity already busy upon the job of putting the work on to someone else.

The social conflict is already in full progress at the very beginning of a numerous society, and it goes on through all the rest of history. No such temperamental adaptation as seems to have occurred in the case of the ant and the worker bee has ever been achieved by man. That is the point where he differs most widely from the economic insects. These creatures have produced a real worker type, a multitude of individuals who seem to have no other desire in life than to toil in certain definite ways and live and die for the collective good. The insect worker works by instinct. Humanity has never produced a real worker type. None of us toils by instinct. Mankind can produce with ease classes prepared to give orders, disdain work and enjoy privileges, but the workers remain not a class but a residual mass, subordinated without enthusiasm, betraying no essential willingness for a subordinate rôle. That is why it is so unjust to tell the sluggard to go to the ant for moral instruction. The ant *likes* work for its own sake. It is morally incapable of inaction.

One thing that has stood in the way of such a separation of our species as we find among ants and bees is the varying economic processes of the human community, which have called sometimes for one type of toil and sometimes for another. And we shall show as this work proceeds, that the resistance in the human soul to a life of mechanical toil has lasted long enough and proved stout enough and is operating now under such new conditions as to make it improbable that a human "worker" type will ever be evolved at all. We are not travelling the same road therefore as the economic insects. The resemblance of our society to their societies is more apparent than real. Man is travelling a road of his own that no form of life has ever trodden before, towards unprecedented destinies.

§ 6. *The Rest of the Historical Overture*

This dawn of human economic association has been treated with a certain fulness here because of its great structural importance to the rest of this work, but the further history of the expansion and complication of mutual help and service must be dealt with more compactly. It must be not merely descriptive but psychological. The whole science of work and wealth indeed, that is to say all economics, is ultimately psychological. Human beings are associated through their brains, and, except in the very early stages of family life, in no other way. They are associated, not by instinctive mechanism and innate class differences as the social insects are, but by different idea systems in what are otherwise closely similar animals. The science of work and wealth is the history and analysis of these operative systems of ideas.

In his temples, laws, customs, man has left us, fossilized, as it were, the data to reconstruct these idea systems that have served to bind him to his fellow men. The history of human communities—political history, that is to say—is, as the *Outline of History* shows, fundamentally a history of developing means of communication and the possibility and realization of larger and larger communities. It is the story of a secular change of scale in the dealings of man with man. The economic history of mankind must be *pari passu* a history of the growth, changes, and replacements of the inducements, beliefs, symbols, and methods that have made social coöperation possible and determined the character of its development. The common worker in the early communities before the dawn of written history, like the common worker now, must have gone about his work because somehow he found himself *there* and his work was what it seemed he had to do. If he had no instinct for work, he had acquired a habit of work, he acquiesced in its necessity. And backing up that sense of necessity in his mind, and arresting any primitive impulse to revolt, there were tradition, religion, awe, there was a belief in ruling Powers, in gods or a god, justifying the scheme of things, a "synthetic personified sense of the Tribe" as the god of the Tribe, as lord, director, and protector. Behind the taskmaster loomed the temple and the possible anger of these gods. To rebel against work was to go out of life into nothingness.

This religious tradition took on the individual's developing ideas and emotions as he emerged from his infantile subjection to mother and father. His childhood was prolonged by it. He grew up out of sonship to his father only to become one of the "sons" of the tribal founder or the tribal god. He never emerged completely from the mental habits of sonship. He never became a free, self-centred adult beast like the primordial *Homo.*

This was not a trick played upon him. It was the way everything grew up about him; it was the way things had come about. It caricatures and modernizes those early social phases to suppose that priests, secular rulers, and leading people were not equally subject in their minds to their lord and god, or that they could release their minds to the extent of being cynical about the personal advantages given them by the general faith in a tribal symbol. They played their part in perfect good faith, not questioning the fairness of their advantages. They were the elder brethren among the sons, and they recognized obligations commensurate with their privileges. They felt that the god was on their side, but also that the god was standing observant over them.

But at some quite early stage the developing human community was invaded by another and harsher conception of relationship. Side by side with the sons of the god and their sisters and womenkind appeared another sort of human being, more definitely cast for the rôle of toil—the slave.

The domestication of animals and the domestication of strangers must have involved very similar mental processes. You took the pups of the wild dog and the children of your enemy and subdued them to your purposes. Mutually destructive tribal warfare passed by a series of variations into tribute-levying and actual conquest and class enslavement. The *Outline of History* tells of the going and coming of conquering rulers over the early civilizations. That had begun when the curtain of history proper rises. It was already established. The nomadic tradition, becoming militant, would impose itself upon the agricultural tradition, and the armed monarch would rule beside the priest. The change in the social structure was not great. Successful wars would bring captives and gang labour in their train. A harsher type of toil would spread and prevail in the larger communities, a

type of toil more consciously under human compulsion and
mentally less acquiescent.

But we can deal only in the broadest outline with the development and interplay of ideas in what we now call the ancient
civilizations. The relation of the everyday working life to the
temple and the symbols of authority can be traced in Sumeria
and early Egypt and in those strange survivals of the tradition
of a remote past, the Maya, Aztec and Peruvian societies. It
was one social pattern—with variations. The cultivator was the
base and main substance of the community. Proprietorship, like
sovereignty, still undefined but apprehended, vested essentially
in the god or god-king or chief of the community, and balanced
against or overruled the customary property of the worker in
the thing he worked upon, land, ship, utensil or what not. There
was community ownership vested in god or chief and there was
user ownership, the ownership of implements. A third type of
ownership manifests itself in relation to personal adornments
and precious objects. But man in the early societies was not
very clear in these matters; he was not very clear about anything; he knew nothing of exact definitions and logical thought;
he probably did not distinguish types of ownership or detect
the various roots of the "thine and mine" idea. For thousands
of years ideas of possession, deference, authority and subordination grew definite or fluctuated and were modified in relation
to this or that new occasion.

Through a long procession of favourable centuries interrelated systems of tradition established themselves in the minds
of men, and the social man whom we can still understand without any great difficulty was gradually and surely established in
the Old World, in Egypt, in Mesopotamia and in Central Asia.
Dynasties came and went, and conquests stimulated or deflected
the process of civilization. Language extended its range and
became more precise. The word won its way slowly against the
visual image as the chief implement in human thinking and
feeling. Pictorial representation opened the way to writing and
an increasing definition and fixation of words. Slowly, through
scores of centuries, the symbols and metaphors which still frame

our thoughts were hardened and set by time. The mental and emotional dispositions of *Homo sapiens* in the great warm river valleys, became more and more akin to our present "humanity."

Age by age, man sharpened and fined his words and idioms, as age by age before he had sharpened and fined his flints. As thought grew fine and exact, the more primordial thinking of the earlier mythologies took on a monstrous and incredible quality. The ancient gods and legends began indeed to puzzle their inheritors. Men, feeling their way to the methods of reason, to generalization and abstraction, looked for more "reasonable" explanations. Twenty-five centuries ago in Greece the modern mind was already pecking its way out from the shell and membranes of tradition and mythology in which it had been incubated—profoundly unconscious of its origins. A fresh phase was beginning in human life. The age of exact reasoning was dawning.

And about twenty-five centuries ago that extension of economic contacts and the development of trade and trading classes and trading cities which had been going on with a comparative gradualness from the days of the first localized civilizations, quickened very considerably. Money and the money idea became increasingly operative. It brought profound and subtle changes into economic life. Money relaxed and released property and made credit processes of a quite unprecedented rapidity possible. Men could now undertake impossible payments and pile up debts as they had never done before. Usury grew. Some day the science of work and wealth, the new realistic political economy, will gather all that is available about the methods of early trade before currency and accounting and find what there is to be found about the trading, for example, of Cnossus and Tyre and Sidon. It seems to have been plain barter. Then the appearance of new, more abstract methods will need to be traced. The onset of money and reckoning was a very cardinal event in man's development. The money community which came into existence in the first millennium before Christ, was an altogether more mobile form of association than the barter and service civilizations that had preceded it.

In the *Outline of History* the Roman republican and imperial system is treated as the first instance of a "money" community. Its economic operations were far more extensive and fluent than those of any preceding great community, and it arose out of a sea conflict between two commercial republics, and not upon the basis of a great alluvial area inhabited by cultivating peasants and conquered by nomads, as the "ancient" despotisms had done. It carried the Western world forward into larger and less stable social methods. China, India were far less affected by money and continued to revolve in the traditional alternatives of conquest and dynastic change for another thousand years.

Religion in the Roman Empire was less integral to its social and economic life—more aloof and less intimate. Human society had no longer the same need of its binding power. Money was providing a new nexus. Religion, as people say nowadays, became "spiritualized."

The extending Roman system made a greater use of the slave gang than any previous system and staggered so soon as its wars were no longer a source of captive toilers. The expansion of the city of Rome and its citizenship was by the scale of world history a rapid and unstable expansion. It never really worked out the conflict of methods between serf, slave, and wage labour. Its wealth was hectic, and it consumed its population. Its crash was a stupendous event for mankind. Disorganization came from within, and the barbarians tumbled into the ruins— with an air of conquest. The common people, sunken from the normal free farmer level, had no spirit to resist the Hun, the Northman, or the Arab. For them it was only a change of masters.

Our modern world arose out of the wreckage of that crash, and so it is that the history of Rome must play a larger part in this overture than any Eastern history. The professors of the science of work and wealth, who will presently be teaching our youth, will some day examine the expansion and collapse of Rome as essentially an economic process. Here we have to go with less than scientific assurance. The thesis of the *Outline of History* is that the facilities for insolvency provided by ill regulated money, the inherent impermanence of a slave system, the failure to develop a representative governing system as the Empire grew—or even to realize that such a thing was needed —the failure to produce sympathetic coöperating "educated" classes in sufficient abundance, difficulties in communication, the nomadic wedge in the Danube plain, and possibly climatic changes and epidemic diseases, all contributed to that series of disruptions and reunions and disruptions which makes the history of Europe and western Asia, the history of the Empire in the West and East, throughout the Middle Ages. The monetary system was too loose and elastic, and the administrative system not responsive, elastic and sympathetic enough for the Empire to work. Gibbon's analysis of the Decline and Fall is all too deeply coloured by his anti-Christian bias, for Christianity, that amazing mélange of ancient rituals with new spiritual ferment, was a symptom rather than a cause in the vast, unsound expansion and collapse of the first great money-credit system. The *Outline of History* tells for how brief a period the Roman Imperial System really worked, and to the *Outline* the reader will have to go for the divergent fates of the Latin and Greek Empires, for an account of the barbaric driftage of the Dark Ages, and the slow resumption of order as the feudal system crystallized out of the confusion.

The Social and Economic History of the Roman Empire, by M. Rostovtzeff, 1926, is a work of great learning and acute analysis. It is a very important first step in the analysis of the Roman downfall. His conclusions (p. 486) are that: "None of the existing theories fully explains the problem of the decay of ancient civilization, if we can apply the word 'decay' to the complex phenomenon which I have endeavoured to describe. Each of them, however, has contributed much to the clearing of the ground and has helped us to perceive that the main phenomenon which underlies the process of decline is the gradual absorption of the educated classes by the masses and that consequent simplification of all the functions of political, social, economic and intellectual life which we call the barbarization of the ancient world. The evolution of the ancient world has a lesson and a warning for us. Our civilization will not last unless it be a civilization not of one class but of the masses. The Oriental civilizations were more stable and lasting than the Greco-Roman because being based chiefly on religion they were nearer to the masses." To which we may add that these civilizations were also simpler in structure and less permeated by those social solvents, money and credit operations.

With the Church and the Holy Roman Empire, with the development of states and kingdoms and the rise and fall of powers and empires in Europe and Asia we need not concern ourselves now. For that too the reader must go to the *Outline*. Our concern is rather with the fate of the productive and business ideas and methods of the Roman and Byzantine world, throughout the long scrimmage of the Decline and Fall. What was holding out in Constantinople, in Venice, in such perennial places as Marseilles, and in Egypt and Persia, in the way of buying and selling and hoarding and credit, while Goth, Hun, Northman and Moslim swept to and fro? Here we can put the question, but we can offer no complete answer. No one can tell us yet, even in the roundest and most speculative figures, how the volume of trade in the Mediterranean varied between 300 B. C. and A. D. 800. We do not even know how populations expanded and contracted during those times; and indeed we knew nothing exact about populations until the dawn of the present era.

And again, what the routine of daily life was like, how people kept house in castle or shrunken town during the worst of these centuries, is only vaguely known. The peasant dug and harvested and hid—as ever—as he is doing now in China. And he was made to work and yield to his brigand master. But where did the leaders, the brigand nobles and brigand princes get their clothes and ornaments made? Who did the dressmaking for the ladies of the Merovingian court, and how was it paid for? Had it all shrunken back to the worker who was kept in the household—who worked for keep, protection and small rewards? A little band of workmen gathered about every castle and manor and increased as order and prosperity returned. Manifestly some sewing and painting and carving and hammering and building were going on right through those ages of confusion.

Here we do but summarize the facts of that survival. And then came the slow economic recovery that becomes traceable after the eleventh century, the steady recovery of overland trading in mediæval times, the rise of mercantile shipping and overseas trade, the outburst of exploration, and the reappearance of wealth. A multitude of towns emerged to prosperity and importance; the Rhineland, Provence, and northern Italy led in the revival of an agreeable productive life in the West. The artizans multiplied, and the peasant went to market more abundantly. Would that we could refer here to some thorough and penetrating comparison of the developing monetary and banking systems of the rapidly healing world with those of the past! But such a comparison has still to be made. Two new devices in human affairs presently began to play an increasing part in the world's restoration; representative government and joint stock enterprise, at first unlimited and then with limited liability; and here again, to take us beyond mere general remarks, there is a call for some synthesizing mind.

The economic spectacle changes in its character more and more as our historical review approaches our own time. History was not repeating itself; history never repeats itself; but men have a curious disposition towards historical repetition. Statesmen and churchmen, as the *Outline* tells, wasted the energies of the Western world in a hundred fantastic attempts to recall the vanished Roman Empire. As persistently that Empire refused to return. Only after 1918 did the world escape finally from that retrospective obsession. Amidst the political and traditional confusion of a thousand years new forces and new orientations grew continually more evident. A greater world, indifferent to tradition, was coming into being. Before the close of the eighteenth century, man had already come to a knowledge of the whole round globe on which he lives, and was rapidly developing his means of access to every part of it. Unprecedented "empires" extended into regions Cæsar never knew. Organized science appeared and invention quickened. It was prosperity coming back to mankind, but with a new face and new methods. A new world-wide productive, trading, financial and monetary system was growing up.

Trade expanded continually from the sixteenth century onward, population increased, and the industrial revolution arrived. There was a vigorous search for productive energy. And at first for "hands." The idea of tapping natural sources of mechanical power was scarcely stirring as yet. Problems of business and social organization exercised imaginative minds. One could quote Fielding benevolently finding work for poor children and laying the foundations of factory sweating, and Defoe with great enthusiasm depicting a purgatorial land of hope for Moll Flanders in the West Indies. Many quite good men, in their zeal to get people working, were advocating every variety of compulsory toil. Las Casas, the champion of the oppressed American Indian, introduced the Negro to America and the questionable benefits of Christian teaching.

But slavery was hard to revive, because no sweeping conquests were in progress, and so wages labour became widespread and at length almost universal. There had been a long struggle in the fifteenth century after the pestilences had depleted the labour supply, and particularly the urban labour supply, to retain the serf at his task and hinder his wandering off in search for wages, but wages servitude had won. Gang slavery reappeared indeed in the plantations of America—to fight a losing battle. There were a conscience and a criticism abroad that the Roman world had never known; and forces beyond its utmost imagination, new slaves without souls or resentments, were coming to take over the toil of the subjugated. The first of these new slaves which came to the rescue of the old was Steam. With the first hum and clanking of power machinery, with the bitter servitude of the machine minders to the inventions that will at last abolish such poor creatures altogether, our historical overture to the contemporary human panorama must culminate and end.

CHAPTER THE SECOND

How Man Has Learnt to Think Systematically and Gain a Mastery over Force and Matter.

CHAPTER THE SECOND

HOW MAN HAS LEARNT TO THINK SYSTEMATICALLY AND GAIN A MASTERY OVER FORCE AND MATTER

§ 1. *Directed Thinking*

BUT before we go on to the actual panorama of present things, we must, if the whole spectacle is to be made understandable, go a little more fully into one particular aspect of history, the history of human thought. Human thinking has passed through several stages in its evolution, and most of us repeat those stages in our individual lives. The way we do business with each other and set about the affair of life is conditioned altogether by the way in which we think. Most of us do not think enough about thinking.

We have explained how round about five and twenty centuries ago the appearance and wide use of money and monetary credit in the world produced a new epoch in human affairs. It was an epoch of enlargement and extension. Mainly through the action of this new flux, money, the huge, unstable Roman system and the associated Byzantine system were able to develop—and collapse. But much more than the expansion of a novel political and economic system occurred at that time. These political expansions and instabilities were reflected in men's thoughts about life and divinity. These were intellectual consequences of far greater and more permanent importance than the material changes. In the *Outline of History* the appearance of syncretic and universal religions, for example, is traced to the expansion of these empires; they destroyed the prestige of the local and national gods. The idea of widespread brotherhoods and world unity dawned.

And simultaneously came a slower and ultimately still more important change in human affairs, though for a time it did not have anything like the same conspicuousness amidst the general appearance of life. This was an intellectual movement, a change in the way in which man did his thinking and came to his conclusions. He began to be more careful of the mental processes through which he took hold upon things. He began to think about thinking, to take care about his thinking and to learn to think.

That was destined to have gigantic effects later on. We are indeed living amidst its gigantic effects, but at the time, for twenty centuries indeed, this intellectual revolution and reconstruction was an affair of the study and classroom, and the mass of mankind knew nothing about it. Even those who were concerned in it may not have realized its full importance.

Let us be perfectly clear about this "learning to think." Children, like primitive man, have still to learn to think; they do a large part of their thinking by imagination. That is, so to speak, the natural way with the untrained mind. Their thinking is a flow of images with which impulses to act are connected. Images and scenes are suggested and give rise by various forms of association to others. The whole flow is pervaded by a sense of wilful activities. It is spontaneous and uncontrolled. Many people in adult life are able to recall a time in their lives when they did all their thinking in that fashion. Many adults never think in any better way.

In the mental flow of child or savage, moreover, things are not distinguished very clearly from persons; they are thought of as quasi-persons. That is another great difference between the untrained and the trained mind. All things are liked or disliked; they can be friendly or inimical. The world of primitive thought is a drama in which the thinker conceives a rôle for himself. The flow of fantasy proceeds and gives an agreeable or disagreeable quality to this or that imagined line of action, which is followed or rejected accordingly.

The thought of the young child, the thought of the primitive mind, is a type of mental activity differing from dreaming only in its closer touch with reality, in its more frequent checking

THE CONQUEST OF SUBSTANCES

A TYPICAL industrial plant such as is found on the outskirts of any great city. This particular picture shows part of a coke by-product system. The stack in the foreground is coal.

THE CONQUEST OF POWER

BUILDING part of a giant hydro-electric system. This is one of the pipes which will lead water to the turbines.

through the waking senses. Otherwise it is a quite undisciplined
and undirected flow. There is hardly any use in it of generalizations and abstract ideas. There is no critical element asking,
"But is this sound? Is this true?" Everything presented in the
flow that is not itself physically real is apprehended in a symbolical and often a personified form. The idea of the winds, of
the seasons, of the tribal organization, of the obligation to do
right, for instance, appears under the guise of personalities
or personal relationships. Everything is supposed to *do* something. Everything that happens is supposed to be *done*. The wind
blows. It seems natural to ask: Who blew it? The river flows.
Who poured it out? The sun rises. Someone has driven it up
the sky. So we get Boreas or Auster, Father Tiber, Apollo, the
charioteer of the sun. Every tree must have a spirit, just as
man has a spirit, and how can there be thunder without a
Thunderer? Father and Mother, at this mental stage, furnish
patterns for the imagining of gods. Jove-pater stalks across the
universe terrible and incalculable—with an immense beard and a
voice of thunder. We cower to the bosom of the Earth Mother,
mother of all the gods. She is the nourishing Mother, the Cow-
goddess Athor, Mother Nature. The unsophisticated savage
remains a child throughout life. To the end of life the primitive
mind thinks in this way. Throughout the opening cycles of human
history there was no other method of thought. All mankind
thought then as our children think now.

This corresponds to what Comte called the mythological
phase of human development. It has recorded itself in a vast
mass of imagery in language and of images and pictures in the
world. The gods and monsters who sprawl across an Indian or
Maya sculpture frieze are thoughts embodied. Osiris, Horus,
Anubis, and Isis express ideas of command and obligation and
of good and evil for which man could devise no simpler, less
encumbered expression. The eyes that a savage paints on the
prow of his canoe betray this same entanglement of his mind
with personality.

Only very gradually, as minds ripened and as mankind ripened,
does an exacter discrimination and disentanglement of essentials

appear, and logical thinking begin. The mythological passes insensibly into the metaphorical. With an increasing vocabulary, abstraction becomes possible to the growing mind. We *disentangle*. Goodness and benevolent power in the world can be thought of without evoking the figure of an armed and crowned chieftain bearing all the symbols of majesty; a boat can be considered as a floating contrivance which does not need an eye. The mind begins to arrest and examine its flow of association; to classify things in this way and then in that; and to pick out what is necessary from what is accidental and incidental.

On that follows "logical" thinking. Man, as he "grows up," begins to reason things out instead of dreaming them out. He begins to control his predispositions and observe a logical coherence. He restrains and criticizes his impulsive judgments and responses. He struggles to control and direct their sequences. He begins to squeeze the inessential associations out of his metaphors and symbols. The Athenian philosophical literature, culminating in Plato and Aristotle, records man's definitive adoption of what psychologists call *directed thought* as distinguished from *undisciplined thought*. The paraphernalia of personification which was once necessary had become an inconvenience and a burden. Gods, demi-gods, demons and fates faded into figures of speech and receded from the arena of judgment, while concepts of a more abstract order, forces and matter, atoms and reactions, were adopted to replace them. Much that was inessential still lurked in the new terms and abstractions, but the effort to get rid of that inessential element continued.

So, in that phase of human development which opened about six centuries B. C., man definitely ceased to take the results of his mental processes for granted. A scrutiny of those processes began. He had found them clumsy and inexact and he had set himself to sharpen them as once his ancestors had set themselves to sharpen flints. He had set himself to chip off the unnecessary.

And also he had ceased to take the world of appearance about him for granted. He had begun to scrutinize and question his world.

In the *Outline of History* Plato is taken as the typical exponent of a novel and inspiring idea, that man is able, if he will, to change his way of living. Aristotle stands beside him in that account, as the first organizer of the collection and classification of knowledge. They questioned custom, and they questioned appearance. Each of these men was in reality greater and less than this, but it is convenient here to use their names and their outstanding qualities as landmarks. We pick them out to simplify our story. In these two men we find the human mind turning upon its primitive methods and seeking a clearer and more serviceable form of interpretation, that will give, they realize, a hitherto unimagined mastery over fact and one's practical reaction to fact. Man, as they embody him, man in the Athenian phase, wrestles with his impressions, classifies them, seeks to clear and order them by exactly defined words, because he is realizing that ignorance is danger, and knowledge, power. He is changing from responsive imaginations to logical thinking, directed towards the attainment of practical working truth.

The psychological chapters of the *Science of Life* deal rather more fully than is possible here with this substitution of orderly and directed thinking for the symbolism and imaginative play that was once the only human method, and which is still perhaps the most ordinary way of thinking. And in the *Science of Life* how this arose out of the still more primitive blind try and thrust of the animal life is explained very simply and clearly. Animal behaviour, it is shown, has three main stages of complexity. ("Main stages," we write; not distinct and separate stages.) First, instinctive and conditioned responses; then, imaginative thought before action; then, logical thought before action. It is unnecessary to repeat that fuller exposition here.

This change-over from a mental life that was merely experience-checked imagining to an analytical mental life aiming at new and better knowledge and leading on to planned and directed effort, is still in progress. It is the greatest change in the methods and nature of conscious life that has ever occurred. It is still only partly achieved. Over a large range of his interests man has still to acquire the habit of thinking with self-control and precision.

§ 2. *The Criticism of the Instrument of Thought from the Beginnings of Directed Thinking Onward. Nominalism and Realism. Experiment. The Renascence of Science*

The philosophers of the Athenian and Hellenic communities of the sixth, fifth, fourth and third centuries B. C. inaugurated the logic-restrained and question-guided thinking of the modern world. But, as we have said, it was a beginning only. It was not the whole stride that had to be made, and we must not exaggerate even while we recognize its essential significance. Man did not, at that time, fall suddenly into a perfected way of thinking. He sought precision. By no means did he attain it. Day cannot come without a dawn, but the down is not the day.

That age of intellectual vigour in Greece marks the breakaway from mythological imaginative interpretations, and it marks also the first repudiation of tradition. The Utopianism of Plato is the first announcement of man's ability to depart from tradition in his acts and institutions. The Science of Aristotle displays a realization of the need for, and the possibility of, attaining a growing orderly body of tested knowledge and directive ideas, for the use of our race. It was to be new and increasing knowledge. That widening departure from tradition is the fundamental subject matter of this book. We are only carrying out to-day the intellectual release that Athens began.

Let us state clearly the full importance of that release. The *Science of Life* deals fully with the appearance of *tradition* in human evolution, shows how it was at first a progressive innovation and how greatly it accelerated social development, how it dispensed with the slow attainment of hereditable characters through mutation and selection, and also how it is now giving place to a still swifter process of social adaptation, due to the systematic interrogation of fact, organized research, and *planned development* that was latent in the new way of thinking. This transition from tradition to deliberate planning which is now in progress, is at least as great an event in evolution as the transition from unassisted heredity to heredity-plus-tradition which carried man above the level of the brute. The man who

orders his knowledge and thinks things out is as far above the
natural man of impulse and traditional usage as the latter is
above an ape which has not even tradition but only instinct.
They represent three successive stages of vital adjustment.

The Hellenic world conceived and shaped the instrument for
modern thought and prepared the human mind for that widening breach from tradition, that forward-looking attitude, to
which it is now committed. But, outside certain fields where the
need for observation and experiment was limited, Greek
scientific achievements were, by our modern standards, small.
Greece made only the first step towards effective knowledge.
There were many more further steps to be made before even
such mental efficiency as we can boast to-day was attained. The
instrument of modern thought was invented and shaped in the
Hellenic age, but it had still to be sharpened and relieved of
many clumsy associations. A long succession of active brains had
still to work upon that task—a task that is still far from completion.

Moreover, that bright beginning in the eastern Mediterranean
was hampered, checked and arrested by unfavourable political
and social conditions. The *Outline of History* tells how the
small and scattered band of original thinkers, which constituted
the whole intellectual life of the Hellenic world, was slowly
swamped and stifled by the conservative traditions of Egypt
and overwhelmed by the vast expansion, disturbances and collapse that constituted the history of Roman Imperialism. That
first intelligentsia, the Hellenic intelligentsia, never arrived at
any sufficient facilities for conducting experiments or exchanging
and discussing observations and results. Indeed, it had a very
insufficient sense of the need for multitudinous experiments. It
was overconfident of this new process of logical thinking it had
developed, and unsuspicious that the new method had its own
peculiar dangers and pitfalls.

What were the imperfections of the new method of directed
thinking? What was still unsatisfactory about logical reasoning
as the classical world understood it?

That there was an unsatisfactoriness appears plainly in certain of the dialogues of Plato, but in a manner and with an application that does not fit in very conveniently to contemporary needs. The essence of the unsatisfactoriness that appeared was this: that there was a question how far words were *accurate*. Were words as true as material facts, or truer, or less true? If they were truer, then a logical conclusion was truer than an experience, and that, on the whole, was the classical assumption.

I write "on the whole" because this assumption was then already being questioned. It may be difficult for many minds to realize that any people have ever been disposed to think that words were truer than experienced things. But the fact is that not only have men in the past continually tended to treat words as more real than material facts, but that now, at the present time, men, you and I included, are tending to do exactly the same thing. We suspect and resist that tendency now, but many people have so far given way to it as to believe that in words they had a means of penetrating beneath experience and appearances down to profounder truths. The tangle between the One and the Many, between the Ideal expressed by the word and the Individuals assembled under the word, arises out of this disposition. It was only through the toilsome discussion and bickering of many generations of men in the later Middle Ages that the processes of this directed thought, which was and is still replacing the more primitive uncriticized flow of associations, were cured, to some extent, of its early disposition towards an independent arrogance, a false profundity and overconfidence, and recalled to a closer relationship to the verities of life. As briefly as possible we will put the bare elements of that great debate before the reader. He may then be willing to admit that those "Schoolmen" who wrangled through the centuries were doing a very indispensable work, too little appreciated by this contemporary world of ours—which indeed could never have existed without their wrangling.

Everybody has heard of this wrangling, of the great mediæval controversy between Nominalism and Realism, but the ordinary educated man, because of his insufficient and misleading education about such matters, is still all too ready to suppose that it was some extraordinary, remote, dry-as-dust conflict of pedants, that can have no possible interest for him. He thinks it was a dispute about some dead issue which has no possible bearing upon his life. He has not been told the truth of the business. That conflict has never really ceased because it has not yet been fought to a definite conclusion; it is still going on all about us under an endless diversity of masks and forms, and there is not a thing in our social, political and economic life that would not have been profoundly different if these controversies had never arisen.

The essence of this vast dispute between Nominalism and Realism which was already beginning in the Greek discussion between the One and the Many, and which is still far from a final conclusion, may be stated in a few paragraphs. Indeed, one may get very near the heart of the matter in a sentence. We have already said that there are three ways of thinking about words; one may think they are truer or less true than fact, or that they are *accurate* and fit fact exactly. For the Realist the word was truer than the experience; for the Nominalist the experience was truer than the word.

The human mind is a very imperfect instrument, just as the human eye is a very imperfect instrument. And just as the eye is prone to "optical illusions," so the human mind has its innate disposition to certain intellectual illusions. Chief among these is this disposition to trust to words, to names; the disposition, for example, to regard any unreal conception to which a name has been given, or any group of things to which a name can be given, as being thereby made actual and different from all other things. The mind trusts too much to the symbol or word it has adopted. The *name*, the *word*, which is man's implement, can easily become his master. He is disposed to believe that things that are called by the same name are necessarily all alike and altogether alike. He falls into that sort of acceptance very readily. He is always slipping into the error of confusing similarity with identity, and supposing that things that have one common quality or a few common qualities have all their qualities alike.

So he is apt to believe that all atoms or all herrings or all sheep or all Englishmen or all sovereign states, are exactly and in every detail alike because they are spoken of by the same word. By that word they are made one. He takes refuge from the infinite variety of existence in the *word,* which he can then reason and dogmatize about. He will say "all sheep" do this or "all Englishmen" do that—meaning that mostly they do. His untutored disposition is to treat the name of a group of things as though it expressed something fundamental and essential, and to ignore the endless variations that shelter under every common noun. This assumption that a name has something real and quintessential in itself, that there is an ideal and perfect sheep, for example, over and above all individual sheep, is the essence of philosophical Realism. The denial that a name is anything more than a label put upon an assembly of more or less similar but never identically similar things is the essence of Nominalism.

There is, we must note here, an unfortunate conflict between the common use of the word "realist" and its proper original meaning. The contemporary reader has to be warned of that difference in usage if he is not to misconceive all this section. In the great controversies of the Middle Ages, the Realists were those who followed this more natural but deceptive human tendency to treat names as expressing something more real than actual existences; while those who held that names were not in themselves real, that they were *only* names, labels just stuck upon things for our mental convenience and susceptible of infinite shifting and alteration, were called Nominalists. The Realist believed only in the reality of words and the general ideas they embodied; the Nominalist believed only in the reality of things and individual instances. The Realist believed that all individuals are imperfect specimens of the perfect "type"; the Nominalist ignored the perfect type. The mediæval Realist was what we should nowadays call an idealist, a Platonic idealist; the Nominalist was the facty man.

This is evidently almost the exact opposite of our modern use of "realist" and "realism," and in order to keep this distinction before the reader's mind, we spell "Realism" here, when it means the philosophical teaching and not insistence upon "actuality," with a capital R. That vast necessary controversy that went on in the Middle Ages was essentially a struggle of the human mind to escape from the innate vice of Realism, from the phantoms, the delusions created in the mind by primitive uncorrected Realist thought, and to look directly and discriminatingly at things themselves.

"Very nice," says the modern Nominalist, after the most clenching deductions, "and now let us try if it is so."

Both sides in that huge wrangle went far and stated excessive cases. Roscellin, an extreme Nominalist of the eleventh century, for example, held that a name, a word, was no more than a *flatus vocis,* vocal wind. But from the time of William of Ockham onward (fourteenth century), and indeed from the time of Abélard (twelfth century) the recognition grew that names and classifications might carry more or less weight and convey more or less truth. Words had to be scrutinized. There might be false as well as true conceptions in the mind. Some words were truer than others, they implied a higher degree of similarity than others, but none were as true as fact. When every name, every word, was marked with a note of interrogation, the way of escape from Realism lay open.

To escape from Realism is to escape from hard classifications, from the harsh judgments, assurance, uncompromising attitudes and dogmas that arise from hard classifications, and to move towards qualified statements, the examination of individual qualified statements, the examination of individual instances, enquiry, experiment and careful verification.

Here we will not attempt to follow the fluctuations of that immense dispute. The practical defeat of Realism over large areas of human interest was obviously a necessary preliminary to the release of experimental science. You could not get men to look at reality until verbal Realism was abandoned. It was so much easier to deduce your beliefs from first principles than to go out to make observations, and according to Realist ideas it was a sounder process. The protest of Roger Bacon was the outcry of a Nominalist in a Realist age. The Realist still ruled completely in the universities and over the teachers for a century after his death.

It was Roger Bacon who was first to ascribe to experiment its proper importance in the pursuit and discipline of knowledge. It was he who first insisted clearly that logical processes must be constantly checked by facts. On that account we take him as we took Plato and Aristotle—as a landmark in human development. He serves to mark a further step in the escape of the human mind and will from their original limitations. It was not so much what he did as what he said that gives him importance. His own actual experimental achievements amounted to barely anything at all. But he was almost the first human being to stress the supreme importance of verificatory experiment in the search for knowledge. He stands out as, in effect, insisting that no words could be trusted without the test of experiment.

His writings led straight to the scientific method of extending and using knowledge. One hears a great deal about the "scientific method," and it is often spoken of as though it were a distinctive method of thinking. But it is not a distinctive method of thinking, but only a distinctive method of using the logical method of thought already in existence, but of using it in a new spirit, a spirit of distrust. Your logic might prove that a thing should be so; your experiment then had to prove that it was so. "Observe, try, record, speculate logically, try out your speculation, confirm or correct, *communicate to other investigators, hear their communications, compare, discuss logically,* establish and so onward"; this, for all practical purposes, is the method of science. Apply as occasion arises. Eschew all *a priori* methods, for you do not know enough about your brain to trust it to work without this constant experimental checking. Check it by other brains, but above all check it by facts. Distrust every term, every name, you use. Logic is very serviceable as an aid to judgment but not as a final judge. All the terms you use *fit loosely on fact.* That is the key persuasion behind the experimental method. Keep trying back to fact. Such was the working scientific method of the nineteenth century, that age of material progress, and it is still the working scientific method at the present time. It is a repudiation of all philosophy that is not perpetually verifying its propositions.

Upon that working philosophy, upon that insistence that every assertion must be checked by fact and by the scrutiny and corroboration of other eyes and ears and minds, all the material triumphs of the scientific worker during the last century have been made. He sets himself to master the things at hand as thoroughly as possible. That is his essential and personal job. If there are limitless implications in these immediate things, he believes that they will unfold themselves and become plainer as his work proceeds. But he will not anticipate such progressive revelations. He will not trust his mind except when it remains in the closest touch with fact and with the concepts of his fellows. He will not tolerate the philosophies that merely project the peculiarities and obsessions of the human mind upon the universe, and declare that this is Truth. The rôle of philosophy from the point of view of the scientific man is not the attainment of wisdom but the perpetual accompaniment and criticism of man's thinking—to avoid follies and remove obstacles.

The detachment of the human mind from its Realistic predispositions remains incomplete. Mankind still believed in the fixity of animal and vegetable species—which were supposed to vary about a perfect type—until less than a century ago, and in the identical similarity of atoms until a quarter of a century ago; and in the world of international politics the Realist way of thinking holds almost undisputed sway at the present time. That intellectual error lies at the root of the greatest dangers that threaten our race. Men's hearts may be in the right place, but their poor heads are still befogged by the magic of names. Plainly a man who takes the Nominalist way and regards such a word as "France" as merely a name covering a great area of country, climatic and social associations, and about forty million human beings of very diverse kinds (numbers of them not even speaking French), will regard international politics from an entirely different angle from a Realist who finds in the word France something more real and vital than any single individual or thing that contributes to the ensemble of that idea. "Russia" is another magic term of this sort for the Realists; "Mother India" again, or the "Old Country," whichever it is. Since we do not teach the significance of these words "Nominalist" and "Realist" in our schools, nor give any sort of training in analytical thinking, we are Nominalists or Realists as our mental temperament or luck may determine, and the Nominalist and Realist of contemporary life, all unaware of this difference in the very elements of their thought, find each the other stupefyingly obtuse. Each cannot see what is the matter with the other's mind. The Realist "patriot" calls his brother Nominalist "traitor" or "cosmopolitan scoundrel," and the like, and is amazed that he does not wince; the Nominalist humanitarian calls the Realist obdurate dogmatist or romanticist and accuses him of a perverse taste for contention and blood.

At a considerably higher level we find the contemporary mathematician who has still to learn the real meaning of "experimental verification," and who is habituated to treating the schemes of concepts in his brain as truer than fact, at odds with the modern biologist. Still constrained in the logical net, he shakes his head at the "unphilosophical" ease of the latter's mental movements. He objects to conclusions that are not final and exactly proved. He has not learnt to rest in a provisional conclusion, and clings to the delusion that purely symbolic processes can win truth from the unknown. His symbolic processes never do win truth from the unknown, but he fancies that they justify an attitude of disapproval towards the pragmatical acceptances of practical science. But in the long run perhaps even the mathematicians will become scientific.

The Nominalist emancipation of the human mind proceeds slowly, but it proceeds; the boundaries of once hard classifications become transparent and manifestly provisional. The discovery of Evolution, the realization, that is to say, that there are no strict limits set to animal and vegetable species, opened the whole world of life and its destiny to Nominalist thinking. The realization by the world of mathematical physics that the universe can be represented as a four-dimensional universe of unique events has abolished the conception of a quantitative equivalence of cause and effect and made every atom unique. Only the indifference of school and college to current thought has prevented every thinking person from becoming a Nominalist by the present time.

§ 3. *The Practical Nature of Renascent Science*

Two fundamental ideas came with the experimental method in the renascent world of the later Middle Ages, to qualify, extend and empower the first great releases of the Hellenic period. One of them is the *changeableness of substances* leading on to the possibility of changing them, and the other is the possibility of *deliberately releasing power*. Neither of these ideas is in evidence in Hellenic science. They were latent in it, perhaps, but they were not in evidence. Their appearance in effective action marks a profound difference between the Old World and the New. The deliberate "Conquest of Substances" and the deliberate "Conquest of Power" are entirely characteristic of our modern world.

There were deep enquiries into the nature and constitution of matter in the ancient world, such as the wonderful guesses of Lucretius, but these were speculative exercises of the mind, prompted by the desire to explain, rather than the passion for effective knowledge. The science of Aristotle is largely descriptive. The herbalist sought practical knowledge, but to the Old-World mind substances were what they were, just as plants and animals were what they were. You knew about them, but you did not probe into them. And neither was there research for power. Curious mechanical toys were made—and there at the curious stage they remained. There was little experimental work, and the philosopher did not deign to share in and scrutinize the practical secrets of the metal worker and suchlike artizans. Archimedes would not have the construction of his practical contrivances recorded. They were beneath his dignity as a philosopher—mere artizan tricks. The highest aim and the only honoured aim of that earlier science was to know.

It is only as the obscure, secretive science of the late Middle

Ages emerges to publicity and discussion that we find these new conceptions of *interference with substance* and the *release of force* in action. The alchemist we discover looking for the elixir of life and the transmutation of baser metals into gold. From alchemy chemistry developed into "iatro chemistry," the chemistry of medically useful substances. All the ancient aloofness of the philosopher gentleman had disappeared by the dawn of the new time. Roger Bacon is full of practical promises, they made the substance of his message, and Francis Bacon died through a chill contracted when making a crude experiment upon the preservative use of cold. He got out of his coach to stuff snow into a fowl.

The science of this new phase was concerned not with the essential nature of things as the old had been, but with the properties of things and what you could do to them and with them. It was more modest because it did not set itself to explain, and yet it was bolder because instead of merely accepting and describing, it set itself to use and alter. It did not pontificate about fact; it grappled with fact. It was philosophically more modest and practically more courageous. It sought practical ends and presently, and almost inadvertently, it found itself penetrating far more profoundly into the nature of things than the exalted philosophers of the Hellenic world had ever been able to do. But that profounder knowledge came by the way; it was found by the wayside to actuality. Science did not even stoop to conquer. It stooped to practical things and conquest ensued.

This modesty of approach and this bias towards practical issues may have been forced upon renascent science by the religious intolerance of Christendom. If so, there is something to be said for intolerance. The Hellenic philosophers had nothing to forbid their seeking fundamental knowledge, but in the late Middle Ages scientific enquiry could only be released by that compromise of the later schoolmen which distinguished sharply between "spiritual" truth which was the *higher truth,* and rational truth, the everyday truth of normal experience and the secular mind. In that way the reconstruction of astronomical ideas which has gradually released the human imagination from an earth-centred universe to the immensity of space, and the realization of organic evolution that has opened to man the limitless vistas of time, have been possible without a conflict to the death between science and religion. There have been disputes and discussions of a very far-reaching kind, there have been forced recantations like Galileo's and martyrs like Bruno, there have been skirmishes in the Garden of Eden and quarrels about the Gadarene swine, but the combatants have never finally clinched. At the close of the nineteenth century science worked upon lines that implied a conception of the universe which was rigidly fatalistic, side by side with the picture of free-will, unqualified initiative and moral responsibility, presented by the religious teacher. It was an intellectual incompatibility which did not interfere very greatly in the steady extension of the multitude of substances that were being made available for human purposes or in the continually increased utilization of extraneous power. Science worked and religion attended to the immaterial needs of mankind.

§ 4. *Ultimate Truths Are Outside the Diagrams of Experimental Science*

In recent years very extensive readjustments have been made in the general formulæ which the man of science has used to simplify and systematize his facts. These readjustments have occurred mainly in the world of physical science; they have affected the steady advance of biological and social science very little. It is the professor of physics who is most concerned. The philosophical concepts that have served to guide and sustain his enquiries hitherto have been, so to speak, under repair. He has had to alter his general diagrams.

The reader will have heard endless echoes and repercussions from these enquiries into philosophico-scientific technique, even if he has not deliberately studied them, and so it is well to explain how far they concern us and how far they do not concern us in this work.

Some recent experiments and observations have jarred heavily with the general philosophical ideas that have hitherto satisfied and served the scientific worker. His diagrams have had to undergo a considerable revision. They were much too naïve and "obvious." In certain fields he has had to question the essential reality of that framework of space and time in which he—in common with the man in the street—has been wont to arrange his facts. He has had to scrutinize the ideas of time and eternity afresh. He has been brought to consider Euclidean space as only one of a great number of theoretical spaces, and to replace it by other and subtler concepts of space that seem more compatible with these recently observed facts. The old issue between predestination and free-will has in effect been revived in terms of mathematical physics. Is the universe a fixed, rigid time-space system, or has it movement in still other dimensions? Is it a continuous or an intermittent universe? The mere asking of such strange questions is very exciting to the speculative mind. But they do not affect the practical everyday life, either of the individual or of mankind, and we note these interesting developments of modern thought here as fascinating exercises for the intelligence outside our subject altogether.

It may be that we exist and cease to exist in alternations, like the minute dots in some forms of toned printing or the succession of pictures on a cinema film. It may be that consciousness is an illusion of movement in an eternal, static, multidimensional universe. We may be only a story written on a ground of inconceivable realities, the pattern of a carpet beneath the feet of the incomprehensible. We may be, as Sir James Jeans seems to suggest, part of a vast idea in the meditation of a divine circumambient mathematician. It is wonderful exercise for the mind to peer at such possibilities. It brings us to the realization of the entirely limited nature of our intelligence, such as it is, and of existence as we know it. It leads plainly towards the belief that with minds such as ours the ultimate truth of things is forever inconceivable and unknowable. It brings us to the realization that these theories, the working diagrams of modern science are in the end less provisional only

THE CONQUEST OF SUBSTANCES
Coal unloader at the Berwind Coal Docks, Superior, Wisconsin.

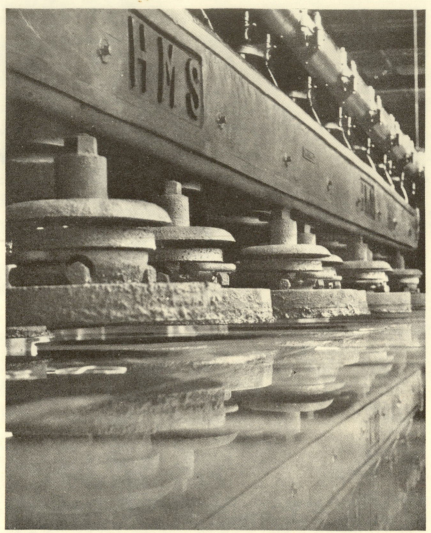

THE CONQUEST OF SUBSTANCES

POLISHING sheet glass. Under this grinding and polishing machine the glass, in two trips under the wheels, one for each side, is given a smooth finish. In grinding, more than thirty different sorts of abrasives are used, from coarse sand to the most delicate rouge. The abrasives are arranged in a precise order and so proportioned that they give the highest polish obtainable.

in the measure of their effective working than the mythologies and symbols of barbaric religions.

But it does not give us any present escape from this world of work and wealth and war. For us, while we live, there must always be a to-morrow and choice, and no play of logic and formulæ can ever take us out of these necessities. To be taken out of these necessities would be to be taken out of existence as we know it altogether.

It is impossible to dismiss mystery from life. Being is altogether mysterious. Mystery is all about us and in us, the Inconceivable permeates us, it is "closer than breathing and nearer than hands and feet." For all we know, that which we are may rise at death from living, as an intent player wakes up from his absorption when a game comes to an end, or as a spectator turns his eyes from the stage as the curtain falls, to look at the auditorium he has for a time forgotten. These are pretty metaphors, that have nothing to do with the game or the drama of space and time. Ultimately the mystery may be the only thing that matters, but *within the rules and limits of the game of life,* when you are catching trains or paying bills or earning a living, the mystery does not matter at all.

It is this sense of an unfathomable reality to which not only life but all present being is but a surface, it is this realization "of the gulf beneath all seeming and of the silence above all sounds," which makes a modern mind impatient with the tricks and subterfuges of those ghost-haunted metaphysicians and creed-entangled apologists who are continually asserting and clamouring that science is dogmatic—with would-be permanent dogmas that are forever being overthrown. They try to degrade science to their own level. But she has never pretended to that finality which is the quality of religious dogmas. Science pits no dogmas against the dogmas of the ghost worshippers. Only sometimes, when perforce science touches their dogmas, do these latter dissolve away. Science is of set intention superficial. It touches religious dogma only in so far as religious dogma is materialistic, only in so far as religious dogma is a jumble of impossible stories about origins and destinies in space and time, a story pretending to a "spirituality" that is merely a dreamy, crazy attenuation of things material. And even then does it touch these dogmas only because they involve magic irrational distractions, interferences and limitations of the everyday life of man.

I wish that there was a plain and popular book in existence upon the history of scientific ideas.* It would be fascinating to reconstruct the intellectual atmosphere that surrounded Galileo and show the preëxisting foundations on which his ideas were based. Or ask what did Gilbert, the first student of magnetism, know, and what was the ideology with which the natural philosophers of the Stuart period had to struggle? It would be very interesting and illuminating to trace the rapid modification of these elementary concepts as the scientific process became vigorous and spread into general thought.

Few people realize how recent that invasion is, how new the current diagram of the universe is, and how recently the ideas of modern science have reached the commoner sort of people. The present writer is sixty-five. When he was a little boy his mother taught him out of a book she valued very highly, *Magnell's Questions*. It had been her own school book. It was already old-fashioned, but it was still in use and on sale. It was a book on the eighteenth-century plan of question and answer, and it taught that there were four elements, earth, air, fire and water.

These four elements are as old at least as Aristotle. It never occurred to me in my white-sock and plaid-petticoat days to ask in what proportion these fundamental ingredients were mixed in myself or the tablecloth or my bread and milk. I just swallowed them as I swallowed the bread and milk.

From Aristotle I made a stride to the eighteenth century. The two elements of the Arabian alchemists, sulphur and mer-

---

*But *Man and His Universe*, by J. Langdon Davies, is good, readable and suggestive, and Ginzburg's *The Adventure of Science* also comes very close to my wish. I may add Holmyard's *Chemistry for Beginners* and Alexander Findlay's *Spirit of Chemistry* as agreeable books for the general reader who would like to expand the matter of this necessarily very brief section. Finally as the proofs of this book pass through my hands, my attention is called to a still closer approximation to my desire in E. A. Burtt's *Metaphysical Foundations of Modern Science* (1925).

cury, I never heard of then, nor of Paracelsus and his universe of salt, sulphur, mercury, water, and the vital elixir. None of that ever got through to me. I went to a boys' school, and there I learnt, straightaway, that I was made up of hard, definite molecules, built up of hard definite indestructible atoms of carbon, oxygen, hydrogen, nitrogen, phosphorus, calcium, sodium, chlorine, and a few others. These were the real elements. They were shown plainly in my textbook like peas or common balls suitably grouped. That also I accepted for a time without making any fuss about it. I do not remember parting with the Four Elements: they got lost and I went on with the new lot.

At another school, and then at the Royal College of Science I learnt of a simple eternity of atoms and force. But the atoms now began to be less solid and simple. We talked very much of ether and protyle at the Royal College, but protons and electrons were still to come, and atoms, though taking on strange shapes and movements, were intact. Atoms could neither be transformed nor destroyed, but forces, though they could not be destroyed, could be transformed. This indestructibility of the chameleon of force, was the celebrated Conservation of Energy, which has since lost prestige, though it remains as a sound working generalization for the everyday engineer.

But in those days, when I debated and philosophized with my fellow students, I was speedily made aware that these atoms and molecules were not realities at all; they were, it was explained to me, essentially mnemonics; they satisfied, in the simplest possible arrangement of material models and images, what was needed to assemble and reconcile the known phenomena of matter. That was all they were. That I grasped without much difficulty. There was no shock to me, therefore, when presently new observations necessitated fresh elaborations of the model. My schoolmaster had been a little too crude in his instructions. He had not been a scientific man, but only a teacher of science. He had been an unredeemed Realist, teaching science in a dogmatic Realist way. Science, I now understood, never contradicts herself absolutely, but she is always busy in revising her classifications and touching up and rephrasing her earlier cruder statements. Science never professes to present more than a working diagram of fact. She does not *explain,* she *states the relations and associations of facts as simply as possible.*

Her justification for her diagrams lies in her increasing power to change matter. The test of all her theories is that they work. She has always been true, and continually she becomes truer. But she never expects to reach Ultimate Truth. At their truest her theories are not, and never pretend to be, more than diagrams to fit, not even all possible facts, but simply the known facts.

In my student days, forty-five years ago now, we were already quite aware* that the *exact* equivalence of cause and effect was no more than a convenient convention, and that it was possible to represent the universe as a system of unique events in a space-time framework. These are not new ideas. They were then common student talk. When excited journalists announce that such intellectualists as Professor Eddington and Professor Whitehead have made astounding discoveries to overthrow the "dogmas of science," they are writing in sublime ignorance of the fact that there are no dogmas of science, and that these ideas that seem such marvellous "discoveries" to them have been in circulation for more than half a century.

No engineer bothers about these considerations of marginal error and the relativity of things, when he plans out the making of a number of machines "in series" with replaceable parts. Every part is unique indeed and a little out of the straight, but it is near enough and straight enough to serve. The machines work. And no appreciable effect has been produced upon the teaching of machine drawing by the possibility that space is curved and expanding. In this book, let the reader bear in mind, we are always down at the level of the engineer and the machine drawing. From cover to cover we are dealing with practical things on the surface of the earth, where gravitation is best represented as a centripetal pull, and where a pound of feathers

---

*See, for example, my own undergraduate essay in the *Fortnightly Review,* July 1, 1891, "The Rediscovery of the Unique"; and see also L. Silberstein upon "The Time Machine," 1894, in his *Theory of Relativity* (1914), p. 134.

weighs equal to a pound of lead, and things are what they seem. We deal with the daily life of human beings now and in the ages immediately ahead. We remain in the space and time of ordinary experience throughout this book, at an infinite distance from ultimate truth.*

§ 5. *The Organization of Research*

Let us consider how this collection of working diagrams up to date, this practical thing, Science, is perpetually being added to and perpetually being clarified and made more serviceable.

There was a time not so very long ago when an isolated man of independent means might still conduct investigations of primary importance and make great additions to knowledge or profound changes in ideology single-handed. A man like Cavendish, the great chemist, or the Abbé Mendel, could work on his own resources and could leave notes and observations behind him to lie undeveloped and disregarded for a long time. But now we think a great deal more in each other's minds than we did. It is often difficult and sometimes impossible to trace the authorship of modern key phrases and words and terms. Who, outside a small specialized world, knows, for example, who first used "genes" or "auto-suggestion" or "metapsychics" or "values"? No doubt the answer is to be given in each case, but few of us trouble about the answer. The new term is thrown out, and suddenly we are all using it. We do not want to be bothered about questions of copyright. Patent rights in a new terminology are no longer recognized. A score of men turn a corner at about the same time and at once indicate their sense of a new direction by the same inevitable phrase that no one had ever dreamt of using before.

To-day, in an increasing number of subjects, teamwork research prevails, and in many it is the only possible method. In

---

*Our discussion of the relations of science to human life, philosophy and belief in the four preceding sections has been necessarily very bare and swift. The reader who would like a longer and fuller treatment of these questions will find it in W. C. D. Dampier-Whetham's *History of Science and Its Relations with Philosophy and Religion*.

the *Science of Life* the rapid production of valuable results by the teamwork in genetics under Morgan in New York is described.

A history and discussion of the social and economic basis of scientific work from the very beginnings of scientific thought would be profoundly useful. Where did scientific questioning really begin? The priesthoods of the early civilizations had a considerable accumulation of knowledge. How had it been accumulated and reported? It seems to have undergone a slow but steady progressive development. Gradually the archæologists, and especially the Egyptologists, are disentangling the material to answer that question. For the last century or more workers, in Egypt especially, have been getting together and cataloguing and classifying the material for the understanding of these remote mental processes, but now, and with the inspiration of a psychology suddenly become boldly speculative and analytical, we are more and more able to realize the current assumptions and reconstruct the thought of past periods.

I doubt if the Egyptians had any idea of research. I suspect that even a very intelligent Egyptian or Sumerian priest supposed that everything was known that could be known, even if he and those about him did not know it all. He had no suspicion of limitless seas of knowledge accessible but unexplored. For him there existed already—Wisdom. All one had to do was to learn and learn, to seek out mighty Sages and learn more. And if he observed something that he had never heard of before, then I suppose he put it on record not as anything new but as a mere provisional replacement of some part of the mosaic of Wisdom that had got mislaid. I doubt if any Egyptian priest, however original, ever thought in the form of fresh discovery. Even when they were most original the ancients were always, they thought, restoring Wisdom. They were, they imagined, in conflict not with virgin ignorance but with corruptions.

Knowledge and skill, conditioned by such views, advanced slowly, backing forward and bowing to the past. Maybe that here or there a man had a momentary glimpse of the limitless seas of things still unknown that lay outside of and encompassed

Wisdom,—that Wisdom knew nothing about. But not for long
did that glimpse last. Such a thought, if it occurred at all, must
have traversed the mind of an Egyptian priest, very much as a
terrified mouse dashes across a room. It was there. It was gone.
Even to-day the intelligent visitor to Egypt, walking through her
long colonnades, recalls something of the fixed recurrence, the
finality, to which the world of the great dynasties had attained.
Everything was known, they supposed, and across the dark
river waited Anubis the Accuser, Horus the Saviour, and—if the
scales did not condemn the pleading soul—eternal bliss with
Osiris, stereotyped also forever. That was life. That was all.

It seems plausible to suppose that the first scientific ques-
tionings began where traditions came into conflict. My own
coarse guess is that the southward swirl of the Aryan-speakers
across the Asiatic and Mediterranean civilizations did much to
loosen the roots of old ideas, that the clash of strange languages
led to a new curiosity about meaning and so to logical analysis,
and that the development of a class of independent, prosperous,
but not too opulent people with leisure made the play of doubt
effective. They sat about and talked and reasoned a little; they
wrote, and copies were made of what they wrote. They began
to ask such questions as, "How do we know what we know?"
Much of that discussion was forgotten or lost again. When at
last the story of enquiry and record is fully traced out it will
seem marvellous how narrow and precarious were the first
springs and rivulets that have swelled to the science of to-day.

What was the first dawn of associated scientific work? The
Museum at Alexandria, perhaps. All associations in the ancient
world had to be religious associations, or they were regarded as
dangerous conspiracies. The Alexandrian savants therefore
dedicated themselves to the Muses. They were patronized by
the Hellenic Pharaohs. What well-nigh imperceptible drops in
the general flood of contemporary human acceptance were these
Hellenic sages who set out upon such enterprises as the measurement of the globe! How flimsy was the thread of occasional and
precarious letters that linked minds in Alexandria with kindred
minds in Athens and Syracuse!

The renewal of the scientific process in mediæval Europe is often ascribed rather absurdly to the dissemination of the Greek literature, after the fall of Constantinople to the Turk. But science died in Imperial Rome with all that Greek literature at hand. Some necessary freedom or protection had disappeared. Nobody was, in fact, left free to care for it. The revival was due much more to the reappearance of certain social types, and particularly of *secure, freely thinking, independent people,* people of "means," stimulated by, but not absorbed in public responsibilities. They could give curiosity play and amuse themselves with dreams of magic discovery. Half seriously and a little furtively these fortunate amateurs took up the search for the secret of transmuting metals and the mysteries of longevity. We have noted the new streak of practicality in the science of the Renascence. The "curio" came before the museum; the pottering odd experiment before the definite enquiry.

Embryonic modern science was closely mixed up with art. Philosophy wrangled. Art observed. Dürer and Leonardo were scientific pioneers. The universities droned along blindly with the oral teaching of traditional wisdom; they were on the side of tradition. Modern science owes few of its initiatives to them.

Mercantile motives and the vast raids of the Mongols set the process of geographical exploration at work again. It had been suspended from the days of the Roman ascendency. Its effect in effacing the delusion that everything was known extended far beyond the geographical field. The unrest and doubt that spread out from this Mongol thrust was probably much more important than the Greek stimulus. The revival of Greek studies at the Renascence did not so much start new ideas in men's minds as confirm and stimulate what was already stirring.

The difference between the mentality of a sixteenth-century gentleman of intellectual tastes and a mentally vigorous Egyptian priest must have rested primarily in the relative realization by the former that there was a limitless, accessible circumambient unknown. There the sixteenth-century gentleman was in advance of the priest. But also he was intensely individu-

alistic, and there he seems to us nowadays to have been less
"modern." The priest had a sense of belonging to an organized
system; albeit it was a tradition-preserving system. The found-
ers of modern science worked for a time almost independently.
They met first in the early academies: the Academia Secre-
torum Naturæ of Naples, 1590, suspected of the black arts
and closed by the Pope; the Academia dei Lincei, of which
Galileo was a member, 1603; the Academia Naturæ Curiosorum
of Madrid, 1657; the Académie des Sciences, incorporated in
1666 after thirty years of informal meetings (including
Descartes, Gassendi, Pascal); the London Royal Society (1662,
after informal meetings dating from 1645), and presently a
variety of specialized scientific societies.* But they assembled
under no sense of obligation, just out of fellow feeling, for the
social gratification of their curiosity, and perhaps also for the
sense of a possible need for mutual protection against the hostility of the traditional. The greatness of Bacon's *New Atlantis* lies
in the clear recognition by its author of the need for coöperation
in research.

The first modern coöperation in research seems to have been
made under the auspices of royal and wealthy persons, to form
collections and horticultural and zoölogical gardens too expensive for a private purse. There the royal and wealthy of the
seventeenth century recall the memory of Asoka and the
Ptolemies. To begin with, laboratories were individual and
private. The first men to earn a living by experimental science
were, I suppose, the assistants of scientifically inclined gentlemen. They emerged to distinction like the groundsmen and
professionals in the games of cricket and golf. Until they could
teach their employers. . . . Then gifted young men began to
be "discovered" and assisted in their own investigations, and
research institutions appeared. The accumulation of facts and
generalizations presently led to public lectures and movements
for the diffusion of scientific knowledge.

The material for this story is still scattered in hundreds of

*M. Ornstein's *The Rôle of the Scientific Societies of the Seventeenth Century*
(1928) may interest the reader who would like more detail here.

biographies and collections of letters. It is all very recent, an affair of three centuries at most. But when it has been collected and arranged the compilers will have done their task ineffectively if they do not display a steady change of attitude on the part of those who were engaged upon that accumulation, towards the knowledge they had procured and tested.

Only in moments of insight and exaltation did the curio-collecting nobles and gentlemen of the sixteenth and seventeenth centuries realize this mighty new directive system they were evoking. This amusing and surprising little pet creature, this Natural Philosophy of theirs, was to grow into a dragon that would sustain the world, but of this they had no idea. For the most part science was a toy or an ingenious way of discovering new money-making activities, and presently it became a useful weapon for teasing the parsons. Or it aroused wonder. By imperceptible degrees we shall find the idea of scientific research as an important public function entitled to systematic support, and the associated idea of science as a devotion and a primary end in life, creeping into the record. Science ceased to be a recreation and became a pursuit. These new views about the importance of science have arrived very recently; within the lifetime of many who are still living.

Such stories as that of the Smithsonian Institution in Washington, of the Institute Pasteur, of the London Royal Institution, and of the Rockefeller group of endowments, would repay a careful scrutiny. They would reveal progressive stages in which men say more and more distinctly, "This Science is a great and mighty business." From such beginnings followed the progressive public organization of research.

The activities of the gentlemen who launched Natural Philosophy upon the world, needed to be supplemented by work of a coarser type before it could realize its vast potentialities. There were practical men, mostly millwrights and often of no education (Brindley could scarcely read and could write only with difficulty) who understood the pressing needs of the day and the practical difficulties in the way of overcoming them far better than the learned. They experimented in a crude practical way.

To their help came some Natural Philosophers (Rennie and Smeaton were F. R. S.) and also some military engineers bringing traditional skill of a certain kind. Out of this contact and collaboration arose the civil engineers. The civil engineers bridged the gap between pure science and practical application; they linked the toy with the needs.

Scientific research is still in its prentice stage. It is still undergoing rapid change and development, and still greatly encumbered with military, naval, and other patriotic entanglements. Its organization for intercommunication is complex and imperfect. The Institute for Intellectual Coöperation at Paris, with Madame Curie as instigator, has directed its attention to this latter group of problems—I know not with what energy, resources, or effect. Organized world-wide research is still a promise rather than an achieved reality, and yet every year the astounding harvest of science and invention increases in mass and length and breadth.

It is interesting to glance at the relations between the scientific process and the older and newer universities of the world. Belatedly those venerable seats of learning which preserve the university tradition in its greatest purity gave their recognition to the new knowledge and, as far as they could, made it amenable to the established routines of syllabus and oral lecture, notebook and examination. They did not receive it humbly; they tried to annex it and assimilate it to their ancient concepts of learning. They did all they could to give it a quality of "scholarship." Enquiry was taught as far as possible as if it were traditional Wisdom. Chairs were set up for this and that, the boundaries of "subjects" were marked out, subjects that could, in fact, coalesce or split into a score of fragments in a year or so, and "degrees" were instituted in science just as they had been for centuries in the "fixed" subjects of erudition. The universities conferred "degrees" of Bachelor, Master and Doctor of Science; that is to say, bachelors who knew some, masters who knew most, and doctors who knew all. They arranged for the young to pass from the innocence of the first year undergraduate to the complete and final knowledge of the robed and hooded Doctor. He was then to be considered a finished scientific *scholar*. Scientific men were appointed to professorial chairs, and the universities, by an insistence upon oral teaching and administrative duties, sought to wean them from too sedulous a pursuit of research.

Only very reluctantly would these venerable institutions recognize the primary importance of research and the essential insignificance of scholarship to the man of science. Abraham Flexner, in *Universities, American, English and German,** shows how much leeway modernization has still to make up. The constant fluctuations and extensions of the scheduled sciences, the perpetual eruption of crude *new* matter, worried the learned mind extremely and are still a cause for reproach on the part of scholars. They complain that science never really knows its own mind. It is perpetually correcting itself, perpetually superannuating its generalizations, never achieving a classical finish in its statements, never becoming Tradition. . . .

Slowly they are learning better now. University science becomes more and more scientific. The grants, the endowments and workers multiply. The science side grows ever greater and overshadows "scholarship" more and more. Knowledge is no longer despised because it is new, nor revered because it is mellow.

Scientific research in a review of human activities must be regarded not only from the point of view of a collective function, but also from the individual's point of view. Research work in itself becomes a career nowadays. It is clear that if the progressive development of human society is to continue, there must be a steady increase in the proportion of scientific workers to the total population. Very little attention has been paid to the social types and classes from which these workers are now drawn and the spirit in which they approach their unending coöperative task.

Scientific research is the modern form of the religious life. It gives courage and a fundamental serenity. It is the securest refuge from the distresses of the human soul. The laboratory becomes the pathway to great adventures and limitless service. Its interrogations may send off men and women to every part of

---

*Quoted in *Nature*, April 18, 1931, p. 543.

the world and direct them to the strangest experiences. Its pay and endowment are the least of its rewards.

But we are anticipating issues that will be better developed at a later stage. Let us turn now to the practical consequences of the scientific scrutiny of human conditions. The main practical sciences of the eighteenth and nineteenth century were chemistry and physics; the study of *substances,* that is, and the study of *force and movement.** The one has led to a vast increase in the materials used in social life; the other to a systematic conquest of natural power.

§ 6. *The Conquest of Substances*

It would be a fine large task in itself to compile a great book, a Book of Substances, giving a really full and orderly record of the subjugation of matter to human needs, a review of all the stuffs out of which Man shapes the tools, implements, machinery, clothing, furnishing, housing, bridges, all the impedimenta indeed of our civilization. It would tell how man has passed from the flint to stainless steel and the sterilized scalpel, and from the walls of the rocky cavern, or a shelter of tree branches and leaves, to towering steel-framed buildings of reinforced concrete. Man was once an animal which picked up things by luck and took them and used them for what they were; he has become a planning creature, making and shaping objects more and more after his heart's desire. That in brief would be the theme of that unwritten book.

Such a Book on Substances would open with a résumé of the materials used by the earliest men we know. The list would be a brief one. Some of the Hominidæ below the human level may have made a free use of sticks and unshaped stones, and may have already begun the shaping of flints. Animal substances, tusks, teeth and bones particularly, and skins, with some rude anticipations of leather-dressing, were added to these primary

---

*Under chemistry we here put botany, which was at first not so much a biological study, a study that is of *living* things, as a systematic development of the lore of the herbalist, with a view to the recognition of plants and the use of plant materials.

elements of the human equipment, and also clay, as a pigment to smear and as a substance to mould and dry. Vegetable fibre began to be twisted and woven. The first traces we have of *Homo sapiens* show him at this stage. The early Neolithic people had already a pretty taste in stones and were finding gold and setting a high value on it. Mining began before the Neolithic period. Palæolithic peoples mined for flints. Their workings are to be found in many places.

At first metals were only known through chance finds of gold and copper and meteoric iron, and then came the discovery of how to reduce certain metals from their ores. The first metallurgists worked in copper and bronze, and then came iron. The furnace improved. The furnace opened the way to glasses and enamels. A large field of knowledge, still rapidly growing, would have to be explored and summarized for this history of human materials. The Deutsches Museum at Munich gives models of primitive mines and the hearths and furnaces of savage people. It shows in a charming model, negroes smelting iron ore. It gives a series leading up to the blast furnace. It unfolds in an illuminating series of exhibits a complex stream of stories about metal winning—for every metal has its own history. The furnaces tower up, their interiors blaze more and more blindingly, the conquered and chastened metals pour more and more obediently to the casting.

All these advances, if one traces them carefully and intelligently, were prettily interdependent. One step here depends on the completion of a quite different step there. Ancient biology, for example, was greatly retarded in its development by its unawareness of the possibilities of magnification by properly shaped glasses or globular water flasks. It never suspected animalculæ therefore. Steel was known, iron was known, but neither was handled in large masses, and so the ancient world knew of steam only as the moving force of curious toys. The simple and obvious idea of railways which must have occurred to road makers again and again could find no material for its effective realization in the ancient world. A sort of rails—stone wheel tracks—are found in such excavated Roman cities as Pompeii and Pæstum.

At that point the railway idea sat down, baffled. It had to wait a couple of thousand years before the rolling mill could turn out iron rails.

This History of Substances we have imagined, would go, comparatively speaking, at an ambling pace even up to the opening decades of the nineteenth century. Man's building operations at that time were still determined by the properties of a few building stones and a few types of mortar and cement, his clothing was either natural wool or silk or cotton, his dyes were "natural" dyes, his list of metals and alloys had hardly grown since the Roman Empire, and his steel was a kind of hard iron. And then came novelties. He began to work iron and steel upon a larger scale. The use of coal in metallurgical operations assisted that. That again led to a control of steam power. At the great museums of South Kensington and Munich the relationship of the development of the steam engine to a large handling of iron and steel is manifest. *Puffing Billy,* that early locomotive, is built up of a patchwork of plates of iron bolted together. It has become almost comic in its clumsiness to modern eyes. The relatively large modern engines are built up of castings, many of which would outweigh the entire *Rocket* or *Puffing Billy*. The first *Puffing Billy*—there were several engines of that name—weighed three tons without fuel or water, and with four wheels it broke the cast-iron rails provided for it and had to have the load redistributed over eight wheels. (The vanadium high-test cast-steel frames of the electric locomotives recently built for the Norfolk & Western Railway, U. S. A., weigh nearly 9.8 tons.) Side by side with the name of Watt, the name of Wilkinson the iron founder should be remembered. The one could not have developed his ideas without the other.

Tinplate and coal gas were other cardinal events in the reawakening phase of human affairs. Rubber, wild rubber, crept into trade and industry, an unimportant stuff at first, destined to become a gigantic interest. In my childhood you rubbed out pencil marks with it. It had little more importance than that. Petroleum was a considerable find that also falls within the last seventy years.

Towards the middle nineteenth century the tempo of the narrative in our Story of Substances would quicken perceptibly. New metallic elements were being investigated; new alloys tried. Rubber began to be put to new uses and mixed with this and that. Such artificial substances as vulcanite and ebonite, combinations of raw rubber and sulphur, were being made and tried out for all sorts of purposes. The idea of artificial substances inspired a growing multitude of patentees. The deliberate conquest of substances was being undertaken. Every day new substances were being discovered and led into the factory.

The headlong substitution of "made" materials for "natural" materials during the last sixty or seventy years is an extraordinarily important fact in this present summary. At the opening of the scientific period, man was still going humbly and submissively to the rock or the plant or the sheep or the silkworm and taking what was given him as the directive and limiting conditions of the building or weaving. Now he makes his pastes and pulps into whatever texture or fibre he needs. Once steel was steel, a rather uncertain but powerful substance. Now, as we will tell later, there are hundreds of kinds of steel, and each knows precisely what is expected of it, and in understanding hands behaves accordingly. An array of once undreamt-of new metals has come in to enrich the resources of metallurgy.

In order to exhibit this array with anything resembling completeness, a sedulous canvass of great groups of industry would have to be made. So much novelty is continually being poured into industrial life that if we were to be up to date we should have to go to the fountain-heads. And also we should have to take stock of all the new raw materials, formerly unused, which are the basis of this ever increasing array of made and prepared substances.

But it is possible to sketch out one or two striking developments that have occurred in the list of industrial substances during the last century, and this shall be done in the next section. That Book of Substances I have just projected for an actual encyclopædic *Science of Work and Wealth* would be a filling up of the gaps and an amplification of the particulars of this and the following section.

But it would go further. It would take up the question of quantities, a thing we cannot even begin to do here. To make the story complete there would have to be an estimate of the visible and probable supplies of ores and of animal and vegetable substances, of oil and coal. That would be—in other words—an outline of Economic Geography and the distribution of present and potential supplies of raw material about the earth. This would broaden out at last so as to amount to a résumé of the chemical composition of the entire globe, considered as a ball of raw material for economic exploitation.

§7. Some Typical Modern Materials

We will not attempt any complete inventory of useful materials here, but let us at least stroll about the human warehouse and see what is lying about in it and what invention and discovery have recently brought in and made available.

If it were possible to summon the whole *Science of Work and Wealth* into existence here, if we could thrust out our hands and eyes into the year 1940 and turn over the two or three hundred thousand pages that may then exist, we should find long, fascinating chapters devoted to the story of coal and oil, the story of iron and steel and of the metals and non-metallic minerals. There would be long descriptions, stage by stage, of mines and foundries, of the processes by which lead, tin, and other familiar metals are brought at last, tamed and submissive, to our hands. Modern discussions of the better utilization of coal would have produced their inevitable fruits. The already rich and eventful history of the distillation of coal, the story of gas and of the by-products of coal gas, would have had new chapters added to it. The oil chapter would tell of the refinery and of another great multitude of secondary materials arising out of oil. Here we can but intimate and sketch. We should read of copper refining—for the electrification of the world depends on copper; we should be told of the conquest of aluminium and of all that its lightness and strength make possible. On tin, they say, the food supplies of our urbanized world depend. But there the aluminium container and the "paper" carton may save the situation.

Had we limitless space the account of the distillation of coal would lead on to a description of aniline dyes, one only of the endless outcomes of that distillation and that would carry us on to an account of the dyes of former days, how rare and limited they were, and we should realize the great outbreak of colour in dress and furnishing and of scents and medical substances— as well as of frightful explosives—that the modern chemist has made possible. How did the colour of a ballet or a pantomime scene in the early nineteenth century compare with that of one to-day? I believe we should find it was extraordinarily flat and unsubtle.

Under the heading of nonmetallic minerals we should read in that great collection of details we have imagined, an account, for instance, of the finding and trade in various precious and semi-precious stones and a little about diamond cutting and why it fixed its headquarters for so long at Amsterdam. No such discursiveness is possible here. And then there would come a survey of the materials of the potter and the glass-maker and the comparative study of the ancient and modern cements. A brilliant array of modern pastes and enamels would follow. The vast architectural possibilities of reinforced concrete would be touched upon. But its fuller treatment would be better left for our chapter on the housing of mankind.

I seem to see before me a vast display of exhibits to comprehend longcloth, paper, celluloid and a multitude of other such substances, brought together under the heading of "The Utilization of Cellulose," the substance of the ordinary vegetable cell wall. One branch of that utilization is the production of artificial silk. Hundreds of ingenious minds, crystallizing their results in thousands of patents, have led step by step to this one new item in the world's clothing.

The world's production of artificial silk in 1927 was more than 125,000 tons. A quarter of a century before, artificial silk was unknown. The story of artificial silk is a story of steadily accelerated invention. Réaumur, in 1734, suggested that artificial silk might be made from the solution of a gum. But the chemical knowledge of the time was insufficient to develop the suggestion. A hundred and twenty years later Andromars made cellulose nitrate by treating cellulose with nitric and sulphuric acids. This could be dissolved in a mixture of alcohol and ether, and when it was forced through a fine orifice, the alcohol and ether evaporated, leaving a filament of nitro-cellulose which could be converted into cellulose again without appreciable loss of form. That thread was the clue to the practical achievement of an artificial silk fibre.

For a time the technical difficulties of manufacture remained insuperable; Andromars' artificial silk fibre was a scientific curiosity and nothing more, and then a Frenchman, Chardonnet, worked out a commercial process. His attention was drawn to the matter while a student under Pasteur, when the latter was pursuing his famous investigations into silkworm disease. For thirty years Chardonnet struggled with his problem and at last worried through to success. He took out his first patent in 1884. His process is still in use, though the cost of the alcohol and ether was at first a serious disadvantage. Effective methods of recovering these had to be discovered.

A parallel process in which cellulose was dissolved in an ammoniacal solution of cupric hydro-oxide was worked out in France in 1900.

In 1902 Cross and Bevan discovered viscose, or zanthate of cellulose, a new and better material for the fibre, and from that time things went swiftly. By 1927 viscose formed 84 per cent of the world's artificial silk output. Three years later the same chemists invented the acetate process by which celanese is produced. All varieties of artificial silk are now known as *rayon*.

The raw materials used are cotton linters—the short fibres produced when cotton is "ginned" to remove the seeds; or wood pulp, obtained from spruce—usually *Picea excelsa;* and an abundant supply of pure soft water. From these materials not only rayon but also artificial horsehair, wool, narrow ribbon exquisitely delicate and fragile, films, sheets, and plastic masses of cellulose or cellulose acetate are now obtained.

When treated with camphor, cellulose forms celluloid, the material of camera and cinema films, of trinkets, toilet requisites, and toys, of collars, of cutlery, brush, umbrella and walking-stick handles, and of a thousand and one things, formerly made in bone, ivory, glass, china, leather, cotton, linen, wood, or metal. A sheet enclosed between two sheets of glass forms the unbreakable material used for the wind screens of motor cars.

Compounds of cellulose and acetic acid (the acid of vinegar) are used as "dope" for aëroplanes. They form a durable, glossy, and extremely tenacious film over wood, metal or fabric, and are replacing other forms of paint and varnish on account of the more attractive finish. Thin sheets of this material are used for wrapping food, and a film deposited on wire gauze forms a substitute for glass. All this variety of substances have been won from wood pulp and cotton refuse in the last fifty years.

It would be an interesting special study to trace the progressive introduction of animal and vegetable substances to industrial use. Leaving the ore heaps and chemical works behind us we should carry out our survey to the open, to the plantations and forests and wildernesses, where the "first state" of our substances is to be found. Some day we shall have precise estimates of the wild wastage of fine timbers that has gone on, and industrious students will have put in order the records of the modern search for fibres and paper, pulps and vegetable and animal oils. A history of materials if it is to be complete must also pursue the fur trapper and tell of fur farms and of the tragedy of sealing. How far is man killing off the whale and the ivory animals? There have been very hideous massacres of penguins for oil; it is a particularly moving story of waste and cruelty.

There is an interesting story behind this vehement search for animal and vegetable oils. Fifty years ago the chief demand for such oils came from the soap industry. Nobody thought of eating them or could have eaten them.

Soap is essentially a sodium or potassium salt of a fatty acid. The fatty acids are present in animals and plants in combination with glycerine. When these glycerides are treated with caustic soda or caustic potash the soda or potash displaces the glycerine, and soap is the product.

Tallow, obtained by boiling animal fat, was used for centuries for soap-making as well as for candles. Palm oil from Africa and olive oil from the Mediterranean region were employed for the choicer toilet soaps. And of these oils there was enough and to spare, until margarine became an article of manufacture. Margarine, however, is also made from animal oil, vegetable oil, or mixed oils. The principal raw materials are the oils of the cocoanut palm kernel, cotton seed, soya bean, or other plant products, and the fatty tissues of the caul and kidneys of cattle. These ingredients are mixed with skim milk which has been pasteurized and inoculated with lactic acid forming bacilli to make margarine. Most people over fifty can remember the introduction of this new synthetic and cheaper rival to butter and recall the prejudice it aroused.

Now the manufacturer of margarine soon outbid the soap-boiler for the better qualities of oils and fats. A scarcity arose, more particularly of the harder oils or fats. The difference between soft (fluent) oils and hard oils or fats is as a rule a difference in the amount of hydrogen they contain. The former have less hydrogen than the latter. It was the hard fats the margarine makers and the soap makers wanted and struggled to obtain.

The chemist in his laboratory, at that time, could produce a hard fat from an oil by the addition of hydrogen. But his processes were difficult to carry out on a commercial scale. The problem was solved finally by employing a general reaction discovered by Sebatier and Senderens. They passed hydrogen through the fat heated to a temperature of 140°C. to 200°C. in the presence of a finely divided metal such as nickel. Not only did this harden the oil, but it deodorized it. So suddenly not only were soft oils turned to hard, but whale and fish oils, which formerly had had a limited utility owing to their objectionable smell, were brought to the aid of the soap-boiler and butterman. The balance of supply was restored, and the quantity available was enormously extended. To-day whale oil can not only be used for soap, but also for margarine, salad oil, and other articles of food. So black olives lie wasting now in the olive orchards of Provence while native labour gathers the material for the world's salad oil in the East Indies and the African forests, and the whalers of the Southern seas supplement their efforts.

While the invention of margarine captured a great supply of hitherto unassimilable oils and fats for food purposes, the story of milk products shows us the reverse process of utilizing a periodically excessive supply of nutritive material for industrial processes. Milk has a constituent called casein. It is an albuminous substance similar to the white of egg. It is the curd which is precipitated when rennet or a dilute acid is added to milk, or when milk sours naturally. When dried it forms a white powder, and of this powder about ten thousand tons are now produced annually in the United States alone.

The buttermilk or skim milk from which it is obtained has a limited value as a food for domestic animals. But the white powder is used in confectionery and certain manufactured foods, in cosmetics and ointments, as an adhesive material for glass, china, paper, wood, and other substances, in printing and sizing cotton fabrics, for waterproofing paper, and for making distempers.

When the dried powder is compressed and then hardened by soaking in a solution of formaldehyde, it can be machined and polished. Alone or mixed with various filling materials or colouring matter, this moulded and indurated material imitates ivory, horn, bone, tortoise-shell, amber, ebony, and ornamental minerals like malachite. It is fashioned into toilet trinkets, inkstands, cigarette holders, the handles of cutlery, brushes, and umbrellas, and scores of other articles. The colouring and translucency of many of these things are exquisite. How many people realize that the manicure set and the morning milk have a common origin?

Another series of artificial substances of great modern importance are the synthetic resins. Natural resins are gummy liquids which are exuded by trees, especially conifers. Amber is a fossil resin that has been valued since prehistoric times. But that is not the amber you will buy nowadays in the Rue de Rivoli. Resins differ from gums in being insoluble in water, and they are extensively used in varnishes. It has been found possible to make substances similar to natural resins by acting with formaldehyde on phenol and other products of coal tar or by subjecting these products to the action of heat, light, alkalis, or strong acids. Other synthetic mixtures are also made, to which coal tar does not contribute. Some of these false resins become harder and insoluble under the action of heat. The natural ones exhibit a contrary behaviour. These artificial products are used in varnishes and as insulating material for electrical apparatus. Since they will withstand a high temperature they have an advantage over rubber, ebonite, and celluloid. Bakelite, for example, which has become popular in a hundred varieties of bright-coloured ware, retains its form and properties when most other materials would soften or decompose. It is one of the most important insulating materials used in the electrical industry. Another variety of resin is made from urea, or from thiourea, a by-product of the gas works, treated with formaldehyde. This can be tinted and is used for table and decorative ware of extraordinary delicacy and colour.

The American petroleum industry dates from 1859, when Colonel Drake drilled the first well at Oil Creek in Pennsylvania. Before that enterprise the American output (used as fuel) was only 2,000 barrels a year. To-day it is more than 900,000,000 barrels, or nearly 500,000 times greater and more than 70 per cent of the output of the world.

Petroleum is a complex mixture. By distillation at successive temperatures, the oil refiner obtains gases, naphtha, illuminating oils, lubricating heavy oils, and a residue of coke, pitch, or asphalt. Naphtha, on redistillation, is separated into petrol or gasoline, commercial naphtha, and benzine, used in dry cleaning. Similarly illuminating oils and lubricating oils yield different grades, each suitable by quality or price for a particular purpose. The heavier oils yield vaseline, petroleum jelly, and other now familiar substances. Paraffin wax, so largely used in the electrical industry—and for chewing gum!—is separated by cooling.

But the constituents do not exist in the proportions required by the modern world. The light oils have become more valuable than the heavy oils. So the heavy oils are subjected to the process of "cracking." A quick rise in the temperature of the still causes them to decompose, with the formation of lighter oils. In this way the production of illuminating oils, and particularly of petrol or gasoline, has been greatly increased during the last twenty years. A natural balance has been adjusted to meet changing human needs.

And so building up that spectacle of the world's activities which is the object of this work, we must add to the scientific experimentalists and research institutions we have already evoked as the nucleus of the modern economic world, a multitudinous array of toil and enterprise. We must fling across our canvas an impression of mines and foundries scattered about and digging into the skin of the world, innumerable quarries of every sort of stone, oil fields with their gaunt cement works, brick fields, the production of clay and feldspar for potteries, coal mines, peat cutting, forestry, and lumbering, saw mills and paper mills and a spreading increasing variety of plantations for rubber, sericulture, cotton, flax, hemp, sisal, factories for cellulose products and all the widespread extraction and preparation of the stuffs out of which the appliances of civilized life, its tools, machines, houses, clothing, and so forth are made. Here, except for our glance at margarine, we will say nothing of food. With food production we will deal later. That is the task of hundreds of millions of cultivators, the fundamental task of mankind, but here already we have millions at work of every race and colour, in every climate, winning and assembling the crude materials of modern industry in ever increasing variety and abundance.

A special chapter of outstanding liveliness in that great Book of Modern Substances would give the history of plantation rubber—with the Congo, Putumayo, and the Stock Exchange in the picture. They are not in our picture as yet, for we have still a long way to go before we come either to the tragedy of defenseless peoples invaded and forced to labour by alien enterprise, or to the problems of overproduction and planless cultivation in our still essentially haphazard world. But here we may at least glance at the happier aspect of a new substance woven into our economic life. A hundred years ago rubber was as unimportant as electricity. The very name reminds us of its chief use, the rubbing out of pencil marks. (Have we not all of us in our infantile artistry suffered from the sulphur streak of the cheaper kinds?) Or the stuff served as the material of a bouncing ball. The Spaniards found the natives playing with solid rubber balls when first they reached South America.

The extensive utilization of rubber dates from 1839. Then it was found that heating rubber with sulphur (vulcanization) made it stronger and more elastic. With more sulphur still it became harder and even brittle. In my boyhood ebonite was used for trinkets, and the incorporation of paraffin wax and other petroleum products with rubber had begun. Ebonite toys were irritatingly brittle. Very fine rubber, containing oil, was in use for such things as the tubes and teats of feeding bottles. And it was in silk-elastic also and particularly in those dreadful and now happily vanished objects, spring-sided boots.

That was about all I can remember of rubber sixty years ago. It was still a mere accessory substance. It would hardly have been missed had it vanished altogether. Consider what has happened since then. Consider its use for electrical insulation alone. If by some miracle rubber suddenly ceased to exist, what would happen to our streets and homes? Silence and darkness. The telephone would cease to ring. Seven eighths of the wheeled traffic would stand immobilized in the streets. Within a lifetime rubber has passed from the status of a supplementary elastic substance to a position of fundamental importance.

At first it was a wild product, it was made from the latex of various forest trees and plants of which *Hevea brasiliensis* was the chief. It was collected, often under dreadful conditions, in Brazil and the Congo Free State. (We shall have a grim story to tell later about that.) In my childhood a few thousand tons of this ball rubber was all the rubber output in the world. Under the pressure of new demands, of which the bicycle tire was the chief, the price rose, the hunt for wild rubber became more urgent and cruel, and the total product rose towards fifty thousand tons by the end of the century. Meanwhile the economic botanists of Kew were working out the problems of its cultivation. It was first successfully grown in Ceylon, and there followed a boom in rubber plantations; they multiplied in Malaya, the Dutch East Indies, Ceylon, Indo-China, India, Siam, and tropical Africa. The output of the cleaner and better plantation product has risen to over six hundred thousand tons, and prices have fallen until further production has become unprofitable. The quantity becomes the more impressive, and its bearing upon human work becomes plainer, when we remember that rubber is derived from a milky fluid which trickles at the rate of four or five pounds a year from cuts in the bark of trees, into small vessels hung beneath the cut. From that sticky treacle its drawn-out threads pass now to weave intimately and indispensably into the entire fabric of contemporary civilization.

All this, which we treat in a few brief crowded pages of evocation here, would unfold in a full and complete *Science of Work and Wealth* into a great mass of clear and well illustrated descriptions. This section is the intimation of a great volume. It would have to be a volume if once it began to expand. This material is the sort of thing that must be done either very fully or very compactly. There is no middle distance for a landscape of staple industries. Either you must see them from a remote distance, a reek of tall chimneys, clusters of strange sheds and retorts, tangles of conduits, gigantic dumps, a distant rumble of trains and machinery, or you must go right up to the blinding heat of the electric furnace and the intimate roar and beating of the machines. You must count the chimneys, weigh the fuel and assemble the records of output. At present we are doing no more than an aërial reconnaissance of all this side of human life.

As Crawford's admirable antiquarian work has shown, a man

in an aëroplane cannot only see more deeply into the sea than
a man in a boat, but he can observe a multitude of land secrets,
old ridges, ancient roads and enclosures, and differences in soil
and texture that are altogether hidden from the man in the field.
But the airman can see nothing of the daisies and knows nothing
of the lurking life in the hedges and by-ways. Here we are, so
to speak, aëroplane economists, more concerned with the past
and the general hang of things than with particular instances.

§ 8. *The Story of Iron and Steel*

But though we have every desire to avoid overwhelming the
reader (and the writer) by masses of detailed technicality, there
is one chapter in the vast catalogue of modern substances which
is so integral to our account of the modern world, that we cannot avoid treating it with some particularity. This is the development of the iron and steel industry which was vitally necessary
to the conquest of mechanical power.

In 1700, iron was made in Britain with charcoal in small blast
furnaces. Steel was got by heating pure wrought Swedish iron
in contact with charcoal. This *blister steel,* so called because the
process of manufacture resulted in the formation of blisters on
the surface of the metal, was broken up, bound into faggots, re-
heated and beaten to *shear steel.* That was the only iron and
the only steel in England, and there was not very much of either.
How much, we do not know. In other countries matters were
at as low or a lower level. Bars, fetters, railways, small cannon
were the largest workings of iron; a sword blade or a breast
plate was the maximum piece of steel.

In the early eighteenth century coke began to replace charcoal
in the blast furnaces. Coke permitted heavier charges, heavier
charges involved longer contact with the fuel, and a more fluid
iron was produced. Coal-fired reverberatory furnaces appeared
after the middle of the century, and puddling and rolling followed. Foundry and forge tended to concentrate on the coal
fields, and industrial units grew larger. Shear steel gave way to
cast steel for many purposes, on account of the relative cheap-

ness of the latter, so soon as crucibles could be found capable of standing the high temperature necessary to melt steel. But shear steel (double shear steel) is still used—for high grade carving knives, for example, and suchlike purposes. With this new abundance of steel, cutlery, fine-edge tools, steel springs became abundant in the world, facilitating scores of new processes and making hundreds of new conveniences possible.

By 1800 the world's output of iron and steel was perhaps over six hundred thousand tons.

By 1820, the production of pig iron in the world passed the million mark. Crawshay of Cyfarthfa could not turn out five hundred tons of bar iron in 1787; in 1812 he produced ten thousand tons. That was how things were going.

This flow of iron and steel into human resources made itself apparent in a number of useful things that had hitherto been impossible. In the latter half of the eighteenth century, not only was wrought iron being largely used, but cast iron was being extended to a number of purposes. The first iron bridge (cast iron) was constructed across the Severn in 1777–79 by Abraham Darby. An iron canal boat was built and launched by Wilkinson in 1787. Cast iron was used for tramway rails from 1767, and wrought iron on the Stockton and Darlington railway in 1825. Iron in quantity had solved that problem of the railway, which had entirely baffled Roman civilization.

In 1788 about half the pig iron produced in England was puddled. The steel was made almost wholly from imported iron, and employed only for cutlery, tools, and springs. The amount must have been relatively small. Nowhere in the world was steel used for anything but cutlery, tools, weapons and springs.

Cast iron, wrought iron, shear steel and cast steel were all available for human use in 1800. There were several grades in each. The quality depended upon the purity of the ore, whether the fuel was coke or charcoal, and upon the judgment of the workman. The purest ore was Swedish magnetite, but there were also inferior varieties of iron from Sweden. Some ores contain phosphorus, and iron containing this element is "cold-short," or brittle when cold. It was used for little but nail-making. Iron melted by coke was liable to contain sulphur. This caused "red-shortness," that is to say brittleness when red hot.

A sample of steel in those days was found to be suitable or unsuitable on trial. Even rough chemical analysis was hardly available as yet and quantitative chemistry had still to come. A sample was examined by breaking and noting the fracture. That is still used as a rough test to-day. But there were neither testing machines, nor quantitative methods of analysis, nor metallographical methods. No organized knowledge, in fact, but merely empiricism and experience.

Neilson's invention of the hot blast in 1829 introduced an economy in fuel and enabled the Scottish blackband ironstone to be smelted. The temperature of the blast was raised to 600°F. That was a great achievement for the time. To-day temperatures of about 1800°F. in the blast furnaces are not unusual. Wrought iron continued to be made by the laborious process of hand puddling for many years. In 1856–60 the Bessemer process of blowing air through molten pig iron to burn out impurities and then adding carbon and other ingredients to make steel came in, and for the first time steel became cheap and available in bulk. Castings of steel up to 25 tons became possible. The open hearth appeared in 1864, a gas-fired furnace in which pig iron and scrap iron are melted in an oxidizing atmosphere. Steel castings of over one hundred tons became possible, and the quantity of metal produced increased and increased. From one American open hearth two hundred tons of metal have been pouring every three or four hours since 1927. We have several hundreds of tons of steel to-day for every ton of iron or steel the world could produce in 1800.

Each advance in the size of iron and steel castings opened up new possibilities of handling and utilization. Lifting appliances for heavy weights, for example, could only exist when metal was available in huge castings. Otherwise you could not make a sufficiently big crane. In 1800 not more than a ton or so could be lifted. To-day 5-, 10-, and 20-ton cranes are common and castings of 50 or even 100 tons may have to be moved. Generally any casting of more than 100 tons is made in two or more parts to be bolted together. But a 50-ton mass can be handled with more ease to-day than a single ton lump in 1800.

In America 11 per cent of the steel produced is used in the form of pipes. The production of pipes was a very difficult process in 1800, and little if any iron pipe was made. There are two methods of pipe-making to-day: either a flat sheet is rolled and the edges are welded in a longitudinal joint, or the metal is rolled over a pier to form a cavity and a seamless tube is produced. Seamless iron pipes are also made by means of centrifugal casting. The high pressures now being tested in power stations (600 pounds to 1,200 pounds per square inch) would be impossible without seamless tube. So one thing leads to another, and impossibility after impossibility crumbles away before the advance in substance control.

The electric furnace came into use in 1890. It is largely employed in the manufacture of the alloy steels used in motor-car construction, and for the stainless steels. Since it asks for water power rather than coal, it has been extensively developed for tonnage steels in Italy, where there are 200 furnaces in operation. The high frequency electric crucible furnace has been introduced since 1927. With this, the highest classes of tool steel can be produced. It contrasts very vividly with the crucible furnaces it is replacing. Formerly you had men standing astride white-hot coke furnaces, enduring the most terrific temperatures as they lifted out the pots of steel by their sheer unaided strength. Now, at the pressing of a button, eight times the quantity of metal is poured out, in a fourth of the time.

The world output of pig iron in 1927 was 85,270,000 tons, and there had been an increase in every decade since 1800. The production of steel in the same year 1927 was 100,180,000 tons. This disproportion is due to the fact that large amounts of steel scrap and iron ore are used in steel making and that a considerable amount of steel contains elements other than iron and carbon. The figures are not comparable. Steel has largely replaced wrought iron for all constructional work and for parts of machinery where strength, resistance to shock, and durability are required. We may compare the 85,270,000 tons of pig iron with the annual output of 650,000 tons in 1800. It is 131 times as great. But the increase in the quantity of steel would be even more striking if the figures were available. To-day we have hundreds of tons of steel for every ton of either wrought iron or steel available in 1800.

And meanwhile steel, which was a distinctly mysterious iron product in 1800, has had its composition studied, analyzed and controlled.

In 1800 steel was just the substance of a knife blade or a sword. It was one substance, so far as was known. But now we have on our economic bill of fare not one steel but dozens. There are first the carbon steels. These contain iron and carbon with only traces of other elements: phosphorus, sulphur, silicon, manganese. All tonnage steel (steels made in large quantities) contain 0.3 per cent and upward of manganese. There are seven grades of carbon steel known as: extra soft, structural or mild, medium, medium hard, hard, spring, and carbon turning-tool quality. It is the first two grades which have so largely replaced wrought iron. The softest cannot be hardened. It can be case-hardened. (Case-hardening consists of heating the metal in contact with carbonaceous material whereby carbon is absorbed, giving a surface of harder steel.) It is workable either hot or cold, and is used for thin sheets, which are cold-rolled, rivets, which have to be beaten out, pipes which have to be bent, and smith's bar.

Structural steel is used for bridges, boilers, and railway rolling stock. Medium steel is used for shipbuilding and machinery. Medium hard for large forgings, parts of locomotives, car axles, rails. Hard steel for wheels, tires, wood-cutting tools, etc. All these carbon steels can be forged and machined, but with increasing difficulty as the carbon content rises. From medium steel onwards the quality depends largely on the heat treatment to which they have been subjected. Hardness is increased at the expense of ductility, and is often accompanied by brittleness.

The following table from the Encyclopædia Britannica indicates the kind of variation:

Material	Ultimate strength
Rivet steel	50,000 lbs. per sq. in.
Medium hard	75,000 " " " "
Spring after quenching	200,000 " " " "
Spring steel	150,000 " " " "

These seven grades have a total extreme difference of carbon content of only 1.2 per cent (from 0.08 per cent to 1.2 per cent). They illustrate the extraordinary effect of minute quantities of this element on iron, and they show the remarkable accuracy with which metallurgical operations are now conducted. A hundred tons or more of metal may be poured into a mould and not differ from the required proportion of carbon by more than 0.1 per cent. Other elements, particularly manganese, nickel, chromium, tungsten, molybdenum, cobalt, and vanadium, when present in certain proportions, have a powerful influence on the qualities of steel. Manganese in quantities below 1.0 per cent strengthens and toughens iron. Very strong castings are made with 1 per cent to 2 per cent manganese.

Silicon steel, or to be more precise silico-tungsten steel, is used for long-span bridges, boilers and in shipbuilding. It has a strength greater by 10,000 pounds per square inch than other kinds used for boilers. Its ultimate strength is 120,000 pounds per square inch, and a test piece stretches 23 per cent before breaking. A 0.9 per cent carbon steel with 1.65 per cent manganese, undergoes very small distortion during heat treatment (hardening and tempering) and is used for dies and gauges. Hadfield's manganese steel has 11 per cent to 12 per cent manganese, and 1.0 per cent to 1.2 per cent carbon and was for long the toughest material known, though it has now given pride of place to the austenitic nickel chrome steels. It resists shock and wear, and is used for tramway points, dredger buckets, crusher jaws, and the like purposes.

A carbon steel tool has a relatively low limit of cutting speed. If the speed is too high it becomes hot, loses its temper and its

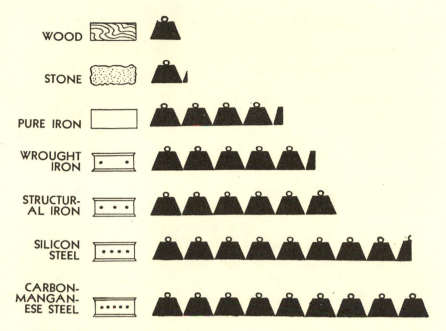

WOOD

STONE

PURE IRON

WROUGHT IRON

STRUCTUR-AL IRON

SILICON STEEL

CARBON-MANGAN-ESE STEEL

THE GROWING STRENGTH OF MAN'S MATERIALS

THE size of his structures, and the scope of his activities, have depended to a great extent on the materials which man has had at his command. Each weight in this chart represents a load of ten thousand pounds to the square inch. To develop from wood or stone, the earliest building material, with a useful strength of about ten thousand pounds per square inch, to the latest steels, which will carry ninety thousand pounds and more, has taken many hundreds of years. There are harder and stronger steels known than the carbon-manganese alloy shown above, but they have as a rule other qualities which make them undesirable for general structural uses. The figures for strength are from the United States Bureau of Standards.

edge. Higher speeds were found to be possible with the tungsten-manganese alloy invented by R. Mushet between 1860 and 1870. This was self-hardening by heating to a high temperature and cooling slowly. Similar steels containing tungsten and chromium were used in America. It was supposed that the temperature of hardening should not exceed 815°C. to 845°C. But Taylor and White (Bethlehem Steel Co., Pa., U. S. A.) after twenty-six years' research discovered in 1900 that if heated to 1040°C. to 1100°C. its hardness was greatly increased, and the tool would cut at a red heat without loss of edge. This was the first of a number of high-speed tool steels. No need to cool off; no need to slow down: they drive on. In some cases cobalt is added to these steels, and it will be news to many readers that there are now several high-speed tool "steels" which do not contain iron. Stellite, for example, has cobalt 55 per cent, tungsten 15 to 25 per cent, chromium 15 to 25 per cent, and molybdenum 5 per cent. More recent and more important now than stellite is tungsten carbide.

The practical consequence of man's conquest of these new materials may be gauged by the fact that, with a particular quality of steel in the lathe and the same depth of cut, a plain carbon steel cuts at 16 feet per minute, an air-hardening steel cuts at 26 feet per minute, or, after quenching, 60 feet per minute, and a modern high-speed steel 100 feet per minute or more. With softer material and lighter cuts a speed of 150 to 175 feet per minute is attained. Under favourable conditions tungsten carbide will remove the metal at over 300 feet a minute. The writer has seen it cutting cast iron at as high a rate as 400 feet a minute.

I will not dilate here upon nickel, chromium, and nickel-chromium steels. The effect of each element is to toughen steel and to enable hardness to be secured without brittleness. They are more effective in this when used together. Stainless steel has more than 10 per cent (often 13 per cent) of chromium. Nickel steels are used in bridge and structural work generally and for boilers. They are heat-treated for guns, engine forgings, and shafts. Chromium steels are used for projectiles, grinding rolls, and roller bearings, and with nickel or vanadium for armour plate, or, heat-treated, for axles, machine parts, and gearing.

At one time aëroplane and automobile were entirely dependent on tungsten steel, because it was the only steel possible for the permanent magnets in the magneto until chrome steel (for cheaper types) or cobalt steel became available. Tungsten can be produced in a ductile form and is then used for the filaments of electric lamps. It has entirely superseded the earlier carbon filament, and it made wireless telephony and broadcasting possible. The earlier forms of thermionic valve essential to a receiving set could not have existed without tungsten. . . .

But enough of such facts have been given for our present purpose. We must draw back before the serried facts overwhelm us. The little steel sword blade of our great-grandfathers has become the framework of bridge, railroad, ocean liner, sky-scraper, and ten thousand other things. In a locomotive or motor car to-day you will find a score of different steels, all beautifully adapted to the work. I will not attempt to estimate the hundreds of thousands of patents, the scores of thousands of inventive minds, that have gone to the making of this one chapter in the multitudinous history of substances. I have left the tale abbreviated, cut down, and only half told, and side by side with it could be set a score of parallel tales.

An adequate Book of Substances alone would make a stupendous volume. You would never read it; you would only read in it. You would insist upon a comprehensive index and go to it ever and again for a fact. Here you have been given all and more than you need. One adviser has already remarked that some of the pages immediately preceding this read like "extracts from an article in the 'annual review' of a technical journal"— and how else could they read? And such a Book of Substances would give only the material basis of the spectacle of human activities, the material basis only of the life of work, wealth, and enjoyment we are setting ourselves to survey. It would be only an introduction to the more crowded books that would follow it. Happily our main argument is possible without the actual production of that interminable catalogue.

§ 9. *The Conquest of Power. Sources of Power*

And now we come to a group of facts so important to the modern world that, as I have told in the Introduction, I thought of calling this entire work by its name, the *Conquest of Power*. There is also a reverse title to that: the *Abolition of Toil.* Yet it is not merely that mechanical power has replaced toil over a vast proportion of the field of human effort. That is only a part of what has happened. There has been an enormous *addition,* an altogether disproportionate extension of the energy available for human ends.

We have distinguished in man's history a prehistoric, casual-living, sub-human stage; a stage in which social life and tradition appear and human life is retrospective and ruled by precedent and historical legend; and this present third stage in which we are living, with science and design rapidly ousting tradition from its domination over human life.

The age of tradition was also the age of toil. The traditional social life is and always has been pyramidal, with a mass of toiling workers as its base. This modern life that opens before us seems likely to have an entirely different structural scheme.

Toil, like tradition, is a distinctively human thing, made possible by the intricate reactions of the human cerebral cortex. Toil is sustained work done against the grain and giving no essential satisfaction in itself, done because the individual indisposition for it is overcome by some more powerful system of motives. A few of the more intelligent gregarious animals have also been made to toil by human compulsion, horses, oxen, and the like, but outside the list of these exceptions there seems to be no real toil in animal life. Most living creatures will not stand toil. They will resist to the death. The "workers" of the ants and bees are not toilers: they work by instinct; it is what their structure dictates and what they want to do. The scarabæus, rolling its dung balls, is no more toiling than the nightingale singing in a tree.

But human *"toil"* is not instinctive, not as people say a

"*natural*" thing. Work may be a natural thing. Much human work, the work of a sincere artist, writer or inventor, for example—expressive work, as we call it—is not toil in the sense in which we are now using the word. It does not go against the grain. But the spectacle of human history shows us a long succession of generations in which a great majority of the community was *subdued to labour*. The muscular force of this labour class, doggedly applied, was the main source of power, the driving force of the social mechanism. The community could not have gone on without that subjugation.

In a brief century or so science and invention have rendered the bulk of this muscular exertion superfluous. It is no longer necessary that man should virtually enslave his fellow man; he has found new slaves, gigantic slaves, out of all proportion mightier than the human hands and muscles that hitherto have thrust and moulded obdurate matter to human ends.

A complete history of the Conquest of Power* would open with a brief review of the sources of power in the early civilizations. It is a meagre list of accessories. Except for the department of transport, wherein wind and stream and pack animal played important parts, for a certain limited use of wind wheels and water power as well as beast power for grinding and irrigation it was human muscle that kept things going. Even on the sea the galley was preferred to the sailing ship.

From this review of the ancestral equipment the record would pass on to the pryings and guessings of more ingenious spirits of the Middle Ages. At the time such enquiries must have seemed the oddest, obscurest, least important of activities.

Each machine was a curiosity because it was unique. It was designed for a particular purpose. This purpose loomed so large that it obscured the general principle. Whatever the motive power—wind, water, horses, or bullocks might be used—it was part of the machine. The first idea of a Prime Mover, capable

---

The Quest of Power, by H. P. and M. W. Vowles (1931), gives the story from windmill and water wheel onward, very interestingly and in ampler detail than was desirable here.

of driving a variety of machines, appears in the work of
Leonardo de Vinci.

The sixteenth and seventeenth centuries produced a number
of pioneers whose work, like so much pioneer work, was more
notable for its failures than for its successes. But as children say
in the game of "hide and seek," they were getting hotter and
hotter. Then, suddenly, like a new and splendid theme taking
possession of a musical composition, deliberate invention and
discovery break into human history.

That fuller story of the Conquest of Power we are imagining
would note the early attempts to use steam, and it would "feature" James Watt very prominently at the opening of the new
phase. It would trace the increasing efficiency of steam generating. It would give pictures and descriptions of the older and most
modern types of steam engine. The steam turbine has opened a
new modern chapter in. the history of steam. From the turbine
the Power Book in the *Science of Work and Wealth* would pass
to a second type of power production, the internal combustion
engine, in which the intervention of steam is dispensed with and
the explosive combustion of a jet of gas or a spray of finely
divided liquid is applied directly to give the thrust of the
engine.

How rapid this development has been may be illustrated by
a few facts. The "Otto" gas engine of 1876 was the result of
100 years of effort, largely fruitless, except for the temporary
success of the Lenoir engine six years earlier. The fuel was town
gas—far too expensive for large scale use. Dowson in 1878 exhibited a gas producer in which cheap coal slack was employed,
and Sir Frederick Bramwell prophesied that within fifty years
the gas engine would replace the steam engine as a source of
power. He was wrong. He underestimated the world's capacity
for power. He did not foresee the variety of purposes to which
power would be applied. It was not clear at the time that steam
engines of ten, twenty, and to-day of over fifty-thousand horsepower would be built.

At that time the oil engine had not appeared. Daimler invented
his petrol engine in 1884, the year that saw the first steam tur-

bine. Parsons' first patent for a reaction turbine was followed a year later by De Laval's patent for an impulse turbine. Priestman invented the first medium oil engine in 1885, and in 1892 Diesel patented the heavy oil engine with which his name is now inseparably connected. The first Diesel was built in 1895, but it took twenty years to work out the subsidiary problems of this type. These three stages in the evolution of the oil engine used successively cheaper forms of fuel, while the actual consumption of fuel in medium and heavy oil engines per brake horsepower has been reduced since 1890 by more than one half. In the last few years the oil engine has been ousting the steam engine in a hundred different fields. The heavy oil engine competes now with the steam engine in driving factories, in pumping, the production of electricity, in the propulsion of ships, and is even threatening the steam locomotive. How great the success has been for ship propulsion is indicated by the fact that in 1930 the world's output of new steamships was 148,176 tons, and of motor ships 1,468,235 tons. The Italian motorship Augustus, built in 1927, is 32,650 tons burden.

The light oil engine made the motor car and the aëroplane possible. Since 1915 the weight per horsepower of an air-cooled engine has been reduced from 3 lbs. to 1½ lbs. The accuracy of workmanship and delicacy of adjustment of these high-speed engines are among the great mechanical triumphs of the age. They run at from 1,000 to 4,000 revolutions a minute. For the sake of simplicity suppose the speed is 1,200. Then there is a revolution every twentieth of a second. In half that time, in one-fortieth of a second, the engine makes a stroke. At each stroke the valves open and air and fuel are admitted, or the mixture is compressed, or it is exploded, or the valves open and the spent gases are swept out. The spark which fires the mixture must take place at exactly the right moment. It must be adjusted to an almost infinitesimal fraction of a second. The inlet valves open and close with marvellous precision. The exhaust valves act in turn, though they are at a bright red heat. High temperatures, high pressure and high speed are here brought into coöperation in a way which would have amazed the engineers of an earlier generation.

Let us explain here a few of the more important developments in the utilization of fuel.

The special advantage of a *gas* is that it can be intimately mixed with the proper amount of air for complete combustion. Only a slight excess is required. A *liquid* fuel possesses a similar advantage. The lighter oils are vaporized before burning, and the heavier varieties are broken up into a spray by a jet of compressed air. Liquid fuels have the special merit that they are easily stored and so can be transported economically over longer distances. The burning of a *solid* fuel is by comparison slow and irregular and from 120 to 150 per cent more air than is required for combustion has to pass through the furnace and flues. The use of mechanical stokers and continuous agitation of the fuel may facilitate the removal of ash and increase the rapidity and regularity, but they hardly affect the excess of air which lowers the furnace temperature.

The distillation of coal in retorts yields gas, ammoniacal liquor, tar, and coke. This process has been in use for the public supply of gas for over a century. A modification of the process in which the yield of gas and liquid products is of secondary importance is employed in the preparation of the hard, dense coke for metallurgical furnaces. Coke-oven gas is now used to supplement the gas-works product for public supply. But coal (usually breeze or slack) and coke can be converted wholly into gas (producer gas or water gas) by blowing air, or air and steam, through the hot material. Gas obtained by the distillation of raw coal contains mainly hydrogen (about 40 per cent), methane (21 to 28 per cent), and carbon monoxide (8 to 15 per cent). The new low temperature carbonization process gives percentages of 29, 49, and 8 respectively. From 5 to 8 per cent of nitrogen is present also. Producer gas is carbon monoxide, and water gas is carbon monoxide and hydrogen. Both these gases contain a large percentage of nitrogen, which serves merely to dilute the mixture.

Coal contains excess of carbon which can only be converted

into combustible gas by burning in a regulated supply of air. It is this air which brings in the diluent nitrogen. Attempts have been made to convert coal, with the exception of the small percentage of ash, wholly or almost wholly into combustible liquids and gases, mainly in order to increase the supply of liquid fuel, but this work is still in the experimental stage. The competition of gas and petroleum has, however, led to another way of using coal—particularly the breeze or slack, which is too small for many industrial purposes. The material is ground into a fine powder, dried and fed into the furnace through a nozzle by the aid of compressed air. Combustion then takes place, as in the case of a gaseous or liquid fuel, and only 20 to 30 per cent excess of air is required. There were tentative experiments on this method forty years ago, but the main progress has been made in the last ten years. The annual consumption of pulverized fuels is now about 150 million tons. It is used for firing cement kilns, in metallurgical furnaces, and for steam-raising.

All these ways of using fuel aim at economy but do not necessarily involve a reduction in consumption. The tendency is for power spread ever more widely over the world to exploit new or old sources of raw material and to provide increased facilities for transportation and other public services. The capacity to employ power seems to be illimitable. And yet fuel, solid, liquid or gaseous, is not inexhaustible. Oil can never satisfy more than a fifth of the world's present dependence upon coal. And the coal "in sight" will last, at the present rate of consumption, for twenty generations or so. Twenty generations back in our own history takes us to the Hundred Years' War, the Black Death, the First Statute of Labourers, the Peasants' Revolt, and the First Navigation Act. The changes since then have been many and, in a sense, revolutionary. But the changes in the next period, especially as they affect human life and work, will appear more numerous and still more revolutionary to those who will look backwards as we do to-day, but over twice the length of time.

As it nears exhaustion, coal may become more valuable as a source of raw material for the chemical industry than as a means of obtaining mechanical power.

Here, were we aiming at encyclopædic completeness, would be the place for a survey of the automobile and aircraft engines of to-day. In that encyclopædic expansion there would have to be a great mass of information about modern engines and a vast multitude of figures and diagrams. Such details would be interesting to those with a special aptitude for these things; for most readers they would stand unread as reassuring and confirmatory matter, and they would add nothing to our general exposition.

But a point we have to note here is the extreme transitoriness of this phase in mechanical evolution, in which power is derived from the combustion of natural substances like coal and oil. The employment of steam was the means by which man broke through to the idea of power machinery; and it was only with great advances in metallurgical science that the explosive engine became possible. But these advances have now been made, and man turns again to the wind wheel and to water power, to the force of gravitating water, of which indeed since the very beginnings of his economic life he had made a dribbling little use, for water-lifting and the like, but which he could never use properly before our present phase of metallurgical attainment because of the inadequacy of his water wheels and his lack of transmission contrivances. Dr. Herbert Levenstein* speaks of the coal-power and oil-power age, "the age of fossil power," as a mere incident in the economic evolution of mankind. "It will have lasted, when it is over, for a shorter period than the Moorish occupation of Spain."

Now, with the electric current discovered and at his disposal, man has no difficulty in transferring the force of the windmill or water wheel to the most distant points of application, and the advance of metallurgy has converted the flapping wooden wheel of the old-world miller into a mighty interceptor of the rush and weight of stream and waterfall. The economic world turns back from fuel to this ancient and hitherto scarcely exploited resource of water power. So long as the world spins and the sun

*Address entitled "But an Apprentice in Nature's Workshop," Soc. of Chem. Indus., July 15, 1930.

shines and the rain falls, there will be no end to the perpetual renewal of water power. It is the widow's cruse of economic life. So long as the wind blows, the wind wheel also will gather momentum. It is possible that in the near future the use of fuel will be confined to such freely moving mechanisms as ships, cars, and aëroplanes, or to the generation of power *in situ*. From the factory or from the fixed transport line, fuel-driven engines may disappear altogether.

The revival of water power is extraordinarily recent. It waited on the electric lamp, which came about 1880, and on the combination of engineering and electrical knowledge in electric generator design which was only achieved completely within the next decade. It was about 1890 that big hydro-electric power plants began to appear, and they were stimulated in some cases by the discovery of electrical processes of manufacture. Aluminium, carborundum, calcium carbide, graphite, and a host of other things were more economically produced, or could only be produced, by electrical energy. In Ontario and Quebec, where there is no coal, the hydro-electric plants are producing power that would require 30,000,000 tons of coal a year. What would the extent of the manufacture and the facilities for transport in that million square miles of country be like if they were dependent upon coal?

In Canada, water provides 600 horsepower per thousand of the population; in Switzerland, 500; in Norway, more than 700; in Sweden, more than 200; in the United States, more than 100. In Great Britain, the source of power remains the coal supply, and water power accounts for only a very small fraction of a horsepower per thousand people.

Here perhaps we may make a remark in anticipation of the chapter we shall devote to the housing of mankind. People have seen in the easy distribution of power a possibility of scattering population more evenly over the countryside. But in spite of the ease with which electricity can now be distributed over long distances, there is little sign at present that this is going on. Electrical power distribution is tending rather to form concentrations at new centres either near the source of power or where it

is convenient for interrelated industries to use one another's products or by-products. The population map changes, of course, as
the methods of utilizing power change, but so far no dissolution of the great town is occurring.

Are there still any undeveloped possibilities of extracting
power from the movements of air or water? An exhaustive
Power Book would summarize the present phase of the still
unsolved problem of using tidal force. And further it would
have to note and describe one or two odd and as yet imprac-
ticable contrivances for the direct capture of radiant solar
energy. In the Kaiser Wilhelm Institute at Dalhem, Dr. Lange
has run a small electric motor by sunlight, passing the light
through a photo-electric cell. This little motor of Dr. Lange's
may figure in the economic histories of the future as Hero's
steam engine figures in those of to-day.

Many suggestions have been made for utilizing the internal
heat of the earth by means of deep bore holes in the crust. In
an indirect way this source is already being tapped. From steam
which issues from the earth at Ladarello, in Tuscany, Prince
Conti obtains over four thousand horsepower, and there is a
similar scheme under development in California.

A high temperature is not necessary to produce power. A
vapour engine, like the steam engine, requires water at a temperature which will produce vapour, and water at a lower temperature which will condense it. The difference between the
energy of the vapour at higher temperature and its energy at
the lower temperature, is the energy available for external work.
Such a difference of temperature exists in nature between the
warm surface waters of the ocean, especially in the tropics, and
the cold water which flows along the ocean floor from the poles.
After preliminary experiments in Belgium, Dr. Georges Claude
is constructing a large-scale engine based upon this principle on
the coast of Cuba. At Malanzas Bay bottom water can be
pumped from the depth of a mile and a half through a 13-foot
pipe and used to condense the steam given off in a low-pressure
chamber by the hot surface water. There is a difference of 14°C.
between the cold and hot water, and this, it is alleged, will suffice

to run a practicable and paying plant. Here we may have another way of utilizing the heat of the sun on a larger scale than those devices of mirrors, lenses, and so forth, which attempt to employ the concentrated rays to produce a high temperature.

We mention these various notions here for the theoretical interest rather than for any immediate practical value they possess. They help one to grasp the idea of man's return from combustion as his source of power to the spin of the earth, the tides and currents of the seas, differences of velocity, pressure and temperature in the incessant stir of the world machine. All combustion sources are vanishing sources. In the end the rotating planet must become man's sole dynamo, the Prime Mover for all his mechanisms.

§ 10. *Transmission of Power*

Having got his power, man's next problem is the application of it to the task to be done. The power has to work this or that apparatus or drive an implement in contact with material undergoing manufacture; it has to be transmitted to the point where that is done. First our encyclopædia would discuss rope, chain and belt drives in the factory, with the problems of friction that arise, and then come to the use of compressed air and impelled water as power transmitters.

The transmission of power by toothed gearing is very ancient. The "teeth" were wooden pegs driven into the rim of a wheel. From the fifteenth century to the nineteenth actual cogwheels were made of cast iron, brass, or bronze. In the latter half of the nineteenth century they began to be made of steel. But in spite of the teeth being cut as nearly as machinery would allow to the exact geometrical shape, so that they would "roll" upon each other, there were still inequalities which produced noise.

One of the difficulties of applying the steam turbine to ship propulsion was the high speed of the turbine and the relatively low speed at which the screw propeller is efficient. The toothed gearing then available was far too noisy. The noise arose from errors in the machine in which the teeth were cut, and which were unavoidable. Sir Charles Parsons showed how to distribute these errors all round the wheel and succeeded in producing gearing which is very nearly silent, and in which less than 2 per cent of the power is wasted in friction.

Again belts and ropes passing over pulleys have been used for many centuries. They extend the range of transmission from a few feet to a few yards. The range is further extended to a mile or more by the use of high-pressure water. Though electric lifts are becoming more common, there are still many hydraulic lifts in docks, harbours, factories, warehouses and hotels and blocks of offices in large towns. How many people realize that the latter depend upon a public supply of water at high pressure laid under the streets like the ordinary water mains?

During the last twenty years some beautiful hydraulic transmission devices, using water or oil, have been invented. They are used to transmit power to machinery and to control the power transmitted according to requirements.

Compressed air has long been used, though it is not very economical since heat is evolved on compression. Nevertheless, air is found to be convenient for many purposes. The South African mines use nothing but compressed air.

During the war a Roumanian—M. Constantinesco—devised a method of transmitting power through water by waves. The water was contained in a long, closed, flexible pipe, and the waves produced by a series of taps on one end. These are reproduced with little loss of energy at the other. It was used first to "time" the discharge of a machine gun on an aëroplane so that the bullets would pass *between* the blades of the propeller. It has since been applied to rock drills.

The hydraulic and wave transmission devices, together with many forms of flexible coupling of the last twenty years, are ingenious additions to methods which sufficed for many centuries. They are novel in principle or design, and they indicate that neither mechanical ingenuity nor the application of scientific principles is exhausted in this field.

The next subject in order would be the electric generating station and electrical distribution. Our encyclopædia of reference would have to explain how the powerful rotation we have won from steam or water is made a source of electric current. It would expatiate upon the working of a dynamo and give pictures of dynamos and power stations. Then the description would proceed to spread out for us our living wires and cables, marching across country, burrowing underground, carrying power to farm and factory, home and road.

Electric energy was not produced on a very large scale until the late eighties of last century, nor was it transmitted very long distances. To-day, two or three hundred thousand horsepower is utilized more than two hundred miles from the source. The voltage, or pressure, at which the electricity is conveyed has risen in forty years from 10,000 to 220,000 volts. For testing the equipment of such a line, apparatus yielding electricity at 1,000,-000 volts is employed, and a flash of artificial lightning 17 feet long is produced by its discharge.

Wonderful it is to reflect that a hundred years ago the very idea of a power station distributing driving force to road, car and factory, lighting and heating cities, and so forth, would have been incredible, and that even the "power house" with its rackety steam engine, driving the machinery in a factory by band transmission, is not a hundred and fifty years old.

§ 11. *Points of Application*

Consider now the various points of application of this power we can distribute so widely. The domestic and agricultural ends it serves are very diverse. But for most industrial purposes the point of application is the tool. In our second chapter, § 7, we have described how the development of steel alloys has permitted a more and more rapid use of tools. We have noted already in our historical introduction, how improvement in one field waits on improvement in another. Here in the correlation of metallurgical exactitude and tool precision we have a modern instance. Our story of the machine tool is a history of ever increasing speed and precision.

In the eighteenth century the art of working in metals was

in a very primitive state. The cylinders of some of the early engines were of wooden staves, held together with iron bands, like a barrel. Before Watt entered into partnership with Boulton, he complained bitterly of the lack of skill displayed by mechanics. Some of his cylinders differed from circular section by a quarter of an inch! The machines used for boring them were that much clumsy and inaccurate.

Maudslay, towards the end of the eighteenth century, improved the lathe. But the most important step towards precision was taken by Whitworth. He introduced standard screw threads and made a machine that would measure to a millionth of an inch. The test piece could not be touched with the finger if an accurate measurement was required. The warmth of the hand caused it to expand by an amount which was measurable by the machine. Sellers rendered similar service by standardizing screw threads in America.

The next stage towards accuracy was the introduction of gauges. Rule and callipers were not sufficiently delicate, so the work was tested by standard rings, plugs or notched pieces of metal. Then limit gauges came into use. It is easier to machine a piece of metal *between* two dimensions than to an exact dimension. So gauges were made in pairs, and the work was made larger than one and smaller than the other. Work is now accurate to within a thousandth or a two-thousandth of an inch.

Parts of machines made in this way are interchangeable. It was no longer necessary to make a single machine. Parts could be made in dozens, hundreds or thousands, and stored. Any set of parts, selected at random, could then be assembled, and they would fit as perfectly as if they had been made individually for the purpose. Mass production became possible. Sewing-machines, typewriters, cash registers, bicycles, and a host of things became plentiful and, with the advent of automatic and semi-automatic machinery, relatively cheap. The process was extended upwards to heavier machinery. To-day a motor car and a 250 horsepower Diesel engine are assembled in the same way as a cash register.

Before passing to the stores, the parts are inspected to ensure that they are within the prescribed limits. In some cases an optical test is used. The part is projected in profile upon an enlarged drawing on a screen, and any slight departure from accuracy is revealed. The drawing is usually made with double lines representing the limits allowed, and if the image falls between these lines it satisfies the conditions. This method was introduced recently in a works where gauges had been used for years and had acquired errors. Machines failed to work properly, the cause was discovered, and the projection method convinced men who were both to believe that the fault lay in overconfidence in a traditional practice.

Automatic and semi-automatic machinery has been evolved by making it self-acting, first in respect of one motion, and then in respect of another. It has been built up slowly, one step at a time. For a human being to repeat these motions in exactly the same way required an almost superhuman capacity for taking pains. Few craftsmen possess the delicacy of touch, the patience, and the conscientiousness to produce the parts by the methods in use seventy or eighty years ago. But with artificial aid, accuracy is largely independent of individual human qualities. The machine makes the machine. Operation requires little effort, muscular or mental. It has become machine-minding, and women, girls, and boys have largely replaced men.

How wonderful it is to watch some of these machines at work! Some of them, fed with bar or strip steel at one end, turn out nuts, bolts, screws or washers by the thousand. A big machine is fed with little rods of wood at one end. These are next seen stuck in holes in a travelling belt which winds over pulleys. This belt moves so that the ends of the wooden rods are dipped in hot paraffin wax; then, after an interval for the wax to set, in a composition; and finally delivered as matches neatly packed in boxes. Another machine takes in tobacco and paper and delivers cigarettes, filled, rolled, wetted and sealed almost faster than the eye can follow. The Barber Knotter, used to join up a new set of warp threads to an old warp, will pick up the two threads and tie them together with astonishing accuracy and speed. If it fails once, it does not pass to another pair of threads, but makes a second attempt with the original pair, and with a

THE CONQUEST OF POWER

MUSCLE SHOALS GENERATING PLANT on Wilson Dam. Close-up of a spillway.

WILLIAM RITTASE.

THE CONQUEST OF POWER

A GIANT hydro-electric generator in the power plant at Muscle Shoals, Alabama.

second failure, a third attempt. After the fourth failure the machine stops, and the operative is called upon to adjust it.

Or take another exhibit. The world now consumes more than six hundred million electric lamps every year. The tube from which the bulbs are blown is drawn out continuously from a furnace which operates twenty-four hours a day. A single works may turn out ten thousand miles of tube a year. The machines not only draw the tube but cut it into lengths. Another machine receives the tube and converts it into a bulb ready for receiving the filament.

Automatic machines are not exactly an innovation, but their use received a great impetus during the war. Before those feverish years, the employment of such machines increased only slowly. They were employed for a few articles for which there was a large demand. Men are naturally conservative, and many manufacturers would have continued to follow traditional methods if they had not been forced by military necessity to adopt new ones. One result was relative cheapness of production. Another was the creation of a productive capacity far exceeding the demands of a world at peace and financially crippled.

Millions are unemployed now because a proportion can supply the present needs of mankind. To this issue we shall return later. Here we will throw out a question or so that will reappear for adequate treatment in the later parts of this work. Is this gradual shrinkage of employment to continue, or can the work be spread over a larger number of hands by reducing the hours (or years) of labour, and providing work for all? How will that square with our present business methods? For some chapters these questions must remain floating questions, until we have opened up several new series of considerations that are essential before we can even suggest an answer.

CHAPTER THE THIRD

THE CONQUEST OF DISTANCE

CHAPTER THE THIRD

THE CONQUEST OF DISTANCE

§ 1. *The Increasing Range of Modern Life*

THE preceding chapters have been, as it were, prepara-
tory to the essential material facts we have to consider.
We are now in a position to set about our summary of
man's activities, our actual world in its present phase of
evolution from local and transitional to world-wide and measured and planned economics.

In the next three or four chapters it will be convenient to use
that non-existent *Science of Work and Wealth* to which we have
already made reference, as though it were a work actually at
hand, even more frequently than we have done already. And
also these museums yet to come must be invoked again and again.
We go through these chapters in great danger of technological
avalanches. Whenever the detail becomes too abundant and
threatens to encumber the development of the general argument, or where material has been altogether unattainable, we
will wave a hand towards phantom galleries or carry over by
a reference to the encyclopædic contents of that imaginary work.

When some years ago I made the first rough notes for this
work, I planned to begin with food. I thought we could open
our survey with the present food supply of mankind and tell
how man eats—and how he gets his food. That had an attractively fundamental air about it. One must eat to live. And the
rest follows. But so soon as I came to the detailed planning of
this part it became evident that we must first deal with the transport systems of the world. The world a century or so ago
was living upon food that grew at its door. The modern eater in
the great modernized communities stretches his hand halfway

round the world for every other mouthful. This increase of range is a prior consideration to any treatment even of the eating, much more of the clothing or housing of mankind.

Extended range of action is indeed the key idea to almost all the great problems with which mankind is at present confronted. In the *Outline of History* it is shown how this has acted as an expansive force politically and how the salvation of man from the ever more destructive and disorganizing activities of war is now only possible through the establishment of a World Pax. The revolution in transport has made all existing governments provisional. It has "abolished distance" and jumbled them up together. In this work we must extend these political conclusions to the whole of the economic life. It has become infinitely easier to-day for a New Yorker to trade with a man in Pekin than it was for him to trade with a man in Maryland a hundred years ago. It is necessary to say something of the processes by which things have come to this pass before we can study the developing consequences.

§ 2. *Railway and Steamship*

A full and exhaustive account of world transport would have to begin with a brief review of transport in the past and the progressive escape of mankind from geographical limitation. Here we can but glance back for a moment to our historical opening and say something about the more or less concurrent invention of wheel and road. The Hittites had roads. The great Persian roads that figure so importantly in classical history were but an extension of that more ancient system.

What seem to have been the primary civilizations had, however, little need of road or road transport, and in Mesopotamia and Egypt road systems remained undeveloped. These first states grew up upon the courses of great rivers, and the river was the connecting link that bound the village to the city and the cities into a state. Man learnt to navigate on these rivers before he put out to sea.

For a long time sea communications were too precarious for essential economic interchanges. There was overseas trade in ornaments and luxuries generally, in rare metals and substances and the like. Probably kidnapping and slave-trading played a large part in the early stages of overseas merchandising. The seaman could lapse very easily into piracy; the shore trader become a wrecker. And early navigation was a very marginal and subsidiary thing to the general economic processes of that time. The general life would have lost only a gleam of colour and a touch of variety if there had been no sea trade at all. There was one exception in the case of Rome during its period of maximum expansion, but otherwise overseas shipping was not a vital organ in economic processes.

Coming on from the older phases of human prosperity to the modern renewal of progress it is interesting to note the development of the canal system in the opening phase of the new industrial age. It will serve to remind us of an important fact already noted in the *Outline of History,* that the industrial revolution preceded the mechanical and scientific one. They were two separate processes which became confluent. One had a precedent and the other was new. There had been an industrial revolution and a factory system (book-copying, e. g.) in Rome. And these eighteenth-century canals also were the revival of a very old idea which had been worked out in China ages before.

But a new intellectual activity was afoot. A certain William Smith, an engineer engaged in canal-making in England, noticed the relations of strata and fossils in the earth in which he worked, and evoked stratigraphic geology as a by-product. He gave body and reality to the speculations of the scholars and philosophers. The traditional cosmogony, the literal authority of the Bible and much else, was drowned by accident in the waterways of the English Midlands. Research and innovation were thereby disencumbered from a very heavy obstruction.

The Marquis of Worcester's *Century of Inventions* (1663) was an early indication of the essentially practical stir that distinguished the intellectual revival of post-mediæval Europe from the phase of Hellenic vigour. That book described a vague, unrealized steam engine, the intimation of what was at hand.

The steam engine arose as a pumping engine, a clumsy mechanical Dinotherium. The first one in use was Savery's, in 1698. For a whole century the steam engine did little more than pump. It came out of the mines at last (1803) to meet with the old obvious idea of rails and give us the railway. A road steam carriage had already been made in France in 1769 by Cugnot. The steam railway had become possible because iron rails had become possible. But it was still extraordinarily clumsy by present-day standards, because the conquest of the necessary substances was only beginning. Stephenson's *Rocket* was made of "cast and wrought iron and a small amount of brass, while, as Sir Henry Fowler has pointed out, specifications for fifty-five separate metals are now required for a modern locomotive."* An encyclopædic *Science of Work and Wealth* with unlimited illustrations would have space to tell the subsequent history of the railway in full and "feature" its more vivid episodes. It would show by period maps how the railways, once they were begun, spread through the world like nerves in a developing embryo. Let us give, at any rate, a few salient facts from this mechanical drama and leave such filling in as the reader who is specially interested in this field needs, to his further reading.

September, 1930, witnessed the centenary of the opening of the first railway, in the modern sense of a public steam railway, between Liverpool and Manchester. There had been tentative railways or tramways with steam locomotives in colliery districts and on the northeast coast nearly twenty years before this event. But though George Stephenson was an ardent advocate of steam traction, the use of that method on the first railway was decided only at the last moment, after competitive trials. The result was so convincing that a number of lines were constructed during the next few years. At first it seems to have been the capacity, and the speed over short distances, rather than the increased range that attracted attention. The new lines were short. They had a strictly local value, and some of the large systems—the Midland more especially—were created by the amalgamation of small and relatively local concerns.

---

*Sir Richard Gregory in a lecture on "Science and Labour."

Passenger traffic, also, was underestimated. The advantage
of carrying heavy stuff in big loads loomed so large in men's
minds that no one seems to have realized the importance the
new methods of transport would assume for travel and journey-
ing. And so, too, no one visualized the social and political influence of the new means of communication. These unforeseen
consequences as they were revealed stimulated the expansion of
railways enormously, and railway development became a mania
in the thirties. In 1825 Great Britain had only 26 miles of line;
in 1850 there were more than 6,600 miles; in 1870, more than
15,000 miles; in 1890, more than 20,000, and to-day, 24,000.
France and the United States began to experiment with steam
locomotives in the year that the Liverpool and Manchester railway was opened. Germany and Belgium were five years later.

From these beginnings the railway spread rapidly over the
world. Content at first to join up neighbouring centres, engineers
soon began to visualize lines which would cross continents and
bring distant peoples into direct and easy communication. The
first transcontinental line spanned the United States in 1869, rising 7,000 feet above sea level in the Sierras, crossing 700 miles
of desert and hundreds of miles of country inhabited by tribes
of hostile red men. The last spike of the Canadian Pacific was
driven in November 7, 1885. By the end of the century the
Trans-Siberian Railway was in operation, and the duration of a
journey round the world had been reduced to thirty-three days.
The Australian can now travel by train from Perth to Adelaide,
and Africa is the only continent still incompletely spanned by the
iron road.

By 1924 there were nearly 238,000 miles of line in Europe,
316,000 miles in North America, 55,000 miles in South America,
81,000 miles in Asia, 37,000 miles in Africa and 30,000 in
Australasia. North America and Australasia now have more
than 22 miles for every 10,000 of the population, Europe 528
miles and Asia only 0.8 miles. The ratio of mileage to population is naturally highest in a large country with a thinly scattered population. In Africa it is low because there are so few
lines. Gold, diamonds and wild forest products make small

demands upon transport. Cultivation of the soil and manufactures are necessary for abundant railway expansion.

The story of these engineering achievements, of the knowledge and skill which have been employed, of the hardships and dangers from rigours of climate and pestilence which have been incurred, would fill many volumes. The way has been blasted along the face of vertical cliffs and through the hearts of mountains. Stephenson had to pump water out of the Kilsby tunnel on the London Birmingham line for eight months. The first of the great Alpine tunnels, under Mont Cenis, seven and a half miles long, occupied fifteen years in construction. The St. Gothard Tunnel, twelve and a half miles long, took ten years. The temperature at the working face arose to 100° F., and water entered at the rate of 3,000 gallons an hour. The Simplon, of the same length, but begun a quarter of a century later, required only eight years—the result of improved appliances. The Gravehals tunnel on the Bergen-Oslo Railway is only three miles long, but involved thirteen years of labour. Steep gradients on the Jungfrau Railway and on the Canadian Pacific between Hector and Field have been overcome by spiral tunnels inside the mountain.

Rivers have been crossed by tunnels and bridges. The boring of the Severn Tunnel occupied thirteen years. Four times water flooded the workings and brought progress to a standstill. In some subaqueous tunnels the excavation has been only a few feet below the bed of the river. The men have a "shield" behind them and the water is kept back by compressed air. In 1880, when the Hudson River Tunnel was under construction, the air blew out through the river bed, water rushed in, and twenty men lost their lives. A "shield" is used in driving through soft ground whether water is present or not. And so accurately are the surveys made that the deviation from the true direction is trivial. In the 12½ miles of the Simplon Tunnel the error in direction was 8½ inches, and in level only 3½ inches. The Hampstead tube had an error in direction of ¼ inch and in level of ⅛ inch. The amazing "truth" of the base of the Great Pyramid, the sides of which, over 750 feet in length, have only a mean error of 3/5 of an inch from those of a perfect square, has long been a marvel to posterity. But this is better.

The railway evoked the great bridge. Before 1850 the longest iron span was that over the Wear at Sunderland—234 feet. The Britannia Tubular Bridge over the Menai Strait (1846–50) has two spans of 460 feet. The Brooklyn Suspension Bridge (1870–83) has a span of 1,596 feet, and the Williamsburg Bridge (1895), a mile away from the Brooklyn, a span of 1,600 feet. That towering mass of steel, the Forth Bridge, was opened in 1890. It has two spans of 1,710 feet, and for twenty-seven years this was the greatest distance which engineers had attempted to cross in one leap. But in 1917 the Quebec Bridge, which crosses the St. Lawrence in one span of 1,800 feet, was opened for traffic, after a disastrous failure ten years earlier. The present stage in bridge-building is illustrated by the magnificent arch across Sydney Harbour, and the still more magnificent structure spanning the Hudson River.

Throughout the growth of this network—more than three quarters of a million miles in a century—steam traction retained its supremacy and is only now being seriously challenged by electricity and the Diesel engine. In the little *Rocket* were embodied all the principles of the modern locomotive, though not its size and form. It had coupled driving wheels, a tubular boiler, and the exhaust steam was discharged up the chimney to increase the draught.

As the volume of traffic increased, locomotives have become larger and more powerful. Size in Great Britain is limited by the distance apart of the rails and the height of tunnels and bridges. The pioneers who determined these conditions did not imagine the future boldly enough. Brunel alone, whose mind ran to big things (he was the designer of the *Great Eastern*), adopted a 7-foot gauge for the Great Western Railway, but Stephenson's curious choice of 4 feet 8½ inches had secured too strong a hold for this to become general.

Though the locomotive, on this account, could not be made much larger, it could be made more efficient. Various improvements were made in the valve gear which controls the admission of steam to the cylinders. Then the boiler, and especially the firebox, was improved. Compounding, by which the steam was expanded successively through the cylinders, was introduced, chiefly in countries where the cost of coal justified the additional expense of construction and maintenance. With the higher pressures rendered possible by boiler plate of higher quality, compounding became more common. Then the steam was superheated on its passage from the boiler and more power obtained from the same quantity of fuel. The increased pressures now being used for stationary engines (there is a power plant in America using steam at 1,200 pounds the square inch) are spreading to the locomotive. Until 1895 the pressure did not exceed 160 pounds on the square inch. Then 200 pounds was tried. While a common pressure to-day is 250 pounds per square inch, there are several using steam at 350 to 400 pounds. Experimental engines using steam at 850 to 900 pounds are under trial, and at the time of writing one is under construction which will use steam at 1,700 pounds—more than three quarters of a ton on every square inch of internal surface.

These improvements have been made possible by metallurgical advance, and they have been stimulated during the last twenty years by the increasing cost of fuel, the competition of electricity and the influence of the Diesel engine. Steam-turbine locomotives and Diesel locomotives are already the subject of experiment. Apart from main principles, the modern steam locomotive is an amazing contrast, not only in size but also in performance and complexity, to the simple little engine that satisfied the Manchester to Liverpool trials, 100 years ago.

The development of railways depended upon their capacity and speed as compared with other forms of transport, and speed with safety depended not merely on power, but also on effective control of train movements. Traffic was at first regulated by "policemen" with flags and lamps, and later by the familiar semaphore. When these signals were worked mechanically they were "interlocked" so that a wrong signal could not be given.

The invention of telegraphy by Wheatstone and Morse per-

mitted the movement of trains to be flashed almost instantane-
ously along the line, and enabled the approach of a train to be
anticipated with a far greater margin of time. This stage was
reached in 1850.

The range of signalling was again increased when signals were
operated by compressed air or by electricity or the two in combination, and to-day the elimination of human error is being
achieved by the use of automatic methods by which the train
gives its own signal of approach, or picks up the signal and
stops of its own accord. Eleven thousand miles of road and
8,500 locomotives in the United States were provided with
automatic train control apparatus by 1928.

Meanwhile the amenities of railway travelling have been
enormously improved. The open trucks for third-class passengers
had a very brief existence. Seats have been upholstered, carriages
warmed, and facilities for eating and sleeping provided. In spite
of isolated instances to the contrary, the punctuality of trains
is extraordinary. The cheapness and range of railway travel
have enormously enriched life for millions who, in an earlier
age, would have been doomed to a narrow and monotonous
existence.

On the other hand, railway transport is inelastic in many
respects. The units are large, the demand cannot always be
foreseen, and the fixed track limits the area from which passengers can be drawn. For this reason road transport has become a
serious competitor, and it is perhaps unfortunate that the motor
bus developed so much later than the steam locomotive. Instead
of coöperating in the provision of a close network of economical
and efficient transportation, the railways may buy up the bus
services as they did the canals, solely for the sake of maintaining the returns upon lines which are, or threaten to become, un-
remunerative.

But it is in goods traffic that railways stand in greatest need
of improvement. There is, perhaps, no more uneconomical ap-
pliance than a railway truck. It has been estimated that one per
cent of a truck's life is spent in running full, three per cent in
running empty, and ninety-six per cent in standing in sidings.

Before the war British railways were laying down sidings at a far greater rate than running tracks. They were becoming warehousemen—of empty trucks. On the Continent and in America nearly all wagons belong to the railways. In Great Britain about half of the 1,280,000 belong to private owners. Railway company trucks stand empty, heavy capital expenditure is involved in sidings, and time is lost in sorting out trucks when required. In common with many other aspects of industrial activity, transportation has grown upon altogether too narrow lines. It has neither been planned with vision nor administered with enterprise. It is burdened and cramped by tradition and routine, and each form of enterprise tends to treat an alternative form, not as a collaborator to be encouraged, but as a competitor to be crushed.

Why, people are asking, should the railways be cluttered up with coal trucks for the home trade in districts where canals are lying idle? Why invest capital twice for the same purpose? The annual fuel requirements of any particular area can be forecast with tolerable accuracy. Coal could be stored. A steady stream of barges would convey the requisite quantity to many districts, and enable a seasonal demand to be met by uniform production at the coal face.

Transport by canal, railway and road has developed independently, and it needs now to be organized as a whole, as coördinated and coöperating rather than as competing units. And road or cross-country motor transport needs to be used to provide existing networks with a finer mesh, and to extend the systems into areas, rich in natural resources, which have not yet been able to bear the capital cost of a permanent way.

The first electric railway was exhibited by Siemens at Berlin in 1879. But electric generators and motors were then in their infancy. Ten years were to elapse before big machines were available, and another ten before many of the details of transmission were worked out. The Liverpool Overhead Railway and the City and South London Railway were opened about 1890. Then several short lines were converted from steam to electricity. Meanwhile the New York, New Haven & Hartford and other

American electric lines were opened, and electrical working adopted for the tunnel sections of the Swiss railways.

The advantages of electricity were more obvious, and the difficulties of introduction and operation less in the case of short suburban and interurban lines with a heavy passenger traffic. By distributing motors along the train, the grip on the rails was increased. Electricity secures quicker acceleration than steam, and less time is lost in increasing or decreasing speed when leaving or approaching a station. It had obvious advantages, too, on underground lines and in long tunnels which are difficult to ventilate. As the power from a large central station is more flexible than that of a steam locomotive, there were also advantages in the use of electricity on main lines with steep gradients. And so the new method of traction has gradually invaded the domain of the steam engine.

That, however, could not be done in a day. It required cheap power such as can be obtained most economically from falling water. Hydro-electric development was a powerful stimulus. Then there was an enormous field to be explored. The most economical pressure for the transmission of electrical energy; whether it should be direct or alternating current, and, in the latter case, whether it should be single-phase or three-phase; the most satisfactory method of communicating energy to the train; the best type of motor: these were only a few of the questions which had to be investigated. Each one of them carried a mass of detail in the design of auxiliary devices. Throughout the nineties and beyond, the patent offices were busy in registering new ideas.

The most wonderful achievement during the last ten years is the equipment of automatic sub-stations. The line is divided into sections of a dozen miles or more in length, and each section is supplied independently with energy from the central power station through a sub-station. The sub-station contains machinery or apparatus for transforming the high-tension current into one of low enough tension to be communicated to, and used with safety on, the train. The overhead lines are liable to have produced in them surges of electrical energy from lightning flashes;

the sub-station machinery may be overloaded by too many trains on the section, and a number of irregularities may occur which formerly required an operator to observe them and make the necessary adjustments. This is now unnecessary. The sub-station can be, and often is, entirely automatic. When an irregularity occurs the machines correct themselves or stop. And the man in charge of the control station can see, by glancing at coloured lamps on a board, whether each control device is doing the work for which it was designed.

As yet we are only on the threshold of this phase of transportation. Omitting urban and interurban lines, there are only 6,500 miles of electrified track out of 563,000 miles. The United States has less than 1,500 miles out of more than 236,000 miles of line. Great Britain has 400 miles out of 20,000. Italy has made use of her immense hydro-electric resources in the streams which flow down the southern slopes of the Alps. She has 670 miles of electric railway out of 12,500 miles. But the greatest development has been in Switzerland. The figures—595 miles out of 1,852—hardly reveal the truth. No less than 67 per cent of the track is electrified and 85 per cent of the trailing-ton miles is accomplished by electrical power. Man has been observing, experimenting, discovering, for scores of generations. Within the last three he has achieved the railway, and within the last one the electric train.

We turn now to the modernization of shipping and the struggle of the sailing ship against extinction. The story of shipping is a continuing story of growth in size, power, and speed. We will not dwell here upon the safety and comfort of modern ocean travel, and we can speak only in general terms of the main economic and political effects of ocean transport. As the *Outline of History* insists, the second British Empire, that is to say, the present British Empire which arose after the separation of the United States, is essentially a steamship empire. It came with the steamship, and with the appearance of air transport and the diminishing importance of the steamship in world communication it is bound to undergo great changes either of adaptation or dissolution.

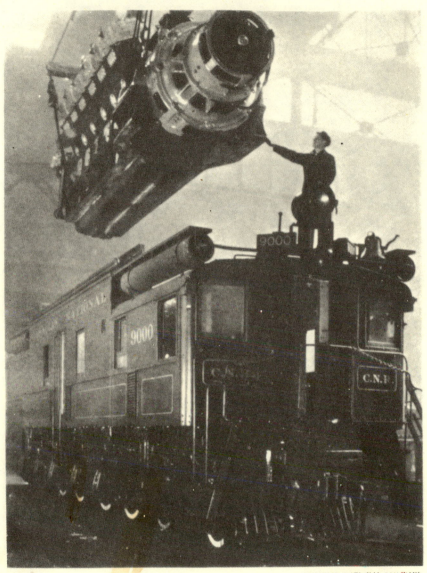

A MODERN DESCENDANT OF THE *ROCKET*

THE oil-electric engine of the Canadian National being lowered into place. This locomotive, the 9000, will take a heavy train across the continent in sixty hours, an unprecedented speed, at infinitely less cost than heretofore.

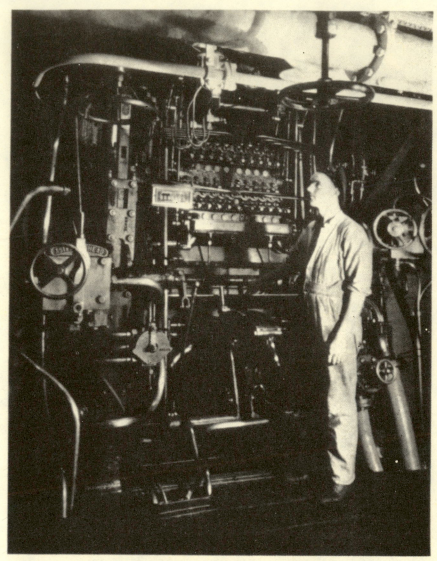

OIL OUSTS COAL

ONE of the battery of Diesel Engines on the new motorship *Britannic*.

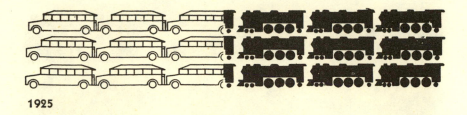

1925

1929

THE ROAD DEFEATS THE RAIL

THE changes in transportation habits that new modes of locomotion have produced.

Each bus represents one hundred million passengers carried in the United States by busses during the year.

Each locomotive represents one hundred million passengers carried in the United States by railways during the same period.

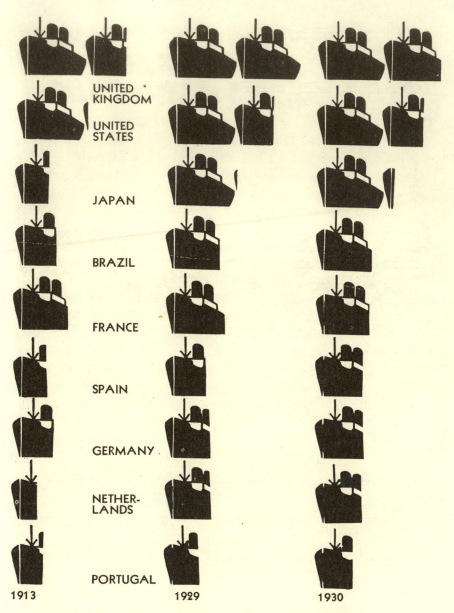

UNITED KINGDOM

UNITED STATES

JAPAN

BRAZIL

FRANCE

SPAIN

GERMANY

NETHER-LANDS

PORTUGAL

1913   1929   1930

THE WORLD'S WATER-BORNE COMMERCE

HERE, for the year before the war, and for the two most recent years for which figures are available, is a graphic delineation of the world's water-borne commerce as indicated by shipping entries for the principal maritime countries. Each ship represents fifty million registered tons entered. Domestic shipping is not included.

The steamship phase has so far lasted little more than a century. In 1777 a Frenchman bought one of Watt's engines and used it to propel a boat along the river at Lyons. Symington exhibited a steamboat on Dalswinton Loch in 1788. The *Charlotte Dundas* clove the waters of the Clyde in 1802. Fulton's *Clermont* navigated the Hudson in 1807. By 1823 more than 300 steamboats had been built in America for use on rivers and lakes, while in Great Britain steamers came into use in a tentative way for coasting and cross-channel trade. The first vessel using steam crossed the Atlantic from America in 1818. But in this and later ships steam was used only as an auxiliary to sails. Steam, as the chief agent of propulsion, dates from 1838.

While all steamships have increased from these beginnings in size, power and speed, those built for the Atlantic passenger service have undergone the most uniform and extensive development. The Cunarders of 1840 were 207 feet long, with engines of 740 horsepower. From this length and power they increased slowly to 500 feet, and 5,300 horsepower in 1880. In the same interval the average speed increased from 8.5 to 15.5 knots. The greater length and speed were facilitated by the use of steel in construction. Composite ships, with wooden frames and iron plating, were built from 1840, but it was the invention of Bessemer steel (1856–60) which led to the great increase in size. Brunel anticipated events by building the *Great Eastern* of iron, 680 feet long, in 1859; but she never fulfilled expectations, and it was forty years before another ship of her size was attempted.

In the opening of the twentieth century, came a vigorous competition between the German, British and American ship builders for the trans-Atlantic trade, and great floating palaces of 700, 800 and 900 feet appeared. Ships are now on the stocks which will be 1,000 feet—333 yards—in length. The *Leviathan* (U. S. A.) weighs just upon 60,000 tons and is 907 feet long; the *Majestic* (British) is equally huge and is eight feet longer. The *Bremen* (German) is just under 900 feet, but she is narrower and about 8,000 tons lighter.

The earlier vessels were driven by paddles, which take up a

great deal of space amidships and are in the way when entering and leaving dock. The screw propeller was patented in 1836 and first used in 1839. The first large vessel to be provided with this means of propulsion was the *Great Britain,* designed by Brunel. She was 320 feet long and was launched in 1844. But the paddle was not displaced for large steamers until the sixties, and it is still used for boats which ply on rivers and lakes. Paddle vessels of nearly 8,000 tons are used on the Great Lakes to-day. Twin screws were tried from 1862, but only obtained popularity on the fastest boats. The maximum growth, however, in size and speed, could only be attained by the use of three and four screws.

Meanwhile, an ever increasing economy was sought in the engine room. The compound engine was introduced in 1854, the triple-expansion engine in 1873, and the quadruple-expansion engine in the last decade of the century. Further economy was secured by the steam turbine first tried for ship propulsion in 1894. The first merchant ship was provided with turbines in 1901. There were, at first, many difficulties and disappointments. There were difficulties arising from construction which were overcome by improved materials and design. The high speed of the turbine and the low speed at which a screw propeller, working in water, is efficient, were conciliated by improved gearing. Alternatives to toothed wheels which have been tried are the Foettinger hydraulic and the electric systems. In the former the turbine drives a centrifugal pump, which forces water through a water turbine on the propeller shaft. In the latter the turbine drives electric generators, and the propeller shaft is driven by an electric motor.

Again, in contrast to the steam turbine, operating with or without a reciprocating engine, and acting through gearing, water power or electricity, is the Diesel engine. Until after the war the Diesel engine had only been tried on cargo boats of relatively low tonnage. But it has been applied far more widely than steam for cargo vessels, and has invaded the field of the turbine on passenger ships. The *Britannic* has Diesel engines of 20,000 horsepower, and an Italian vessel, similar engines of

27,000 horsepower. During 1930 the increase in the world's steam tonnage was 148,176, and of motor tonnage 1,468,235— an amazing development in less than fifteen years. The advantages are simplicity, compared with the turbine and its auxiliaries; smaller storage space for oil than for coal, and fewer men required to run the machinery. So far as shipping is concerned, an oil age has already begun.

During the last year nearly 70,000,000 tons of shipping have been available for the world's needs. They have enabled human beings of different races and tongues to meet and mingle. Raw materials have been carried nearly round the world and exchanged for other raw materials and goods. But until fifty years ago most articles of food were perishable. Apart from a somewhat limited trade in live cattle, meat, fish, fruit and vegetables had to be consumed within a few hundred miles of their source. Only salted food could be kept for any length of time. The preservation of food by cooling it below the temperature at which the bacteria of putrefaction were active began in the middle of last century. The first cargo of beef was sent from America to England in 1877; the first cargo of mutton came from Australia in 1880. Scientific investigation has fixed the most suitable temperature for preserving every article of food for which there is a distant market. Many foods have ceased within the last thirty years to be "seasonable." The world dines at one table, and the fare is vastly richer and more varied than it ever was before. Could anything illustrate more simply or more forcibly the difference created by the railway and the steamship? Mining and manufacture lead to great concentrations of population which far exceed the food-producing capacity of the immediate neighbourhood. Yet they labour for the rest of the world, and the rest of the world supplies them in greater abundance and variety than they could produce directly for themselves. But this is anticipating our next chapter.

We may glance here at the question of freight charges, and particularly at the ideas of David Lubin and the more experienced work of Sir Arthur Salter. Lubin dealt with the question of freights before the war; he wanted to fix them instead of leaving them to a complex process of haggling; he wanted an international transport at fixed rates on the model of international postage. His suggestions are full of mental invigoration.

Salter's work, *Allied Shipping Control,* arose out of his experiences with transport problems during the war. Enormous economies were effected by putting all the allied shipping under a common direction. At one time American wheat was going to Italy, while Indian wheat was passing it *en route* for England. The wartime pooling of shipping put a stop to such absurdities —"for the duration." The American wheat was turned aside to London, and the Indian to Italy, and thousands of miles of transport were economized. "For the duration." Thereafter everything was allowed to lapse back into the hands of the private profit-seekers.

A complete survey of transport by rail and sea would give typical pictures and descriptions of modern docks and transshipment methods. It would involve a great history and description of harbours. At first these were the natural mouths of rivers or sheltered bays, with staging of timber or stone to facilitate loading and unloading; then, in the order of elaboration, a bay sheltered from the waves by an artificial embankment or sea wall. The sides of the river or the shores of the bay would next be excavated to provide a number of huge tanks, separated or confined by massive concrete walls. On these walls appear cart tracks and then railway sidings, and at length miles of railway, bigger and bigger open sheds, tall warehouses, machinery for pumping and for loading vessels with astonishing speed and economy of human effort, great chutes for loading a ship with ore or corn carried in bulk. (On the Great Lakes 12,508 tons of ore have been loaded in 16½ minutes, and unloaded in 3 hours and 5 minutes.) Corn is poured into a ship down a chute and sucked out of it through great tubes from which the air is continuously withdrawn by a fan—waterfalls of grain, and reversed waterfalls with the grain pouring upward.

Provision has to be made not merely for cargo but for the repair of ships. Where it is not considered desirable on the ground of expense or urgency to construct a permanent dry dock, a floating dock is used. There is one at Southampton, and another at Singapore, either of which will accommodate the largest ships. A floating dock is like an immense box, open at the top and ends. Or it may be likened to a steel trough. The sides and bottom are hollow and are divided into compartments into which water may be admitted or from which it may be pumped. The dock is sunk by admitting water, the vessel is moored over it, the water pumped out, and as the dock rises the vessel is lifted out of the water. The Southampton dock is 860 feet long and will lift 60,000 tons; that at Singapore has a lifting capacity of 50,000 tons. They are floating factories, portable shipyards, equipped with workshops and machinery to enable any kind of repairs to be carried out. That at Singapore was towed all the way from the Tyne. There or elsewhere you could, if necessary, build a ship.

Another great item in the spectacle of modern transport is the development of ship canals and particularly the development of Suez, Panama, the Manchester Ship Canal, the St. Lawrence chain and the Kiel Canal. To the present generation all these great waterways are accepted with little emotion or understanding; to our parents and grandparents they were objects of awe and admiration. Conceived in earlier times merely as substitutes for roads or rivers, canals in the latter half of the nineteenth century became also links in oceanic communication and terminal extensions which enabled oceanic transport to penetrate deeply into land areas. A few canals by-pass tempestuous or dangerously crowded seas. To the first class belong Suez and Panama; to the second the Manchester Ship Canal and the St. Lawrence chain, the Amsterdam Canal, and the New Orleans Industrial Canal; instances of the third type are the Corinth and Cape Cod canals. In a number of cases the canal route is not only safer but shorter.

The Suez Canal, opened in 1869, occupied ten years in its construction. It was merely the last of many efforts, none completely successful or permanent, to connect the Red Sea with the Mediterranean. The history and legend of these efforts cover more than three thousand years. Before work upon the existing canal was commenced the proposal was debated for more than half a century. It was accomplished by the labour of a quarter of a million men and the expenditure of twenty million pounds. Half as much again has been expended in widening, deepening and otherwise improving it. In 1870 only 451 ships made the passage. By 1927 the number of ships had increased to 5,545, and the tonnage was 28,962,048. How would trade have developed in the Mediterranean and the Far East, and what would have been the political history of Europe had it never been undertaken?

The history of the Panama Canal would afford material for a modern epic. The earlier years were grim with tragedy. De Lesseps, elated with his conquest of the sands of Suez, utterly underestimated the magnitude and difficulty of the task in Central America. In spite of heroic efforts, he failed. Between 1879 and 1887, no less than £66,000,000 was sunk in the enterprise, and 16,000 men died from disease. The United States government took over responsibility in 1904. By 1914 it had completed the work at a cost of £75,000,000. Two factors contributed to the American success. One was modern medical and sanitary service—particularly the steps taken to prevent mosquito-borne disease; the other, military discipline. There was a tendency among the civilian engineers at first employed to quarrel with one another or to leave for more remunerative posts. To secure loyalty and continuity President Roosevelt replaced them by military officers. Military officers could neither disobey orders nor seek other employment. In 1927, 5,475 ships with a tonnage of more than 27,000,000 used the passage. There is thus a peculiar symmetry in the flow of traffic through the Suez and Panama canals, the easterly and westerly exits from the North Atlantic system.

The Manchester Ship Canal has enabled that city, situated 45 miles from the sea, to become the third port in Great Britain. A similar but far deeper penetration is effected by the chain of canals along the St. Lawrence, and the Welland Canal between Lake Erie and Lake Ontario, still under construction. A small ship can now be loaded at Manchester and discharge its cargo at Chicago. A limit to the size of vessel is imposed at present by the St. Lawrence canals which permit only a 14-foot draught. It is proposed to deepen the channels throughout the whole length, and the next generation may see the largest cargo vessels moving athwart the south Lancashire landscape and so out to sea, and ending their journey by passing through cultivated fields for hundreds of miles to a port a thousand miles from the ocean.

The traffic on these inland waterways is amazing. The Sault Sainte Marie, between Lake Superior and Lake Huron, carries more than 85,000,000 tons a year—more than Suez or Panama.

On these narrow ribbons of water traffic is concentrated. Dispersed on the wide oceans is a mass, stupendous by comparison, whose total bulk defies the imagination. Millions of horsepower and hundreds of thousands of men are moving thousands of millions of tons from those who have to those who need, with ever increasing speed and no regard for distance. No central mind directs this world circulation; and yet a routine is perceptible which suggests conscious coöperation and a purpose clearly seen, an order, as it were, crystallizing out of chaos. Can the inorganic world with its atoms and molecules, its crystalloids and colloids, show anything more wonderful or inexplicable than human transport at its present stage of development?

There is another aspect of the development of great ships and controlled shipping and water transport at which we can glance here only for a moment. That is the elimination of human suffering that has gone on at the same time. We do not mean simply the heroic sufferings of shipwreck and famine and natural disaster; those we can in a sense tolerate. But it is certain that in the past the small sailing ship far from land, remote from the influence of women and children and all social restraints, was all too often a pit not simply of deprivation but of cruelty. The galley slave was a slave, but throughout the eighteenth and early nineteenth centuries the sailors, often beguiled aboard, were among the poorest and most evilly entreated of labourers. Almost inadvertently science and invention have lit and cleansed those miserable caskets of oppression beneath the tall masts and the bellying sails of the old order of things at sea.

§ 3. *The New Road and the Airway*

A new chapter of the history of communications is opened when we consider the modern revival of the road. The macadamized road was the high-water mark of roadmaking in the pre-railway era. With the coming of the automobile a new phase in the history of roads opened, roads of a harder, firmer type appeared, more or less freed from the filth of horses and the disintegrative beating of their hoofs. The internal combustion engine, rubber tires and new road surfaces have interacted in the evolution of our modern road traffic, a multitude of illuminating problems of traffic control and of road- and town-planning have arisen and are arising out of this evolution. But of town-planning we will write later. A full encyclopædia of *Work and Wealth* would have to expand copiously upon such problems as the possibility of a closer coöperation of road and railway through the transfer of large package units from chassis to truck.

And then we turn our attention to the air. The very recent but very complex story of the achievement of mechanical flight has still to be written. At present the organization of air services in a practicable form is enormously hampered by the jealousies and frontier impediments of the seventy-odd petty sovereign divisions with which our developing world is still entangled. *The Science of Work and Wealth* would have, of course, a full and fully illustrated review of the latest development of aircraft and it could weigh the merits of the airship against the aëroplane. Here, we must say to the reader, is a way of going wherever you like about the world, very swiftly and agreeably, so soon as you are sufficiently tired of the traditions of nationalist and imperial conflict, to turn to these new powers and conveniences.

The internal combustion engine lies at the root of both these developments, the automobile and aviation. They came in a necessary sequence. The automobile was the inevitable predeces-

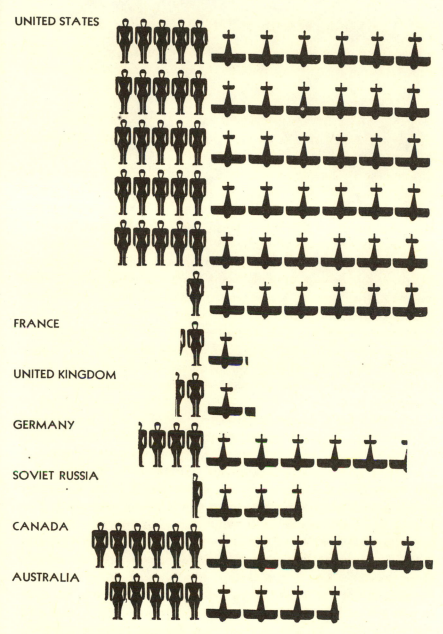

UNITED STATES

FRANCE

UNITED KINGDOM

GERMANY

SOVIET RUSSIA

CANADA

AUSTRALIA

THE STATE OF CIVIL AVIATION

EACH plane indicates one million miles flown, and each figure indicates twenty thousand passengers carried. Only the principal flying countries are shown. It is interesting to note that during the period shown, more than seven hundred million passengers were carried by railroads in the United States, compared to less than half a million carried by plane. The statistics on which this chart is based were compiled from United States government sources, and are for the latest year available, 1930.

sor of the airship and aëroplane. Until a fairly reliable light engine had been worked out upon the ground, where sudden stoppages did not involve disaster, sustained flying was no more than a dream. The early "gliders" in the gliding machines, Lilienthal, Pilcher and Chanute, were plainly and consciously preparing for the advent of an efficient engine. So soon as sure and sufficient power was available, both flying and the navigable balloon became inevitable.

The automobile story is still a confusion of claims and disputations. Gottlieb Daimler (1885–86) was early in the field, but it is alleged that Siegfried Narkus in Austria had made and driven a four-wheeled car with an internal combustion engine as early as 1875 (Encyclopædia Britannica). By 1897 a lot of people were busy making experimental cars of various types, in France, Germany, England and America. To show the manner of the growth and do justice to these experimenters would require furlongs of museum gallery. It took a dozen years and the toil of many thousands of inventors before a really trustworthy car, that would not only take its driver out but bring him home again, had become a marketable commodity. In 1897 there were ninety cars upon the roads of the United States; in 1906 the hundred thousand mark was passed, in 1913 the million and in 1928, twenty-one million. There is now (1931) a car to every seven people in the United States and to every sixty people in Great Britain and France.

The aëroplane followed fast on the car. The world of inventors was in labour, so to speak, with the automobile in 1896–97. That was the great time of road trials and freaks. The corresponding years for the aëroplane were 1909–11. By 1903 Wilbur and Orville Wright had already added a petrol motor to the gliders with which they had been experimenting since 1900 at Dayton in Ohio. They were certainly flying in 1905. Santos Dumont flew in 1906, and Farman, at the Voisin works at Issy near Paris in 1908. In July, 1909, Blériot flew across the English Channel, and from that date onward the record is crowded with flights of increasing length and height. The Atlantic was first crossed in 1919 by Alcock and Brown.

The very earliest speculations on the possibility of mechanical flight were based upon flapping wings. The significance of soaring, with wings placidly outspread, was not at first apparent. And though Sir George Cayley in 1809 stated the principles upon which a heavier-than-air machine could be employed, a hundred years elapsed before this became an accomplished fact. The balloon, invented by the Montgolfier brothers at the end of the eighteenth century (1783)—lifted by hot air, hydrogen or, after 1821, coal gas—had buoyancy, it was capable of lifting a load up into the air, but its direction was that of the wind. In 1852 Gifford fitted a steam engine to a balloon and propelled it at five or six miles an hour. But a larger machine, built three years later, came to grief. During the Franco-German War a balloon which had a propeller worked by eight men was used. In 1885 Renard and Krebs constructed an airship, *La France,* propelled by a nine horsepower electric motor. This machine flew over Paris and attained a speed of fourteen miles an hour. But that was about as far as the lighter-than-air machine could go until the internal combustion engine came to its assistance. This association became possible at the dawn of the twentieth century. In 1901 Santos Dumont flew a navigable balloon, like a fat flabby fish, for seven miles out and home, round the Eiffel Tower.

The earlier French airships were "non-rigid." They consisted of a lozenge or fish-shaped envelope containing the gas, and the car for pilot, passengers and machinery was suspended from a net, embracing the fragile gas container. The "rigid" type, in which the fabric is stretched over a sausage-shaped metal framework, and the gas is contained in "ballonnets" in separate compartments of the larger vessel, was developed in Germany by that great experimentalist, Count Zeppelin. He was at work before the end of the nineteenth century. He was the first to make a rigid airship (of aluminium covered with silk and linen and containing hydrogen). It made successful flights before the end of 1900. But his Zeppelins remained very tender and fragile for ten years. It was only with the invention of duralumin (an alloy of aluminium) in 1909 that a really adequate, strong and light frame for a rigid airship became possible. Duralumin has five times the strength of aluminium and is nearly as light. During the war France and Great Britain developed non-rigid types of airship, and by 1918 the latter country had several hundred of them for scouting and coastal patrol. Italy showed a preference for semi-rigid ships—non-rigid envelopes stiffened by a metal keel. Germany, keeping the lead Count Zeppelin had given her, went on building rigid airships of the largest size and using them very effectively, and until 1916, when the L 33 was brought down near London, there was no information available outside Germany as to their design and construction.

Experimental work with large airships is less easy than with aëroplanes; airships are infinitely more costly to build. They are relatively fragile, and when a disaster occurs they are more expensive in human life. Until hydrogen can be replaced by the non-inflammable gas helium, the menace of fire will always be associated with them. Helium is the next lightest element to hydrogen, and although abundant in the sun's atmosphere, it is on earth a gas of rare occurrence. It is found in various natural gases and in the water of some mineral springs. It is widely distributed, but only in very small amounts; it is obtainable in considerable quantities in America alone. The supplies are manifestly limited, and this puts yet another obstacle in the way of general airship development.

The armament competitions of the opening decade of the twentieth century, and then the war, were tremendously stimulating to both airship and aëroplane construction. At the outset of the conflict aëroplanes were used only for reconnaissance and to mark for gunfire. By the end of the war an elaborate system of air fighting existed, and night after night great air raids—in which the big aëroplane of the Handley Page, Gotha type presently ousted the more vulnerable Zeppelin—bombed the belligerent populations behind the fighting lines.

The Peace of Versailles released the accumulated possibilities of the civil transport aëroplane. The first regular air services had already been established before the war in Germany in 1912, when rigid airships were used. By 1920 there were three British and two French companies providing cross-channel services by means of aëroplanes. The British interests were subsequently (in 1926) concentrated in Imperial Air Services, Ltd., which operates between England and France, Switzerland, Germany, and Belgium. British Empire routes were also established in Africa, the Near East, India and Australia. But the British Empire is not very happily planned for air transport. Britain has a very central maritime position, but the main air services of the future are more likely to radiate from the centres of the great land masses of our planet. By 1926 the route mileage of the world's air transport had reached 50,000, and the number of miles flown in that year along these routes was nearly 17,000,000. This progress testifies not only to great improvements in the design and construction of the machines, but also to the increase in efficiency of the internal combustion engine. In 1915 the lightest water-cooled motor weighed 4 pounds per horsepower, and the lightest air cooled engine 3 pounds. To-day the weights of these engines are more than halved.

Apart from transport, the aëroplane is being used for many economic and administrative purposes. Vast areas where the population is sparse and means of communication poor are being surveyed from the air. In 1925 and 1926, 120,000 square miles were mapped by aërial photography in Canada. Rivers and coast lines and routes for new roads and railways have been surveyed in the United States, and in Australia the extent and form of the Great Barrier Reef have been recorded. The forest areas of Germany, Canada and other countries are being determined in this way. Mineral resources in Africa and the United States are being investigated. Town surveys have been made in the United States and Germany. The Canadian Salmon Fisheries are being policed by aëroplanes, and cotton and other crops are being sprayed or dusted with insecticides or fungicides by low-flying machines.

Few people before 1918 could have believed that archæological work would ever be undertaken in an aëroplane. But thanks mainly to the energy of one man, Mr. O. G. S. Crawford—who learnt the business as an aërial photographer at Arras during the war—the aëroplane has become now a most important instrument in reconstructing the life of the past. An aërial photo-graph reveals details in the texture and quality of the ground which are totally invisible to a man on the surface, and the long unsuspected vestiges of ancient settlements and the pre-historic layout of the land have been elucidated to a very re-markable extent in this way.

From its very beginnings, civil air transport has found itself entangled amidst the narrow political boundaries of the past. An International Convention for the Regulation of Aërial Naviga-tion was ratified by many countries in 1922. This was followed by an International Commission for Air Navigation on which twenty-five states were represented. The Commission acts as an advisory body to the governments which send representatives on such questions as customs, licenses and certificates of air-worthiness, and the establishment of lighting systems and the provision and dissemination of meteorological information—a strange complex of fiscal, legal and scientific services.

It is plain that we are still only in the beginnings of this new age of road and air transport which the internal combustion engine has made possible. The new highroad and the airway are at about the stage the railway had reached a century ago. The actual mechanism, the automobile or the aëroplane, that is to say is in existence in a working state. It is the development of the network that has now to be undertaken. Over great parts of the world the normal automobile cannot yet be used because of the want of modern roads. Either it must be replaced by auto-mobiles of a special type and toughness—like the Citroën cars used in the North African desert and the crossing of Central Asia—or it cannot be used at all.

Still more is regular and trustworthy air travel restricted by ground conditions. Night flying and long distance cannot be con-sidered safe until invention and organization have collaborated to anticipate and deal with the at present very heavy risks of fog. But, as we shall see in the next section, conquest of fog by the development of beam wireless and particularly of the new micro-rays, to which fog and rain are transparent, is close at hand. There is also needed a great effort in the development and application of meteorological science, so that the aviator may plan his route with assurance, free from the dread of adverse surprises by rain, snow, fog and tempest. Only by evolving a cosmopolitan organization can meteorology achieve that manifest task before it.

Week by week, year by year, at this point, at that, the road map and air route map of the world are being elaborated and redrawn, and every change in these maps involves political, social, and economic consequences of the most fundamental order. The transport framework of a new world system is being pieced together in spite of a thousand traditional antagonisms and impediments.

§ 4. *The Transmission of Fact. The Present Moment Becomes World-Wide*

But this chapter is concerned not simply with Transport, but with all methods of communication. We are considering not only how men and things can be moved about the modern world, but also the movement of information and ideas. Mankind seems to be approaching a phase when we shall realize and think almost as if we had one mind in common. Political disorder and various sorts of uproar delay the attainment of that phase, but there is an element of inevitableness in its advance. We move towards a time when any event of importance will be known of almost simultaneously throughout the planet. Everywhere it will presently be the same *"now."*

The story of communications, written regardless of any limitations of space or time would deal with signalling, with semaphores, smoke signals, practised by every savage people from the Picts to the Polynesians, and the like, and then go on to the story of electrical communication, with the electric needle, the telephone, the dawn of radio communication and the possibilities of the wireless transmission of visual impressions, as its chief episodes.

We may perhaps glance at a few facts in this latter story. It all falls within the compass of a century and a half. Until the end of the eighteenth century few of the phenomena of electricity were recognized; its nature was a subject of speculation rather than organized experiment. Volta had shown how to produce a continuous current of electrical energy in 1793. In 1819–20 Oersted discovered that a wire conveying a current would deflect a magnetic needle; in 1825 Ampère studied the forces exerted between a current and a magnet and between two currents of electricity; and in 1832 Faraday showed that when a current was started or stopped in one wire, another current in the opposite direction was "induced" in a neighbouring wire. At the time these things, the germs of all the telegraphic and telephonic developments of to-day, seemed curious minor facts.

Soon after Oersted's discovery, attempts were made to transmit messages by the deflection of a magnetic needle. In 1820 Ampère constructed a telegraph which had twenty-six wires and twenty-six needles—a wire and a needle for each letter of the alphabet. It was not until 1836 that a measure of success was achieved by Gauss and Weber in Germany, and Cooke and Wheatstone in England. Wheatstone's first instrument had five needles, but these were reduced to two, and in 1845 to one. The letters were arranged on a dial, and the needle pointed to a particular letter, according to the signal received. The instrument had the merit that no special knowledge or skill was required to operate it.

Meanwhile Morse, in America, adopted a different plan. He devised a code of "dots and dashes" by sending a current along the line for a shorter or longer period and recording them by a pointer, or "pencil," which pressed against a moving strip of paper while the current flowed. His first patent was taken out in 1835. By 1851 there were fifty companies using the Morse code in America. In Europe the needle instrument prevailed, and the Morse code and system did not come into use until 1861. In 1853 duplex telegraphy was invented. By this method two messages could be sent simultaneously over the same line. Edison invented quadruplex telegraphy, by which two messages can be sent in each direction simultaneously, in 1874. These are two out of scores of refinements which increased the speed and range of electric communication. The needle instrument and the dot and dash apparatus were supplemented, and to some extent superseded, by printing telegraphs, in which each letter is produced in type on a moving strip of paper. During the last twenty years it has become possible to transmit fac-similes of letters and photographs.

Transmission under water demanded elaborately constructed and insulated cables, and created many unexpected problems. England and the Continent were joined in 1851. A cable was laid between Ireland and Newfoundland in 1858, but it broke three years later. The first permanent Atlantic cable was laid in 1866. More sensitive recording instruments than those which sufficed for land lines were required. These were found, first, in the mirror galvanometer, and secondly, in the siphon recorder, both invented by William Thomson, afterwards Lord Kelvin. The siphon recorder has a siphon dipping into a vessel of ink. The long limb of the siphon, drawn out to a fine point, rests upon a moving strip of paper. The signals are received by a sensitive galvanometer with a suspended coil of wire instead of a needle, and the deflections for dots and dashes are in opposite directions. These deflections are communicated to the siphon, which traces a straight line so long as no message is coming through, and a wavy one when signals are being received. The dots were indicated by waves on one side, and the dashes by waves on the other side of the line.

By the aid of a number of subsidiary devices, the speed of cable transmission has been increased from 15 letters a minute in 1858 to 2,500 letters a minute at the present day. There are now more than 3,000 submarine cables in the world, with a total length of about 300,000 miles, and 21 of these lie between Europe and North America. The whole of that network of intercommunication has been established within eighty years— the lifetime of a single individual. It has effected a revolution in method of government and in the conduct of business. It tends to make the world one unit to a greater extent even than the railway or the steamship. It permits of instantaneous decisions in places remote from one another. It annihilates time—in some

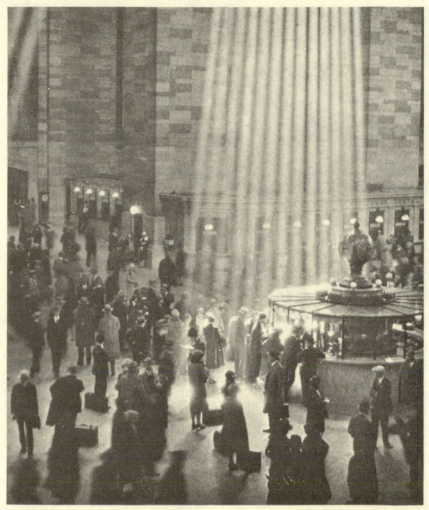

HUMANITY IN MOVEMENT

THE Grand Central Station, New York. It is estimated that more than sixty-eight million people used the terminal in 1929, of whom forty-seven million were passengers. The remaining twenty-one million used it as a thoroughfare to the surrounding office buildings, hotels, and streets, or to meet and bid good-bye to passengers.

THE PRINTED WORD

FED by a giant roll of paper, huge presses like the one in this picture print, cut, fold and pour out a continuous stream of newspapers ready for distribution. The white arrows show the direction of the moving papers.

cases it antedates events. An incident in the Far East may be known in England before the hour by Greenwich time at which it occurred.

The transmission of human speech, with its vowels and their consonantal modifications, was a more delicate matter than the transmission of dots and dashes. From 1854 onward inventors were busy on this problem. Some means had to be devised to cause an electric current to vary with the vibrations of the human voice, and then to reproduce these vibrations at the receiving end. The problem was solved in 1876 by Graham Bell. Briefly, his apparatus consisted of a transmitter and a receiver with a connecting wire. The transmitter was composed of a flexible ferrotype disc, a disc that is of very thin sheet iron, gripped by its edges and fixed opposite the end of a magnet. Round the magnet was a coil of wire through which a weak current of electricity flowed. When a person spoke to the ferrotype plate it was set in vibration. Its approach to and recession from the magnet altered the magnetic field and caused corresponding alterations in the strength of the current which set up similar vibrations in a disc in a similar instrument at the receiving end. The chief modification since then is in the transmitter. This consists of a box with a flexible disc on one side. It is filled with granules of carbon, through which passes an electric current. A person speaking to the disc causes it to vibrate, and the vibrations are communicated to the carbon granules. This causes variations in resistance and consequent variations in the strength of the current.

So it became possible for one person to speak to another at a distance, and the next step was obviously to devise methods of getting into communication with the person with whom speech was desired. Here again was a new field for invention and enterprise. Switchboards through which a number of subscribers could be put into intercommunication were devised. The first was set up at New Haven, Connecticut, in 1878, with several thousand subscribers. In London in the same year the subscribers were less than a dozen. To-day there are about 20,000,000 telephones in the United States, or nearly 16 for every hundred of the population, and there are more than 30,000,000 telephones in the world.

The distance over which messages could be sent increased. Many improvements had to be made in auxiliary apparatus before long-distance telephony was possible. For long-distance lines, the feeble currents which represent speech have to be reinforced by valves such as are used in wireless telephony. But with no unreasonable delay the chief towns of Europe and America were brought into communication, and the human voice was carried across the wide seas. In the towns the telephone operator is gradually being displaced for local calls by the automatic exchange, a wonderfully ingenious arrangement by which any subscriber can call up any other in the area by "spelling" the number on a dial.

But now a new phase in communication was to appear—the transmission of signals and speech without connecting wires. This development began in the mind of a mathematician and in the laboratory of a professor of physics. Like the preceding developments, it was a triumph of pure science. In 1865 Clerk Maxwell published his electro-magnetic theory of light in which he suggested that electricity was propagated through space by a wave motion similar to that of light. About 1887 Hertz detected these waves. It was known that when electricity jumped across the gap, a spark was produced. It was known, too, that when the discharge took place between large metal plates or coils of wire the spark was not a single flash, but a series of flashes caused by the electricity surging backwards and forwards millions of times a second. This surge in the circuit which contains the spark sends out waves. Fitzgerald had suggested in 1883 this method of producing electric waves, but there was no way of detecting them. Hertz formed a circuit composed of two conductors "connected" by a straight piece of wire with a gap in it. The conductors were charged with electricity by an induction coil—a coil similar to, but larger than, that which thousands of people have used for administering "shocks" to their friends. When the spark jumped across the gap, sparks also passed between pieces of metal placed very close together in other parts of the laboratory. The electric waves had reached them, a similar surge was set up, and with each oscillation a spark passed.

These pieces of metal served their purpose for confirming the existence of the electric waves and enables their properties to be studied. But a more suitable form of detector was invented by Branly, and in 1896 Marconi took the step which rendered possible the wireless transmission of signals. He connected one of the terminals between which the spark passed to a long wire slung in the air, and the other terminal to a metal plate buried in the earth. The "earthed" aërial radiated waves far better than any other device, and has remained an essential element in wireless transmission ever since.

Marconi brought his apparatus to England and demonstrated its practicability over a distance of 1¼ miles on Salisbury Plain. Before the end of 1897 he sent signals 14 miles. In 1899, messages were sent 85 miles. In 1901, received by an improved detector, messages passed between Poldhu in Cornwall and St. John's, Newfoundland, a distance of 2,000 miles. In their course the waves kept to the curvature of the earth, surmounting a "hump" of the Atlantic 125 miles above the direct line joining the two stations. This result could not have been predicted by the scientific knowledge then available. The practical test revealed a new fact of enormous importance to future development. Electric waves would spread over the surface of the earth and be within range of millions who had the means of detecting them.

Further advances were rendered possible by new devices, more especially by the thermionic value which could be used not only to detect signals but to amplify them. We have no space here to describe these devices, nor the hundreds of others which played their part in the development of wireless telegraphy.

We pass on to the next stage in this amazing story of achievement—the transmission of speech. For this purpose the original Marconi system of producing waves was unsuitable. The sparks were violent intermittent disturbances which produced short trains of waves, each of which rapidly died away. If you throw a stone into a pond it sets up a train of ripples on the surface. If you then throw another stone in the same place, another train of ripples is set up. If, instead of throwing a stone, you dip your hand into the water and move it rapidly and regularly up and down, you will send a continuous stream of waves over the water as long as you keep up the motion. If the movement upwards and downwards of the hand is slow, the distance from crest to crest of the waves—the wave length—is longer than if the movement of the hand is quick. It was the persistent hand and not the occasional stone, that voice transmission, as distinguished from signal transmission, required.

An alternating electric current flowing with extraordinary rapidity and regularity up and down the aërial was necessary to produce the continuous waves required for wireless telephony. Several rival systems of wireless transmission produced waves of this kind, and a new method was available after 1913, when it was discovered that the valve, hitherto used for detecting and amplifying the signals, was itself capable of acting as an oscillator and of radiating electric waves. The transmission of speech was then achieved by imposing on the continuous waves much coarser variations corresponding to the vibration of the human voice. The speaker's words are received by a microphone, which is really a sensitive telephone transmitter. The electric current flowing through the microphone is modified by his voice and conveys these modifications to the outgoing wave. This wave conveys the modifications to a distance, where they are rendered audible in a telephone receiver or a loud speaker. Such, in brief, is the general procedure by which wireless telephony has been accomplished.

By 1920 our world by land and sea was everywhere throbbing with dots and dashes and living words. For half a dozen years Europe and America had been in wireless telephonic communication. The British government had projected a chain of wireless stations. The most remote parts of the Empire were to be brought into communication. All over Europe and in North America there was intense activity, when suddenly the whole practice of long-distance transmission was changed by a most curious circumstance.

No branch of applied science has ever exercised such a fascination for the man in the street as radio transmission. Advance had been so rapid, the field was so new, that the physicist and the engineer had not swept it clean. They had left things to be discovered—mostly new arrangements of the parts, of which there is a bewildering variety. That was a great opportunity and stimulus for the gleaning amateur experimentalist. But while opportunities for private experiment in reception were unlimited, those for experiment in transmission were limited to wave lengths which did not interfere with public service. For public use, the relatively long waves were monopolized, for the earlier investigators had found these to be the most effective for their immediate purposes.

Consequently the amateur was forced to use short waves. But he was not necessarily limited to short distances. In 1921–22, American, British, French, and German amateurs were communicating with one another across the Atlantic with far less power than that required by the big stations. Through their efforts it was realized that for the longest distances the short wave is the more effective, and the cost of equipment less. This was especially the case when it was further discovered that with a special form of aërial the short waves could be radiated even more effectively in the form of a beam with very little spreading. This beam aërial consists of a number of parallel wires hanging vertically and in a straight line. If the row of wires is north and south the waves are radiated east and west. If the row is east and west the waves proceed north and south. They form a beam with a very slight divergence, whereas long waves spread fanwise over a wide area. If similar, but more numerous, wires are hung behind the others, they form a screen, and the waves are radiated only from the front. This beam wireless has the same relation to the long wave wireless, that a focussed searchlight has to an unshaded arc light. By beam wireless England is now in regular communication with South Africa, India, Australia, Canada, the United States and other countries. Long-distance lines in America also employ this method.

In April, 1931 (says *Discovery*, May, 1931), a new "ultra short wave" radio equipment was demonstrated. Conversations were exchanged between Dover and Calais on a wave length of only eighteen centimetres, using aërials of less than an inch in length, with a power of half a watt—which is just sufficient to light an ordinary flash-lamp bulb. In this new apparatus, the sound of the speaker's voice at the transmitting station is carried to a "micro-radion" tube where waves called "micro-rays" are generated; the waves oscillate at a rate of sixteen hundred million times a second. After concentration by an ingenious combination of two reflectors into a fine pencil of rays, somewhat similar to the rays sent out by a searchlight, the waves are transmitted into space. An important feature of the micro-rays is that they are not subject to the "fading" effects encountered in ordinary wireless transmission, and they are not absorbed by rain or fog, as is the case with light rays. The demonstration has shown that wave lengths of between ten and a hundred centimetres can be used for commercial transmission. This gives a great range of difference in transmission and nearly a quarter of a million micro-ray instruments will be workable without any one of them interfering with another.

Wireless communication was rapidly adopted for use at sea. All ships making long voyages are equipped for it, and by the direction finder they are able to ascertain the point of the compass from which signals come. It is also destined to facilitate aërial navigation very greatly. An airman can already find his way to the aërodrome through darkness or fog by noting the direction and strength of signals which are continually emitted for his guidance. And these new micro-rays will manifestly play a large part in the complete development of such vitally necessary facilities. The aëroplane of the future will have micro-ray eyes, and it is within the limits of scientific possibility that that which these radio eyes will see may be translated again into direct vision for the pilot.

The broadcasting of entertainments began in Canada in 1920. In 1922 the British Broadcasting Company was formed. In America, many broadcasting services were established by private enterprise. The isolated farmer, the aged and infirm, the sick are brought into touch with the world. The colonial settler, a hundred miles from a railway, can hear during his dinner hour the weather forecast, the crop reports, market prices, as well as many things remote from "the daily round, the common task." In Europe a man may, by merely turning a knob, hear music in variety, or speech in one of half a dozen tongues. What is distance? Where are political boundaries when man can speak to many men across a thousand miles of space?

The possibilities are boundless. And yet as we go to press official announcement has just been made of a difficulty which may, for a time, block progress and largely frustrate the efforts of all these scientists and inventors. The ether is becoming over-crowded. Powerful stations, broadcasting variety entertainment, are so increasing their range as to interfere with reception thousands of miles away. Even signals of distress from ships at sea are said to have been drowned. There is a destructive competition going on in the ether which in the end will benefit nobody and lead to nothing but a deadlock unless it can be solved by international agreement.

Yet manifestly more is still to come. Television is already possible on a small scale. The unsurmounted difficulties here are still immense. To appreciate these, consider the simpler case of transmitting a photograph by electricity. The original picture is divided into a number of minute squares. Each of these squares is illuminated in turn by a spot of light until the whole photograph has been explored. The light reflected from the surface will vary in intensity according to the light or shadow of the part illuminated. This reflected light falls upon a cell sensitive to light—a vacuum tube having the inner surface coated with a metal that changes in resistance as light falls upon it. So, as the spot of light runs over the picture and explores it, the current through the cell varies with the light and shade and conveys these differences to the outgoing waves. At the receiving end these waves act on a mirror galvanometer which regulates a minute beam of light in an otherwise darkened chamber, falling successively on a series of small areas of a piece of sensitized paper. This paper, on development, yields a copy of the original photograph. This process of transmission may take ten or fifteen minutes.

In television a distant person or object has to be explored in the same way by a spot of light. That is not difficult. No photography is involved. At the receiving end corresponding spots of light, of greater or less intensity, according to the light and shade of the original, have to be thrown on a screen with such rapidity that the last has appeared before the first has faded from view. When anyone looks at an object, an image is formed on a sort of screen—the retina, at the back of the eye. This image persists, after the object has been removed from sight, for one tenth of a second! On this elementary fact of the persistence of vision the cinema rests. But see the limiting time conditions imposed on television! The distant person or object must be explored ten times a second, and the transmitted image formed on the screen with the same rapidity. The apparatus must be capable therefore of working at least three thousand times faster than that used for transmitting a photograph. The difficulties in achieving this rapidity are partly mechanical, and partly they lie in securing a sufficient intensity of light to illuminate a large area. At present the transmitted picture could be contained on a postcard.

But who dares say that these difficulties will not be overcome? The time may yet be when a man will talk to another a thousand miles or more away, and each may be able to see, life size, every movement of the lips and every changing expression that indicates the other's mood. Everyone in that concentrated and intensified world will be living, so to speak, in the next room from everybody else and able with little effort to step into that next room to speak to a friend or make an explanation to remove a misunderstanding. The whole world will be a meeting place.

§ 5. Print and Film

This recent and dazzling development of electrical communications which has made the present moment world wide must not blind us to the major importance of that larger organization of human communications which is concerned with the establishment of ideas, the supply of ordered knowledge, the maintenance and development of common understandings—namely, the printed word. Electrical communication is a matter of the past century; the book has been developing for more than two thousand years; the newspaper, in its modern form, as an addition to the world's mental power, is a thing scarcely two centuries old.

We live in the light of a hard, crude alertness to events. It is a glaring and unshaded light, which casts strange shadows, but it is light. Few of us realize the darkness and the remoteness from current reality which characterized the minds of our great-grandparents. They had a few well printed books, bound in leather and handsomely out of date, a small news sheet, and a monthly magazine as their chief sources of information. That was all.

The *Outline of History* tells in brief the main factors in the story of the book, because an outline of human history is necessarily a record of continually growing communities, and necessarily it deals with communications as matters of primary importance. Such figures as Alexander, Cæsar and Napoleon are mere passengers carried about by the real moving forces of life; the use of cavalry on the Persian roads, a new system of monetary trading, the sailing ship and the highroad. The entire contents of the *Outline of History* might easily be rearranged under five successive headings: (1) Before Speech (2) Speech (3) Writing (4) the Printed Book (5) Mechanical Transport and Electric Communication, each indicating a revolution in communication and involving a new, larger, and more complex social organization. The printed book and map revolutionized the world at the Renaissance; the newspaper followed hard upon manageable paper and printing.

And here again our museums come to our aid. This time we can refer to actual museums. There are already many miles of galleries treating of the making and use of books. There are also vast collections of filed newspapers, and now such of the primitive machines as survive are being taken care of and found floor room. In these museum galleries it is possible to trace the first origins of the press in the classical white notice board, the "album," in the news letter and news sheet, and go on from that, step by step, until the throbbing great printing machinery and the stir and rush of a well equipped newspaper office are brought before our reader.

We dare not embark upon the story of newspaper work and the adventures of newspaper men. Interesting it would be to trace the thrill of excitement from the moment of a crime to the arrival of the reporter and the headline proclamation to the world. How is reporting done? That would be a queer chapter in the detailed story of human activities. Our picture, in its fullness, would include the government representative making his communication to the gentlemen of the press and the interesting, tactful and precarious work of a foreign correspondent. The editing and make-up of a paper would be shown.

The rôle of the newspaper in modern life is profoundly important. On the one hand it touches the book, on the other the pulpit, the lecture-theatre and now the radio talk. It is the modern man's daily reminder of things greater than himself, of a life of the race exceeding and comprehending his own. Every day that reminder comes to him. Few of us realize how the intensity of the individual life is diminished and the individual life *generalized* by the newspaper. To that we must return later when we come to review the education, formal and informal, of the modern citizen.

The newspaper is so much with us now that it is already difficult to imagine a world without it. Still more difficult is it to realize what an extraordinary and possibly transitory thing it is in social life—in the form in which we know it now. It does work now vitally necessary to a modern community, and it does it very crudely. It began simply and frankly enough as a purely informative news sheet. It was produced as that and bought and paid for as that. But from the very earliest stages it became evident that it had other uses. It was extraordinarily convenient for all sorts of announcements, which had previously been made chiefly by criers, by notices on church doors and suchlike frequented places, and its use for advertisement became rapidly profitable. It could, in addition to the news it supplied, supplement its interest by the discussion of public affairs.

Its rapid expansion in the nineteenth century was associated not merely with the spread of elementary education but with a revolution in paper making. The rag-made paper of the past could never have been produced in sufficient quantity for the modern press. Wood pulp, wrote Lord Northcliffe in the eleventh Encyclopædia Britannica, is at the roots of the expansion of the modern newspaper. The machinery to produce it in great quantities became available in the last quarter of the nineteenth century, and with that came huge printing machines, folding machines and the like, making the printing and distribution of a couple of millions of copies in a few hours easily possible.

The vast demands of the daily press are being met by a ruthless destruction of forests and have encouraged the planting of quick-growing soft timber at the expense of hard constructional varieties, which are also being exhausted to serve other human needs. It has been estimated that the present European demand for soft woods exceeds the annual growth of existing forests by three thousand million cubic feet.

From the first the newspaper was developed on commercial lines. It betrayed little ambition beyond profits, and little consciousness of the rôle it was playing in the expansion of our new and larger world with which it was being evolved. Its successful proprietors, with a few distinguished and redeeming exceptions, have sought to give such news only as appealed to the commoner sorts of mind, to provide excitement and entertainment even at the cost of veracity, and to gather "publics" which would present an attractive field for well paid advertisements. Their temptations have been immense. They have been naturally and necessarily on the side of private adventure against comprehensive control. They have a bias against an orderly commonweal. Our press is an adventurer's press. Few newspapers have any interest in supporting or defending a soundly organized public service, nagging attacks on public services are a world-wide newspaper feature, but every newspaper has an interest in a shabbily conducted, privately owned transport system which is advertising to keep its passengers in a good temper, or in a purveyor of quack medicines or trashy foodstuffs sustaining a legend of merit by a lavish expenditure in display. No newspaper again has any interest in the exposure of fraudulent or adulterated commodities, unless such an exposure will frighten or flatter the owners of competing articles, to its profit. It has no organic links with political issues. Serious discussion may easily bore its readers; ridicule and caricature of men in difficult positions are not only easier to do but more acceptable to the ordinary man. It can offer or refuse, it can in fact sell, "publicity," that most precious commodity, exactly as it is disposed. The marvel is not that the ordinary modern newspaper succumbs too often to these manifest temptations, but that it has not been altogether overwhelmed and degraded by them, that it still in its way, performs something of its necessary function in the new community. It does, as we have said, generalize its habitual reader and open his mind, however crudely, to a wider, more various life beyond his own.

But what needs to be made clear and is by no means clear to a generation born amidst newspapers and brought up on them is the extremely recent and the extremely provisional nature of the press as a social and political organ. Nobody seems to have foreseen how the community would be generalized by letterpress and by a universal habit of reading, and still less did anyone scheme or contemplate such a task of sustained information and direction as a better form of newspaper might undertake. The newspaper, a mere petty excrescence upon life in the early seventeenth century, is discovered to be a necessary part of our modern social organization. Now that we have it and observe it we realize that it is not only a vitally important organ, but also one still in the process of development and social adjustment.

The cinema, with its recent development, the talking cinema, destined it would seem at a not very distant date to be modified and mitigated into the artistic "sound film" in which talk will play a minor rôle, is a more modern and even more startling case of a new, important method of intercommunication gone very seriously astray. So far it has been developed chiefly on its "amusements" side. The story of the cinema is a worse record than that of the newspaper so far as the waste of serviceable opportunity through triviality of conception goes. Its obvious uses for educational purposes have still to be developed. The universities and schools of the existing régime lack the vigour and enterprise to control this new and powerful instrument for the distribution of mental impressions.

To that we must return later. A broad treatment of modern education will be the culmination of our enterprise, and in this chapter it will suffice to mention only the development, manufacture and distribution of the "movies."

Our imaginary economic museum, in its immense and spacious fashion, will have room to give an account of the making and display of a typical talkie-movie from the moment of its invention to its final disuse as a superannuated film. (I grow more and more pleased with the storage accommodation of these museums of ours.) And here again we shall be forced to note the inconvenience of outworn political traditions that now hamper, and may continue to hamper indefinitely, the world-wide spread of ideas by the cinema, in the interest of national antagonisms and national profiteers, the quotas, the customs dues and all the "blackmail of frontiers."

Another system of world communications, the international post, shows a better spirit at work. The creation of the Postal Union, marks a phase of sanity breaking through the chronic spites of nationalism. The growing facilities of letter transport over great distances were first realized in America, and in 1862 the United States suggested a conference which was held in Paris in 1863. Wars interrupted the movement for some years, but in 1875 the first International Postal Convention was signed at Berne and the Postal Union brought into being. It has survived all the stresses of conflict that have since torn the world, and to-day, so far as letters go, our planet is practically one. Forty billion letters pass through the organized postal services of the world, besides newspapers, books and parcels in great quantities. One scribbles a letter in a room in Manchester or Chicago and with a minimum of delay it starts on its journey, to a solitary Pacific island, to a factory in Soviet Siberia, to a boy on a battleship, to a prisoner in a jail. More than a hundred million letters a day are rustling about the world.

This Book on Communication again, like the Book of Substances and the Conquest of Power, is given here in the briefest outline. But the *Science of Work and Wealth,* rest assured, if and when it comes into existence, will give by its unrestrained pictures and descriptions an illimitable store of interesting and curious detail, helpful but inessential and quite impossible to summarize. And when the *Science of Work and Wealth* has laid down the world's roads and railways, launched its fleets and traced its multiplying airways through the blue, it will turn round and tell the reader just how he can travel to the ends of the earth, how he may talk to and see his friend wherever he is upon the planet, and what are the facilities and conditions for sending a ton of goods from anywhere to anywhere.

And so the scale and tempo of the modern process will be set for the survey of feeding, clothing, housing, protecting and keeping in health and order, that will follow.

CHAPTER THE FOURTH

THE CONQUEST OF HUNGER: HOW MANKIND IS FED

A MODERN ORCHARD

A THOUSAND-ACRE orange grove in Southern California, typical of the wholesale food production of to-day.

THE MODERN PORK BUTCHER

THE General Foods Company packs pork chops in a cellophane-like substance, boxes them and passes them through a freezing chamber, 50° below
zero (lower picture). The side of the freezing chamber is removed in
the picture at the top to show the boxed chops (light band in the middle
of the picture) between the upper and lower rollers that carry them along.

CHAPTER THE FOURTH

THE CONQUEST OF HUNGER: HOW MANKIND IS FED

§ 1. *The World Eats*

EVERY day upon this planet about 1,900,000,000 people eat, and eat at least enough to keep themselves alive. In no part of the civilized world now does death from starvation figure as a dominant item in the mortality list. There may be many deaths to which wrong or insufficient nutrition is a chief contributory cause, in India and China, particularly—some million or so a year. But by the scale of 1,900,000,000, the deaths from actual starvation do not bulk large. We come now to the fashion in which this primary need of the species *Homo sapiens* is met.

It is doubtful if ever before the world has carried and fed so immense a human population as it does to-day. Even in the most prosperous and fertile phases of the early civilizations it may be questioned whether the total came to much more than a few hundred million, and the boldest estimate of the numbers of our race in late Paleolithic and early Neolithic times would probably fall within the compass of a million or so; who were far more closely occupied by the food hunt and for the most part much nearer famine than any human community to-day. As for still earlier stages of our evolution, have we not already called attention to the fact that the great apes must needs be rare and unsocial creatures because each small group of them requires square miles of rich tropical forest for its food supply? Throughout all history until the present age famine has been a periodic experience. To-day, in spite of the world's immense unprecedented population, it is a restricted local accident.

The Neolithic Age was an age of more food—and of proliferation up to the limits of the food supply.

§ 2. *Fertilizers*

In Chapter I we have stated the broad facts, as they are known to-day, of man's agricultural beginnings. If we were to expand the subsequent history of food production until we came to present conditions we should next have to compile a history of the growth of agricultural knowledge and method.

So soon as agriculture passed beyond the flood lands of the great rivers, where the soil is annually renewed and refreshed, the fact of soil exhaustion pressed for attention. The soil demanded intervals of rest and refreshment. The history of agriculture tells of the passage from natural husbandry with resting fallow lands, to the realization of the value of legumes, beans, vetches, etc., in restoring fertility to the soil, to the modern rotation of crops, and so on to the systematic restoration of soil by natural and artificial fertilizers. From that it goes on to modern intensive cultivation with every possible artificial assistance and acceleration of nature's generosity, and to the scientific breeding and feeding of animals.

The story of artificial fertilization falls broadly into three well marked stages. By 1840 the labour of botanists like De Saussure and chemists like Liebig had shown that in addition to air and water, four materials were essential to plant life—nitrogen, phosphorus, potassium and lime. The replacement of these elements after cropping began to be studied systematically. An empirical use of fertilizers already prevailed. Manuring with natural products, with humus (mould), dung and lime, had been practised for centuries. Now it was realized that the necessary nitrogen, phosphorus and potassium could also be introduced from other sources. The developing science of chemistry set itself to discover and prepare the most suitable forms of these additional plant foods. The first factory to make a successful chemical manure was opened by Lawes in 1843. Liebig had made an earlier attempt, but his enterprise was a failure because he fused his materials together and rendered them insoluble. The fertilizer prepared by Lawes was superphosphate of lime, obtained by treating bones or mineral phosphates with sulphuric acid. Bones also began to be used directly, ground up more or less finely; mineral phosphates were employed; and the Basic Bessemer and Siemens processes for steel-making provided basic slag, supplying phosphoric acid, particularly useful for pasture on heavy soils.

Potash was obtainable only by burning wood (pot-ashes) and seaweed, until the discovery of immense deposits at Stassfurt about the middle of the century. It is now obtainable from flue dust in certain industrial operations, and other natural deposits are being worked. An attempt is also being made to recover it from the bed of the Dead Sea.

The first phase of the nitrogen industry (1839–68) was the use of guano, the accumulated droppings of sea birds, mostly from Peru. Then—as the guano deposits approached exhaustion, nitrogen, combined in a suitable form and in large quantity, was discovered near the surface of certain arid areas in Chile. The ordinary saltpetre is nitrate of potash; Chile saltpetre is nitrate of soda. With the development of gas manufacture this source was supplemented by ammonium sulphate. The ammoniacal liquor obtained during the distillation of coal is neutralized by sulphuric acid. These were the only sources of agricultural nitrogen until 1906, when synthetic nitrogen appeared.

Artificial fertilizers, and the restoration of fertility by a rotation of crops, are at present used mainly in the intensive farming adopted in thickly populated areas. They are not employed in the vast wheat-growing regions of the world. The ultimate effect of growing the same crop year after year without making up the loss is exhaustion of the soil,* and nitrogen compounds are so soluble that if they are not used up quickly they are washed out. At the British Association Meeting in 1898 Sir William Crookes emphasized this tendency to soil exhaustion. He pointed to the growing demand of the world for wheat, and

---

*It might be inferred that continuous cropping led to a continuously declining yield. This is not so. The field at Rothamsted, cropped with wheat year after year to which no fertilizer or manure has been given, has yielded about 12 bushels an acre since 1875 without showing any tendency to diminish further. The experiment began in 1852 and a decline occurred in the first twenty years, after which the field stabilized. *Carr-Saunders.*

the limited supply of mineral nitrates. And it was he who first suggested the abstraction of nitrogen from the inexhaustible store in the atmosphere.

Lord Rayleigh had shown a few years previously that when an electric discharge passed through air, oxides of nitrogen were formed and could be isolated under proper conditions. By 1907 a process based on this reaction was in commercial operation. The fertilizer produced by this process is calcium nitrate. Another method was found in which nitrogen was passed over lime and charcoal, when calcium cyanamide was formed. Put into moist soil this yields ammonia. These original processes are gradually being superseded by one invented by Haber in Germany just before the war. In this a mixture of hydrogen and nitrogen (from liquid air) is passed at a high temperature and pressure over finely divided platinum. The resulting ammonia is then converted into the sulphate or other compounds. One of these, of great utility, both as a fertilizer and in the manufacture of the synthetic resins we have described in Chapter II, is urea.

In 1903 the total output of agricultural nitrogen expressed in metric tons of pure nitrogen was 352,000, and it was all in the form of naturally occurring nitrogen compounds. In 1928 the amount used was just close upon 2,000,000 metric tons, of which 1,019,200 owed their nitrogen to the air.

So much for the scientific and practical development based on a chemical theory of fertility.

But Berthelot, the great French chemist, early expressed a suspicion that fertility was not entirely due to normal chemical reactions, and by 1880 research was actively at work upon this doubt. While nitrates were found to be immediately effective, ammonium compounds were apparently inactive for twenty days.

In 1887 Warrington in England and Winogradsky in Russia detected and isolated special types of bacteria which changed ammonium compounds into nitrates. There are, in fact, two stages in the change, and each is due to a specific organism. One changes the ammonium compound into a nitrite, and the other converts a nitrite into a nitrate. Both of the types of bacteria concerned are called nitrifying bacteria. Ten years later it was discovered that the nodules on the roots of leguminous plants (peas, beans, clover etc.) contain colonies of a third type of bacteria which enable the plant to absorb nitrogen direct from the air in the soil. The last are called nitrogen-fixing bacteria. With their discovery a biological theory of fertility was super-imposed on the older chemical theory.

But even these two parallel explanations are insufficient for the complete account of soil fertility. Since 1900 it has become recognized that both the chemical and the biological changes are dependent upon physical conditions. Temperature and mois-ture are to some extent functions of the physical condition of the soil—the fineness as well as the character of the particles, the closeness of packing and so on. And there is in many cases an optimum state of division and distribution of the fertilizer. The water-holding capacity of the soil, which is no less important than the food supply, is in large measure determined by the physical conditions of the soil particles, for the roots of plants require, on the one hand, water wherewith to supply the leaves, and air wherewith themselves to live. So that if all the soil space is occupied by water the plant dies of suffocation, and if it is all occupied by air the plant perishes by drought.

The farmer of former times discovered by experience the ad-vantages of thorough cultivation, of liming and marling, of natural manures and of rotation of crops. But he did all this by rule of thumb and tradition. He knew nothing of the vast complexity of mineral substances and of living organisms, nor of the marvellous changes that go on in the chambers and corridors of the soil. And it will perhaps be another century before he can interpret these with the same certainty with which an experi-ment in a chemical laboratory can be understood.

§ 3. *The Mechanized and Electrified Farm*

Machinery is rapidly coming to the help of the farmer, and a steady "electrification" of agriculture is in progress. Cultiva-tion for endless centuries was carried out entirely by hand labour and the use of animals. It was always a conservative industry, modifying its methods only in response to some urgent stimulus. The application of machinery to agriculture came later than in mining or manufacture. It marked the change-over from agriculture for immediate consumption to agriculture for marketing. In England the outburst of mechanical invention of the eighteenth century was coincident, in the latter half, with the enclosure of land and the associated revolution of agricultural practice. There appeared the drill (sowing machine), harrow, reaper, winnowing machine and haymaker. A primitive type of threshing machine was introduced in 1798. These machines came into wider and wider use continuously throughout the nineteenth century.

The use of machinery in America dates from about 1850, and in the wide, unbroken stretches of the newer countries there was greater scope for it than in the small enclosed fields of older civilizations. Here the sheaf-binder first saw the light. It not only cut the corn, but tied it into bundles ready for stooking. To-day in the drier areas of California and Australia, where the wheat ripens on the stalk, a machine is used which cuts off the heads and threshes and bags the corn. The stubble is then burnt and its mineral constituents restored to the soil.

In the latter quarter of the nineteenth century the steam engine began to replace horses. The first step was obviously to secure speed and economy of human effort in the heavier and more laborious operations. Ploughing, harrowing, and threshing were accomplished by steam. Because the heavy steam engine pressed heavily upon and consolidated the soil, it was sometimes, and still is, used in a fixed position, and the plough hauled backwards and forwards by chain tackle.

The greatest service was rendered to all agricultural operations by the development of the oil engine. This rapidly came into use for barn machinery, such as hay, chaff, and root cutters, cake and seed crushers. The earlier oil tractors for ploughing and cultivation were heavy machines with the same disadvantages of weight as the steam tractor and suitable only for large farms. But small machines drawing a two-furrow plough soon became available and are now widely used. With a tractor it is possible to plough five acres or more a day as compared with one by a man and a horse. It has been calculated that ploughing absorbs from 15,000 to 20,000 horsepower hours per square mile, and other mechanical cultivators from 7,000 to 10,000 horsepower hours. You must multiply the horsepower by eight to get the equivalent in superseded man power. So while the agricultural population decreases annually in comparison with the town population, the world production of food increases. Machinery, scientific cultivation and the improvement in the strains of agricultural plants necessitate rural depopulation.

Steam and oil power are now being supplemented, and to some extent displaced, by electricity. This form of power is less suitable for many agricultural operations because of the need of a supplying cable. On light land the oil tractor and on heavy clay the steam-tackle plough are preferable. Electrical ploughs or cultivators are, however, used on the Continent and in America under favourable conditions. Current is conveyed by a cable wound on a drum on the tractor. But it is in the farmhouse, yard, and outbuildings that electricity is of the greatest service. Much work, especially with animals, has to be carried out before daylight and after dark. The byres and stables are lighted first. Then the housewife demands a washing machine. Then comes electric dairying. Milk is drawn from the cow by an electric milking machine which absorbs only one sixth of a horsepower. With a herd of fifteen cows the saving in time is one and a quarter hours a day. The milk is now cooled in an electrically operated refrigerator, the cream is separated in an electrically driven separator, and churned in an electrically driven churn. The utensils are sterilized in an electrically heated chamber. If the cow's drinking water is warmed, she yields more milk.

In the barn, electricity is more convenient for driving the various choppers, cutters, crushers and mixers, machines for corn shelling, husking and shredding, grain cleaning and grading, hoisting and elevating, than an oil engine. The tendency is to use separate electric motors for each machine, so that overhead shafting with pulleys and belts is avoided. Out of doors electrical energy is used for pumping, including domestic water supply and irrigation. Add to these such household utensils as cookers, kettles, irons, vacuum cleaners, toasters, and the manifold uses of electricity on the modern farm become even more impressive.

In Sweden experiments are in progress in warming the soil by an underground cable in order to promote early growth. Seeds for garden crops are being irradiated by ultra-violet light, which is also used to supplement sunlight in greenhouses. Poultry houses are lighted morning and evening in winter. The hens thus have a longer daily period for exercise and food. They are found then to lay a larger proportion of eggs in winter when hitherto there have been a shortage and high prices. The total output per hen does not seem to increase; she simply becomes a less seasonal bird. When all the poultry houses in the world are lighted we may expect eggs to be a uniform price all the year round. But the consumer will have to pay the electric-light bill.

Progress in the use of electric energy has been hampered by the scattered population of agricultural areas and the high capital cost of transmission. In the United States this is five times as great per head as for the average town consumer. In England there are electrically operated farms in Sussex, in the neighbourhood of Chester and elsewhere. An extensive experiment is proposed in the eastern counties. On the Continent there has been a more vigorous development of electrified cultivation because of the prevalence of cheap electricity derived from water power. Between 1924 and 1927 the number of farms in the United States supplied with electricity increased by 86 per cent. In the latter year there were 227,442 farms supplied from public sources, and probably a larger number with private plants. It has been estimated that 600,000 or nearly 10 per cent of the farms in America are using electricity in these various fashions we have noted.

§ 4. The Spectacle of Cultivation: The Vineyard and the Bee Keeper

To make a complete picture of contemporary food-getting we should next have to review various special aspects of the business, contrasting new ways with old, in market gardening,

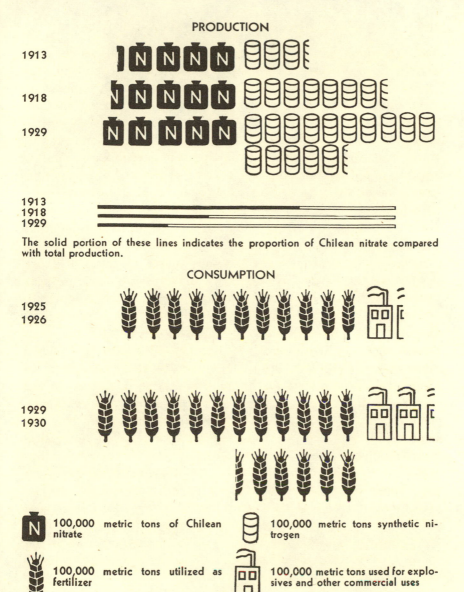

PRODUCTION

1913

1918

1929

1913
1918
1929

The solid portion of these lines indicates the proportion of Chilean nitrate compared with total production.

CONSUMPTION

1925
1926

1929
1930

N 100,000 metric tons of Chilean nitrate

100,000 metric tons synthetic nitrogen

100,000 metric tons utilized as fertilizer

100,000 metric tons used for explosives and other commercial uses

THE WORLD'S NITROGEN SUPPLY

NITROGEN is a vital element in both war and peace. This chart shows its production and consumption before the war and to-day. Until the development of various processes for securing nitrogen from the air, the world's nitrogen supply was largely in the hands of Chile.

in the working of orchards, vineyards, and plantation generally, in dairying, pig-keeping, cattle-ranching, and fisheries. A year or so ago the British Empire Marketing Board produced a wonderful film of the herring fishery showing the journey of the herring from the shoal to the market, but I am afraid it is too Utopian an anticipation to suggest that our encyclopædia should be supplemented by films for use in the study. Whether our science museum will be able presently to provide permanent sideshows of this sort is another matter. Films and moving-picture peepshows are used in the Kensington Science Museum and at Munich. From the cattle ranch, the sheep run and the levelled fields and the quay, from the terraced hillside and the marshalled orchard and orange grove, we should follow the beasts and fish and the grain and the fruits and the roots and so forth on their journey—often now a journey halfway round the world—to become food for the table. We should give a stirring picture of the slaughter houses of Chicago (one of the earliest instances of mass production). We should assist at fish-drying, at the preparation of haddock and kipper, and we should feel the chill of the modern refrigerator car and the storehouse for frozen meat. Jam should have its meed: the fruit-picking, the boiling, and the canning.

The bee keeper, ancient and modern, demands at least a section. We should tell of the passing of the beehive and the end of the annual slaughter of the bees. With the beehive the grindstones of the old windmill have passed away. The world was full of windmills and beehives when we sexagenarians were children. We should have to treat of modern flour-handling and of modern bread-making and biscuit factories. And after food production would follow a review of food transport and methods of modifying and preserving food, chiefly with a view to its use during unproductive seasons or its removal to remote markets. Butter, cheese and such new milk products as condensed and powdered milk must be dealt with, and the preparation of those "cereals" which play so large a part now in the nursery and on the breakfast table. We should need a long chapter on the canning and food-packing industries. Close to that comes the manufacture of meat extracts. Nowadays, not only meat extracts but vegetable juices stand ready prepared for the cook's hand.

I find myself with an assortment of items about the history of feeding that have still to be arranged. Each by itself has its special interest, but the assembled mass of information would be overwhelming. Our complete encyclopædia would have an account of margarine—a long and interesting chapter that would be now—in the history of edible substances. Margarine is edible substance won from the comparatively inedible. It is made from various animal and vegetable oils, so treated as to resemble butter in every respect except its vitamin content. We have told already (Chapter II, §6) how it stole the fats from the soap-boiler, and a full history of salesmanship should relate how the popular mind was won over, by changes of name and novelties in marketing, to the new comestible.

And there would have to be the story of wine. The trivialities of creed and controversy have, alas! estranged Mr. Hilaire Belloc from me, to my infinite regret, though they leave my admiration for his vigorous writing undiminished, or how gladly would I get a special chapter from him on wine, with supplements from colonial agents-general, anxious to recommend their particular brands of Cape hock and Australian Burgundy—Mr. Belloc objecting or not, as the case may be—in vivid footnotes. Nowadays the grapes are often crushed by mechanism, but still in the Province of Champagne red feet dance to music in the wine press. They may go on doing so. I am told that the twigs and seeds get crushed nowadays in the cement presses and yield unhelpful additions.

Beer and cane sugar, syrups and treacle, would give another sunlit chapter to that unwritten encyclopædia of ours. Cocoa and chocolate would have also to be told about. The entire grocer's stock indeed would be traced to its origins and explained. Or rather it must be dealt with at its origins and traced step by step to the grocer's counter. It would be a book of bright little marvels. And the reader, the nine-out-of-ten reader, would never read all that mass of detailed information. He would dip into it and find it amusing until he began to tire. He would skip and turn it over and stop here at this picture and there at a headline. And then he would stop reading. Most of it he would take as read, which is precisely what we are doing here. We are merely taking two steps instead of one. We are taking it as written, and then we are taking it as read. The result is exactly the same.

Now, passing very briefly over the marketing of this food stuff, for marketing is to be dealt with later, we wave a hand to the modern kitchen, with its gas cooking and its electric refrigerators, make the customary contrast with past conditions, and pause at the breakfast table and the dining-room door.

§ 5. *Substitutes and Adulteration*

We freeze food, we store it, we move it over immense distances and modify it in hitherto unheard of ways—and we have increased our gross supply enormously. But certain less agreeable aspects of modern food production must not be ignored in this survey. Science casts a shadow wherever she distributes her benefits. New substances are not always unmitigated blessings. It is impossible to deal completely with the feeding of mankind unless we bring into the picture the ingenuity and industry that are lavished in—how can I put it?—supplementing the supply of recognized foodstuffs by calling in, as unobtrusively as possible, substances less obviously nutritious and appetizing. The harsh word for this is "adulteration."

When I write "harsh word," I have in mind a gentleman charged with supplying a lubricating grease into which he had put 40 per cent of chalk, which, unhappily for the machinery and him, happened to be mixed with iron filings. "Oh," he protested to his barrister, "we don't call *that* adulteration. That is a most objectionable word. We call it 'loading'." In matters of food and drink, the gentler, more acceptable term is "substitution." Originally adulteration was understood to be plain cheating, and the adulterator had little to say for himself when he was found out; his adulterated stuff was destroyed, and he went into the pillory or was branded, nailed by the ear to any convenient woodwork, or otherwise roughly handled.

But the increase of knowledge and human subtlety have complicated this question. The idea of artificial and synthetic foods has a peculiar charm for the practical substitutionist, and the conception of suggestion comes in as a very real help when one is detected in misdescription. There may be substitution in series giving the most remarkable results. In one delightful instance a firm was prosecuted for selling something called lemonade crystals which was labelled "Pure Fruit Juice and Sugar Only." It was shown that neither fruit nor sugar was used in their manufacture. The "accepted substitutes"—ingenious phrase—for lemon juice and sugar in the trade are citric acid and glucose. But this particular firm had procured its citric acid from a purveyor whose idea of an "accepted substitute" for citric acid was tartaric acid. And tartaric acid also by the charitable customs of commerce can have an understudy, and so what this firm of caterers was finally handing out to thirsty little boys and girls was a "tartaric acid substitute"—of which they did not know the composition. Analysis showed it to be dirty phosphoric acid. The label had not only the lying words quoted above but a picture of a large yellow lemon in vivid contrast with a lovely green leaf. The defendants alleged that this was to help people to "realize that it tasted like lemons"—which my informant declares stoutly it did not do. All the more need for the helpful label, the defendants might argue. It is distressing to think of the virtuous teetotaller, who has avoided alcohol as a deadly poison throughout his life, betrayed into the consumption of this sinister brew of glucose and old bones.

This is but an outstanding instance of an all too prevalent disposition to put a brave face upon dishonesty. S. L. Bensusan, the well known writer on British Agriculture, has recently come upon and made a happy use of a private and confidential memorandum issued by the British Food Manufacturers' Association upon Jam.* Jam, Mr. Bensusan protests, should be made of sound fruit and sugar alone. Swedes and vegetable marrow, dyes and so forth, are inadmissible to the housewife's preserving pan. But this federation sets up certain standards for "First

*New Statesman, Dec. 20, 1930.

Quality" and "Second Quality" jams, and its guiding instructions to the patriotic jam-maker leave Mr. Bensusan and ourselves astounded. "First Quality" jam for the British market need not have more than 50 per cent of fruit, and second quality more than 20 per cent. The "fruit" may be brought from abroad in tubs with preservatives; it may be eked out with any old vegetable pulp as an "acceptable substitute," the want of seeds in this pulp may be supplemented by the stale stock of the seedsman, it may be livened up with citric, tartaric and malic acids and brightened with any "permitted" colouring matter, and there it is, First Quality British Jam. What Third Quality Jam for the millions can be like is known only in the deepest recesses of the British Food Manufacturers' Association.

In a systematic treatment of this question we should find ourselves confronted by certain main types of justifications and excuses. There are "preservatives." Some, it is alleged, are quite harmless, but that is no reason why the consumer should not know clearly that they have been employed, just as he has a right to know that food has been kept in a refrigerator. Most preservatives employed seem to be injurious in various degrees, and some are a plain danger to health. Yet they may be arranged in an unbroken ascending order of virtue until you come to the time-honoured practices of salting beef and pork, smoking hams, hanging game and putting sugar or lemon in your tea. Is there any really "natural" food except unmixed fresh raw fruit?

Next to preservatives come various colouring matters employed to restore our confidence in faded and jaded substances. It is a fine line that separates decorative and encouraging from deceitful coloration. It needs a still finer discrimination to distinguish between the modern "flavouring substance" and the herbs in the soup or the mint English cooks put with peas and potatoes. Finally there is the bulk substitution of one cheaper and less reputed foodstuff for another. It is called by the more reputable name, to help the imagination and stimulate the receptive juices of the consumer. Why should they not be stimulated?

You see that this is not a simple case of wickedness and adulteration on the one hand and goodness and no adulteration on the other. We can pass by imperceptible degrees from the poisonous scoundrelism of those lemonade sellers to the makers of the most desirable foodstuffs and condiments and to every sort of innovator in dietary. What of the breakfast cereal? What of the sausage? When Raleigh came to Europe with the potato, did he realize that he was bringing over an "acceptable substitute" for wheat flour?

A constant warfare goes on between two types of alert intelligences in this field of food supply, a conflict which indeed extends far beyond catering into almost every field of human activity. People are being shabbily active and intelligently cunning in the feeding of mankind, and they are spending their lives and finding their profits in degrading human food, but at the same time another active class is making the most strenuous efforts to increase the quantity and quality of human nutrition and to restrain and defeat the sordid interests that would poison and enfeeble us. The campaign for more and better food is a world-wide and on the whole a not unhopeful one. We have already glanced at the conflict of the same factors in the problem of journalism, where we found sordid considerations and unimaginative self-seeking cheapening and corrupting that general supply of information and discussion which is now so necessary to civilized life, and we have found the countervailing forces as yet undefinable and ineffective; but as regards the more urgent matter of food, what we may call antiseptic organization is better developed. There is a great body of legislation for the protection of the people's food in every civilized country; there is an organization of analysts and inspectors.

Our projected *Science of Work and Wealth* would tell in full of the development and organization of this new preventive service—for its beginnings date only from the middle of the nineteenth century. Before that time the only check on adulteration, except for outbursts of popular indignation and municipal action (taking the form of market control), was through the Revenue service, which naturally confined its attention only to the sophistication of dutiable articles. An interesting part of that history would be the passing and working of the Federal Food and Drugs Act of the United States of America (1906). That marks a very important phase in the history of the American stomach, and also in the history of private enterprise. From being a country where private enterprise had carried the adulteration and misbranding of food to extremes, the United States now ranks among the most wholesomely nourished lands in the world.

There is also the American Consumers' Service, Inc., to be noted, which reports to its subscribers on the real value of commodities offered for sale—with especial reference to adulteration.

But manifestly a completely satisfactory food supply for mankind is only possible when we know what is to be scheduled as completely satisfactory food. Scientific food control awaits the advance of physiological science. Until such schedules are produced, legislation must aim mainly at the suppression of misdescription and leave the individual, with such guidance as his doctor can give him, to choose among his poisons. We must still have our substitute lemonade, perhaps—but with a plain intimation of the bones or other refuse from which it derives its refreshing acidity. In the place of that green and yellow picture of a lemon, if a decorative label is still felt to be necessary, a slaughter house or a knacker's yard must be pictured as attractively as the artist can contrive.

§ 6. *Dining and Drugging*

A new chapter opens, and the reader's appetite is revived when we turn from the caterers' stores and the substitutionists' problems to the dinner table.

And here we have to consider not merely what people eat but how they eat it. One interesting change challenges our attention, the gradual replacement of the private dining-room by the restaurant that is now in progress. I do not know if anyone has yet attempted to trace and measure this steady replacement of private by collective feeding.

Feeding used generally to be a very unobtrusive and intimate affair. Even cats and dogs like to turn away from us a little to finish up a bone. The peasant, the small householder of only fifty years ago, either never fed abroad, or on such rare occasions as he did, took his little packet of food with him. The employee brought food with him to his work or went home to eat. Large classes of inferior people were too shy and awkward to eat in strange company, and the banquets of the rich were private. People ate together in the refectories of monasteries and nunneries, in military messes, in university college halls, at public banquets and city feasts. They ate at the dreadful tables of boarding houses. There were almost always associative links to bring the eaters together, except when one was travelling —and travel was rare. But now everywhere the little tables of the restaurants increase, and so does the proportion of meals taken by the average man in promiscuous company.

A pleasant subsection of our encyclopædia or museum would deal with table furniture and decoration. We should see table-cloths and mats and serviettes, china and glass, forks and fish knives and flowers, replacing bit by bit the dipping in the bowl, the loving cup, the trough-like habits of the past.

Equally interesting and laborious would it be to get together a comprehensive account of the large-scale catering connected with this change of habit from secret to open eating. Our encyclo-pædist would have to go behind the scenes of a great restaurant and display the cooks at work and the organization of the service. For the present the interested reader will find much quite trust-worthy information in Arnold Bennett's novel, *Imperial Palace*. Is there a limit to this increase in collective feeding? That we shall be better able to discuss after we have dealt with the development of collective housing, as we shall presently do.

Another specialized section would be necessary for our to-bacco and cigars. Carmen no doubt will demand a place on the scene. We should have to tell how far machinery and the machine-made cigarette have superseded Carmen's nimble fingers. In the days of Dickens most cigarette smokers rolled their own cigarettes; it was a very foreign and rather sinister thing to do. Now few have the skill, and there are hardly any private cigarette machines. I doubt if you could buy one. Who put the pocket "cigarette machine" on the market, and who or what has hustled it out of existence again?

And after all that spectacle of feasting it would be necessary, I feel, to call for doctors and drugs—and here more particularly drugs. Diet from the point of view of health and medical treatment has been dealt with in the *Science of Life,* but if our detailed survey is to cover the whole complex of human activities, the work of the medical man must have proper attention. I have found very great difficulty in weaving the doctor and surgeon into this scheme of human living so far as their normal professional activities go. And the dentist. But I think here is a place for them so far as they are to be considered vis-à-vis with the eating individual.

Much of the physician's work can, of course, be considered and dealt with when the organization of the modern city and the public control of public health is again considered. Surgery again may be made a sort of side chapter to a treatment of scientific research. And there must be a little world of admirable human beings making the beautiful apparatus and instruments that subserve such work. I do not know where we should place it in our encyclopædia, and I find it ungracious and impossible to ignore it. Here, at any rate, with a sort of logic we can note the preparation, manufacture and distribution of drugs. It is, I believe, a very neat and interesting industry indeed. The unobtrusive tabloid and the urbane ingratiating capsule have banished most of the horrors of the dose. The comic writer can no longer wring any laughter from the black draught. We live in a time when the black draught is forgotten. But in the eighteenth and nineteenth centuries it was almost as cardinal in domestic life as "washing day." We still talk of a man "taking his medicine" when he has to face the consequences of some rash act, but in this age that phrase has none of the suggestion of nose held and bold gulping, that it once possessed.

How far the drug industry interlocks with the manufacture of meat and vegetable extracts and with condiments and perfumes, I do not know. To find out and tell the public would be a task as fascinating as it would be laborious. And since no one would read a complete description of this matter all through unless in preparation for an examination, we need not set ourselves to the task. We need do no more than think of the various groups of factories and laboratories, the clean and skilled workers, the bottling machinery and canning machinery busy with ever increasing efficiency upon these myriads of supplementary products.

§ 7. *The Peasant, the Basis of the Old Order*

Having eaten, drunken, and rectified ourselves we can face certain fundamental issues that underlie our description of food production. These issues are indeed fundamental to the whole process of social and economic evolution.

We can no longer dispense with detail by waving the reader to imaginary encyclopædias. We must sit down here to direct and exact discussion.

We will imagine that we have really looked over various voluminous and well pictured descriptions of scientifically planned plantations and that the picture of the organized production over large countrysides, of this or that item upon the daily menu of mankind, is before us. But when the reader goes about the world, particularly when he is in an aëroplane over Europe, southwestern Asia, India or China, he sees no such widely conceived and widely handled areas of production. For the most part he sees the best soil and the most convenient regions parcelled out into extraordinarily small patches and being cultivated by methods that any full rendering of the possibilities of modern production will assure him are antiquated and obsolete. He will find if he enquires into the matter that these little patches are held individually and managed independently. He is in the presence of the most obdurate obstacle to the effective modernization of the world, the peasant. The peasant is the type, symbol and substance of localized traditionalism. He is the basis of the old order and a misfit and anachronism in the new. He, with his whole family, work upon and live upon his holding of land. He and his family constitute an almost autonomous social unit.

A couple of centuries ago, practically all mankind was living on local produce. Foreign trade was a trade in luxuries, superfluities, and accessories. Fosdick, in his *Old Savage in the New Civilization,* cites an account written by a Massachusetts farmer of the year 1786 of his economic life, which has happily been preserved for us. All his meat, bread, vegetables, fruit and (maple) sugar, he grew himself. His clothing came from his own wool and flax and leather of his own tanning. His house was built from his own trees, and he had his own forage. All he needed from the outside world were a few such things as salt, pepper, lead bullets, gunpowder, tools and weapons, and few of these things came from overseas. These needs he satisfied easily by selling a fraction of his wheat or cattle. The human world, save in the regions given over to nomadism, was a world of such small localized cultivators, and its towns, industries, churches and monasteries, courts and armies, such as they were, were all resting in the last resort on the indefatigable toil of the man with the plough and spade, *working in the vicinity.*

There was one important breakaway from this generalization before the modern era, the case of Rome during the mightier phase of the City-Empire. Then the subjugated provinces, and especially Sicily and Egypt, sent a great tribute of foodstuffs in exceptionally large ships to the capital. The economic life of all Italy indeed during the days of imperial expansion, shows a movement of essential produce unequalled in quantity and distance elsewhere in the ancient world. Where there are very large rivers there had also been, since the very earliest days, an important concentration of produce to aliment city aggregations at crucial vantage points. Since the beginnings of history there have been such pre-railway great cities, for example on the Nile, on the Euphrates and Tigris, on the Ganges and the great Chinese rivers.

But these were exceptions to the general state of human affairs. The immense majority of the race was dispersed in a village plus small-town pattern, and each repetition of the pattern was economically autonomous and capable of carrying on by itself, if necessary, for an indefinite time. Indeed, it had to be so autonomous, because there were no means of either taking away or bringing produce in bulk. If production failed, the district starved. In the past men could die of famine in Cheshire while Kent had a glut. And the fundamental dots in this stippled pattern of human society, the individual dots that made the circles of relationship, made the rosette of villages and township, were the hand cultivator, the peasant. Alterations in the status of the peasant there have been again and again. In the story of Pharaoh's dream of the lean kine and the fat kine we have the memory of a deal in which the burthen on the peasant is increased. And the château-burning of the first French Revolution finds its parallel in most of the social cataclysms of the past. The superincumbent pressure is thrown off, and the peasant recovers his surplus produce. But whether the peasant was getting a greater or lesser share out of his total yield, whether he was serf or debtor or free and prosperous small farmer with no master above him, did not in the least alter the fact that the economy of the community was entirely based on him. He conditioned the lives of his tyrants and masters and parasites. They might come or go, they might vary widely, but he remained. He was the essential thing. Nothing in the nature of industrial England or industrial Belgium was possible before the nineteenth century, no countryside carrying millions of industrial workers and having a food production out of all proportion smaller than the needs of the population it carried.

§ 8. *The Passing of the Peasant*

Essentially the modernization of food production means the supersession of this small localized self-directing cultivator, peasant or peasant-like. Here we will speak only of the mechanical organization, the material pressures, concerned in the process. It will be more convenient to leave until later the mental and social stresses this supersession involves.

We have mentioned already the expropriation of peasants in

favour of an estate system with slave labour, as a phase in the Roman development. This probably diminished the total output per head and thinned out the population of the countryside, but concentrated a large share of the produce as profit in the hands of the slave owner. The decline and fall of the Empire, the cessation of the slave supply, meant the restoration of the soil to the peasant.

It was a thousand years later, in the British Isles and under entirely new conditions, that the supersession of peasant holders appeared again. In the south and east of England the dispossession of the peasant was associated with sheep-farming for wool export, but it was also directly related to the appearance of new agricultural methods that superseded the strip husbandry and common grazing of the ancient traditional system. It was not merely that the peasant was dispossessed in England; the more important fact is that his methods were set aside. His labour was economized by production on a new scale. Specialization ended his autonomy. Cultivation was less and less for immediate use and more and more for the market. And his home industries were overwhelmed by town products. In this new process of estate aggregation the countryside population was actually reduced while the surplus of production was greatly increased.

It is unnecessary to trace in detail here the phases of the process that replaced the English peasant almost altogether by the agricultural labourer. It is one typical local instance of a world-wide struggle that is still going on, with many fluctuations and setbacks. It is a fight between the individualist "family farmer" on the one hand and organization and (later) machinery on the other. In Denmark the small cultivator has persisted by a surrender of much of his individual freedom to coöperative organization. He has survived by combination. The English peasant was extinguished before he and his world had reached a level of knowledge and education that made such a voluntary association for collective purposes possible. The English smallholder to-day is a new social type still upon its trial and still learning the lessons of coöperation that the Danish peasant mastered two generations ago. He is not in the old tradition. He is a return to the land.

We may pass very illuminatingly from the story of the disappearance of the English peasant to the struggle that is now going on in Russia. The Soviet government is trying to pass at one stride from conditions that prevailed in fifteenth-century England to an organization of agriculture comprehensive beyond anything hitherto known in the world. A strenuously modern conception of social organization is seeking to impose itself upon a mediæval peasantry, and there is a conscious and acute struggle between peasant and estate—which in this case is a government estate. Upon its issue depends the whole future of Russia. A successful resistance by the peasant spells regression and defeat to that vast experiment. A triumph of large, coördinated cultivation means, on the other hand, an educated countryside, dominated by schools and research stations, and playing a large part in the establishment of a new social order throughout the world.

This primary problem of the Russian revolution, the problem of the peasant, was the main topic in a conversation between the present writer and Lenin in 1920. Lenin was then very hopeful of a progressive organization of publicly owned estates, district by district and province by province. The peasant method of life was to be fought and beaten in detail, first here and then there. The peasant, said Lenin, has great resisting power in his own place, but he has not the nation-wide solidarity nor the alertness to bestir himself to combat an attack on his dearest habits and prejudices when it is going on in another part of the country. So that by concentrating all the resources of the Soviet government first in one province and then in another, all Russia would at last be won to modern agriculture and reconstructed from the ground up. Special, specially favoured, regions were to be chosen for the establishment of great communal estates, which were to produce upon modern lines, and the peasants of unregenerate districts were to be won over to submit in their turn to communal organization by the spectacle of the super-productivity, comfort and vitality upon these estates.

That was the project of Lenin in 1920. It seemed to me a quite reasonable and hopeful method. But it was never pursued. The famine year of 1920–21, the economic blockade of Russia by Western Europe, and the crippled state of Russia's industrial plant, delayed its realization. The necessary machinery was not at hand. The peasants underproduced because they got no satisfaction out of their extra production. The Western world, with its conservative traditions, held aloof, and no machinery or commodities of any sort could be got to stimulate the peasant to toil. The N. E. P. of 1921, the new economic policy, was a desperate attempt to save the immediate situation, a reversion to many of the liberties of private accumulation and ownership that had been abolished. Trading and production for profit reappeared in the towns, adventurers with foreign capital came bargaining into Russia, and the abler peasants grew richer than their fellows again. In a few years Russia began to resemble the United States of a century ago. Profits and social inequality developed on a scale that threatened every ideal and hope of constructive communism.

This temporary arrest of socialization began in 1921. For reasons entirely obscure to me, the development of a socialized estate system in chosen localities did not go on, as it could and should have gone on. There was a delay of eight years. There was a distinct drag in the modernization of Russia for those eight years. The temperamental Slav was, it seems to me, in a phase of lassitude. He dislikes measured steady work; he likes to take things by storm—and many things cannot be done in that way. So, I say, it seems to me; but reputable observers see in that interlude of eight years a period of recovery, necessary for the accumulation of energy for a fresh push forward. Trotsky and Zinovieff protested in 1927 against the gradual recession from socialist ideals, but the protests were set aside. Their protests, said Stalin, Lenin's successor, were premature. The time was not ripe.

Then, in 1928, Stalin awoke to an extravagance of energy. Not by parts, but as a whole, should Russian agriculture be made over. The N. E. P. was disavowed and set aside. The richer peasants, who had been evoked by the N. E. P., were suddenly denounced as the enemies of Russia. They were persecuted, and their children were persecuted and denied ordinary educational facilities. The time was ripe at last. Russia was to be made over by the Five Year Plan, which was to abolish the peasant for ever in favour of the collectivist estate, scientifically controlled. Russia was, in fact, to do in five years what the capitalist system has been painfully feeling its way towards for centuries. Was it, is it, an impossible undertaking? We must remember Russia has the experience of those centuries to help her, American machinery, American agricultural experts in prairie cultivation, and a very real but rather incalculable fund of enthusiasm to draw upon.

We are still watching that effort. It is the most interesting thing in contemporary history. Such pioneer reporters as Henri Barbusse, Maurice Hindus and Frazier Hunt tell of great changes and enthusiasm, infectious enthusiasm; they seem to have felt success in the air. And we get excellent propaganda films full of sunshine, hope and promise to tell us of the Five Year Plan sweeping ahead of schedule time. The screen displayed the building of the railway from Turkestan to Siberia very vividly and told me in continually increasing type:

TURK-SIB WILL BE READY IN 1930
TURK-SIB WILL BE READY IN 1930
TURK-SIB WILL BE READY IN 1930
TURK-SIB WILL BE READY IN 1930

Possibly it is something old or cold or bourgeois in my blood, that mingled a broad streak of scepticism with my appreciation. A question of temperament comes in here, and the reader should know of it. I do not like Dostoevsky or Tolstoi; I dislike the epileptic temperament; I am the antithesis of a Slav, and I bore away at things. I like things done without haste and without delay. I do not like things in front of schedule time any more than I like them behind time. So I doubted. But in May I learnt that my scepticism in this instance was unjustified. Turk-Sib was ready—and seven months of 1930 had still to run. Turk-Sib is running. Good for Russia! Good for Stalin! So far.

So far, because witnesses also return to testify to a terrible misuse of the new machinery, of harvesters taken to pieces out of mere childish curiosity and rusting in the fields, of the new wine bursting the old bottles and then running to waste.

In March, 1930, the Western world became aware of a check in this big thrust that was to carry rural life in Russia with one stupendous rush from mediæval to ultra-modern conditions. The young communists in charge of the transformation were rebuked for excess of zeal; they had driven too hard, and they must relax. All over Russia the Kulaks, the richer peasants, were slaughtering the stock they had accumulated rather than surrender it; their persecution had been not merely unjust but intolerable, and they were in revolt.* The attempt to foment a "class war" between the peasant with a dozen head of stock and his neighbour or his brother or his cousin with less or none, had failed, and the peasants were holding together. Perhaps this was only a first assault and a first repulse. Perhaps these Russian revolutionaries who have been in so extreme a hurry and so convulsive in their methods have learnt deliberation from this check and thrust forward all the more effectively for the lesson.

The Russian experiment will be an enormous stride in the modernization of the world, if it succeeds; but even if it is heavily checked and delayed, or even if it fails altogether, it is only one part of a world-wide thrust towards the single organized human community. Russia is a very forward country because it is also a very backward country. Its issues lie bare and plain. There is none of the complex closeness, the elaboration and masking of conflict between the scientific and instinctive forces, that one finds in the Atlantic communities.

Soviet Russia is double faced. She is communist and instinctive on the one hand, and she is state-socialist, scientific-planning and organizing on the other. She is mediæval and modern, re-

*Between March, 1929, and March, 1930, sheep decreased by one third, and pigs by two fifths, and horned cattle by one fifth. There was a famine of meat and dairy produce. *Farbman* in *Piatiletka. Russia's Five-Year Plan.*

204 The Work, Wealth and Happiness of Mankind

vivalist and cold-blooded. There are, for example, two entirely different types of experiments going on there in agricultural reconstruction, experiments with a curious parallelism and a curious indifference to each other; these are (1) the "Kolkhozy" and (2) the "Sovkhozy." They serve to illustrate a curious two-sidedness that runs through all this Russian revolution. The Kolkhoz (1) displays the old sentimental unwashed sweating "democratic" side, all natural virtue, brotherhood and kisses. The rich peasant is dispossessed, the poor are exalted above him, and the whole village attempts collectivist democratic management—with, however, as Hindus and the propaganda film make clear, a bright young man from Moscow as persuader, adviser and redeemer. On the other hand (2) the Sovkhoz is a state plantation, a really scientifically planned and directed modern large-scale organization of production with disciplined and trained workers—the big cultivations in Turkestan, for example, or the "Gigant" in the Caucasus, the vastest wheat-growing estate in the world, measuring fifty miles from north to south and forty from east to west. One thing cripples the Sovkhozy greatly. The best lands are already thickly settled by peasants, and so they have fallen to the Kolkhozy. The Sovkhozy have to take up lands hitherto uncultivated, either because they are poor lands or at a grave distance from consuming areas. They carry no village population; they are run to produce wheat (or some other single crop) for the towns or for export. The two thousand square miles of the Gigant have a total population, including engineers, families and subsidiary staff, of 17,000—of which, by the by, over 16,000 were under thirty years of age in 1930.

These Sovkhozy make straight for a new world order, but it is very doubtful if the Kolkhozy do anything of the sort. The Kolkhoz seems to be the old Tzarist Mir in a state of emotion. It is Rousseauism pretending to love machinery and taking it to pieces out of sheer childishness, misusing and destroying it. Recently Russia has been sending out admirably made, good-humoured, and attractive films about the new departure, in which peasant beggar women or social outcasts of a highly idealized sort, are represented as suddenly taking control of affairs, adopting all the latest devices of scientific agriculture, and founding and organizing elaborately mechanical coöperative estates. It is quite charming nonsense, but it seems to be sent out in perfect good faith.

Socialism did not originally include and does not necessarily include now any insurrectionary or "primitive" element. Its essence is scientifically planned construction as opposed to individualistic *"laissez faire* and all will come well." It was Marx whose mind was dominated by the prevalent political democracy of his time, who twisted up progress with crudity, and determined this curious Russian "squint," so that we are never quite sure to what Russia is looking and what her next step will be. Russia is, in fact, a vast area of moody and fluctuating economic experiments distracted by two points of view, and for that reason alone even her warm well-wishers—and I am one—are left doubting whether her constructive effort will succeed or will relapse finally into a mere barbaric chaos of insecure petty cultivation at the present Chinese level.

The change in the Russian landscape is at any rate remarkable. Joan Beauchamp, who visited Russia in 1927 and again in 1930, describes it very vividly in a pamphlet, "Agriculture in Soviet Russia," as she noted it from the train. In 1927 the age-long tradition of strip cultivation still held sway, "implements of the most primitive kind" prevailed, "a third of each family's land lay fallow each year," and "each peasant wasted much of his working time walking from one to another of the many strips into which his holding was divided." In 1930 a great proportion of the strips had vanished; they survived mostly close to the towns and villages (no doubt for vegetable growing and townsman odd-time cultivation). Elsewhere the small peasant holdings have been replaced either by vast state farms using the most up-to-date machinery, or by "peasants' collective associations which have gathered together all the horses and machinery they could beg, borrow, hire or confiscate."

"I travelled from Moscow down to the Northern Caucasus during the recent harvest, and it was fascinating to sit at the carriage window and observe all the different methods of agriculture in use as the train sped on. Sometimes we passed through districts where all the land was divided into tiny strips on which men, women and children were working by hand, aided only by the simplest implements. Here a peasant was cutting a strip of perhaps a tenth of an acre of wheat with a sickle, handful by handful, while his wife followed after, gathering the handfuls into sheaves. Next a lad ploughing half an acre or so with one horse. Then we would run into a district where already the strip system had been abolished and fields of wheat, barley, or oats of a reasonable size began to appear. There we passed long lines of reapers, with scythes sweeping rhythmically, followed by women in bright headscarves, bending down to tie the sheaves. At times we travelled for kilometre after kilometre through uncut wheat, waving far away into the distance. On the edges of some of the larger stretches of corn horse-drawn reapers, such as those still used on many English farms, were at work, often following one another in squads of three or four. Sometimes we came upon large pieces of land which the peasants were bringing into cultivation for the first time. In one such field, at seven in the morning, I counted no less than eighteen horse machines about to start work. Wherever the strip system had been abolished a good deal of machinery of the most assorted types was in use, and the method of traction varied almost as much as the type of machine—here and there a tractor, more often a pair of bullocks, occasionally a camel, but most often, horses.

"Most of the villages seemed to consist of one-storeyed mud houses with barns or cowsheds attached, though a number of the newer houses were made of wood with red zinc roofs. In many districts new houses were being built of bricks with zinc roofs, but all appeared small, and very few had more than one storey. Not far from the villages, running along beside the railway for a kilometre or so, there was often a strip of rough grazing land where herds of cows or bullocks grazed, watched by children. Harrowing also seemed mostly to be entrusted to the children, who hailed us joyfully as they sat perched on the harness of whatever animal happened to be dragging the harrow. . . ."

The expropriation of the peasant as it occurred in Britain through enclosures and a change of scale in farming, and as it is being attempted in Russia through governmental socialization, are extreme instances of the release of production from petty individualism. Changes in cultivation over the rest of the world have for the most part been of a less drastic type. In the older countries, still under the sway of the traditions of a long past of peasant culture, we find a great variety of peasantdoms still prevailing, more or less mitigated to fit modern exigencies; here the peasant enslaved by the usurer, here grown larger into an acquisitive free farmer, here in barbaric regions the slave cultivator of a local chief, here sharing profits and here paying rent in kind or money to a landowner inheriting from some sort of expropriating brigand. One widespread result of the war in eastern Europe, in Esthonia, for example, has been the breaking up of great estates and a relapse towards—if not actually to—peasantdoms.

In vivid contrast to the ancient deep-rooted peasantdoms of Europe and Asia are the conditions of cultivation in the new lands that have been opened up to cultivating occupation in recent years: the modern ranch and farm in America, Australia and New Zealand, and the exploitation of new irrigation lands. There the cultivator, starting *de novo* with modern appliances, works directly for the market and not for his own consumption, just as the new Russian Sovkhozy do, whereas the primitive peasant worked entirely for consumption and at most traded only, or yielded reluctantly, the small surplus of his output.

The story of New Zealand is particularly illuminating. As that very modern community rushed into being there was extensive land grabbing. It seemed probable that a big private estate system would be established, with tenant cultivators. Vigorous legislative opposition, and particularly graduated taxation, has checked this tendency. The great estates have to a considerable extent been broken up. But the proportion of small cultivating holders, that is to say, holders of less than half a square mile, has not increased. The increase is in holdings of from half a square mile to eight square miles. With modern coöperative methods of machinery and selling, an active Agricultural Department and state electric power, New Zealand seems to be working out a satisfactory and prosperous modern agriculture with owning cultivators farming upon that scale.

Neither peasant nor landlord appears in the scheme, and the stratum of modern-spirited farmers exercises very considerable political power. For many types of cultivation the large farmer, who will be in effect neither complete owner nor debtor nor rent-payer, but a fairly free occupier, financed through phases of difficulty by a state cultivators' corporation, selling mainly to its marketing board, assisted by its laboratories, sustained by its common services and in the ultimate resort under its control, may prove to be the final best through long ages in the future before us.

Different climates, differences in contour and soil may vary the optimum area for unified farming, from the hundreds or even thousands of square miles possible over prairie regions to the few acres of an orange farm or a vineyard. New Zealand, it must be remembered, is a sheep-farming country where the farms rule large. The unit of enterprise may prove to be much smaller in urbanized regions, where fruit, vegetables, flowers, poultry, and highly manured, intensely cultivated dairy farms will be at a convenient distance from a market. But these are differences in scale rather than differences in spirit. The smaller holdings contemplated will be something very different from the strips of the past, and the worker altogether different in quality and outlook from his peasant predecessor. He will be growing for the market as an item in a comprehensive scheme. The general principle of a limited, controlled and directed individualism with an overriding state landlord runs through all the most hopeful schemes for agricultural reorganization.

§ 9. The World's Catering Is Still Unorganized

There are two other questions, both very speculative, that we have to consider before we leave this subject of the world's eating. The first is how far our present reorganization of our food services upon world lines is still incomplete. It is vast and elaborate, but it is still haphazard. Immense economies and readjustments will have to be made before the constructive intelligence can be satisfied by the state of affairs. Let me quote again from Raymond D. Fosdick who in his *Old Savage in the New Civilization* has said already exactly what has to be said here.

On the surface of the earth there are to-day living 1,900,000,-000 people.

"We know precisely the quantity of food necessary for this vast population. That is one of the additions to our knowledge which the new science of statistics has given us. We know, moreover, where this food is grown and raised. We know the quantity of exports and imports for each of the sixty-five nations of the world. We know the primary and secondary sources of supply for particular countries. We know, for example, the amount of wheat that Germany would ordinarily import from Russia, and Russia failing as a granary, the amount that has to come from the United States or the Argentine. We know the dependency of the United States upon other nations for coffee, tea, cocoa, sugar and many other products, and the dependency of other nations upon us for wheat and beef. In other words, through modern statistics we are able, in our generation, to get a complete picture of supply and demand in relation to the world's food.

"And yet is it an orderly process that we see? Is it a process that has been worked out to obtain a maximum of benefit for the human race and a minimum of suffering and waste? Has organizing intelligence been applied on a world-wide basis to the production and distribution of food? The question answers itself. In spite of all our knowledge, this essential phase of the world's work is a chaos, a haphazard, drifting arrangement in which sheer chance plays far too prominent a part. As if natural hazards like crop failures or animal diseases were not enough, the human race adds to its own confusion by tariff wars and discriminatory regulations and cut-throat competition and a hundred other exhibitions of international folly. Consequently, part of the world is hungry while the rest of the world has food in quantity. Eastern Europe starves while the farmers of our Middle West burn their corn for fuel. Asia is underfed while North America hunts a market.

"Here is a vast problem that is calling for the organizing intelligence of mankind. The field has been surveyed and the factors are known. What we need now is synthetic thinking, constructive brains, a plan, laid down in world terms, that will disentangle and weave together in a common system the complex details of our present arrangement."

There is one powerful argument for a revision of the legal, political and educational traditions that at present rule mankind. That such a revision is pressing upon us is the conclusion to which all this review of human work and wealth is taking us. The next section will reinforce that argument very strongly and underline it with a note of urgency.

§ 10. *The Limits of Plenty*

The second wide question we cannot ignore is the possibility of a progressive exhaustion of essential supplies. As we have shown in the *Science of Life*, every species has hitherto eaten (or starved) according to the current year's resources. A limiting factor in the expansion of life, lies in the restricted and diminishing supply of available phosphorus. And we are now beginning to take nitrogen from the air in the manufacture of artificial fertilizers, a process that may easily attain such a scale as to produce within a few score centuries a perceptible change in the composition of the atmosphere. "The solution of the nitrogen problem by Crookes," says Professor Armstrong, "has brought us nearer to destruction rather than saved us, by hastening the depletion of irreplaceable phosphatic stores. We can clearly foresee in phosphorus the limiting factor to the world's progress." Professor Armstrong is not a miracle of judgment or knowledge, but these words of his command respect. Man is able to do what no other animal species has done: he is able to draw upon the accumulations of energy in the past and to anticipate his normal periodic supplies. He is doing so now, and it is a task awaiting the early attention of research students in economics to assemble and summarize everything that may illuminate the problem of how far man's consumption of food is exceeding his proper income and invading the capital upon which his future depends. In the *Science of Life*, in the Book on Ecology and in the Book upon Human Biology, attention is drawn to this fact that for the last two centuries *Homo sapiens* has been increasing at a rate that almost justifies the phrase "a breeding storm," and it is suggested that even now the human

THE MECHANIZED FARMER

"DISKING" an orchard in the Pacific Northwest with a gasoline tractor. Tractors of this type are used on hilly farms in many parts of the United States for ploughing and other agricultural operations, where a steam tractor would have difficulty in negotiating the slopes.

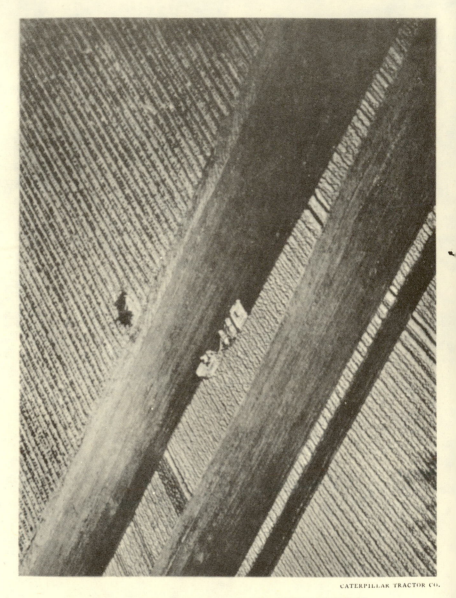

THE LATEST STAGE OF HUSBANDRY
A CATERPILLAR tractor and drag at work.

population may have passed the security point and be greater than it should be for a prosperous sustained biological equilibrium.

We have already raised this question in our outline of a Book of Substances. But now we are able to put the matter in a more concrete form, as a picture of all this feeding and feasting we have displayed, the smoking and wining and drugging, going on without apprehension, prevision or guidance upon dwindling supports over an abyss. It is a primary issue of unknown urgency, calling aloud for earnest and sustained study and for collective controls, conceived not on national or imperial, but upon absolutely comprehensive world-wide lines.

CHAPTER THE FIFTH

The Conquest of Climate: How Mankind Is Clothed and Housed

CHAPTER THE FIFTH

THE CONQUEST OF CLIMATE: HOW MANKIND IS CLOTHED AND HOUSED

§ 1. *The Wardrobes of Mankind*

SO SOON as our 1,900,000,000 people are assured of food, the questions of clothing, shelter and ornament arise. The search for comfort begins. Man—and still more woman—arrays himself against the elements and to encounter his fellow creatures. He dresses, he arranges his personal background.

When first I planned that voluminous undertaking, the *Science of Work and Wealth*—that project which turned out at last to be only the necessary vast eggshell, the phantasmal embryonic wrappings from which this present work was born—I put down the title of two great books. One was to be How Mankind is Clothed, and the other How Mankind is Housed. As soon, however, as the attempts to assemble the material began, it became evident that these two systems of human activity were in fact inseparable. They are both in essence now, man's conflict with climate and the weather. And so far as the treatment of industry goes furniture is one indivisible link. Such substances as textiles and leather would have to come in twice over if the two subjects were separated, though little more than the lie of the seams separates a shirt from a pillow case or a pair of boots from the cushion of a smoking-room armchair. The productive processes are the same. And hat, parasol, umbrella, tent shelter, shed, hut, hovel, and house have, as the biologists say, a plain morphological as well as functional connection. They are all represented by the shell of the snail.

First we should have dealt with the general materials for

clothing and furniture. There would have been an account, an immense account, like endless galleries in a museum, of natural and artificial fibres, and of modern spinning, weaving, knitting and netting. After that would have come the colouring and printing of these fabrics. Leather and skins generally, demand a chapter by themselves. Then would have come the shoemaker, hosier, hatter, tailor and dressmaker. A discursion of fashions follows naturally on that. I think our encyclopædia would have omitted the soul of clothing unless it included an account of dress designers and their methods and profits and a survey of modern dressmaking and millinery as they have developed in such typical centres as Paris, London and New York. That could be made intensely interesting—for everyone with enough money to "dress." How are fashions launched and sustained? And one could tell of the subtleties of "exclusive" fabrics, made only for this or that dressmaker, and of the perpetual stealing of models and infringements of copyright. We could show the rich lady from the Argentine or the United States coming to Paris, and all the decorative traps and lures that are set for her money. We should have a wonderful and amusing chapter here—and I should like to have it written by some student with misogynic tendencies and a meticulous industry.

Such a discussion of dressmakers and decoration, even the suggestion of such a discussion, may seem frivolous to some readers and altogether beneath the dignity of "economic science"; but indeed it is not at all frivolous. The fashions are not merely a sort of decorative crest to the business of clothing mankind. All the world nowadays follows the fashions. There is no stable, staple costume left anywhere any longer. We may glance back at the past when for large sections of the community costume was as prescribed almost as military uniform. That fixity occurs now only in very out-of-the-way places, and every year it is more difficult to find any out-of-the-way places. There have been local reactions towards traditional costume in Spain and Italy, and in Brittany the priest and public opinion are effectively conservative of local modes. Apart from such exceptional cases the treatment of fashionable clothing is an essential part of the treatment of clothing in general. The mannequin parade in the Paris club or hotel links inseparably now with the shopping of the lodging-house "slavey" on her afternoon off, or the gala costume of the Kentish fruit-picker with money to spend. It is all one process of a continually varying demand and a continually stimulated production.

It might be interesting and profitable here to go into the question of what should be included in the modern man's wardrobe. I am not thinking here of the wardrobe of a smart man-about-town. But what should a sailor, or an agricultural labourer, or an engine driver, or a clerk in a modern civilized community possess in the way of hats, shirts, boots, shoes, suits, and ties and collars? And what in fact does an exceptionally prosperous individual of these classes buy for himself nowadays? That ought to be ascertainable, but I know of no one who has attempted to ascertain it. I think we should find a considerable gap between the equipment that is reasonably desirable and the equipment actually possessed in most cases. I think we should find the world is shockingly underclothed to-day by the criteria of either efficiency or desire.

In the first place every worker in a soundly organized community should have proper working clothes, and by that I mean not simply overalls, but such underclothes as are best for him to toil and sweat in. I doubt if the expense and trouble of procuring this working costume should be left to him. They are the concern of the efficiency-seeking director as much as the space and lighting of his work-place. The modern agricultural worker, quite as much as the miner or factory hand, should have his working costume. And men and women are mere industrial slaves if there is not a considerable part of their waking life spent out of working clothes. That means suits and dresses and fresh underclothing into which they can change. The old-time peasant almost everywhere had his or her traditional "best," the go-to-meeting array, the provincial "costume." This was handed from one generation to another. It might be amusing to give a series of illustrations to show how alike those "old-world" costumes were and how distinctive they were felt to be. The modern worker has little need for such parade costumes for feasts and rare occasions, but more for varied personal clothing during his ever increasing leisure. He wants first his sound and adequate "producer" costume as this or that sort of worker, and next his sufficient and satisfying individual "consumer" wardrobe as a free and independent citizen. The Lancashire operative usually has a "berryin' 'at," for funerals and state occasions, a last trace perhaps of the peasant's "best" regalia.

I believe myself that the present underclothing of the world is disgustingly dirty, ragged and defective. A contract to put that right and keep it right would set every woollen and cotton factory in the world enlarging itself and working overtime. And would keep it working overtime until fresh factories arose.

It is not simply for the oily mechanic, the miner and the farm hand, that we have to consider this two-sided wardrobe. There is an old-established but increasing disposition in most of the organized work of the world to put the worker on duty into a uniform. In the past he was usually expected to share or bear all the expense of that. When I was a draper's apprentice the clothing expenditure of the shop assistant's wages was controlled by the fact that the men had to appear behind the counter in a white shirt and collar, black tie, black tail coat and dark gray trousers, or some such similar rig—it varied with the establishment—while the shop woman was under similar obligations. For shop assistants living in, this meant that from a quarter to a third of their wages was earmarked for uniform. In off time there was nothing for it but to go on wearing the same things. As a natural reaction against this obligation, it was the supreme ambition of every assistant to possess a coloured lounge suit. That was the symbol of one's (temporary) freedom, one's citizenship, one's manhood. One felt, when one wore it, no longer a shop hand but a man. One might be anyone in mufti. A select few treasured the equivalent of the peasant's gala costume in a cherished dress shirt or so, a white waistcoat, and a carefully folded evening-dress coat and trousers. They wore this gear at chapel dances and genteel occasions of that sort. Heads of departments got to tweeds and deerstalker caps. Nowadays there are thousands of young men in plus-fours who have never handled a golf club in their lives but who wear them as the outward and visible escape from some quasi-uniform imposing occupation.

I do not know how it is with the clothing of shop assistants to-day. Nor do I know on what terms the hall porters, hotel waiters, bus-drivers, railway conductors, postmen, delivery boys, lift attendants, and the like, that increasing band of uniformed men and women, are clothed. The social effect of the uniform, however, is very plain. The uniform limits both control and obligation. It is no longer an affair of lord and inferior; your personalities disappear in the formalized relationship. The first obligation of the man in uniform is to respect his uniform—as the scientific worker must respect his research or the doctor the public health.

Cheap, smart, stylish clothing, I am told, has revolutionized the factory life of women. The conditions under which girls are asked to work must have a certain compatibility with their clothing. Girls looking as they think like ladies, expect to be treated as they think ladies (working in a factory) should be treated, and the result is an extraordinary rise in the standard of cleanliness, language and manners.

Uniform expresses rôle, and as community-planning develops and the laying out of towns and architectural scheming become more extensive and influential in people's imaginations, the idea of a personal as well as a functional rôle may influence men and women in the direction of "dressing the part" even out of the employment hours. Their costumes will become indications of how they wish to be treated. They will express their conceptions of their own characters. We may be moving towards an age of much more varied costumes than the world has ever known before.

With all this an encyclopædic volume on clothing would deal copiously—in relation, no doubt, to museum displays—and then it would come to the making of the clothes in question. It would deal with the typical varieties of clothing factory, the mysteries of standard shapes and sizes, the processes of distribution and the eternal struggle between the economies of standardization and the incurable craving of every living individual for something distinctive. And so we should come back at last to those "exclusive" fabrics and designs to which we have already alluded. "Exclusive" designs—if we may be paradoxical—may become more general. As workers are released by improved productive methods from staple production, the proportion engaged in the design and making of distinctive clothing may increase.

§ 2. Cosmetics

Before we leave this matter of clothing, it may help to make our picture of social life complete if we say a little more about adornment. No human activities witness so directly to the almost universal resolve, at once heroic and pathetic, to make life gay and lovely as those which constitute the cosmetic industry.

In the last quarter of a century this has become an immense industrial interest. The Washington Bureau of the Census of Manufacturers tells us that for 1929, the factory value of perfumes, cosmetics and other toilet preparations manufactured in the United States alone was $207,461,839. This sum would probably have to be doubled for an estimate of the prices actually paid by the ultimate consumers, for profits in this trade run high, and to this would have to be added the upkeep of 803 beauty establishments, the wages of 13,000 more or less skilled employees, masseurs, rubbers and the like, electric current used in treatment and other expenditures. The gross total at the consumers' end cannot fall short of $500,000,000. In all ages, far back into pre-history, we find human beings have painted and adorned themselves. The Cro-Magnon people painted themselves like Red Indians; all India seems to paint, if only caste marks upon its forehead; nearly all savages smear themselves abundantly. Museums are littered with the rouge cups, trays, manicure sets, mirrors and pots for greases and messes, of the pretty ladies of Sumeria, Egypt, Babylonia, and thence right down to our own times; but never can the organization of human adornment have reached the immensity and subtlety shown by these American figures.

To our fourth chapter we have given the title of the "Conquest of Hunger," and this present chapter goes on under the caption of the "Conquest of Climate." But, as we have noted already in our remarks about dressmaking, mankind is not for a moment content with mere nourishment and covering and shelter. In a world in which, as we have shown, there is a frightful deficiency of underclothing, as many people as can are already striving for beauty, dignity and general effectiveness in their costume, and we have noted how clothing and conditions of employment can react upon each other. Here, under this heading of cosmetics, we face a still franker manifestation that man does not live by bread alone nor build his houses simply to keep warm and dry. This section goes beyond those necessities into another sphere of conquest altogether, the attempt to conquer happiness and beauty. And to keep something of youth still—something more desirable and far more evasive than bread or board.

Let us consider the effort to be pleasing that a modern woman in comfortable circumstances will make to-day. If our present hope that comfort and abundance are spreading down now steadily from class to class is to be justified, this is what most women will be doing in no very distant future.

It is an average well-to-do woman we are describing, intent, she says, upon her duty of pleasing mankind. She goes now to the beauty shop for massage at least once a week, and there, according to her physical condition, she has electric treatment or rubbing with creams, the application of hot and cold lotions; she has her face put under a "mask," an affair of beaten-up eggs and other ingredients which tightens on the face, she has it covered and rubbed with ice. Then her eyebrows must be plucked to a fashionable form, and there must, especially if she is of a dark complexion, be treatment for any casual hair, for an incipient moustache or the like. Her neck must remain round and youthful; it must be treated for sagging, and her hair, even if it does not need to be dyed, must be washed, marcelled, or water-waved and rubbed with a tonic. Good hair tonics are specially expensive. Once a week at least the hands must be manicured, and generally the nails are coloured as well as polished. A little pedicure may come in here. Few people can be trusted to cut and arrange their own toe nails well.

After this weekly or bi-weekly cleansing and refreshment our lady goes home. But she does not go empty-handed. She will need a selection of scents; and she will carry off bath salts, lotions, eau de cologne (costly when well alcoholized), and perfumed soaps. We will say nothing of her dental care, because that is a part of normal hygiene. During the day she will want to clean her face, and this is done, not dairymaid fashion, with soap and water, but with cleansing cream which takes off powder, rouge and dust and prepares the facial ground for reconstruction. Then comes skin tonic or liquid astringent to tighten up the skin, reduce any puffiness under the eyes and remove what remains of the cleansing cream. Then all over face and neck is put a "foundation" or "vanishing cream," and on this goes the powder (there are various powders according to the part of the body), rouge (red, orange, or dark red, according to the type and fashion), lip salve, and "kohl," black powder or liquid, for the eyebrows, the upper eyelids, or just under the eye, or at the hair roots on the temples.

If her face feels tired and there is no time to go for massage, our lady puts on some very expensive "day cream" and lies down for one or two hours. It has quite a wonderful effect, and when it is taken off again with cleansing cream and astringent, the face feels back in its teens. A "muscle oil" also is very helpful in tightening up the muscles of the face, neck and shoulders and diminishing the wrinkles at the nostrils.

After the triumphs of the evening the lady cleans her face before retiring with cleansing cream and liquid tonic. Then, if her face is thin, she puts on a thick, oily, very *nourishing* cream, or if it is fat, a *reducing* oil, and if she can bear it she goes to sleep thus anointed. But if she finds it unendurable she gets up again and wipes it off.

Also she must put cream on her hands to keep them white, and special cream on her nails. And also, perhaps, if she has been

advised to that effect, she will put on a "wrinkle eradicator"—
a band of rubber tied tightly round her forehead—and a "chin
reducer," made by experts, of elastic and herbs, to brace up and
keep her chin muscles within bounds.

But, you will say, this is a very exceptional woman, and indeed
this is a very superfluous section to insert in a survey of world
economics! By way of answer you are referred back to the
figures from the United States Census of Production given in
the opening paragraph of this section. There are a million women
in the United States alone with an average annual expenditure of
something like £100 on these things.

§ 3. *The Dissolution of the Home*

A comprehensive survey of housing would begin with the
housing of the past. That was highly localized both as to design
and material. We recur here to the motif of "delocalization"
which runs through all this work. Housing is now more and
more independent of local resources, though it is still dominated
and will always be dominated by climatic conditions. You can
bring any material now to a place, but you cannot take its weather
away. The partial release from locality produces a certain dis-
cordance in many populated landscapes, because of the incoherent
variety of forms and material now possible, but the weather is
a steadying and harmonizing influence.

Here some very pretty pictures will come to mind. Compare
the slant and structure of roofs in snow country with those in
hot countries and windy lands, the characteristics of marsh,
riverside and seaside building, the variations of window space, of
the height and size of rooms, of the construction of verandas,
loggias, sun traps and sleeping porches with variation in sunshine, windiness and rainfall. There is little need to tell here of
the rapidly increasing comfort of the modern house, because we
are all living through that improvement; consider, for example,
the appearance of the bathroom and the enormous brightening
of the evenings that has come with the electric light.

But the electric wires and the water tap take us on to another phase of the development of modern housing, the enormous development of collective services in the modern community. Water was laid on to the home in London in the seventeenth century, and domestic gas lighting came early in the nineteenth. The cholera epidemic of the middle nineteenth century stimulated the development of drainage and sanitary organization in Great Britain and made the English for a time the propagandists of domestic and public sanitation—until the Americans took the good work out of their hands. Our museum should show the rapid development of domestic interdependence in the modern town and give sections on water supply, drainage, sanitation, the destruction of refuse and the distribution of hot steam (as in New York), gas and electricity. And it will point us also to the household end of the telephone, with its new access to shop, doctor and mechanic. Here too a thoroughly exhaustive account of the decreasing autonomy of the modern home would have a few pictures from the London *Punch* of the eighteen sixties to remind the happy present of the vanished horrors of "washing day." A description of the working of a modern laundry seems indicated here. All these collective services tend to replace the structurally separated house by collective buildings, mansions of flats and the like, and the high and rising value of land in urban agglomerations stimulates this tendency.

And there is another side to this increasing collectivism of modern life, and that is the increasing disposition towards collective housekeeping on the part of women. The modern household is not only invaded at every point by collective services, but it is also assailed and superseded by them. For all its improved facilities, the separate home irks people nowadays more than it did. Women, especially the abler ones, rebel against domestic preoccupations. Men object to a life with preoccupied women. Domestic service, especially in the small household, is more difficult to obtain than it was. It would be interesting to give an account of some country house or château of the eighteenth century for the purposes of comparison. The owner, like Trimalchio in that immortal banquet Petronius has preserved for us, could boast that everything he consumed was grown on his own land

and prepared by his own dependents. Even his town house was served by his own mules and wagons from his own estates. Against this former autonomy of the rich we have to set the history of the modern hotel industry. Formerly "hotel" was the name of a great private town house; the seventeenth century knew nothing of what we call hotels. There were inns. You brought your lackey with you, if you had one, to secure proper service. The real dreadfulness of these inns glares through the fun of such a novel as *Humphrey Clinker*. In Russia, towards the end of the nineteenth century, you still brought your bedding, your tea, and even your provisions to the inn. You do that now over the greater part of India. Over all Asia, indeed, the caravanserai still rules. And these accommodations existed only for travellers. For those making a longer stay there were "lodgings." Fielding's account of his *Journey to Lisbon* describes an actual lodging in the Isle of Wight for the edification of posterity.

Athwart these memories we evoke the advance of the Hotel Industry, as the provision of a care-free comfort and abundance, at first for the very rich, now for the well-off, and presently for most people. We note the hotel branching out into the service flat and mark the progress of the residential club and country club.

With these advances there comes a considerable change in the status and quality of domestic service. From being a personal dependence with indefinite duties and a general obligation to obedience and obsequiousness, domestic service in a flat system becomes definite in its functions and with a certain personal detachment that marches better with modern conceptions of human dignity. In a London service flat or in a London club a modern bachelor is assisted in his domestic affairs by human beings he may neither rail against nor threaten nor burden with unexpected and uncovenanted tasks. But yet their assistance can make him extraordinarily comfortable. He can telephone that his rooms are to be ready before he comes to London, and he will find them in spick-and-span order. A maid will call him in the morning and bring him his morning tea, a valet carries off his disordered clothes to brush and puts out a fresh suit; a newspaper drops into his letter box. He finds his bath prepared. He telephones down to a central kitchen or restaurant for any meal he needs, and it is served him. Tea is served, and clothes are put out for him during the day. If an electric light or a lock goes wrong, a skilled mechanic comes up to set it right. The tenant's utmost trouble in the matter is to ring up the housekeeper or head steward.

He has never "engaged" any of these helpers. He never gives them "notice." Often he does not know their names. He goes away for a month and may find one replaced. He may ask a friendly question about that, but it is not his business. He knows nothing of the religion, politics, private life of these competent professionals. Such a system of relationship would have been inconceivable in A. D. 1850. Then these people would have been part of our bachelor's private household; he would have been their patriarchal tyrant, and they (and he) would have suffered all the limitations and inconveniences of their being fixed upon his back.

§ 4. *The Landscape of Homes and Cultivations*

This secular disappearance of the autonomous household through these double and alternative processes, the collectivization of its services on one hand and collective substitutions on the other, open up the prospect of an entirely new series of patterns in the layout of town and country. The life of the ordinary fairly prosperous citizen tends to divide itself between a town apartment with a stereotyped fashion in its fundamentals and either a country club or an individualized cottage or bungalow, and the large-scale map of our populated regions alters in accordance with these tendencies. The regrouping of urban centres and dispersed out-of-town homes and resorts is going on now with extraordinary rapidity and demands a new planning of roads, open woods and other common lands. The idea of "Town-Planning" is a new one in the Anglo-Saxon world. Before that idea became prevalent, towns grew unchecked. They grew higgledy-piggledy, but their growth never came to any crisis that

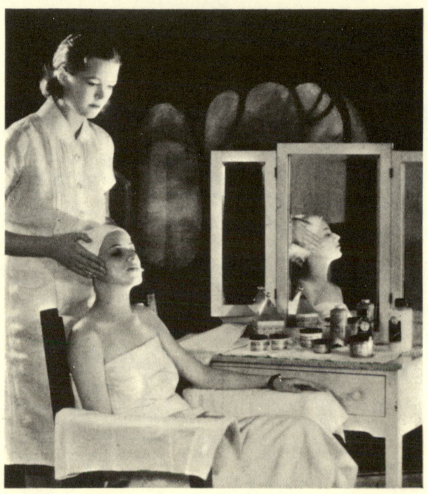

HELENA RUBINSTEIN.

THE MODERN WOMAN CONQUERS AGE AND FATIGUE
A BEAUTY parlour.

NEW YORK: THE UNIQUE CITY

LOWER NEW YORK, seen from the air. Most of the larger buildings show-ing in light colour have been built within the last five years. New York illustrates many of the soaring possibilities of modern architecture; but it may be doubted if the cities of the future will follow its pattern. Its narrow, restricted area, its foundation upon firm rock, and the peculiar social economic conditions that have promoted building upon small lots without a general plan, have given it a bristling verticality that may re-main its own special distinction.

challenged control until the present era of continually advancing
and varying transport facilities. And "Town-Planning" still
remains very uncertain because of the endless devices and
methods of transport that have still to be tried out and judged.

But though Town-Planning came as an afterthought to the
great urban aggregations of modern Europe and America, the
idea itself is an obvious and ancient one. The cities of the old
civilizations were planned, as often as not, as wholes. The idea
came as a novelty to Renaissance Europe and has never since
been lost sight of in Germany. Such eighteenth-century cities as
Karlsruhe were carefully planned. Sir Christopher Wren tried to
plan a new London after the great fire, but he was defeated by
haste, greed and vested interests.

Before the modern housing map can be made out in detail it
will be necessary to work out the proportion of urban and diffused urban population to the country worker and to the de-
localized elements—free to live anywhere—in the grand total
of people whose needs have to be provided for. There will necessarily be great local variations in these proportions and in the
nature of the local activities. They will presently become calculable, but thus far estimate and guesswork have had to be used.
It will become more and more possible, as surveys become more
exact and statistical methods are perfected, to determine the
proper sites for factories and industrial fields and to scheme out
systems of intercommunication between them and the residential
districts, to plot out the great schools, colleges, directive and
research stations, the clinics, the hospitals, rest houses and play-
grounds, the theatres, dancing-places and museums, of an advancing social order. Such a planned distribution of populations
is called "zoning." There are already planning schemes which
regulate the number of individuals in a locality; the Welwyn
Garden City plan, for example. Such regulation is necessary, if
adequate breathing and recreation space is to be maintained.
The Ministry of Health fixes an upward limit to the number of
persons per acre in urban regions in Great Britian.

But all this planning has to be given substance and reality in
a world already covered with fields, hovels, farms, châteaux,

villages, towns, and cities, whose forms and distribution have been determined by an interplay of forces and feelings that have now passed away or changed beyond recognition. We can look about us and see the old towns of yesterday with their cita-dels and fortifications, their casernes and iron-barred palaces, their cathedrals and town halls and market houses, giving place incoherently to the thrusts and pressures of our new occasions. All this dissolving and changing human landscape must be brought at last to the measure of a quantitative survey. And that survey must comprehend the rapid advance in building and engi-neering methods that is going on, and the attempts of power supply and water supply and every extending collective service to keep pace with the changing, experimenting and developing contours of façades of the rehousing of mankind.

Happily, in this field, it is only when we come to political frontiers that we impinge upon the traditions of patriotism and war. The local struggles of expanding municipality with urban and rural district councils, the conflicts of new avenues with an-cient slums, may be severe and intricate, but, at any rate, we do not teach in our schools the inviolable sovereignty of Paradise Alley and Muck Lane, we do not stir up in them a more than religious fervour to remain for ever what they are, nor invoke all the forces of romance and sentiment towards bloodshed in the cause of old insanitary suburbs inconveniently situated upon our outlets, but "rightly struggling to be free." The most formidable obstacle is the individualistic landowner whose obstinacy, greed and defensive energy have necessitated and probably will in many cases still necessitate a long political and legislative struggle.

§5. *Modern Architecture and the Possible Rebuilding of the World*

At a later stage in the development of this survey we shall point out the probability of community-buying taking the place of individual-buying in respect to many commodities and serv-ices. In no field is this more practicable and probable than in the plan and rearrangement of town and countryside. It will be

convenient to anticipate the conclusions of that discussion here
and to review the tendencies of contemporary rebuilding. A
steady enlargement of the enterprises, an increasing boldness
and comprehensiveness are to be noted. The time may not be
very remote when whole districts and townships and cities may
be systematically reconstructed upon one single plan.

Most people have still to realize the vast extensions of available material, the changes in method and outlook that have come
to the modern architect. The most fundamental change is the
replacement of natural materials by reconstituted and artificial
ones, and particularly the development of the steel framework.
In our story of the steels we have noted the development of
structural steel. Most steels will corrode unless specially protected, but the metallurgist may be trusted to deal with that difficulty. So far, steel frameworks have been made in large forgings
and riveted together, but now welding is coming into use,
particularly in America. New alloys, lighter to handle and fix,
may be counted upon with confidence. Even now buildings can be
made upon a scale and of a complexity beyond the utmost imagination of the builders of a hundred years ago. Before our age
the technical problems of architecture were concerned chiefly
with the piling up of weights. Great buildings were really
"stately piles." Now they can have a new openness, grace and
variety, and they can soar up to heights unthought of before.
They can also be built with what a hundred years ago would
have been an incredible speediness.

Up to the present the original mud hut has been clearly traceable in modern building. Cement, mortar, the dried brick are all
mud at one remove. All building has hitherto been a wet process.
Now it becomes the "dry" putting together of fully fabricated
parts. And as R. A. Duncan has pointed out in his essay in
*Science and the Art of Architecture,** building is ceasing to be
a skilled handicraft and is becoming an affair of mass production, far more rapid and capable of rearing much more massive
edifices.

In the place of massive walls of brick and stone, hollow walls

---

*Journal of the Royal Institute of British Architects, June 7, 1930.

of metal-sustained composition are not merely possible, but most practicable and economical, so that a room can be like a vacuum flask and maintained at a steady temperature impervious to heat or cold; it can be lined with soundproof materials; or it can be built of tinted or clear toughened glass and saturated with sunlight. And while the house of earlier times was a mere accumulation of masonry boxes with clumsy fireplaces for ventilation and staircases from floor to floor, the modern building becomes more and more like an engine, with tubes for air, hot and iced water, sanitary apparatus of all sorts, wires for heating and lighting, telephones, speaking tubes and the like. The house of a hundred years ago compared with the modern house is half-way back to the cave.

Steel frameworks are already a great stimulus to rebuildings, especially the rebuilding of big blocks of offices, warehouses and retail stores. Because steel-frame construction is quicker than any other method, the capital invested becomes remunerative in a shorter time, or a business is not interrupted for so long a period. It is also cheaper than any other form, and that also encourages rebuilding and expansion. The rigid framework permits of lighter walls, less weight, a taller building with a greater capacity on a given area. A steel-frame building has a greater range of upward extension than one of stone or brick. The spaces between the framework may be of very light material—hollow porous blocks—especially in the upper stories. The steel framework permits a much larger area of window space and therefore larger rooms. This window space means better day lighting, especially in the murky atmosphere of northern manufacturing towns. The side and back elevation of the newer warehouses in Manchester, for example, appears to be "all window."

Many steel-frame buildings have masonry fronts; but the masonry is only a veneer. The "bricks" or "blocks" used to fill the spaces between the steelwork have often no structural qualities—they are merely "fillers."

For dwellings man still builds with little bricks, like the men of old. It seems difficult to replace the small rectangular "block" by the "slab" which is suggested by the vertical walls. But "wooden" bungalows are frequently covered wholly or partially and lined and ceiled with asbestos cement sheets, or covered with roughcast sheets which consist of a thin cement sheet mounted on expanded metal, like a coarse wire net. For interiors three-ply board is being used, and cheap panelling employing this material is now available. Slates are rapidly disappearing as roofing material, and the slate quarries languish. But tiles are more varied in pattern and colour, and may do much to produce beauty even in a small dwelling.

When there are museums to do justice to the march of structural knowledge, the ordinary man will realize what a large amount of vigorous experiment and innovation is in progress. I spoke the other day to an architect of the problem of noise in flats, and he rattled off a list of devices and compositions to meet that one trouble; Cabot's quilt, acousticon plaster and a score of others. But so far, where there is glass, it is difficult to bar out noise from the exterior.

It is small wonder that not only young men and women with an artistic and constructive drive in them, but also business men, financiers and publicists concerned with the problems of human employment, turn their minds more and more definitely to the immense possibilities in comfort, creative work and beauty and happiness of this ever renascent art. Before them a by no means insurmountable barrier of social and business usage and political stupidity stands in the way of a complete reconstruction of human habitations, in which only a few lovely, memorable or typical buildings now in existence will be spared. At this stage in our work this may seem a very bold prophecy, but when the reader has got through our twelfth chapter he will probably be quite ready to accept our very confident prophecy that, *if our present civilization does not crash,* it can hardly avoid this stupendous rebuilding. It is not only that man *can* do it. It is not only that it stirs the imagination as if with trumpets to think of its being done, but, as we shall show, it will *have* to be done to sustain the economic working of our world. We shall have to rebuild to keep the economic machine running.

As it is, England is being rebuilt at the rate of a complete new world in a hundred years, and the economic life of a New York skyscraper is estimated at thirty years. A friend reading this passage foretells a licensing of buildings which will require the clearing of the site when the license expires.

The layout of that rebuilt world is also amenable to imaginative reconstruction. In the first place considerations of economy point to a continuation of the present processes of agglomeration. Plumbing, sanitary convenience, power distribution, and so on, all necessitate close grouping. Transport facilities release even the horticulturist, the flower and vegetable grower from the necessity of sleeping and living in his spare time close to his work. To resort in fine weather to the sea, the forest and wild, the open country, is a very powerful desire in most human beings, but that can be gratified by the use of tents and light pavilions and need not prevent the concentration of permanent habitations in handsome soundproof, sweet and clean compound buildings. A village, a town, a great city need no longer be an accumulation of huts, hovels and discordant, inconvenient old houses. Now it can be planned and made as one complete architectural undertaking.

This is not any sort of Utopian dreaming. It is going on now. Everywhere in the world building schemes are becoming bolder and more comprehensive. The ever more deliberate organization of industry, the scientific reconstruction of factories, with which we shall deal in Chapter VII, advance step by step with the progress of habitation. We can foretell with as much assurance—subject to the one proviso we have already made—that the twentieth century will be the Era of Rebuilding as we can call the nineteenth century the Era of Railways and Steamships. Let the thoughtful reader of English to whom a great public library is accessible compare the article upon Architecture in the Eighth Edition of the Encyclopædia Britannica with the current edition. It is a different subject; it is an account of a different world.*

---

*The reader who finds this section attractive will probably like to read Le Corbusier's *Urbanism* (translated into English by F. Etchell as *The City of Tomorrow*).

§ 6. *The Lighting of Town and Countryside*

One of the least obtrusive and yet one of the greatest, biologically speaking, of all the great changes in human life that have occurred since 1800 A. D., has been the immense development of artificial lighting. Quietly, steadily, a little more every year, the evening lights have been turned up. To anyone from Stuart or Georgian times who might return to contemporary life, nothing would seem more remarkable than the night-time brightness not only of interiors but of streets and roads. And it is a change still in progress. What we have is only an earnest of the lighting still to come.

Man is a daylight animal. So were his ancestors, and so are all the primates. We are creatures that see with an unparalleled and exquisite precision in a good light. But we are in darkness and groping at a stage of illumination when most other mammals can still see effectively. So while the carnivores prowl and the herbivores creep to their drinking places, the gorilla squats with his back to the tree in which his family nests, and man goes into his cave or camp or clearing with a fire to keep off inimical beasts. From twilight to dawn, except when the full moon comes with its magic and excitement, or when he talks and wrangles or indulges in some mystical singsong or dance, savage man is out of action. Dawn rouses him, and sunset dismisses him.

This daylight phase of human life lasted almost to our own times. Man was busy from dawn to sunset—"for the night cometh when no man can work." The torch, the fire, and the dim oil lamp remained the chief illuminants until the coming of the candle. When one thinks of the crabbed, uncertain lettering of the manuscripts, and the chill small flame of the lamp, one begins to realize the heroism of the student burning "the midnight oil." (How many men like Pepys laid down their pens and put their books aside in early middle age because of blindness?) "Wax candles," says the Encyclopædia Britannica, "are probably of Phœnician origin," and candles massed on a candelabrum were the typical illuminant of temples and palaces (the golden candlesticks of Solomon's Temple, e. g.). The eighteenth century saw the candle at the zenith of its career. Massed candles could give churches, palaces, and public gatherings a soft brilliance that seemed at times dazzling against the background of the circumambient night. But even the roads and lanes about the palace itself were black or had their blackness made visible by swinging oil lamps or transitory linkmen.

A new phase arrived at the very beginning of the nineteenth century with the use of coal gas. The lighting of streets and houses became brighter. There was a simultaneous advance in gas and lamp lighting. Lamp wicks were improved, and better burners devised. At first the gaslight was a naked flame owing all its illuminating power to the incandescence of its own constituents, but later the burning of the gas was used to heat lime to incandescence. The "limelight" has survived as a proverb for the conspicuous, long after its theatrical use has disappeared. Presently petroleum, paraffin, and the mineral oils and fats came to the help of the lamp and candle in their struggle against gas. The gas was enriched by various admixtures. All through the nineteenth century the standard of nocturnal brightness was rising. Lighthouses also were spreading and multiplying about the world and calling continually for brighter lamps. Nineteenth-century London and Paris had already developed a night glare beyond the utmost dreams of Babylon or Rome.

Then came the electric light. Its first form was the spitting arc light fluctuating with its violent flushings, and then the incandescent filament lamp. Jablokoff's arc light (1876) was the first practical arc light. Edison's inventiveness made incandescent lamps a business possibility four or five years later than this, and thirty thousand of them were alight in 1882. At first the filaments were of carbon, and then came the far more efficient tungsten filament. Steadily electric light rivalled and then surpassed all the combustion lights.

Gas made a gallant struggle as an illuminant against its newer rival. Auer von Welsbach, while trying to improve the electric lamp filament, hit upon the modern "gas mantle." This is a mantle of cotton or pumice dipped in nitrate of thorium and cerium and burnt. The thorium and cerium salts are reduced

EVE SPINS NO LONGER

The comber-lap machine in a cotton factory—one of the processes used in preparing cotton yarn for the comber.

THE CITY OF TO-MORROW

PROJECTED towers of Radio City, the great building development by the
Rockefellers between Forty-eighth and Fifty-first streets, and Fifth and
Sixth avenues, in New York.

THE CONTEMPORARY CITY

THE Chicago River, Chicago, showing the new Wabash Avenue draw-bridge in process of construction; the London Guarantee & Accident Co. Building at upper left; the clock tower of the Wrigley Building, right; Wacker Drive in the upper part of the picture, with the Michigan Avenue Link Bridge at left. A hundred years ago there was nothing but mud flats here.

EWING GALLOWAY.

FLOODLIGHTING THE MODERN CITY
The Wrigley Tower in Chicago at night.

to their oxides, thoria and ceria, which become brightly incandescent in the gas flame.

Man has now at his disposal a great and increasing variety of electric-light sources, which continually become cheaper, more powerful and more manageable. He has gaseous vapour lamps in which the current passes through a glass tube of attenuated gas; this tube can be bent to form designs and letterings, it can be as long as twenty feet; its decorative possibilities are immense; such are the Neon tubes whose ruddy orange brightness is a familiar note now at night in every city in the world. This Neon light has great penetrating power in a fog. And there are little incandescent lamps, scarcely larger than pin heads, with which man can explore a hollow tooth, and powerful ones for searchlights that sweep the sky. He can tint and temper these lights in the most various ways. He can make them stimulating, or he can make them restful and tranquillizing. And he has now the utmost freedom in grouping them. Before the electric light came, every light on earth was burning upward; it had to stand on a base; it had to be fed regularly and jealously guarded from other inflammable material. From all these limitations the designer is now released. Now man can put lights under the bedclothes or in his mouth, upside down and where he will.

At the present time, *white* light of the Neon type, extraordinarily cheap, since it consumes practically no current, is becoming available. Neither lamp manufacturers nor power companies hail its advent with delight, and its application therefore is being delayed, but sooner or later it must come into use.

Upon all this "conquest of darkness" there follows a vast revolution and extension of the possibilities of architecture, housing, and living generally. A room at night can be lit more delightfully than was possible even with sunshine in the days before electricity. Colour can be thrown upon walls and buildings and changed and varied. There need be no permanent patternings on walls or scenery; everything can become a screen for projected lights, form, and colour. Great advances have been made in the science and use of reflectors, and light can be concentrated upon this or that special point or poured out (in flood

lighting) over wide surfaces. Already a number of fine buildings have come into existence, built as much for flood lighting
from beneath at night as for the slow creeping of the downward daylight across their façades. The time is upon us when city
life at least will have all the assured freedom of vision and movement that daylight alone permitted in the past.

And nocturnal light spreads out upon the highroads—and
upon the air routes—from the city to the once black and silent
countryside. We have now upon the highroad a sort of symboli-
zation of the conflict between individualism and collectivism.
When the automobile first came, it was rare, it had to travel at
night upon roads whereon it never encountered another light
except a distant house window, the lantern of a carter, or the
glare from the eyes of a startled sheep or cat. All the driver
wanted to do was to see ahead of him. There was a steady
competition to produce continually more brilliant and far-
reaching lamps, until head lamps became veritable searchlights.
That was all very well until the automobiles multiplied. Then
headlight dazzled headlight, and automobiles had to feel their
way past each other, dipping their lights, turning them down,
going slow. The night highroads became confusing and distressing and dangerous to drivers. The local authorities and automobile associations accepted and still largely accept the powerful individual headlight to-day and put up reflector signals and
warnings on the country road. But in the towns the headlights
must be turned down, and now the disposition is to spread out
the lighting and light the highroad. Great lamps can be hung
high above it, but the more convenient form of road illumination
now (involving a more exact levelling of the roads) is cheap
white flood lighting at a level below the car body. It seems
highly probable that the time is near when the automobilist will
save his headlights for the lane and by-way, and that the great
roads of the future will run lit and silent, luminous white bands
across the night landscape. Instead of the continual conflict of
individual glares there will be a steadfast light along the track.
There will be collective lighting instead of personal lighting.
Amidst the dark landscape flood-lit houses will shine like glow-

worms, and indolently wandering searchlights pick out trees and shining waters. One will have to go far from the artificial brightness of the roadways to recall the clear softness of moonlight or the bright stir and glitter of the stars.

Among other consequences of the present revolution in lighting will be the probable disappearance of those lonely workers, the lightship men and the lighthouse keepers. For now anything that can be moored or fixed off a coast can have its lighting controlled from the shore; there is no need for the imprisonment of men to tend those lights.

§7. Protective and Regulative Services of the Modern Town and Countryside

A survey of the layout of population in town and country would be incomplete unless something was said of the marshalling and protective services of the modern community. The older civilizations fought fire, imposed sanitary controls over epidemic disease and filthiness generally, and kept order in the streets only in the most rudimentary fashion.

One might write a history of civilization in terms of police and public order, in which attention would be concentrated throughout upon the growth of organized controls and protections in the developing body politic. I cannot decide in my own mind which is most symbolical of social organization, a lighthouse, a cadastral map, a ship's wireless apparatus or a traffic policeman. But I incline to think it is the traffic policeman. The stage is not so very remote—indeed, it is still theoretically in existence in most countries—in which every man was expected to do his share in keeping order, suppressing fires and performing similar public duties whenever he was called upon. Sheriffs, constables and so forth, came into existence primarily as directors and marshals of the common effort and became the nuclei of special forces only by degrees. In the small, highly localized, toilsome but uneventful countryside community of the past, there were few real strangers, crimes were almost family events, and the necessity for an organized control of such things as traffic, public cleanliness, and personal safety did not appear. The great towns of mediævalism in Europe, India and China were dark, insanitary, dangerous tangles, and it did not seem they could ever be anything else. But the change in human methods of communication which has made all the world neighbours has conversely made the man in the street a stranger, and the organization of his protection and direction struggles to overtake the sweeping reconstruction of our homes and ways and roads that is now in progress.

The city, to begin with, we may note, was a planned and unified affair. It centred on the *arx,* it was walled and well organized, the brain and heart of a small countryside. The typical Greek city was this; even Rome was this in its beginnings. The sanitary planning of kingly Rome or Cnossos was sound and adequate. But so soon as political organizations enlarged to the scale of kingdoms and empires, cities began to lose their figures and spread. It is only now that the modern architect and the modern policeman are setting out to get these vast, loose, flabby monsters into shape again.

The story of the modern police, after the historical retrospects usual in such studies, would begin in good earnest in the seventeenth and eighteenth centuries. Crime and the mob were getting out of hand during that period with the growth of a larger economic framework that admitted of quicker escapes, ampler hiding places and less controllable gatherings. A large part of police duty was, to begin with, repressive. Mobs out of hand, rioting, was a marked and distinctive feature of eighteenth- and early nineteenth-century history. The first French Revolution became a riot on a large scale until a whiff of grapeshot cleared the streets. The nineteenth century saw the steady development of a police not simply of repression but of order. Any history of police would have to note continually the steady increase of directive duties and the relative diminution of the more primitive repressive functions. Less and less does a modern police constrain us to do this or that, and more and more does it become a service of specialists associated with the layout of roads and habitations, dissolving congestions, arresting annoy-

ances, averting dangers, assisting people to do what their education has presumably disposed them to do.

I think in an encyclopædic expansion of this present survey
there might be a long and interesting chapter on fire-fighting,
tracing its organization from primitive neighbourly helpfulness
to the splendid disciplines and equipments of to-day. In the uneventful life of the newspaper-less past a fire was not without
its consolation of excitement. It must have stirred up everybody
and been a nine-days' wonder. People must have talked of all
they did and thought and felt. And who set the place alight?
The cloth hall of the town of Thaxted in Essex still preserves
the iron hooks on long poles that were once used to drag the
thatch from burning houses, and some of the water buckets that
were passed from hand to hand along the street. From that sort
of thing we have ascended stage by stage to the watchtowers
and ever-ready engines and fire escapes of a modern great city.
And the ordinary man in the street is no longer a helper but
a nuisance at a fire. Precautions against fire were admitted very
reluctantly to the list of public functions. The earlier fire
brigades were paid or kept up to the mark by insurance companies. Great fires sweeping away whole quarters of the con-
gested cities of the time, are normal incidents in the history of
the Middle Ages. They are much less important relatively under
contemporary conditions. It is lamentable to note how much of
the records of the art, literature and science of the past has been
destroyed by fire. The Great Fire of London swept out of existence all the apparatus of Gilbert, that most interesting of all
our scientific pioneers. Fires at Dantzig, Copenhagen and Peters-
burg did much to diminish the tale of early telescopes, and all
Volta's original apparatus was destroyed by a fire at Como.
Priestley's library and apparatus were destroyed by mobs in
1791, another aspect of inadequte protection.

The agglomeration of the modern community in cities, residential districts and organized areas of production, not only
created a new need for systematic regulation and protection but
raised also another set of problems through the wearing out of
its fabric and its accumulation of waste material. In addition

to the activities of constructors, engineers, builders, furnishers, and the like, in addition to the activities of police and firemen, there are the perpetual repairing and replacement of material that go on, the wrecking and removal of outworn buildings and other structures, the removal of débris, the dustbin and the dust destructor. There is a vast industry of salvage in the modern social organism. I am told by a competent adviser that the Waste Trade, considered altogether, is the fifth greatest industry in England. It salvages everything from old iron, rusted girders, scrapped machinery and brick rubble, to bottles, bones, rags, worn-out tyres. It is a filthy and at present ill-organized service in which much sweating, insanitariness and dishonesty prevail.

The defilement of scenery is one of the minor evils that arise from the ill regulated extrusion of waste materials. I would like to give a picture of that once beautiful corner, the Pont de Nice at Grasse, to illustrate that point. The picture would not reek and smell, however, and so it would give only a very imperfect idea of how a backward municipality may still defile the world. This dump engenders a plague of flies and forms a sort of club and prowling place for a miscellany of mongrel dogs. In the Middle Ages excrement, waste and débris lay where they fell; filth and rubbish were everywhere, but they were diffused. The effort to banish these offenses precedes the effort to destroy them and leads to hideous concentrations. While I cry aloud at the Pont de Nice, my friend Bernard Shaw bewails with equal bitterness the dumping of London rubbish at Welwyn. But in this field too the type that prefers service to profit is at work, the community is not content, and steadily things improve. An encyclopædic *Science of Work and Wealth* would have a huge illustrated section on scrapping, housebreaking, salvage and the manner in which the struggle against foul offensive accumulations is being waged to-day.

So we add to our growing catalogue of human activities the increased multitude of people engaged in building and building regulation, in planning layout and in rebuilding and rearranging habitations, in keeping roads and drains open and working, in maintaining every sort of security and order, in preventive hygiene and in the suppression of fire. Here too we must glance at the hospitals, with the ambulance organization and at the medical profession. These are the scavengers of damaged and scrapped humanity.

We have surveyed now—superficially enough but sufficiently for our present ends—all production, all transport and all the services of order; we must next note, as compactly as possible, a third main mass of occupations, *distribution*.

CHAPTER THE SIXTH

How Goods Are Bought and Sold

CHAPTER THE SIXTH

How Goods Are Bought and Sold

§ 1. *Old and New Shopping*

HERE we make our first step from the appraisal of the mechanism and material of civilization towards social psychology. Hitherto we have studied the forces and materials of production and considered how things are got and made and consumed. We have come now to a point where the question of their distribution has to be considered. We have to take up the relations of the consumer to the producing organization.

Had we the limitless pages of an encyclopædia to fill we would give here a picture of an Egyptian market, tell something of the desert trade in the early empires, and glance at the export industry of Cnossos in jars, beads and so on, making such guesses as are customary of the spirit and motives of the buyers and sellers. Trade in luxury articles went to the very boundaries, went beyond the boundaries of the known world. Imperial Rome had trading stations in India, and thence probably commodities drifted off into the unknown. With a brace or so of historical students to help us we might go on to an account of the Venetian and Levantine trade of the Middle Ages and the commerce that kept the mule passes over the Alps open and in repair. How much of that remains to be deduced and inferred? What sort of caravans and companionships followed the ancient "green roads" of England that are still traceable over her hills? What occasions brought them? The refrain of the slow breaking-down of barriers, the slow transition of economics from local to cosmopolitan would run through all that history.

The markets of 1750 were emerging gradually from a still

very local and limited condition of things. Trade beyond the local bounds remained very largely an affair of luxuries, delicacies, accessories, and smallish manufactured articles. Spices for pickling winter provisions were important. But cotton, tobacco and sugar were beginning to travel in considerable bulk across the ocean. Guns and pistols, cutlery and fine textiles, went back in exchange. Wine and oranges moved north from France and Spain. Voltaire distributed the watches he was teaching the Swiss to make, by letters of recommendation throughout the courts of Europe. Enough business existed to sustain a system of wholesale markets and exchanges.

It was by insensible degrees that this system accommodated itself to the ever increasing bulk of material handled and to the increasing importance of the masses, the peasant, and the labouring "proletariat" as purchasers. It is quite recently that the masses have been thought worth while catering for. Before the middle nineteenth century, shops hardly existed for anyone below the prosperous middle class. For instance, there was no such thing as a furniture shop to cater for poorish people. Such poorish people went to sales and got second-hand stuff. The home in which I was born was furnished about 1855. I do not believe there was ever a new thing in it. It was a second-hand outfit, half-worn carpets, slightly damaged chairs; even our library was replenished at auction sales. Everything was "good" but in decay. And all the food and domestic material came from little individual shops, each with methods and characteristics of its own. Mrs. Bean's butter we thought better than Mr. Martin's, and there was nothing to touch Mrs. Bean's tea. She got it out of a great canister and weighed it and packed it up in a paper parcel. Soap was weighed and cut off; mustard one got from the chemist, also weighed for every purchaser. It would be very interesting—and in places rather pathetic—to trace the appearance and development of the great "popular" department store and the ousting of the small, independent shopkeeper.

Three main types of modern distributive organization exist. First of all comes *the department store,* the concentrated giant store with an immense radius of delivery, to which people go for clothing, furnishing, provisions, *et cetera*. Then the *chain stores,* the syndicated shops for more immediate necessities, the multiple shops everywhere at hand, that now supply tobacco, everyday groceries, milk, meat and so forth. And, as a special and important type of department store, in Europe, and particularly in Great Britain, we have the machinery of *coöperative buying,* by coöperative societies, the surviving tangible fruits of Robert Owen's socialist beginnings. In management and organization, this third class tends to resemble the department stores, the difference being that the object of the coöperative administration is ostensibly for service and not for profit. Gains in the coöperative shop are understood to reduce prices or they are returned to the members of the society as a "dividend."

An interesting type of store is the Woolworth type, in which a miscellany of articles is offered at a uniform price. These stores cut prices by eliminating travellers and advertisement and buying lines of goods by the million direct from the manufacturer.

The activities of the man behind the counter do not end with his handing out the goods demanded by the consumer. If he does less weighing and packing and measuring nowadays, he does more selling. Every capable shop assistant is alert, not only to remind you of any need you may have forgotten or suppressed, but also to "introduce" new goods to you that you have never thought of getting before. He is a propagandist of consumption. Through all distributing organizations—least so, perhaps, in coöperative stores—runs this idea of salesmanship. Salesmanship tries not only to make things attractive to you, but also it seeks to make buying easy for you. And in the last few years, in pursuit of the latter end, it has evolved the Instalment System. This marks a new phase in distribution. Great multitudes of people are now in possession of goods that they partially own. They have paid an "advance"; they pay for two or three years to complete their purchase, and meanwhile, in case of default, the seller has the power of recovering the goods.

There was considerable criticism of instalment selling in its early stages. Young people, it was thought, might sink into debt at the outset of life, sacrifice economic freedom for immediate advantages of comfort and equipment. They would lose the power of discontinuing or changing their employment, lose, in fact, the right to strike. But this line of thought disregarded the fact that at the worst they would have to surrender a partially used and paid-for commodity that otherwise they might never have possessed. It was also held that in a time of depression the supplying companies would cease to receive the bulk of their instalments, and that they in their turn would be unable to observe their obligations to the banks that had financed their enterprise.

Tested in America by the very grave slump of 1930, these fears seem to have been exaggerated. Buyers have kept on paying; resumption of the goods involved has not increased. In the United States three quarters of the automobiles sold are sold now on the instalment system, and furniture, refrigerators, radio apparatus, pianos, washing machines, important books at a high price, jewelry and suchlike goods, are largely marketed upon the new lines. When it comes to perishable articles such as boots and fashionable clothing the security is manifestly not so good; the instalments must be spread over a shorter period, and, by taking up references and exacting collateral guarantees, the methods of the seller approximate to those of the ordinary private loan monger. About 13 per cent of the retail trade in the United States is instalment selling, and its annual total is estimated at £1,200,000,000.

The social consequences of this new method of distribution are still a matter for speculation. Instalment buying seems likely to diminish savings, hoarding and popular investment. Instead of putting money by to get something, people will get something and then pay for it with the money they would otherwise have put by. They buy first instead of buying last or not at all. There is a quickening of the production, distribution and consumption of goods.

§ 2. *Teaching People to Want Things*

And now we have to bring into our picture one of the most highly illuminated aspects of modern economic life, advertisement. There is great need of a history of its wide extension, new methods of appeal and increased penetration during the past half century. That history would deal with media, the newspaper, the circular, the shop window and the bookstall, the wayside house and the railway carriage, the roadside board and the hoarding. It would glance up at the aëroplane writing advertisements in smoke across the sky with letters one mile or so long. It would consider the advertisement side of the cinema and radio. There is deliberate and open and there is also masked and incidental advertisement. There is a point when advertisement ceases to attract and begins to irritate or bore. People can be habituated to disregard an advertisement. I have already written a rather amateurish essay on the psychology of advertisement in *The World of William Clissold.* But there are serious books on the subject: Professor Dell Scott's *Psychology of Advertising;* T. Russell's *Commercial Advertising;* H. L. Hollingsworth's *Advertising and Selling;* Sir C. F. Higham's *Advertising, Its Use and Abuse,* and works by H. Gale, S. R. Hall, A. T. Poffenberger, E. K. Strong, and others.

Turning now from the methods to the social function of advertisement, we may point out how necessarily advertisement is a part of the replacement of individual by widely organized marketing. The old trader and his shop were known in the neighbourhood. The talk of the countryside was their sufficient publicity. But the new trader may be at the other side of the mountains or the other side of the world. As he cannot show his face, he must show a placard. He has to create a giant, a nation-size or world-size personality, for himself and his commodity. The common man to-day buys his screw of tobacco or his packet of cigarettes from a Briareus as big as a continent. Picturesque and amusing as the methods of advertisement often are, this side of the question is far less important and interesting than its aspect as a new system of intercommunication and its bearing upon social psychology. The advertisement organization of to-day can spread the knowledge and use of a new commodity and all the changes in habit and custom a new commodity may bring with it, with the utmost rapidity throughout the world. It can break down social habits and usages in the most extraordinary way. It can suggest new conveniences and economies of time and labour, indulgences such as cigarette smoking and gum chewing, taking a daily bath or resorting to winter sports. It can make us feel uncomfortable after our coffee or doubtful whether our throats are not suffering from a previously unsuspected irritation.

The story of cigarette advertisement should be amusing and edifying. Half a century ago Europe knew nothing of the machine-made packet cigarette. Then it spread with incredible rapidity about the world. It was found that there could be such a thing as de-advertising a commodity. One day a certain firm was so ill-advised as to proclaim that its particular brand did not "irritate the throat." Hundreds of thousands of people thought that over, coughed in an investigatory and suspicious manner, and gave up smoking cigarettes.

At present it seems arguable that there is great waste and overlapping in this field of activity. And it is only slowly and recently that a genuine system of ethics for marketing generally and salesmanship in particular has developed. Is it necessary to protect the public more strongly than it is protected at present against misstatement and furtive falsehood in advertisement? In Great Britain there is a considerable general legal control and much effective local legislation against sky signs, tiresome processions, flashing lights and other irritating media. In the United States much has been done through the federal government's control of interstate trade to check lying and unwholesome suggestion in advertisements, more particularly in the advertisements of medicines and drugs. America moreover is the centre of the Associated Advertising Clubs of the World, whose motto is "truth in advertisement," and furthermore, this association has established a National Vigilance Committee to keep the profession above reproach. In the future it is quite possible that the check upon the statements of Briareus, as he hands out our goods, will be much more stringent. The main body of the advertising profession will certainly be on the side of such a censorship. Competition in falsehood ultimately discredits all advertisement. It may be possible to bring side by side sample advertisements for the last century and the present time, to show the advance in dignity and integrity that has already occurred.

The extension of professional advertising from marketing to politics and the public service will open up another issue of very great interest. For the modern man the daily newspaper already fills to a certain extent the place of a daily religious service. It takes him out of himself and reminds him of all the world. It makes a miscellaneous appeal. Formerly, in the days of fixed traditional attitudes the newspaper took the side of some definite party in politics; it discussed morals and public affairs in its "contents," and its advertisements were mainly marketing—and invitations to entertainment. But now it is much more "newsy" and much less educational in its contents, and on the other hand the advertisement columns become a forum for appeals and proclamations of collective importance.

But here we are passing away from marketing and looking again towards the question of public education. We will go no further in that direction now. All our later chapters will point towards education, and finally the chapter on Education will crown and complete our work. But to our growing enumeration of human activities we now add the placard and the handbill, the aëroplane writing across the heavens, the sky sign flaring and blotting out the stars, the displayed advertisements of the newspapers, the monstrous letters on the cliff face, the hoarding making its discordant proclamation athwart the rural scene, the rain of samples, the pestering cigarette tray, the perpetual nagging of our wearied attention in railway carriage and street car and restaurant and hotel room, the bawling loudspeaker, the interlude advertisements on the cinema screen (in France more particularly) and the association of the radio (in America) with advertisement. And every one of these things means a swarm of people busy in making and diffusing the glad tidings of goods to be bought; a whole world of clamant activities.

§ 3. *Fluctuations and Vagueness in Distribution*

The present distributing methods of mankind are in a state of violent fluctuation. Fifty years ago most commodities reached the consumer through three well defined stages. First the producer, whether manufacturer or grower, sold his produce to the wholesaler. Then the wholesaler sold to a retailer, who either sold in a shop or hawked the goods about the country. The retailer unpacked and repacked the goods; he cut up the cloth and calico, he chipped up the sugar loaf, weighed out the tea and butter. This seems, under modern conditions, of which increased efficiency in advertisement, packing and postal enterprise are the chief, to be at least one stage too many for stability, and the history of distribution for the past half century is largely the history of a struggle to squeeze out some one of the three stages. The manufacturer brands his goods and advertises them to the consumer; he may even, in the British boot trade, e. g., distribute through his own shops; retail shops unite to buy directly from the manufacturer; or as a third way to the desired end, the wholesaler cuts out the retailer and breaks out as a system of chain stores. Chain stores may thus arise either as wholesalers' shops, manufacturers' shops, or by an enterprising retailer adding shop to shop and cutting out his wholesaler.

In America there has been a great development of mail-order houses selling their goods, not by displaying them in shops, but by describing them in catalogues and circulars which are distributed by the million. Mail-order houses appeal to a scattered population; they do for the country people what the great department store does for the concentrated urban population. The illustrated and explicit price list takes the place of the department displays.

Every modification in methods of communication and carriage is felt at once in the distributing world. Each involves changes, novelties and abandonments, in warehousing and storage. The architecture of warehouses varies with improvements in handling. The old-fashioned retailer kept his goods on his premises and showed samples in his shop window. Now a dealer will keep a brightly lit showcase in a railway station, a hotel, an arcade or an exhibition of goods; he will receive your order by post in an office miles away, and pack and deliver your goods from some quite remote centre.

The breaking-up of the old retail-shop tradition has also broken up the ancient traditions of the shopman. Formerly, in England and America, he was indentured as an apprentice, for four or five years learnt the "art and mystery" of selling, lived on the premises and worked upon time-honoured precedents. As businesses grew in size and the personal contact between the employer and the apprentice diminished, the instruction of the latter in merchandising became more and more a pretense, and as the standard of living in the community rose, the long hours, the bad food and crowded housing of the living-in system became less and less tolerable. Now apprenticeship and living-in die out, and a vast variety of salesmen (often specially trained by their employing firm) take the place of the old "shop assistant."

The present existence side by side of old types of shop and new marketing experiments leads to a vast amount of overlapping in the distributing trades. In England there is a shop of some sort for every forty-five inhabitants, and one person in every twenty-five is a nonproductive distributor. This seems a very heavy burthen of not very skilled activities upon the general population. Our world is in fact full of goods (with sellers behind them) looking or wandering about rather vaguely in pursuit of the consumer. A typical instance of the planlessness of our distributing machinery is the wild multiplication of petrol pumps along the roads, twice as many as are needed, since the coming of the automobile. For half these adventurers struggle, failure and frustration lie in wait.

No figures are available of waste through the deterioration of unsold goods, especially in the provision trade. Indeed, the science of distribution is still in a very backward, merely descriptive state. The general impression among financiers and business men, is that distribution in the modern community is loose, unstable, adventurous and very wasteful. But that is not the fault of the distributor. It is not only that shopping and selling change with the progress of transport and mechanism generally and with facilities for advertisement, but, as we shall see later, that customers are also in a state of flux. Purchasing power drifts from class to class. The rich and the middle class change not only in taste and in intelligence but in character. The process of monetary deflation (which we shall explain later) shifts purchasing power from the customers of one type of shop to those of quite another sort. Inflation will provoke a feverish buying of "valuables" to hold against a rise. Deflation tempts the possible customer to restraint, to save his or her money.

E. A. Filene tells us that "the average article sold by department or other retail stores to-day costs the consumer two, three, four, often six or eight times its production cost." This does not seem to be a very exact average, but the statement is very illustrative of the huge unprecise interception of money due to the uncertainty and experimental disorganization of the distributing machinery of the modern state. This high cost to the consumer is not, Mr. Filene says, due to profiteering, it is due to waste. He quotes research work by C. N. Schmalz (Harvard Bureau of Business Research) to show that the net earnings of a series of department stores studied, varied between 1.1 per cent loss and 1.6 per cent gain. His own ideal seems to be a combination of department stores with chain stores. He would have great department stores at all the centres of distribution, and each department, for boots and shoes, automobiles, watches or what not, would be in a chain with the same departments in the other great store buildings throughout the country. This vast organization would deal directly with the producers; the middleman would be cut out entirely. This is "mass distribution" to balance mass production. As a third factor in the modern distribution of goods Mr. Filene advocates the credit union system, by which groups of employees and neighbours guarantee one another for the repayment of emergency loans. All these are expedients for bringing the individual buyer into a less wasteful relation to Briareus and eliminating secondary middlemen, credit retailers, loan-mongers and the like parasites upon popular distribution. At a later stage (Chapter X, §7) we shall have something to say about collective buying.

§ 4. Coöperative Retailing

A note is necessary here on that very distinctively British method of distribution, the coöperative store. This is an attempt to replace the retailer by a combination of consumers, and it is practicable and efficient just as far as its members represent a stable and homogeneous community, with similar needs and similar habits and ideas. Then in the case of such commodities as coals, boots, groceries, ironmongery, it can effect great economies. The members are the owners of the organization, and the profits made on the trading—or as coöperators prefer to say, their surplus payments—are returned to them as a "dividend" in the proportion of their purchases.

In Britain there are 1,364 of these societies, varying in the number of their members from a score or so (in a small village society) to a quarter of a million. They vary as greatly in their range and enterprise. Many are little more than profit-sharing grocery stores; others are complete profit-sharing department stores and carry on bakeries, laundries, dairy farming, and a multitude of services and productive activities. They run libraries, travel guilds, schools, dance halls, entertainments, periodicals and building societies. About £3,000,000 of house property is owned by coöperative societies in Britain and they carry £7,000,000 of advances made to members for the purchase of their own houses. This various multitude of voluntary associations is federated to the Coöperative Wholesale Society (there is a separate C. W. S. for Scotland), and there is a Coöperative Union of Great Britain and Ireland for legal, educational and propagandist purposes. The retail coöperative societies of Britain employ upward of 170,000 workers, and their gross sales in 1929 were £217,000,000 of which nearly one-tenth was returned to the purchasing members as "dividend." About one in eight of the British population is a member of a coöperative society, which means that over one third of the family households of Britain buy more or less of the goods they consume through coöperative retail stores.

In Finland, Denmark, Belgium and Switzerland coöperative retailing is equally well developed, and the rest of Europe north and west of the Danube is not far behind. The coöperative movement in France was originally and is still mainly a coöperation of producers with which we are not at present concerned. Consumers' coöperative societies in France number over two million members which works out at below one family out of five or six in comparison with the British one in three.

Nothing to compare with this great network of distributive machinery is to be found in the United States. The life of the common man there is far more individualistic and adventurous and less stable, defensive and protected than in Europe. He buys on his own. For the year 1928 the retail buying in the United States has been estimated at forty-one thousand million dollars. Of this only one hundred million is ascribed to coöperative retailing. More than half of the grand total was affected through small private adventure shops which are perpetually opening, going bankrupt or closing down. Not one in ten of such small businesses struggles through to a success in America. The rest was done by great profit-seeking systems, department stores, chain stores and mail-order organizations.

So much for coöperative retailing. But it is only one aspect of the coöperative movement. The broader implications of that movement will be dealt with more conveniently after we have considered the general conditions of productive employment in the next chapter.

CHAPTER THE SEVENTH

How Work Is Organized

R. H. MACY

MODERN RETAILING

A GREAT department store during the height of the holiday rush. (New York.)

MODERN INDUSTRIALISM AND THE TROPICS

A WOMAN worker on a rubber plantation in Ceylon engaged in tapping
rubber. The collecting cup is at the base of the tree. Thence the latex
starts on its journey to the highroad, the electrical distributing system and
a multitude of vitally important uses in the modern world. She is as
integral to the new system as a banker or an engineer.

CHAPTER THE SEVENTH

How Work Is Organized

§ 1. *Putting the Personnel into the Picture*

ONLY in the preceding chapter have we begun to take what is called the "human element" into our account of the world processes of production, distribution and ordered life. We have been looking hitherto not so much at peasants and farmers as at fields and estates; we have reviewed factories and warehouses rather than workers and traders. Even in the agricultural sections where we have displayed the strips, the peasant type of cultivation passing away and giving place to estates and large farming, we have said hardly anything of the peasant giving way to the agricultural labourer. We shall have quite a lot to say about that before we have done. And were all the science of work and wealth that we have summarized thus far, actually assembled and written and illustrated in all its confirmatory but oppressive vastness, we should still have no more than a display of factories running like automatic toys rather than as complexes of human coöperation; we should see the automobile in mass production being built up bit by bit upon its endless band, the biscuit passing magically from dough to box, and so on through a thousand industrial process series' without a hand to help it. Now we have to enter a fresh field of description. It is time we brought working human figures into this world spectacle of cultivation and production we have evoked.

What we have to consider now, the marshalling of workmen, foremen, managers, directors, experts and experimentalists in due order, might be treated in reference to any one of ten thousand different series of productive operations. Each would have its own characteristics, but each would exemplify the same broad facts of industrial organization. We might, for instance, survey the working of a modern engineering plant, a shipyard, a factory for making typewriters or cash registers or clocks and watches. Or we might give a distillery or cement works or a shredded wheat factory. Essentially we should deal with it now as a "manned" factory, a factory considered as a human going concern. For each or any of these concerns an account could be rendered of employees, their types, their numbers; how they are directed by foremen, how all the various groups are co-ordinated by the manager and his staff. An adequate survey of a modern factory would include a discussion of the housing, feeding and sanitation of the staff; its recreations and rest places, its welfare organization and casualty stations. We will not ask yet what inner forces hold the wills of all this personnel together; that is for a next stage in our surveying. *Why* they do it all, comes later. First we must ask *what* each one does.

In doing this we leave our museums behind us. They have been most useful so far as a system of reference, but now they fail us, and we push into a region where as yet no comprehensive museums exist. The Science Collections at South Kensington and the Deutsches Museum display the material organization of modern production with great completeness. You may, for example, see the layout of a whole machine shop in either, presented as a working model. You can make the wheels go round. Everywhere there are working models of machinery. Compressed air and electricity are used, and the visitor can put the wheels and so forth in motion either by pressing a button or in some cases by putting a penny in a slot. For certain types of boy, and even for some modern girls, such museums are a preferable substitute for Paradise.

But no figures of workers animate these factories and machines in motion. Imagine, however, that this idea of working models has been carried on to a further stage and extended to the provision of model plants, in which minute workers are seen carrying out their operations, and the business and labour handling of the raw material are traced to the finished product in terms of living individuals. In such a model we should see not only "the wheels going round," but also the little figures which pull over the levers to set them going. Little coloured threads could run from the captains to the noncommissioned officers and men of this personnel. At the side of each model plant would be diagrams of the numbers, pay and hierarchy of the workers. Such models may or may not be practicable. Imagine models of local industries conceived on this plan, animated "personnel models" to adorn the local schools of every industrial region. The intelligent youngster could say not merely as he does now, "This is what happens to the stuff and that is how the wheels go round," but "This is father," and "That is the person I intend to be," and later on such a youngster would go to work with a sense of participation in a complex team job that few of the myriads which industry annually swallows now possess.

Whether such industrial models can really be made or not, I do not know; but the idea of them is also the idea of our present approach to Organization. We begin to put in the human figures in our panorama of human work. We have to pass in imagination through the field or the machine or the selling service, note the gang leaders and foremen, and so come to the manager's office, the board of directors and the departments of research and suggestion.

Illustrated descriptions of typical industrial plants at work bulk large in that encyclopædic dream, *The Science of Work and Wealth*. But we need not wait for them now to discuss the broad questions these organizations raise and illuminate. The pictures, the descriptions, the models remain to be made, but for the present they can be taken as given. Even before this substantial preparation is realized, it is still possible to open up the main issues of staffing and management in general terms.

§ 2. *Guild and Trade Union*

Let us begin our survey of the personnel of production and distribution at the base, with the individual who actually ploughs, sows, reaps, tends beasts, hews coal, stokes furnaces, lays bricks, saws timber, spreads cement, weaves, hammers, casts, blows glass, tends machines, handles goods for sale, fetches and carries, packs parcels, enters items into books, typewrites, transmits telephonic or telegraphic messages, steers ships, guides vehicles: the fundamental *worker*. How is the worker put to his job, paid, ordered and kept going?

The modern world grows to-day, day by day, in unbroken succession out of the old world of toil, and the tradition of the worker is still one of subjugation and compulsion. He or she behaves and is treated as inferior. During the ages of toil the fundamental worker was either the cultivating peasant, a pressed man, a serf or a slave outright. We have considered already the new forces that tend to wrench the practical ownership and control in agricultural production from the peasant and to make him an agricultural labourer and so industrialize agriculture. We have stated the essential facts of this process as it is displayed by Great Britain and Soviet Russia. We have noted too—though as yet only in the most general terms—the liberating effect of money in the past, and how in our present organization the wages worker plays a rôle in mine and factory and plantation which replaces and renders unnecessary the individual and gang slavery of the past.

Yet to this day the crack of the whip and the rattle of the chain haunt the thoughts of many people when labour is discussed. To many it seems impossible that anyone would work unless want and hunger stalked the unemployed. The worker they think has to be kept down and compelled. They cannot imagine contented and participating labour. But there are others who can, and their faith and their efforts to realize their conviction play an important part in the making over of the world that is now in progress. The conditions of the modern worker are still undergoing rapid development as the scale and mechanism of production and exchange expand and evolve, and any account of the labour organization of mankind, however full and detailed, which fails to recognize that every method and institution of to-day is provisional and entirely transitory, will necessarily be losing value from the very moment it is made.

The full *Science of Work and Wealth* would have to include

some elaborate masses of fact about the mutations of the labour
institutions of the world as machinery and power have developed. There are three main strands of evolution interweaving
in this reorganization of work. First, there is that industrialization of the peasant with which we have already dealt. Next,
there is that numerical expansion of the craftsman class of
mediæval life, and that change in the scale and nature of its
activities which has given us the mass of skilled, and the greater
mass of semi-skilled, manufacturing workers of to-day. And
thirdly, there is the struggle of the unskilled worker, the economic successor of the gang worker, the mine slave, the galley
slave, the plantation worker, the excavator, the pyramid builder
of the old order, towards a tolerable life: a struggle in which
he is helped by the steady substitution of mechanical power for
the muscular ingredient of his task. The broad drift is towards
a fusion of all three types of worker into one huge body of semi-
skilled workers working at their various jobs under skilled direction, and having a common type of mentality and an unprecedented sense of solidarity. The incessant changes in the method
and apparatus of production are abolishing many types of the
highly skilled craftsman, and the universal spread of education
is bringing the black-coated, white-collared clerk down—or to
put it more truly, is bringing the semi-skilled worker up—to a
common level of respect.

Neither the peasant nor the gang worker of the past developed any autonomous organization worth consideration; the
one was ruled and directed, so far as he was ruled and directed,
by his owner, his lord, his creditor and the market demand, and
the other was herded to his task by his overseer. But the more
intelligent and more valuable craftsman has always organized
locally throughout the ages in the local interests of his craft.
The societies he formed in the days of the Roman Empire do
not seem to have survived the general débâcle of Western economic life in the Dark Ages, but with the gradual return of
social order and prosperity, associations of craftsmen appeared
side by side with merchant guilds. Manufacture was handwork;
the productive group was a small one, a master, a journeyman or

so, and a prentice or so, all hoping to become masters in their turn, and the craftsman guild concerned itself chiefly with the restraint of competition and the material and spiritual welfare of its members.

There was no essential and permanent antagonism then between employer and worker.

We know very little of the internal organization of such larger enterprises as cathedral building, the greatest collective effort of mediæval times, but there is little record of labour troubles in these undertakings. The lore of the masons was elaborately secret, and the literature of freemasonry throws little light on the actual working of the job. The cathedrals, however, grew very slowly by modern standards. Evidently they were not so much the work of crowds as of not very considerable bands of men levying their pay as the pious provided it, and doing their work year after year. The cathedrals were early instances of what we shall refer to at a later stage as "collective buying." The original "secrets of the Freemasons" were probably geometrical drawing, quarrying and chisel work combined with the political and religious activities necessary to keep that collective buying alive.

Many productive arts remained purely domestic throughout the Middle Ages. It was only in the fourteenth century, with the general broadening out of life and a steadily increasing volume of trade, that the increasing size of the unit of production released the possibility of antagonism between employer and worker. The number of journeymen relative to the number of masters was increasing to an extent that opened up the possibility of remaining journeymen for life to most of them, and with that they began to organize to maintain wages and keep down the tale of hours for the working day. The fifteenth century saw a considerable amount of trouble upon such issues.

The devastation of Germany by wars and the enlargement of trading and productive operations in less troubled regions of Europe ultimately submerged most of the industrial organizations of mediæval times. They were elaborate in their methods and inadaptable. Machinery crept into use, and already in the seventeenth century, before the advent of power, the process by which capital accumulated and some small producers prospered and grew while others declined and fell into employment by the former, was well under way. The gap between master and man widened: it became a class distinction. The industrial revolution —with its "division of labour"—preceded the mechanical revolution with its economy of force and attention, by some decades, and at first the mechanical revolution did no more than emphasize and exaggerate this process of class differentiation. In one branch of industry after another, work began to be done no longer by the hands of individuals but in squads, in companies, in battalions.

The first organization of the new scale industry was directive; it came from the entrepreneur. He planned his merciless factories and arranged the duties of overseer and time-keeper. The character of the new industrialism departed more and more widely from the traditions of mediæval craftsmanship in the direction of gang work. The first organization of industrial labour, suffering under these conditions of degeneration, sprang from no preceding organization. It was entirely defensive. It was the outcome of intolerable distresses. It was a fight against long hours and sweated work, a fight against the mutual competition of hungry workers and against the advantage this gave to the bargaining employer. At first such organization was illegal, and the long story by which the collective bargaining of the workers won its way to recognition is to be read in the Webbs' *Industrial Democracy* and the Hammonds' *Town Labourer, Skilled Labourer* and the *Rise of Modern Industry*. The trade union began its career, regardless of craftsmanship or the need and quality of the product. It was an urgently necessary protective fighting organization to protest against long hours, insufficient wages and the individual degradation of the industrial worker. It spread easily and naturally to many fields of unskilled labour, where the workers could be easily assembled, and less easily to such workers as the scattered seamen, and still less easily to the agricultural labourer.

By the nineteenth century there was already a wide gulf in

interest and feeling between the directive and exploiting elements in industrial production on the one hand and the worker on the other. The nature of that gulf is of vital importance in our present study. For many years it has been an antagonism—on both sides. A great majority of employers have been attempting more or less consciously to get the most out of their workers and to pay them as little as possible; the reciprocal effort has been to lighten toil, shorten working hours and raise pay. Throughout most of the nineteenth century this warfare has smouldered or raged over the whole field of employment. The employer has fought for the right to discharge at will, to lock out as he chose, to play off the urgencies of the unemployed at his gates against the resistances of the worker within. The chief weapon of the employed has been the strike. Here again an expanded treatment of the law and practise of industrial conflict, the organization of militant unions, the conflict around the open shop, the history of great strikes would make a vast, tragic section of our encyclopædia in which many acutely interesting passages would be embedded in a dry tangle of highly technical detail. To-day all the lower ranks of workers in our industrial plants are potential strikers; and the special organizers and officials of the trade union and of its more militant dissentient subsections must be shown in those working models of ours, flitting obscurely but effectively round and about the industrial plant. They maintain a certain standard of life against the exigencies of work. Our picture will not be complete without them.

At any time almost any of these concerns, these coöperations, these great services, of which we have imagined a series of working models under our eyes, may begin to run slowly or stiffly or stop, stop short for an hour or a day as a warning strike, or stop at the onset of some conflict that will be fought to a finish. The average annual loss in working time actually caused by strikes is often grossly exaggerated. Professor Carr-Saunders puts it—for the thirty-two years between 1893 and 1924—as about the equivalent of one day's holiday each year. Their more serious effect is the dislocation they may cause in completing or obtaining contracts.

This relationship of antagonism between employer and employed is the most important fact of our present phase of economic development. It has been manifest in the past, but never to the same extent. Is it an inevitable relationship in a modern economic system? In the middle nineteenth century there were many who thought it was. They believed that the economic process could not go on without a margin of want and the resentful resistance of the worker. They displayed a stern fatalism for others and were happy to feel themselves luckier and more deserving than the common run. But there are various schools of opinion which deny that necessity. The Communist would obliterate the employer and so solve the problem. He carries out the idealism of democracy to its economic conclusion. He believes that in some way the masses can exercise a directive will over economic life that eliminates all need for compulsion and changes the spirit of direction. Work, when the mystical dictatorship of the proletariat has given place to its still more mystical goal of the classless, the homogeneous, community, will be spontaneous and joyful. It is not a very explicit doctrine, and so far Communist rule in Russia has not so much as manifested a stormy disposition towards it.

But quite outside the adherents to the Communist creed there is a growing multitude which is convinced that this great antagonism in our economic life is not essential, that it marks a mere phase in evolution, that it can be reduced almost or altogether to a vanishing point, that without any violent revolution or breaking up of society, while carrying on with the world as a going concern, there may be a steady reconstruction of the economic life of our species that will produce a willing and effective coöperation of everyone engaged upon it. These more hopeful spirits can point now to a great number of instances where better pay has been proved to mean happier and better work, where shorter hours have been more productive than long hours, and where the spirit of coöperation has been evoked to mitigate or replace the crude compulsion and resistance of the first harsh phase of modern industrialism.

§ 3. *Industrial Democracy: Workers' Control*

In studying the progressive organization of the semi-skilled labour which is becoming the main labour mass in town and in the countryside alike, a very great number of more or less parallel efforts have to be considered, all aiming at the restoration of a sense of participation on the part of the worker.

The nineteenth century was the age of democratic ideas. It was pervaded by the assumption that the maximum of justice and directive wisdom was to be attained by a universal uniform distribution of votes, and so we find such a book as the Webbs' *Industrial Democracy* (1897) filled largely with an account of the quasi-parliamentary administration of labour organizations. The problem of the control of the secretary was a grave one from the beginning, and all sorts of constitutions have been devised to prevent executive councils and officials getting out of hand. The secretary can bully and dominate because of his close and continuous knowledge of the society and the difficulty of tracing his acts and assembling a meeting competent to judge them. He has also great opportunities of selling his society. But the secretaries of all societies are necessary evils, and a great book could be written upon their inconvenience and disloyalties.

Industrial Democracy, for all its thirty years and more of life, is still the best general introduction to the development of labour organizations and to their main type of defensive activity; the insurance of their members against discriminatory treatment, their collective bargaining, their experiments in regulating hours and processes, restraining the competition of boys and non-members, insisting upon sanitation, securing protective legislation, and so forth. In the past third of a century great advances have been made in the state enforcement of sound labour conditions, and much that was once a matter for trade-union regulation is now the subject of legal enactment. Here again the mass of fact is vast and tangled, and an encyclopædic *Science of Work and Wealth* would give an ordered array of statistics as useful for reference and confirmation as it would be unattractive to any but the highly specialized reader. Every great industrial country presents its own distinctive method of approach to these problems and has its own types of solution.

The industrial democracy of the nineteenth century was defensive and restrictive; it meddled little with business direction except to object when the interests of the worker seemed to be threatened, but since the beginning of the twentieth century there has been a strong disposition to incite the organized worker to usurp or assume (whichever word you prefer) some or all of the functions of the directorate. This re-unification of industry by the upward extension of the workers' will, was formulated in England in the opening decades of the twentieth century as Guild Socialism, but the idea, in many variations, of the autonomous organizations of masterless coöperating workers has spread all over the world. What is practically the same conception of workers' control has played a considerable and not very happy part in the industrial experiments of Soviet Russia, and there were various very substantial attempts to realize it in Italy after the war and before the onset of Fascism. We have no space to tell in detail of the formation, struggle and failure of the National Guilds in Great Britain after the war, nor of kindred experiments in other countries. The British National Building Guild of building-trade workers executed a number of contracts between 1920 and 1922 and did good work before it got into financial difficulties. For a time the "shop steward," a representative of the workers in the discussion of various details of method and discipline with the employer, assumed an importance he has not retained. He was a war-time product who acted for the workers during the emergency disablement of trade-union organization.

A sore point in the existing relations of employer and employed is the general absence of any judicial process in the dismissal of workmen. If the employer comes down to the works in a temper he can still sack the first man he sees. In Germany an attempt has been made to remedy this. Statutory works councils have been set up in all establishments above a certain size. These councils consist of workmen only, and whenever a man is dismissed they can examine into the circumstances and if they think fit they can bring the matter before a special court. If the employer cannot show that the dismissal was dictated by the economic position of the concern or cannot prove that it was "just," he must either reinstate him or pay compensation. See Guillebaud, *The Works Council—A German Experiment*, 1928.

In America the restriction of immigration since the war has cut off a bountiful supply of cheap and helpless labour and produced very great changes in labour conditions. From a state of harsh conflict and forcible suppression there has been a powerful thrust towards constructive experiments. For example, employers have organized their workers in "company unions," comprehending all the workers in a plant, electing employee representative councils or work councils. These company unions develop what are called "welfare features," such as the sale of the company's securities to its workers at rates below those to be got in the open market and the purchase of insurance to cover all the workers employed by the concern against sickness, old age and death. This type of organization tends to break up the old nation-wide trade unions and runs (says the Encyclopædia Britannica, Article, *Trade Unions*) to a membership of several millions.

Another type of experiment lies in the direction of a trade union undertaking the responsibility for production. The business in return gives the union a share in the gain from increased output. This method worked so well between the Machinists' Union and the Baltimore & Ohio Railway Co. that it has spread to a number of other railway systems in the United States and Canada. Similarly the Amalgamated Clothing Workers' Union has taken over many of the duties of management and supervision from the manufacturers, has studied and effected considerable economies in production, and done much to educate and increase the efficiency of its members. This tailors' union has been outstandingly successful; it has accumulated funds, made loans to employers and carried through a big coöperative housing scheme in New York City.

§ 4. *Profit-Sharing*

Another line of attempted reconciliation between the "two nations" of employers and employees, a line of reconciliation proceeding from the initiative of the employer, lies in profit-sharing, a peculiarly French invention. A French profit-sharing system was in operation as early as 1820 and there are a number of such businesses still active. The Paris Bon Marché has a scheme at work dating from 1880 by which all its share capital is now in the hands of past or present employees. Similar schemes have been operated in Great Britain and America following upon French precedents. The employees of the British Gas Light and Coke Company, the largest gas company in the world, have acquired £750,000 of its ordinary stock as their share in its profits. The Zeiss works in Jena, manufacturing glass lenses, are run on a profit-sharing scheme that has proved a great success.

But such successes are exceptional in the history of profit-sharing. The method has many drawbacks; its outstanding successes are few and generally due to the enthusiasm and integrity of the managing employer; it does not increase and spread through the general body of industry. It fails to excite much enthusiasm in the ordinary worker, who is apt to consider it as a mere complication of his pay, and the trade unions regard it as a method of shelving the proper adjustment of wages. It raises many delicate and debatable questions about what are profits and what are receipts from the consumption of capital, and what proportion of the annual surplus may legitimately go back into the business for depreciation and expansion. It is in fact an encumbering quasi-benevolent device; it leaves the primary functional opposition of employer and employed untouched, and we note it here mainly to distinguish it clearly from the essentially structural innovations, the real resumptions of responsibility and participation by the organized workers, that have sprung from the Guild Socialist conception.

§ 5. *Continuous Employment and Waiting About: the Possibility of Lifetime Jobs for All*

One chief hardship of the worker in the modern industrial world is the uncertainty of his employment from day to day and in many cases from hour to hour.

Comfortable prosperous people know little of the tedium, wretchedness and disappointment that have characterized and still characterize, great fields of employment through the "waiting about" forced upon the workers by the chancy, *undercalculated* and inconsiderate nature of a large proportion of industrial operations. Men have to stand at dock gates, waiters queue up outside restaurants, men and women sit inactive in clothing shops waiting for work to be given out, they assemble in silk-weaving establishments, in steel works, glass works and so on, *earning nothing* until they are beckoned to their task. Until recently it was not even the custom to pay actors and actresses for rehearsals. Few prosperous people realize that to be an out-of-work is often as binding and far more tedious than to be in employment. They think of being out-of-work as a leisurely, free state, disagreeable only through its concomitant of want.

One might imagine from this that one great objective of trade-union effort would be to secure continuity of employment. But that has not been the case. There are alternative evils to be considered. Labour under contract is hampered in the strategy of collective bargaining. And a contract for continuous employment without definite conditions for treatment may become very easily a practical slavery. The ancient English contract with farm servants for a year, the yearly bond of the Northumbrian coal miner, the annual hiring of the Staffordshire potters, have now, for that reason, become matters of history. It is only when the contract is amplified by a very rigorous definition of the rights and remedies of either party, when there is a well defined schedule of the customs of the trade and the precise duties of the worker, that the latter can feel secure against aggressions and deprivations. We find therefore that the worker is forced to choose between two uncertainties: uncertainty of continuous earning on the one hand, and uncertainty of treatment on the other. His adjustment between these two sets of considerations is a complex task which is still going on.

Contemporary industrialism has been evolved in relation to a labour class numerically always in excess of the demand for its services. Industry has been wont to take in workers as it needed them, by the hour, day or week, and to drop them again directly they were unwanted. The community had to carry these workers for the primitive type of employer during his intervals of relative inactivity, and he was never called to account for their upkeep. Such education as these workers got was provided either by charitable bodies or the general community, and when they were disabled or superannuated they again went on to public resources. There was little or no recognition of the indebtedness of the employer to this floating population of impoverished people which served to cheapen his labour supply. That did not come into his figuring. The drain they made on the general resources was not charged to him.

Education in the early stages of the industrial revolution was trivial, poor relief was a minimum, and it was only as the standard of efficiency and economy rose, as education became public and expensive and assistance for the out-of-work increased, that people began to think of any bookkeeping as between the social cost of the worker's birth, life, and death and the finance of industry. The common man of to-day has become a much more manufactured and costly product than the common man of a century ago. Then he was, one may say, a wild product, like a chance mushroom in a meadow; the employer picked him and consumed him; now he is a cultivated product, and the organized community which has made him asserts its right to control the exploitation of his abilities.

Professor Carr-Saunders calculates that the cost of producing a boy for the labour market in Britain (1930) is well over £350. The government returns show an educational expenditure of £100; food and clothing amount to at least £200, and rent and social services certainly add another £50 to the total.

The industrialist of the early nineteenth century lived like an animal that ranges in the woodland; he reaped his profit with no thought of whence it came and with an unshaken confidence in his own right to live. But all that has changed and continues to change. The industrial concern is becoming more and more dependent on public resources for the quality and intermittent support of its labour supply, and the world at large grows impatient with the factory's habit of absorbing and then excreting workers into the general community without the slightest regard for social decency. Sustained unemployment means degeneration; and the right of industry working for private profit to take the young people society has provided, has civilized and to some extent educated, use them intermittently for a term of years, and throw them out in a state of diminished usefulness in order to avail itself of younger, fresher and cheaper material, is being questioned more and more acutely.

The possibility of greatly reducing casual and short-term employment can be approached not only from the point of view of the public services, but also from the point of view of the employer. Casual labour is rarely loyal or zealous labour, and a considerable effort is being made by many employers to diminish or eliminate it altogether from their works. As I was planning this section a significant document dropped into my letter box, an American publication, the *Survey Graphic,* giving an account of the labour organization of Messrs. Procter & Gamble, a firm of soap-makers (about whose products and standing I know nothing). This firm claims to guarantee a minimum of forty-eight weeks' employment in the year to ten thousand employees. It is not quite clear if they have other employees outside the privileged ten thousand, but if so, they are apparently probationers and few in number. This is a very interesting and plausible claim, and probably it is the anticipation of something likely to become much more general. There is no reason why that much foresight should be practicable only in soap-making. Messrs. Procter & Gamble are satisfied that they reap a full reward in the increased good-will of their people. Any business organization capable of figuring out its production as exactly, they say,

LEWIS HINE.

THE WORKER AND THE CITY

A worker on the Empire State Building, which towers more than a thousand feet above the streets of New York. In the background is the Hudson River, and beyond it the New Jersey shore.

THE COLOURED WORKER

A COTTON picker in the fields of the Southern United States, who is just as much a part of the contemporary industrialism as the Diesel engine.

may reap a similar reward. That seems acceptable. It depends entirely on the figuring out.

It appears reasonable to argue that this "waiting about," this immense amount of slack in the economic machine, this running waste of unemployed hours and energies, is neither a necessary nor a permanent state of affairs. Its continuance is due to the statistical insufficiency in our body politic. But the trend of things is all towards sounder statistics and better forecasting.

Let me throw out here a broad thesis for the reader's consideration. The total life product of a worker, the money earned during the working years, should be equivalent to all that worker's expenditure and all the expenditure upon that worker, including the overhead charges for directorate and government, from the cradle to the grave. If it is less, he is a parasite; if it is more, he is being robbed and is carrying nonproductive social elements upon his shoulders that he ought not to carry. These seem to me to be sound propositions, giving a definite intimation of the way in which economic life may and should be measured and organized.

In the more calculable days that lie before mankind the economist should be able to state with ever increasing precision the amount of productive work required from every citizen to earn his life subsistence and his freedom for the residue of his time and energy. As these estimates become more precise it will become possible for the State or for some world-wide labour organization to make a deal with the ordinary worker, to undertake to find him or her employment for as many years as it may be necessary to work off that contribution, and to guarantee a life income in return. Such an organization would be responsible to the worker for his maintenance, and it would make its arrangements with the public or private service or production concerned, for his employment.

§ 6. *The Amelioration of the Factory*

Turning now from the current methods of employment for the mass of workers in our human ant-hill and the way in which these methods may develop, let us consider a very interesting field of enquiry and experiment which falls under the term "Scientific Management." This term we owe to Frederick Winslow Taylor, and as exemplified by him it was essentially a reconstruction of industrial processes after a close study and analysis of every step in the process under treatment. For example, he dealt with shovelling in a large steel plant, watched and timed workers, tried out movements and showed that they were using ill-chosen shovels, lifting excessive weights here and insufficient weights there, and missing the easiest way of performing their tasks. By altering the types of shovel used and carefully teaching the shovellers, such an improvement in the process was made that the average wages of these men was raised 63 per cent while the cost of handling was reduced 54 per cent.

Another research of Taylor's led to great improvements in the transmission of power by leather belting and to the redesigning of lathes. The same methods applied to the general planning-out of work to be undertaken, led to conspicuous economies in the moving about of material, the elimination of delays when stuff had been used up and more was required, the arrangement of work spaces in the order of maximum convenience and so forth.

Particular attention was given to prevent machinery standing idle. Inactive machines, vacant floor space, swell the overhead charges without adding to the product. Work thus closely watched can no longer be left to the old type of foreman. Its direction becomes educational; the foreman must be, to a large extent, a teacher and demonstrator and a specially trained and skilled man.

So in our review of contemporary human activities we must add now to the worker, foreman, shop steward, overseer and suchlike traditional officials in all really organized businesses, a new small group of very important people who are planning, watching and charting the processes of production. From the point of view of the worker, his task is made less laborious and troublesome but more effective. He is to work in the best air and the best light; his temperature and comfort and mental tran-

quillity are studied to enable him to give his best; he is relieved
before the fatigue stage sets in. Such are the concepts and
methods that are spreading now throughout the industrial
world.

By way of contrast to efficient modern going concerns, a study
or so of early nineteenth and Victorian enterprises might be
very useful and entertaining. The material for such studies, I
should imagine, must still exist in abundance—accounts, balance
sheets, plans of layout, estimates—but how far it has actually
been digested and made available I do not know.* I may be
wrong here. Perhaps more than I think of the directive intelligence of the smaller, more limited and more controllable business of from fifty to a hundred years ago was carried about in
people's heads; perhaps the great part of Victorian management went undocumented, its once living records long since de-
cayed in the cemetery.

In our modern plants we shall certainly find not merely a
more adequate documentation, but a distinctness and definition
of parts in the organism which were either unorganized or absent
in the more primitive economic structure of the nineteenth century. There are, for example, the beginners who replace the old
apprentice fags, those who are indeed working in part but who
are also in part learning. For them the factory is half a school,
a specializing school. For them there must be a special teaching
and controlling staff. The modern factory has to deal with the
general educational organization of the community in a spirit of
give and take. The educational authority has to come into the
business as the protector of the 'prentices to see that they are
really taught and not used merely as cheap junior hands, and the
industry seeks to extend its influence into the schools to secure
a better type of worker in its shops.

Another modern section in a business organization outside
the everyday round is the research staff, concerned with the
systematic investigation of problems arising out of the work and
in the search for novelties, improvements and economies. Both

---

*Such men as T. G. Ashton, G. W. Daniels and others have made studies on
Victorian cotton, wool, brass and iron production. *H. J. L.*

these sections are correlated nowadays with great educational and investigatory organizations outside the works, with the school, the technical college and the scientific side of the university. The days when it was possible to distinguish sharply between business organizations and public educational and social institutions have passed away.

In America such great industrial organizations as General Motors, the Ford Motor Company and the Westinghouse Electric Manufacturers have established training institutions to meet their own particular needs, and these interlock closely with exterior schools. For instance, we find the University of Cincinnati, Antioch College in Ohio, the Institute of Technology at Flint (Mich.), and the Technical High School at the city of Dayton (Ohio) all in close coöperation with the General Motors organization at Dayton. The engineer students pass to and fro between the shop, the classroom and the laboratory.

The increasing correlation of the organizing forces in the factory with public research and education to-day is well displayed in that pioneer institution, the National Institute of Industrial Psychology in London.* Here, under the direction of Mr. C. S. Myers, there is a continual coming and going between school, employer and public official. "Planning" is studied, that is to say, the layout of plant, the routine of processes, the storage and transport of material. Fatigue is exhaustively scrutinized: its relation to hours of work, to lighting, to temperature, to the movements of air in a workroom. Winslow Taylor's ideas are adapted now to this new industrial process and now to that. In addition, work is going on continually with the object of making a trustworthy classification and tests for nervous and mental types, so as to fit the job to the worker and avoid the distress and wastage of setting the wrong sort of individual to an uncongenial job. Employers send applicants for posts under them, to the Institute for tests and examination, instead of trusting to their own casual impression of the aspirant; parents may bring youngsters for advice as to the choice of a *métier*.

---

*The ruling ideas of the Institute are set out in *Industrial Psychology*, by C. S. Myers and others (1929).

At first the work of Winslow Taylor and the larger enterprise of the London Institute were regarded with considerable suspicion by the workers themselves as being no more than an attempt to put them under increased pressure and reduce employment. Winslow Taylor, in his classical instances, seems always to have insisted that the workers concerned should have a substantial share in the economies effected in the form of increased wages. The question of the reduction of employment is one best deferred to a later stage, but the dread of any increased stress through "Scientific Management" is already dispelled. The Institute has got a number of expressions of approval from workers with whom it has dealt. Says Factory A: "Could we not have more like this? It has made it a lot easier for us." "It feels much safer now; we can get on with the work much quicker." Factory B echoes: "It is much better now; we can stick to the job without being fussed about." "It's fair now; it divides the work up—share and share alike." And a worker from Factory C says: "When we heard of the changes you were giving us, we were that glad we all felt six foot high. . . . I wish you had been here when I was a girl; I wouldn't look the old hag I do now."

It is interesting to contrast the conditions of the actual worker at work, now and in the past. The toil of the Lancashire cotton-mill hands or the sweated Sheffield cutlers of the early industrial period was immeasurably inferior in ease, dignity, comfort and leisure to that of their current successors. Already it is difficult for us to realize how enormously and needlessly cruel were the relative ignorance and inexperience of the pioneer age of power production. With no profit to the employer worth talking about.

In 1830 England was leading the world in the development of the new industrialism; she was the supreme industrial country. Let us see the price in humanity that she was paying, recklessly and needlessly, for that ascendency. In those days a cotton hand would be getting from four shillings to five shillings and sixpence a week, his wife three shillings and his children from one shilling each, upwards. The budget of a family of weavers who were paid at the current highest rates showed that after rent and working expenses had been deducted from their earnings of eighteen shillings, ten shillings and tenpence a week was left for the food, clothing and other needs of seven people. This is rather more than the amount available for the same objects in the families of the lowest paid unskilled London labourers in 1912. But four people had to work sixteen hours a day to earn it, as against one man working a ten-hour day. Moreover, bread cost then sixpence halfpenny for a four-and-a-half-pound loaf of household or brown bread. Many families, although in full work, were obliged to obtain relief from the parish.

This sample cotton operative at the age of thirty could probably already look back upon over twenty years of toil in the mill. Six or seven was the age at which most children started to earn, although some began younger. Our man might at that date have been one of the pauper children sent from all over England by their parishes to a life indistinguishable from slavery in order to relieve the local ratepayer, for that practice was not stopped until 1816. Or he might have been a child whose father had been told that if he would not bring his children to the mill he could not be allowed parish relief. Once brought there, the child would have been obliged to work thirteen, fourteen, or fifteen hours a day for six or even seven days in the week and all the weeks in the year. Factories were known where girls of eighteen worked eighteen hours a day for five consecutive days a week; others where workers were often kept on all night. Even seven days' work was exacted. The engines, it is true, were stopped on Sundays in order that a Christian population might go to church, but the children were required in many cases to turn up as usual and clean machinery. Such were the wages, such the hours, under the leading industrial state of the world only a hundred years ago.

From time to time the Commons, urged by the better employers, passed Acts limiting the working hours of apprentices to twelve, but no method of enforcing them was provided, they were not carried out, and outside the very best mills, real relief did not come except in the matter of night work, until the passing of the Acts of 1847 and 1850. For all those interminable working hours the children stood, or walked, or crawled under the machines, collecting cotton waste. One employer, known as humane, calculated that his children during their work walked upwards of twenty miles. They also walked from their beds to the factory and back again. There were meal-times—an hour and a half in all—for adult workers, but not for children. They had to clean the machines and to eat their food as they worked among the oil and dust and flue. If they grew too tired, the overseers beat them to keep them at work; their fathers beat them to keep them awake so that they should not fall into the machines. Everyone spat to get rid of the flue that settled in their lungs—it was stated in evidence before Sir Robert Peel's committee (1816) that when spitting failed to achieve this purpose emetics were freely given.*

We are told to-day that there has been exaggeration in the attacks made on the early factory system, that many mills were clean and airy, so that the operatives who worked in them were better off than those who ate and slept and worked in the damp cellars necessary for the home weaving of cotton, that brutal masters were an exception, and that the children of the home-workers toiled as long and were often more cruelly treated than those who were at the mercy of employers and overseers. That may be true. The English are a kindly race, and the presence of onlookers is always a check on cruelty. It is certainly true also that the housing conditions of the time were sufficient to account for any amount of typhus, typhoid and tuberculosis.

Here is a description of a district in Spitalfields inhabited by weavers in the year 1840; Manchester is described as "even worse." "Ruinous buildings, streets without sewers, overflowing privies and cesspools, and open ditches filled with a black putre-fying mass of corruption infecting the air for miles round, render the district the abode of disease and death. There are streets and alleys from which typhus fever is never absent the year round."* And the new machines brought their own occupational diseases—consumption from the cotton flue, stomach diseases

---

*Hammond: *The Town Labourer,* p. 158.
*"Report on Handloom Weavers," 1840, p. 681.

for the weavers who sat pressed forward against the beam of the loom, cancer for the mule-spinners, consumption again for the girls on worsted spinning who, "exposed to a constant spray of water from the frames, were compelled to spend the greater part of the day in wet clothing; and the introduction of hot-water spinning merely increased the heat and dampness of the air."*

Flax mills were described as even more unhealthy, the Sheffield grinders were killed by steel dust, the metal-workers were blinded by sparks. Every trade seems to have produced its own scourge. And the new machines were run so fast that it was painful to keep up with them; accidents were continual; when workers were killed in the course of their employment they were not thought worth the trouble of an inquest. Many factories were dirty, dark and airless; in many the workers were locked in, at a temperature of 80°, without water—forbidden, in fact, to drink—without lavatories, and under what they certainly regarded as a prison-like and brutal discipline.

As for brutality, it has to be remembered that the wage-earners were helpless. In the huge new towns there was no public opinion, and no custom to protect the men in any established rights. They might not combine to negotiate with their masters or even to secure that these latter observed the law. Each individual must make his own bargain for employment, those who complained were prevented from obtaining fresh jobs and had nothing to keep them from starvation but the workhouse. In such an atmosphere blows and brutal punishments seem normal. Nor had the worker any help from public opinion. Respectable people, with their minds still obsessed by the thought of the French Revolution, regarded him as a potential Jacobin.

Even the physical consequences of these inhuman conditions roused in the comfortable classes not pity but repulsion and fear—their very diseases and deformities set the industrial classes apart as alien, sinister and dangerous. The only possible method of dealing with them seemed to be violence, and it was an age of evictions, transportation, whippings, treadmills and

*Pinchbeck: *Women Workers and the Industrial Revolution*, p. 137.

pillories; capital punishment was inflicted for any felony. To go out on strike was commonly treated as an offense.

The only possible answer for the victims was to return savagery for savagery. Magistrates were terrorized so that they were afraid to convict rebellious operatives, and employers and their agents were intimidated so that they dared not give evidence. The first standards of fair treatment set up, the unions, were maintained so far as they could be maintained by a reign of terror.

Turning to the vital statistics of the industrial operative of a hundred years ago we find that whereas miners seldom lived beyond fifty, the weavers were said to die soon after forty. At thirty-five their earning power began to decline. Slaves must have been very cheap indeed before any slave-owner would have thought it good management to kill his men so young. But then the slave-owner had to buy his slaves, while the community in the opening phase of industrialism gave its young without fine or fee into the hands of the industrial employer.

A hundred years ago things were at this stage in England. But in this still disunited world things do not move forward at a uniform pace, and one land after another blunders through the same experiences as its fellows—knowing little or nothing of the lessons they have learnt. China industrially is a hundred years behind western Europe, and there to-day one can see a population entering upon an entirely similar phase to that from which the men, women, and children of industrial England are emerging.

The silk factories of Shanghai to-day can show conditions which vary only in detail from those of the British industrial revolution. The children who crawl in them do not choke their lungs with cotton, but they scald their fingers picking cocoons out of pans of boiling water and die of blood poisoning in consequence. The smell must be worse than that of the dirtiest cotton mill that ever defiled Lancashire, for it is added to by unwashed babies slung under the frames and the putrefying insects in the cocoons. The hours, the wages, the disregard of health are similar—the only alleviating factor seems to be the absence of English winter nights for people who have been working all day in a temperature of 80 degrees.

Egypt, again, tells a parallel story. There came to hand by the same post (January, 1931) the news of a weavers' strike in Lancashire against a proposed lowering of their wages and labour conditions "to meet foreign competition," and an account of the sort of competition they have to meet in a report upon the Egyptian cotton mills of to-day. There we have now, just as we had in Lancashire a hundred years ago, the ill-organized factory, the ill-arranged machinery, because Egyptian flesh and blood is so cheap. "Half the workers are under fifteen and many under nine." . . . "I saw with sorrow in several factories the almost automatic hitting of the children with canes and whips by the overseers as they moved up and down, to spur them on to their work." . . . "There was some hitting of the children on the head, a really dangerous practice." . . . "The mills run from 5 A. M. to 8 or 9 P. M., but no one in authority seems to find it necessary to see that individual young workers, or groups of them, have any regular pause for a meal." . . .

A report upon conditions in the Cairo silk-winding and hand rug-making shops is equally bad. "Tiny children of five and a half years and upwards working like rapid machines in the hand-work shops, with all expression of childhood gone from their faces." . . . In a rug-making shop a child suffering from the painful, dangerous and infectious disease of trachoma was at work, crowded close to other children. In the cigarette and tobacco factories children work among dangerous processes and imperfectly guarded machinery.

Equally dreadful are conditions in the cotton mills of Bombay.

If there is one redeeming feature in this account which differentiates it from the contemporary descriptions of Lancashire a hundred years ago, it is that it is not, as it were, a voice crying to empty heaven, but the evidence of Dame Adelaide Anderson, a distinguished British Inspector of Factories (a social official inconceivable a hundred years ago), published in the *Review* of the International Labour Office at Geneva, a publication effective enough, at any rate, to produce at once assurances from the Egyptian government that steps are now being taken to remedy the worst of these conditions.

It may not need as long as a hundred years, perhaps, to bring Egypt into line with the state of affairs already established in Lancashire. The pace of progress may be quicker for China and India as the world moves towards unification. Here, by way of reassurance, is a description of the newer phase in the cotton industry. The mill described is still not Utopian, but it is sufficiently developed from primitive conditions to show the nature of the new order to which we still seem to be moving.

If a cotton operative of 1831 could be taken over one of the Lancashire mills to-day what would catch his attention first? Probably, the new machines, stately, complex, precise and beautiful compared with the crude mechanisms which enslaved him. Then, surely, the scarcity of human beings. In a room where a dozen great carding machines are delicately gathering up their film of cotton he might see no one at all. The seething, wretched, mill-ground humanity of his experiences has vanished altogether. If he spoke of it he would be told, "There should be a girl about." Minding an avenue of shimmering spindles which would stretch from one side of a broad road to the other he would see two men and a boy. Two healthy men and a well grown boy. The weaving sheds where women work might seem more familiar to him, for women, invincibly possessive, bring little bundles with them into the spaces between four looms where each rules over her tenter, stamp them with their personality, and so to speak domesticate them. But now new looms are coming which will need but an eighth of a man's attention—the old factory swarm is gone forever.

Next our returned cotton slave would remark the light, the extraordinary amount of light, the clear atmosphere, the absence of little children and the air of alertness, intelligence and self-respect that reigns among the workers in a good mill. Noisy it would still be—we are not yet able to control our noises—but he would be shown lavatories, cloakrooms, water to drink and to wash in—the place so arranged generally that our now expensive workers may combine and harmonize to the best effect with the costly machinery they control. If he talked to this generation of his great-grandchildren he would find independence in the place of hopelessness, social humour for his bitter class hatred, and technical interest in improvements for his blind, agonized obstruction to every economy of toil.

But the most fundamental change, productive of these others, is that the worker is no longer an isolated individual or even a member of a helot class. He is a voter, a citizen with acknowledged rights and an acknowledged value, whose state concerns itself perforce with his safety and the decency and cleanliness of his surroundings, sees that he is compensated for accidents, and makes provision for sickness, unemployment and old age. He is also, if he is wise, a member of a respected and powerful union which guards his hours and wages and champions him in any case of ill-treatment or injustice.

This much can be found in any ordinary mill. But our present system can be run to yield far more than this. Cotton has been chosen for description in this work, instead of the mines or the metal industries, to illustrate the worst possibilities of industrialism in a phase of eager, profit-seeking enterprise. In England, moreover, cotton is a hard-hit export trade which handles a low-priced article. It must compete now with the output of India, China and Egypt. Yet such a firm as Tootall, Broadhurst, Lee & Company of Manchester, working with modern conceptions of scientific management and sympathetic intelligence superadded, is able not only to train but to educate the young people in its Bolton mills, teaching, besides English subjects and gymnastics, physics, mathematics and drawing to the boys, and cooking, sewing and housework to the girls. These last domestic arts are taught not only in a modern kitchen, but also in a typical Bolton cottage, so that the pupils may see what can be made of the sort of home they may one day possess. For all the employees of this firm there are a library, games clubs, musical and dramatic societies, a dental clinic and a welfare department.

The firm we have named is merely an outstanding instance of

the civilization of industrialism. It is a leader in a general movement. The process is being universalized slowly, alas! but surely.
Probably very few of our readers have visited the Home Office
Industrial Museum in London. It is not a popular place of resort, but everyday business men of the better type who are building or reconstructing factories go there for warning, advice,
information, and inspiration; problems of industrial diseases and
discipline are brought there by factory inspectors or employers,
and studies are pursued by students of social and economic problems. It is fascinating to see how the orderly trained mind
is extending security throughout our crowded, busy ant-hill.
Here in one place is a grim collection of broken apparatus,
hooks of cranes, chains, bearings, and torn, scorched and
blackened electric fittings that have gone wrong; every one of
these has caused the death of one or more workers; it is, indeed,
a sort of "Chamber of Horrors" in that respect; but every one
of these exhibits has been the basis of an enquiry and vigorous
preventive measures. There are series of studies of, for example,
the causes of explosions in industrial plants, of eye accidents and
their prevention, of lighting in relation to fatigue and eye strain,
of protective clothing, of the particular dangers and necessary
precautions in the pottery, the bakehouse, the laundry, the printing hours, shipbuilding, housebuilding and so on. Veiled by dark
covers that must be drawn aside, there is a terrible series of wax
models; arms and hands, faces and bodies discoloured and distorted by anthrax, lead poisoning, silicosis, dermatitis and a
number of other industrial diseases.

Almost every new industrial process, particularly when it involves new materials, needs to be watched in the interests of the
worker. Working in pitch and paraffin has brought to light unsuspected dangers of skin cancer; the increasing use of chromium
has made chrome ulceration a special problem. There are X-ray
photographs of choked and diseased lungs, and there is an exposition of the precautions, regulations and prohibitions that have
resulted from these studies.

We have just mentioned the disappearence of flue from the
cotton factory. At the Home Office Industrial Museum one may

see how dust, chips, filings and flue are sucked away from the worker and out of the factory atmosphere. Another considerable section of the museum is devoted to the prevention of fatigue, to comfort, rest rooms, sanitary accommodation and kindred problems. The London Home Office Industrial Museum is only one of several. There are similar collections in Milan, Berlin, Amsterdam, Paris, Lausanne and elsewhere. They are not merely in evidence and protest against the headlong, ignorant exploiter. Associated with them is a very definite and increasing element of control and punitive power.

Such is the contrast of a modernized scientific industrialism with the hideous lawless exploitation of the opening phase—in Egypt, India, and China to-day; in Lancashire a century ago—when the promise of the new order is yet masked by the greedy incompetence of the profit-seeking employer and the ancient black tradition that servitude, to be productive, must be ruthlessly imposed. In these industrial museums the spirit of the trained, educated man is made visible, steadily overcoming the dull brutality and rapacity of the primitive entrepreneur. They are among the most significant and hopeful of the signs and portents of that world of organized foresight towards which human affairs are moving.

They will move in that direction more and more rapidly as increasing masses of people grasp the significance of what is going on and throw their influence into the scale on the side of scientific control as against "free" individual profit-making. Steadily, as world unity is organized, the whole of man's industrial life throughout our planet will be raised to the level and beyond the level indicated by that museum in Horseferry Road to-day.

§ 7. *Vestiges of Slavery and Tropical Forced Labour*

The backwardness, the heedless cruelty, revealed by contemporary reports upon the factories of Egypt, India and China is not only dreadful in itself, but it pulls dead against all the progressive forces of the more highly organized European and American communities. On the one hand we have the civilized factory we have just described, and on the other we have the soul-destroying factories of the backward countries, undercutting all but the very highest grade of Lancashire product and obstructing further advance. We have this discord of easy modern productiveness with ancient traditional greed. The responsibilities of the International Labour Bureau at Geneva in this respect alone are colossal. The establishment of a common standard of employment throughout the world remains a distant objective to which we move forward only very slowly.

But there are still graver aspects of contemporary production, due to the present irregular distribution of civilization and order —aspects that cannot be ignored in any survey of contemporary human activities. It is unhappily true, as Bombay and Cairo testify, that civilization does not necessarily follow the flags of civilized states. Modern machinery and commercial greed can outrun the modern administrator very easily. In the darker, the less illuminated regions of the world, the worst impulses of barbarism and modern business enterprise can meet and mingle to produce far more frightful consequences. There is, then, not even the pretense of paid employment; there are outright slavery and a form of enforced production under threats and duress more horrible than any slavery can be.

The extent to which slavery itself still exists is not always realized. Lady Simon, in her book, *Slavery* (1930), puts the number of "owned persons"—that is, persons who may be sold as chattels—at considerably over four million. But these actual slaves do not as a matter of fact constitute a formidable economic threat. They are confined for the most part to Arabia, the northern two thirds of Africa, China, and the wild territories between India and China; they are not employed on industrial work nor even in handling valuable crops for international commerce. Slave labour is extremely inefficient—it is estimated that it takes two slaves to do the work of one free man. It is unintelligent and unambitious, devoid of any incentive to improve. It is not really cheap, for slaves cost money to catch, to breed, to buy, to train and also to maintain. They receive no wages, but they must be fed and clothed, housed, tended in sickness and incessantly supervised. As against efficient modern labour the slave does not pay. Slavery as an economic method is moribund; if it survives as an institution it will be in the form of domestic servitude.

In this form it is still a social problem. The faster it can be stamped out, the better. But it is another aspect of human helplessness which challenges our attention when we are considering threats to the Atlantic standard of life. This is the system of peonage or forced labour. It is in effect, as we shall see, the economic *consumption* of backward and ill-organized races. It is far more profitable than slavery, and in some cases it is even more cruel. There are, at any rate, reasons for keeping slaves strong and well. They possess a money value, and a man must be drunk or negligent, stupid, a miser, mentally diseased, or out of temper before he will damage his own property. Slaves may, of course, fall into the hands of callous or morbid persons. Where they have been captured and marched long distances to the slave markets they must have passed through extremes of suffering. Where women are used deliberately to breed children for sale or sold as prostitutes they must often be among the unhappiest creatures on earth. But each slave, until worn out, is of value to someone. If human beings must be ill-treated or damaged in order to make them work, or killed in order to terrify their companions, it is cheaper not to buy them in the beginning.

PUTUMAYO

The natives who were tortured in tens of thousands and killed or starved wholesale by the rubber companies of the Putumayo and the Congo were not slaves. Technically they were "free" and under the legal protection of governments which rank as civilized. Their freedom only added to their misery. At this moment the Africans who are being flogged and robbed on the cocoa plantations of St. Thomé and St. Principé are supposed to be indentured labourers who have entered into contracts of service of their own free will.* Sir Roger Casement's reports on the Putumayo were written only twenty years ago, and some of

---

*Lady Simon: *Slavery*, p. 144.

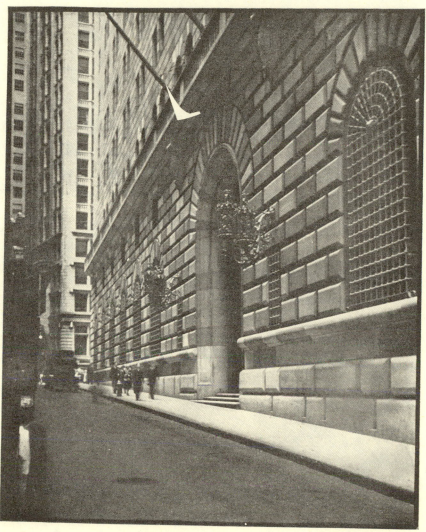

A FASTNESS OF THE MONEY SYSTEM

THE New York Federal Reserve Bank at 33 Liberty Street, New York City.

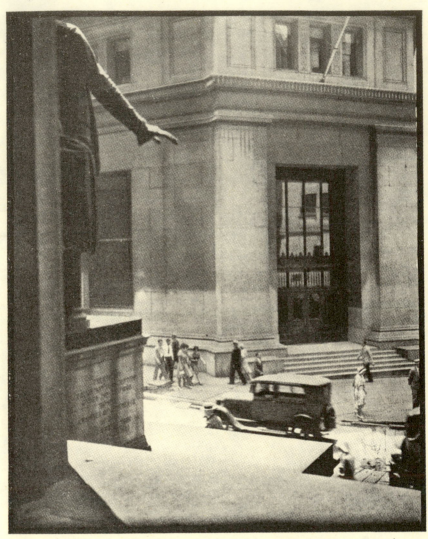

A FINANCIAL NERVE CENTRE
WHICH MAY STIMULATE OR INHIBIT
THE three small windows belong to J. P. Morgan's office, 23 Wall Street.

the men against whom his most serious charges were made are believed to be still alive, free and in possession of their fortunes and probably still engaged in their appalling activities.

The forest-rubber region of Central South America is mainly the watershed of the Putumayo River and its confluents. These waters go on into the Amazon, and they flow through a land of tropical forests. The district of Putumayo belongs to Peru, but it is almost surrounded by Ecuador, Colombia and Brazil, and at the time of Casement's report, in 1910, it was not in fact subjected to any real form of legal government. It is separated from the lower reaches of the Amazon by thousands of miles of swamp and jungle, and from the coast to the west by the Cordillera Mountains.

In 1907 it was inhabited, according to the official estimate of the Peruvian government, by about fifty thousand Indians. They were not warlike people—in fact, that they were gentle, docile, and almost defenseless, is clear not only from the testimony of travellers and missionaries, but from the fact that only once or twice did a few of them venture to revolt against the oppression the economic utilization of rubber brought upon them. Until the last quarter of the nineteenth century they were visited by very few white men. Most of them could call their lives their own. Then adventurers from Colombia began to come down the rivers in search of wild rubber trees, bringing Indians to collect the milk for them. At first these newcomers traded with the natives, selling them rubbish in order to get them into debt, or inducing chiefs to pledge the labour of their clans. When such trading failed to produce as much rubber as they wanted, they resorted to terrorism. Each of these men considered the particular river on whose banks he had settled and the Indians who lived by it as his property: he kept all competition out of the district, maltreated the natives as he chose, and carried off and kept or sold the women and children.* The agents under his authority were half-tamed Indians, usually from some tribe belonging to another river, who were trained as guards and allowed to carry

---

*Annual Report of the Minister of Justice to the Peruvian Congress, 1907, p. 782. Official Peruvian Government Press.

rifles. They themselves were compelled to force the forest Indians to bring in the quantity of rubber which had been fixed by the master and to follow them and hunt them down if they tried to leave the district. In return for this the guards were allowed to bully the natives as they pleased. The women and children were theirs to play with.

By 1910, however, when Casement's report was made, these early Colombian pioneers had almost disappeared, bought out by the Peruvian Amazon Company, which was amalgamated with the firm of Arana Brothers. But the joint firm, largely controlled by Julio Arana, carried on the old methods, though its agents now replaced the independent adventurers. It, too, relied on control by armed Indian guards, of whom Casement stated that though many he met were demoralized ruffians, capable of any crime, others, he thought, ill-treated the natives because they knew that if they did not do so they would themselves be murdered.

It was by mere mischance, from the company's point of view, that his visit was paid at all. In 1904–05 Arana Brothers had recruited about two hundred Barbados natives who were British subjects, and some of these men complained to the British Consul at Iquitos, the local headquarters of the company, that they were not only being refused the right to return, and used as slave drivers rather than workers, but that they were themselves subject to the grossest ill-treatment. These complaints bore out accusations which had been made in a book, *The Andes and the Amazon*,* written by W. F. Hardenburg, a surveyor who had travelled through the district making a survey for a railway on behalf of the Peruvian government, and the British Foreign Office sent Consul General Casement to inquire into the question. He was of course afforded facilities by the Peruvian government and was accompanied everywhere by the Peruvian Amazon Company's principal representative.

His report† confirmed the very worst of the rumors which had

---

*Fisher Unwin, 1907.
†British Parliamentary Papers, Miscellaneous Nos., 1912. References unless otherwise stated are to this report.

been current. The Barbados Negroes—men of a semi-civilized class, some of whom could read and write—had not only been forced to commit crimes against the Indians, but had themselves been the victims of gross ill-treatment. But their own cases fade into insignificance beside what the report reveals of the victimization of the natives. These unfortunate beings, men, women and children, were systematically tortured and flogged. They were flogged regularly, with twisted whips of rawhide, if the loads of rubber they brought in did not reach the weight required, and arbitrarily if anyone chose to flog them. Of the natives Casement saw, he reports that quite 90 per cent bore scars as the result of their floggings—some of the worst scars he found on children of ten or twelve (pp. 33–35). In one house containing the fifteen Indians who served as servants to a settlement he found only one small boy unscarred. Deaths from flogging were frequent (p. 37), due as a rule to putrefaction of the wounds.

After the whip the most common instrument of torture was the stocks—two heavy wooden beams with leg holes cut in them, which were closed down one over the other when the legs had been inserted. Victims were confined in these for long periods, often with their legs forced so widely apart that they suffered extreme pain, and in some stocks the holes were so small that the beams could not be closed without cutting and crushing the flesh (pp. 41–42). Not infrequently natives were flogged when confined in these machines and then left to die of hunger—an eyewitness spoke of having seen them "scraping up the dirt with their fingers and eating it" and "eating the maggots from their wounds" (p. 39). Another method of punishment was to hold them under water until they were nearly drowned (p.38), or to hang them by the neck with their toes just touching the ground until they were almost strangled (p. 39); one witness spoke of men being flogged while in this position. When the rubber had to be transported to the coast, which happened three times a year, the Indians were forced to carry it for about sixty miles, over a path "fatiguing to a good walker quite unburdened," and without any food but what they could bring with them. The principal representative of the rubber company himself told Casement that "hundreds" of them perished during the forced marches. One load of rubber weighed by Casement was just 50 kilos (100 pounds).

Large numbers, too, of the natives were shot, either as reprisals, after the one or two occasions when a revolt was attempted, or from mere wanton savagery. One witness speaks of Indians killed for sport—tied up to trees and used as targets (p. 66). Other individual crimes described by more than one independent witness are too revolting to have been the work of sane men. These dreadful accounts are for the alienist and criminologist rather than for the economic student.

It is obvious that under such a régime the Indian women and children were at the mercy of any white man or native guard who liked to amuse himself with them (p. 46). The Barbados men stated that they themselves were offered native "wives" at every station, but not as a rule allowed to take these women on with them if they themselves were shifted.

The general outcome of this combination of greed and ferocity may be stated briefly: Between 1900 and 1911 the amount of Indian-gathered rubber shipped to England through the Iquitos customs house was almost 4,000,000 kilograms—an amount which must have fetched between £1,000,000 and £1,500,000. The number of Indians deliberately murdered during this time or killed by starvation "often purposely brought about by the destruction of crops over whole districts" (p. 158) was at least 30,000, which is at the rate of under £50 per life tormented and destroyed. In 1906 the population had been estimated at 50,000. In 1911 it had fallen to 8,000. The difference between 30,000 and 40,000 is attributed to deaths from disease. That the coercion was so greatly intensified during these six years as to bring about this average yearly diminution in the population of 7,000 was due to the flotation by the Aranas in 1907 of a British company. In order that capital might be attracted from British investors it was necessary to show a high output, and during 1906 nearly 3,000,000 extra kilograms were extorted from the natives. It is to be regretted that the Aranas' search for British support was sufficiently successful to secure not only money but interest in very influential quarters, and that in consequence the pursuit of the Putumayo facts is not so easy as it might otherwise be.

Since Casement's reputation suffered later from the part that he played in the Irish rebellion, it may be as well to state that the most damning evidence was not taken by Casement alone, but in the presence of other members of the Commission, and often of officers of the company or of the British consul at Iquitos, and that all the allegations made were confirmed by the report of Dr. Paredes, the head of a judicial commission dispatched to the Putumayo by the Peruvian government in 1911. Other reports by Peruvian officials dating back to 1905 are quoted by Hardenburg in his later book *The Putumayo, the Devil's Paradise.** The facts were beyond dispute.

Yet nothing effective was done, and so far as one can learn, nothing effective has been done. Before even drawing up his main report Casement had provided the British government with the names of the principal criminals, and these had been telegraphed to the Peruvian government at a time when most of these men were still openly in the district. They were, however, allowed to escape, some of them dragging with them large numbers of captive Indians either for sale or for continued forced labour in other parts of the forests. Two were known to have crossed the border into Brazil and to be continuing the collection of rubber there. The Brazilian government seems to have made genuine efforts to arrest them but, owing to the wildness of the region, failed in its purpose. Dr. Paredes issued warrants for the arrest of no less than 237 persons, but after he returned to the capital he "ceased to fill any judicial function," and only nine of the warrants were made effective. Even of the nine men arrested, none were brought to trial. Casement, revisiting the country at the end of 1911, found that the half-hearted attempts to plant rubber trees which had followed his former visit had come to an end again. A month later his first report was published by the British government; it had been kept private in order to give the Peruvians some inducement to undertake re-

*Fisher Unwin.

forms, but when it became clear that there would not be any reforms the facts were made public. For a time the press of the world rang with the scandal. The British courts ordered a compulsory winding-up of the British company. Sir Edward Grey instructed British consuls throughout the world to report in future on the treatment of native races within their districts. Then came the war and a multitude of distractions. Facts to-day are hard to gather. What happened to Arana and his agents, and what is happening now in the rubber forests, nobody knows.

CONGO RUBBER

The havoc wrought in the Putumayo district, bad as it was, may be considered as almost trifling and accidental beside the devastation caused by the French and Belgian rubber companies in the Congo. Their individual crimes were no worse—you cannot do more to people than torture them to death—but in every other respect the Peruvians and Colombians are distanced by their European competitors. In the first place, the area of country and the number of victims concerned were very much greater, and the period of misrule longer. The two Congos, French and Belgian, cover an area of 1,600,000 square miles, rather larger than Europe without Russia. In the Belgian Congo the native population was reduced from over 20,000,000 in 1890—some observers, among them the English explorer Stanley, placed it at 40,000,000—to 8,500,000 when an official census was taken in 1911. There seem to be no figures available for the French Congo. They are probably smaller, partly because the area concerned is only two thirds of the other, partly because the French part of the country was never so densely populated. But it seems likely from what evidence we do possess that the proportion of survivors was much the same. In a debate which took place in the French Chamber on February 19 to February 21, 1906, it was stated that according to official documents in one region alone 20,000 natives out of the 40,000 who had lived there were destroyed in two years.

Secondly, the outrages of the Putumayo were perpetrated by a few hundreds of persons working for a private company in a region where no governmental control existed. It was an escape from control. The wholesale massacres of the Congo, on the contrary, were carried out either by the actual forces of the State, or by mercenaries hired by wealthy companies who enjoyed the full support of their governments and were defended by them with ardour in their respective parliaments. The one scandal happened in a remote frontier district; the other was systematically planned in Europe by persons holding exalted positions and was deliberately carried on with the aid of many well known European newspapers, a skilful propaganda, and a widespread system of bribery. The originator, the mainstay and the chief beneficiary of a system which has killed more human beings than the European War, was King Leopold II of Belgium, and every influence which can be wielded by an astute and wealthy king was wielded by him in order to ensure its continuance.

The Congo Free State was formed in 1884, under the name of "The International African Association" "for the purpose of promoting the civilization and commerce of Africa and for other humane and benevolent purposes." King Leopold, who was the head of this association, represented that his agents had drawn up treaties of amity and friendship with the independent native rulers of the Congo, and he persuaded the other European powers to recognize him as absolute and personal sovereign of the greater part of the Congo basin in return for various assurances embodied in the "Congo Act." These included a promise that he would put down the slave trade then being carried on by Arab raiders; a guarantee of "complete freedom" to the trade of all nations, another guarantee against the granting of any trade monopolies or favours, and a general pledge that he would "watch over the preservation of the native tribes." He was enabled to obtain this position of trust partly because he bore the reputation of a wise ruler and a philanthropic man, partly because of the English support which was forthcoming for the son and namesake of Queen Victoria's favourite uncle.

This accomplished, he set about to do four things: assume possession of the land and its products; stop private trading;

especially in rubber and ivory; raise an army among the savage tribes of the Upper Congo, and organize propaganda in Europe. By 1890 he had recruited some thousands of soldiers—in many cases by downright slave-raiding. His circulars* promise bonuses of 90 francs for every man over 1 metre 35 centimetres in height, 65 francs for youths over 1 metre 35 centimetres, and 15 francs for male children over 1 metre 20 centimetres. The next step was to get permission from the European powers to impose duties on merchandise in order, ostensibly, to fight the Arab slave-raiders. There were at that time both English and Dutch firms established on the Lower Congo, and protests were made by them as early as 1890 that the policy of the Congo Free State was ruining private trade and stirring up strife among the natives. The King, however, replied to these protests by a widespread newspaper propaganda, and obtained permission from Europe to exterminate the Arabs, and £1,000,000 from Belgium to carry on the war in return for his leaving her the Congo in his will. He succeeded in driving the Arabs from the Congo and in getting possession of the enormous stores of ivory which had been in their possession. Then he turned to his other objectives.

In order that the reader may form a picture of what his actions effected, he must be told something of the state of the river country and the natives who lived in it as Stanley found them on his voyages in 1879 and 1882. The river banks were at that time the home of a flourishing population which he estimated at forty millions. He saw large numbers of centres of population, each containing from 5,000 to 40,000 people—settlements extended for hundreds of miles along the waterside. The tribes had reached a certain level of civilization—they made beautiful cloths and ironwork, carried on a number of other skilled crafts, cultivated a large variety of vegetables as well as maize and sugar cane, kept their gardens as well as Europeans could do, and were above all enthusiastic merchants who made long voyages up and down the river and maintained trade relations with the distant tribes of the interior. These people were

*Quoted in debates in Belgian Parliament, March, 1905; March, 1906. Official shorthand reports.

savages—there were even among them a certain number of cannibals—but the foremost Belgian historian of the Congo said of them at that time, "They are warriors only for defense; they are one and all traders."* It is as well to stress the fact that their rulers held the land in trust for the tribesmen and "early explorers of the Congo; Catholic and Protestant missionaries with long years of experience in different parts of the territory; British consuls, indeed a whole host of witnesses" testify to the jealous regard of the native population for their rights in land.† This land King Leopold proceeded to appropriate. By an official decree of July 1, 1885, he declared that "vacant land must be considered as belonging to the State."

By vacant land, it subsequently appeared he meant all land not actually built upon, the forests in which the various tribes hunted and collected the raw materials for their trading and their crafts. In 1891, his armies being prepared, he forbade the natives to collect or sell rubber or ivory to merchants, or merchants to buy them from the natives. This practically destroyed the whole private trade of the area, for it was for rubber and ivory that the goods of the European firms were interchanged. Henceforth, any native who collected rubber for anyone but the State was a poacher, and the merchant who bought it of him a receiver of stolen goods. The merchants protested, but with no result, and they were finally forced to abandon their business.‡

Next, by secret instructions dated Brussels, June 20, 1892, the King informed the Governor General of the Congo State that the officials of the State were to "exploit the produce of the forests." To induce them to do this he would pay a bonus on rubber and ivory "proportionate to the cost of exploitation"— that is, the *less* the native received for what he brought the greater was to be the payment to the official.§ When news of these instructions reached Europe, the German government pro-

---

*Wauters: *L'Etat Indépendent du Congo.*

†E. D. Morel: *The Black Man's Burden*, p. 115.

‡The full story of these events may be found in E. D. Morel's three books: *King Leopold's Rule in Africa* (Heinemann) ; *Red Rubber,* and *The Black Man's Burden* (Parsons).

§Official shorthand report, Belgian Parliamentary Debates.

tested that it was a violation of the Congo Act to which Germany had been a signatory. Leopold, in a reply dated December 11, 1895, signed Edmund Van Eetvelde, denied that any bonus was either in existence or in contemplation. It was, in fact, the pivot of his organization.

Next a system of "taxes" was imposed on the natives—they were ordered to bring in certain amounts of ivory, rubber, or whatever produce of value the district produced. When the forests were exhausted the natives were compelled to labour themselves or to bring in food for those engaged in forced labour.* Officials were informed of the amounts they were required to collect and given a certain time in which to collect them. Refusal to furnish the required amount was to be considered as a revolt and punished by force of arms, and by taking hostages.

Under this system, between 1899 and 1906 alone over £13,700,000 worth of rubber was collected by the natives of the Congo.† Within a year of its inauguration the Lower Congo looked "as though a tornado had torn across it and destroyed everything in its passage."‡ The amounts fixed as "taxes" were so great that it was impossible for the tribes to produce them. They refused, or failed, their villages were raided and burned, their women carried off as hostages to be redeemed, if they were still alive, by payments in rubber.

The report of one of the remaining Belgian merchants says, "There is not an inhabited village left in four days' steaming through a country formerly so rich; to-day utterly ruined. . . . The soldiers sent out to get rubber and ivory are depopulating the country. They find the quickest and cheapest method is to raid villages, seize prisoners, and have them redeemed afterwards for ivory." If we add that one or two black soldiers armed with rifles were left as sentries in every helpless village with no one to call them to account, and that as a check on their wasting cartridges they were told in many cases to cut off the right hand

---

*Official shorthand report, Belgian Parlimentary Debates, July, 1903.
†*Red Rubber*, p. 36.
‡*The Black Man's Burden*, p. 120.

or sexual organs of their victims, dry them, and bring them in baskets to their superiors, one for each cartridge used, we have the essential features of the system.* As for these superiors, whether King Leopold's own officers, or the officials of the great companies to whom he had farmed out part of his territory, it may be as well to add that they were not allowed to resign. If they left their stations they were prosecuted for desertion or died or were killed on their way to the coast.†

For twenty years this procedure was pushed methodically further and further inland under the name of "pacification." In 1903 a traveller named Murdoch, in 1907 another called Scrivener, travelled up the Congo for weeks together without meeting a single human being, past "long miles of ruined mouldering villages thickly strewn with skeletons"‡ where once there had been a dense population. In groups of villages estimated in 1898 to have contained about 140,000 inhabitants, in 1903 under 18,000 were left.§ The country of which these statements were made was part of King Leopold's "private domain."

Matters were even worse in the concessions. The Abir Company—an organization managed by a council consisting among others of a Belgian senator, the Grand Master of King Leopold's court in Belgium, a prominent banker and member of parliament, an ex-governor general of the Congo, and a Belgian nobleman—"enrolled thousands of natives, armed with rifles and cap-guns, to force the rubber output upon the general population. It kept some 10,000 natives continually at work all the year round collecting rubber, and some 10,000 men, women, and children passed every year through its 'hostage houses.' . . . When certain areas became denuded of rubber, the remaining male population was carried off wholesale under escort and flung into another area not yet exhausted, their women handed over to the soldiers."

---

*British Government White Book, Africa, No. 1, 1904.
†*Red Rubber,* p. 88.
‡*The Black Man's Burden,* p. 124.
§*King Leopold's Rule in Africa,* pp. 238–41.

It can hardly be necessary to add to this picture by the enumeration of atrocities. Of course, there were atrocities, tens of thousands of them, there were intended to be—they saved cartridges. And they were filthy and bestial beyond description. One official seems to have punished men who did not collect enough rubber by forcing them to drink the white man's excretion.* Another made the natives eat the rubber if it was badly prepared. The Court of Justice at Boma—there was a court, and great play was made with its existence in Europe—decided that the subsequent illness and death of the Negroes concerned could not be attributed to this as the "introduction into the stomach by the mouth of an elastic substance was not productive of after ill-effects."†

The reports of these atrocities were, of course, challenged. From the first complaints of the European merchants settled on the river to the last debates in the Belgian Parliament, every criticism of Leopold's administration was met by official denials, by a widespread counter propaganda, and by allegations that the criticisms came from corrupt or interested persons or formed part of political plots. Occasionally new "humane" regulations would be published in Europe in order to impress public opinion. In 1903 an edict appeared in Brussels to the effect that the natives were only to work forty hours a month at rubber-gathering. In 1906 three inspectors were appointed. But slowly information leaked out—always disputed, always contradicted by King Leopold's ministers and the heads of the Catholic party in Belgium, in spite of the courageous protests of the Catholic missionaries on the spot.

There is no need to go into the nature of the evidence here—it may be consulted by anybody on the shelves of the Anti-Slavery Society in London. Or the names and numbers of the parliamentary papers, and British and American consular reports which confirm the statements of travellers and missionaries and of officers and officials themselves entangled in the system

---

*Memorial to Congress from the American Missionary Societies, January 16, 1905.

†*Red Rubber*, p. 106.

may be found in Mr. Morel's books. In case any reader has
been made sceptical by war-time stories of atrocities, let him
consider that Leopold II was defending himself and his closest
friends against these charges for over twenty years. In this task
he spared neither time nor influence nor money. And year after
year, in speeches and books, openly published, Morel and the
other principal members of the Congo Reform Association accused him of deliberately inciting, bribing, and even command-
ing his officers and soldiers to wholesale murder, rape, arson,
the feeding of troops on human flesh, mutilation, and torture
of every description. They accused the King of doing this deliberately and systematically, to an accompaniment of lying and
corruption, for the sole end of amassing a personal fortune.
They published the names of many of the responsible heads of
the concession companies; they made their charges specific and
personal in the highest degree. They were well known men living
as a rule in England, whose courts would not have hesitated for
a moment to condemn them if what they said overstepped the
limits of legal proof. And no one of them was ever prosecuted
for libel.

That the Leopoldian régime endured in the Belgian Congo for
twenty years was due to the fact that the man responsible for it
was a king, and a king who had enjoyed until middle age a
reputation for virtue and benevolence. The Congo Free State
had been brought into being amid such torrents of eloquence
about helping the natives that it took ordinary people a long
time to make the necessary complete reversal of their opinions.
From the beginning Leopold had realized the need of a complicated defensive organization at home. Side by side with his
system of terrorism in Africa he built up a system of propaganda
and corruption in Europe. To begin with, he farmed out large
areas of the Congo territory—in all perhaps two fifths of the
whole—to companies of persons whom he thought it advisable
to influence. He kept half the shares in each of these companies
for himself; the rest were held by court officials, journalists,
bankers, judges, etc. These enterprises soon became enormously
profitable. Paid-up shares of the A. B. I. R. Company of a par

value of £4.6.6 were freely dealt in at prices between £700 and £1,000. This in itself constituted a barrier against reform, for every step taken to expose the system brought down the value of the shares—which finally, when reform was complete, fell to a few shillings. In addition, the existence of a market in these shares gave the King an opportunity of placing his inside knowledge at the disposal of journalists, financiers, or politicians whom he wished to bribe. He enlisted the general support of the Clerical party in the Belgian Parliament and the unwavering loyalty of their leader, M. Woeste, by various political concessions, though individual Catholics supported the Socialists in their demand first for reform and then for annexation. In Belgium itself the King had the further advantage that he ruled the Congo Free State not as a constitutional monarch, and not in his capacity of King of the Belgians, but as an absolute monarch and purely in his personal capacity.

Even so he felt unsafe; he needed accomplices against a possible day of reckoning. He lay open to the attack of hostile philanthropists in France, Germany, and England. He therefore set about inducing the French to introduce his system into the French Congo. He employed journalists to contrast the enormous profits made by the great Belgian concessions with the small trade done in the "undeveloped" French territory. A wave of speculation in Belgian rubber shares coincided with this effort and attracted the attention of French financiers. Finally, in 1899, after what a well known French writer described as "scandalous financial and political intrigues, bribery and corruption," Leopold succeeded. Within a year the French Congo had been parcelled out among forty financial corporations each with a thirty-year charter. Many of them were partly financed by Belgian capital, and their directorates interlocked with those of the great Belgian concessionaire companies. An attempt was made to extend the system to French West Africa and the German Kamerun. There were powerful trading firms in the first of these colonies, and they combined with the officials to defeat the proposal. In particular the Governor General of French West Africa, M. Ballay, opposed a system which required "a soldier behind every producer." The German government did grant two concessions to Belgo-German companies, but after a year the privileges of these groups were cut down and further applications for concessions refused.

The French Congo lies to the north of the Belgian—it is a country covering 600,000 square miles and carrying just before the war a population of 5,000,000. At the time when the Leopoldian system was introduced, such trade as existed was largely in the hands of trading firms who had established themselves along the sea coast and on the lower reaches of the river Ogowe. Under the new system the concessionaire companies considered themselves entitled, by their charters, to sole possession of all the rubber and ivory in their respective countries, and it followed that trade in these commodities between the natives and any third party became illegal. The natives were forbidden to approach the trading stations. The local administration—which was to receive a royalty of 15 per cent on the company's output —imposed a tax payable in rubber itself, and to be paid to the companies. When, failing legal redress, a revolt occurred against this new state of affairs, the concessionaires sent out their raiding bands, the government its columns of soldiers, to burn and slay from one end of the country to the other.

In 1905 somebody got hold of a batch of suppressed reports made by officials appointed under the De Brazza régime which had preceded this modern exploitation of the Congo. They were published, and they revealed to the French public a state of affairs the exact parallel to what, by that time, was known to be going on in the Belgian Free State. Here all over again were the murders, the mutilations, the women carried off wholesale for the use of troops, the hostage houses, and the atrocities. Tens of thousands of natives were stated to have perished during these first five years. French feeling ran high at these disclosures. The government of the day was alarmed into sending out De Brazza, the former governor, to report on the new régime. His instructions (since published by his widow) contain passages urging him to make it clear that the French system was not similar to the "proceedings of methodical tyranny" which were being carried on in the Congo Free State.

It is true that the French government had not reserved large areas for systematic exploitation on its own account which could be compared to Domaine Privé or the Domaine de la Couronne on the other side of the frontier, but its administration and its armed forces were supporting the concessionaire companies in a system which was identical to that carried on by the corresponding Belgian companies. De Brazza confirmed this. In a way, this was unfortunate. The English Foreign Secretary —Lord Lansdowne—had suggested that an international conference should be held to discuss the affairs of the Congo, and had the French been able to enter such a meeting with a favourable report in their hands the Government of France might have agreed to it. As it was, France joined with Belgium in resisting the calling of a conference, and the proposal was dropped.

De Brazza died on his way home from the colony; his staff were forbidden to draw up a report from the material they had collected, and all that happened was a three days' debate in the French Chamber (February 19–21, 1906). The demand for the publication of De Brazza's material was defeated by 345 to 167, and although charges naming most serious crimes were made against particular companies, and it was proved that the government inspectors were recommending their dissolution, no steps whatever, either then or subsequently, were taken against them. On the contrary, the travelling inspectors, who had at least reported, though their reports had been suppressed, were removed in 1911.

By that time matters were improving in the Belgian Congo. There is no space in this book for a history of the Congo reform movement, and it is enough to say that in 1908 the Congo Free State was formally annexed by the Belgian government under the name of the "Belgian Congo," and that reforms were set on foot so that the worst features at least of the Leopoldian system disappeared. In 1913 the Congo Reform Association was able to meet in London and to dissolve itself in the belief that its work in the Belgian Congo was done. But in the French

Congo it is feared that matters are still far from satisfactory. The latest account which we have in English is *Travels in the Congo* (*Voyage au Congo* and *Le Retour du Tchad*), by M. André Gide, the well known French writer. These two books were published in 1927 and 1928, immediately after his return. M. Gide seems to have gone out on a semi-official mission with no idea at all in his mind that he would be interested in the treatment of the natives. He says that when he had been there for a few weeks he could think of nothing else. Where the natives were under the direct control of the French government he found them poverty-stricken—sometimes starving—but free, once their rubber tax had been paid. This tax was estimated to take them one month's work in the year. But in the interior, where concessions have been granted, he found the old evils still going on. He arrived at one spot six days after a black sergeant had shot twelve men, massacred fifteen women with an axe, and shut five young children up in a hut and set fire to it.* The native who first brought the news to M. Gide's party was thrown into prison for having done so, but M. Gide was able to get him released and the agent of the company prosecuted—with what result the book does not say.

He also found women, some with babies at the breast, forced to make a great embankment of earth which more than once gave way and buried the women and children at the bottom. This "murderous road" was to enable the representative of the Compagnie Forestière to drive along it once a month in his car. He was told that a month before a native had been flogged to death, in the presence of M. Pacha and M. Mandivier, the company's agents, for not bringing in enough rubber.† A chief told him that he had seen ten men die in a single day as a result of ill-treatment. He found children of both sexes taken away from home with halters round their necks and made to work for six days without pay or anything to eat. Again his informant was imprisoned.‡ He was told by a government medical officer that

---

Travels in the Congo, pp. 65–66.
†*Ibid.*, p. 70.
‡*Ibid.*, pp. 148–49.

the Compagnie Forestière breaks all the sanitary regulations and propagates sleeping-sickness in districts free from it by its system of recruitment; that it is "ruining and devastating the country."

Nevertheless, one gathers from what M. Gide does not say that matters are better than they used to be. From systematic massacre things have toned down to such unsystematic murder as we have here described. But it is difficult to get exact information—or even to find out how many concessions are still held by the companies or what they are doing with them.

This account of the massacre of primitive and barbaric societies by the uncontrolled forces of modern industrialism, enterprise, and finance, threatens to grow out of proportion to the rest of our review of human life. It has run away with the pen. And yet only one side of this monstrous rubber story has been told. There is another, later, rubber history almost as depressing if not as horrible as the story of forest rubber. This is the story of plantation rubber. From blood and torture we pass to dismal servitude. In *Asia* for February, 1931, M. Luc Durtain gave an account of work upon the rubber plantations of Indo-China. It is a description of brutal compulsion and unhappiness, inflicted in this case upon Annamese victims.

From this history of rubber-getting a complete description of this aspect of barbaric servitude to modern economic demands would go on to the long, intricate black record of forced labour in South and Central and West Africa, less atrocious, perhaps, but equally unrighteous and unhappy. From rubber it would pass to gold, to diamonds, to cotton and copper. Everywhere there is the same story of greed, of haste. The same crying need for controls is manifest. It is a history of things unforeseen. It is a crowning demonstration of the diabolical possibilities of uncontrolled and uncriticized profit seeking. Supremely it is a story of the new powers and forces that have come to man, running wild and crazy in a last frenzy for private and personal gain.

King Leopold, that *reductio ad horribile* of the obsolete advantages of monarchy in the modern world, is only a crowned

and glorified symbol of a world-wide undisciplined spirit of acquisitiveness. The new economic life has come upon mankind
unheralded and unpremeditated, and first it caught and enslaved
the poor and the children of Great Britain and western Europe,
and now it has spread throughout the earth. The old traditions
of trade and gain and government are insufficient to control it,
and we are still struggling to discover new forms and methods
of control. It feeds and expands the life of hundreds of millions
which could never have come into existence without it, but also
there are those other millions it crushes and torments.

But there for the present we must leave this part of our
spectacle. At this stage of our survey we are not ready to discuss
any solution of the problems that are raised in these two sections. We must go on for a time with our examination of the
developing new world economy that plays such havoc with the
unprepared; then we must go into the question of the motives
that keep people toiling, seeking gain, helping, oppressing, and
destroying one another. After that we shall be able to bring the
operations of finance and the wealth scramble that are so
largely responsible for these stresses into a rational relationship
with the present governments and the present education of mankind.

Then and only then shall we be able to return with sound
comprehensive ideas to the problem of these sufferings, ideas
which will enable us to measure our hope and plan our activities
for ending such distresses for evermore. In these matters indignation is not enough. Indignation without restraint is little more
than a vindictive impulse to extend the area of a wrong. It is
the clear head and the thought-out plan that will lead us to a
happier world. Let us therefore resume our general description
of the organization of modern production.

§ 8. Rationalization

Any talk of the organization of businesses nowadays will
evoke the word *rationalization* at a very early stage. And just
as *democracy, dictatorship, ideology* and *realism* are all used

nowadays to mean something the reverse or almost the reverse of their original significance, so *rationalization* also is an inverted term. To rationalize has one meaning in psychology, another meaning in the sociological writings of Max Weber, and quite another in the loose discussions of modern politicians and business men. We are using it here in its current popular sense.

It is one of those words which are really easier to understand than to define. Mr. Urwick, in his very illuminating book, *The Meaning of Rationalization,* gives a pleasing variety of "definitions" by a number of people who for the most part do not define it at all. They talk of the "spirit of rationalization" and what it is intended to do. The gist is a repudiation of haphazard—of uncontrolled—"evolution" in a number of fields where it has hitherto ruled; a recognition that planned and calculated design and adjustment are needed throughout the whole world of economic life. Such are the root conceptions of this work, and they are conceptions that have been growing more and more plainly acceptable for some years. Their practical application has been, so far, more effective in the United States and Germany than in Britain, but their discussion has been, as are all such discussions nowadays, world-wide.*

An outstanding, indeed a heroic, exponent of rationalization in Germany was Walther Rathenau. It was the late Lord Melchett who popularized the word in England. At times he used it—evidently with "anti-Socialist" controversy in his mind—almost as if it were the antithesis of nationalization; his reasonable point being that business can be better reformed and reconstructed from within by business men, than from without by politicians. But the word has a much wider sweep than that would give it.

It took some time for the leaders of British financial and industrial thought to arrive at this idea of a planned remodelling of business organization. Their ideas, because they have an older tradition, remain much more "individualist" and "evolutionary" than those of their American and German equivalents.

---

*A clear and interesting sample of the spirit of Rationalization up to date is Donham's *Business Adrift,* with an Introduction by Professor Whitehead (1931).

At the end of the war their first apparent impulse, unhappily too effective, was to escape from all coördinating controls and stampede back to the happy days of detached profit-seeking before the war. It took quite a long time for them to discover that the days before the war were no longer available as an objective, and meanwhile other countries moved forward intellectually and practically.

Rationalization is often confused with headlong amalgamation. It is nothing of the sort. It may be easily possible to carry the coalescence of business organization too far. Points may be reached, varying with the particular industry concerned and with regional conditions, at which the advantages of economies are balanced by the difficulties of management and direction, and beyond these points there may be an increasing loss of vigour and effectiveness with increasing scale. With regard to certain overriding broad services such as transport, the rational distribution of various staple products, and the like, there may be no real essential obstacle between existing conditions and a rationalized world control; but with regard to much of the business of the world the most favourable dimensions for autonomous businesses may be reached at a far less universalized level.

In some, and possibly in many, directions attempts at unified organization may have already been carried beyond a favourable extreme. And they may have been carried in the wrong direction. Combination should aim at material industrial advantages. So far as "rationalization" means that, it is little more than what was known before the war as "coöperation"—in restraint of injurious competition. There should be physical economies; less fetching and carrying, less waiting and delay, a steadier employment of power, a better division of labour, a shortening of time, less "splash," the elimination of intermediate profits. Such are the legitimate ends of the rationalization process. We do, however, find a type of merger which is merely financial, a merger to monopolize a market rather than serve a public better. We can but glance here, anticipating various issues we shall have to raise later, at the way in which national tariff arrangements may facilitate such merely financial profiteering combinations. World-wide free trade and a world-wide common commercial law might result not in an increase but in a break-up of many large industrial constellations, at present operating rather in restraint of trade than for economy of service.

How far the size of an industrial concern may be increased depends also very largely upon the level of intelligence and honesty and the facilities of intercommunication in the community in which the concern is operating. These set temporary and removable limits to super-organization, but there are also very definite maximum limits to every type of control and association, limits due to irremediable mechanical difficulties, just as there are definite material limits to the size of every type of animal and vegetable organism. There is a relation between the intricacy and largeness of a job to be done and the amount of gray matter to be devoted to it. The most powerful mind conceivable cannot give more than four and twenty hours of attention to the details of a task. As the breadth of a control increases, its complexity of intervention must diminish.

In addition to these essential limitations to the concentration of control there is an immense variety of forms of human production and transmission, where the need for a very high degree of detailed freedom is imperative. A very precise limit is set, for example, to the activity of multiple retail shops. They can distribute standardized things, but they are useless or vulgarizing and mischievous when they attempt to deal in objects in which a certain individuality is essential. You cannot have chain shops to sell pictures. You cannot, as another example, have satisfactory mass-produced costumes for women. People weary even of cigarettes, cakes and tea in uniform packets, and where a chain-shop organization has bought up all the groceries of a countryside, it is not uncommon to find little enterprises springing up, "Ye Olde Tea Shoppe," or "Lavender's Parlour," or suchlike quaintness, in which a couple of maiden ladies will sell recommended teas of obscure purveyance and home-made cakes, at Bond Street prices, and do very well by it. Their human inefficiency seems more welcome than the hard, limited certainty of the packet. Similarly, there is always room for the small manufacturer of "special" individual cigarettes in the smarter quarter of any city.

When we come to the selling of any kind of work into which a strong element of artistry enters, the objection to wholesale dealing is fundamental. It would be interesting to find out how far the big general stores of America and Europe, which attempt to deal in everything under the sun, have been obliged to make such departments as bookselling, tailoring, furniture and so forth, autonomous and self-subsisting. It would be equally interesting to find out how far such an industry as that of the dress fabrics of Lyons has had to follow the same process. Distinctive designs are produced exclusively for special buyers who make costumes for a select clientèle, and this must necessitate independent or quasi-independent small manufacturing concerns. I believe that it would be possible to trace a very widespread process of internal decentralization and rehabilitated freedom, in modern production and trade. Many great concerns may prove on examination to be like the present British Empire, an association of practically independent organizations with nothing to link them except the "golden link" of ownership by an overriding company—a sort of parallel to the golden-link function of the imperial crown.

Rationalization, we repeat, is not amalgamation. Economy, research in common, exchange of information, exchange of services, elimination of competition in buying and selling alike, mutual financial accommodation, agreements to share out work so that one concern may concentrate upon this type or model of production and another upon that, these are among the essentials of rationalization. For a conception of economic life that is all adventure and speculation, jostling cut-throat competition for profits, conflict and waste, rationalization substitutes the idea of a planned, statistic-ruled system, adequately and efficiently productive and distributive. For conflicting completely separated businesses, it substitutes the idea of interrelated and confluent businesses. It is in fact Nominalism instead of Realism applied to the titles of firms and the names of undertakings. Because a mass of activities are assembled for a time under one name, that does not mean we are dealing with a permanently distinct organization in conflict with similar organizations. Rationalization sets its face against that delusion; it is indeed essentially a revolt against that delusion.

Naturally rationalization comprehends the idea of scientific management and stimulates its application. Expressing as it does the feeling that for every process there is a best way which is the right way, *it involves the repudiation of the idea that individual profits are the test and end of business success*. The discussion of motive in social life is a very important one; we shall devote to it the whole chapter following this one, but here we must note that rationalization is in effect a renunciation on the part of its advocates of any priority of the owners' profits over the health, vigour and future development of the service or industry rationalized. That is a profoundly significant change of front in the world's business life. And advances upon that new front must bring us at last logically to the realization of the whole world as one organized business system.

§ 9. *The Coöperative Movement**

We have already noted the characteristics of coöperative retailing in our account of the buying and selling of goods. But coöperative retailing is only one aspect of a constructive movement of very great significance in our present welter of economic experiment and reconstruction. It is mainly confined to the more highly industrialized countries of Europe. Differences in phase of economic development have checked its appearance in America. In our account we shall have to glance at various considerations that will be dealt with more directly in our subsequent chapters (VIII) on social motive, (IX) finance, and (X) wealth. It is impossible to consider the coöperative movement as concerned solely with economic method and mechanism.

In its wider sense the term "coöperation" covers all that

*See *Self and Society:* a collection of essays published by the C. W. S.; B. and S. Webb: *The Consumers' Coöperative Movement;* P. Redfern: *The Consumers' Place in Society;* E. Poisson: *The Coöperative Republic,* and Professor Bernard Lavergne: *L'Ordre Coopératif.*

rationalization implies and more also. As Professor Henry Clay points out, "every sort of voluntary association to restrain reckless individual self-seeking, cut-throat competition,"* and the like, is essentially a coöperative association. Price agreements, cartels, trusts, trade unions, employers' associations, all fall within the term.

But when we speak not of coöperation generaily, but of the coöperative movement as it is manifested through such organizations as the English and Scottish Coöperative Wholesale Societies, the French Consumers' Coöperative Societies, and their associated propaganda, then we are dealing with something at once more specific and more far-reaching than any mere combination to control competition. The movement looks beyond immediate relief and economies to a new world, to the Coöperative Republic, the Coöperative Commonweal. It carries its projects of rationalization right up to the social and political reconstruction of the human community. It is a theory of society based on the idea of man as a consumer. The customer has looked at the world, and this movement is the outcome.

Since Britain and France were the first countries to experience the industrial and mechanical revolutions, it was natural that in these countries also the first attempts should be made to stem the destructive effects of the chaotic individualism these changes released. There are records of the coöperative buying of food by workers to protect themselves from the rapacity of retailers before the end of the eighteenth century, but it was only after the end of the Napoleonic Wars that systematic attempts to arrest the storm of reckless competition, of underselling and underpaying, of sweating and social degradation, began in real earnest. Robert Owen in England, and Fourier and Saint Simon in France, are the outstanding figures of that new effort. We owe both the word "socialism" and the phrase coöperative movement" to Robert Owen, and in their early stages the ideas conveyed by these words were closely akin. They spring from the same root. We have no space here for a history of the development and variation of socialist ideas. The

*Economics for the General Reader, Chapter VI, § 3.

basal concept of the coöperative movement as distinguished from other branches of the Owenite stem was the voluntary combination of individuals into associations for producing, buying and selling, for mutual aid and for the education of their children. These associations were to form, so to speak, the nuclei of a new social life amidst the stresses of the old. They were to succeed and multiply and coalesce at last into a new human society. Socialist thought moved away from this idea in the direction of the "social revolution" of the Communists or of socialization through the development of public services (Fabianism). The coöperative movement, on the other hand, seeking to "crystallize" a new world out of the current disorderly liquefaction of the old social order, narrowed down to small voluntary associations.

For some decades the history of coöperation was one of experiments, for the most part unsuccessful. The idea produced, however, devoted workers and thinkers like George Jacob Holyoake in England and Charles Gide in France; it found willing and untiring, unsalaried officials and organizers; it tried and tried again to achieve realization. All men are not self-seekers, or there could be no coöperative movement to-day. Only gradually was it realized that the systematic development of a growing and spreading coöperative organization must begin at the consumers' end. It was in 1844 that the Rochdale society hit upon the idea of a "dividend," which we have already described in Chapter VI, § 4, and found in that idea the way to solvent and efficient coöperative marketing, and about eighteen years later there were enough successful coöperative retail societies in operation to found the still vigorous and expanding British and Scottish Coöperative Wholesale Societies. Concurrently propagandist and educational organizations were formed. From that time onward the history of British coöperation has been one of discreet but steady expansion, until there are now 6,000,000 members of the British consumers' coöperatives representing certainly over 18,000,000 of the population. For a time the coöperative idea in France was applied chiefly to production groups, but in 1885 a nuclear consumers' coöperative appeared at Nîmes, and the movement has now attained to a membership of over 2,000,000. It is strictly a workers' movement. Even in Great Britain it has never spread upward to the middle classes.

The coöperative movement has always been quietly but persistently propagandist and enterprising. And it has always displayed a strongly cosmopolitan disposition. Its tentacles spread throughout Europe and reach to India and Japan. Gradually the difficulties in the way of producer coöperation have been studied and solved. In Ireland, in Russia, Italy and other mainly agricultural countries the unit coöperative society has been a society for the joint purchase and use of agricultural machinery, for mutual credit and for marketing. The Coöperative Wholesale Society trades as a unit with the Russian coöperatives, and British coöperatives farm, manufacture, finance, publish and educate, as well as trade.

And yet one may doubt whether this movement, as it exists at present, will ever crystallize out into that promised new world. That new world, it would seem, needs something more, much more, than is to be found in this sane and discreet extension of membership and activities. It may be overtaken by other forces, more powerfully and rapidly constructive. It is significant that the coöperative movement has failed to take root in America. It has been nipped in its initial consumers' retail phase, as we have noted in Chapter VI, § 4, by the competition of the more vigorous and varied department and chain stores. Trade-union enterprise has anticipated some of its productive possibilities and the greater mobility of the population has been against it. The modernization of economic life has reached such a point in America that the possibility of slow progressive crystallizations has passed.

In Russia all the coöperatives were abolished in 1920, and restored, with a difference, in 1924. How far they can now be regarded as voluntary associations it is impossible to say. In Russia, excluding the Ukraine, they include 15,000,000 members, and they conduct nearly half of the country's retail trade. Their federal organization, the Centrosoyus, conducts great trading operations with the English Coöperative Wholesale

Society. In Italy again the National Union of Coöperative Societies was suppressed in November, 1925, and replaced by state control. The organization ceased, in fact, to be a voluntary coöperation; it became a state machine. While in America economic development had apparently rendered the coöperative movement unnecessary, in the Bolshevik and Fascist State Socialisms its organizations have been seized upon and incorporated with the governmental machinery.

In the perspective of a western European point of view the coöperative movement is seen to grow, but, to be slightly paradoxical, it grows without animation. Professor Lavergne, in his sound and ample book *L'Ordre Coopératif* (Volume I, 1926), is confident of the merits and future of coöperation. By a series of metamorphoses, he says, "the coöperative, formerly a petty district shop distributing small necessities, has become big industry and big business, destined heir of those great public services whose direction overstrains the political State. It is profoundly important to the social sciences to demonstrate that the coöperative principle—which leads towards a happy democratization of incomes—can supplant both the old ideal of State socialism and the more recent idea of municipalization. From the facts, too long neglected, of coöperative progress, the lesson emerges luminously, that both private capitalism and socialist régimes can pass on to a new order which combines their merits and has none of their defects." P. Redfern, in the Encyclopædia Britannica article, cites facts which seem to justify Professor Lavergne. He tells of the International Coöperative Alliance, "a minor league of nations" with 85,000 societies in 36 countries, the International Coöperative Wholesale Society representing 28,000,000 members, of a Special Coöperative party (of five members) in the British Parliament, to which 423 societies with a membership roll of 3,281,971 persons are affiliated. He tells of great educational and propagandist activities. To these we may add Lavergne's account of the coöperatives of communes and municipalities in Belgium to run light railways, electric distribution, and other public services. But in contrast with Lavergne, Redfern ends his article—doubtfully.

There are 6,000,000 coöperators in Britain. What proportion of them see anything more in coöperation than the source of that useful "dividend"? Twenty-eight million adults would be a mighty force to bring about a coöperative world state or at least a coöperative Europe, but how many of that 28,000,000 would even trouble to attend a public demonstration in its favour? The movement has prospered through the passionate devotion of a few hundred or a few thousand men. How far have they imparted their passion to the masses of the movement? For my own part I can testify that, though one English adult in eight is a coöperator, and though I talk freely with all sorts of people, I have never heard any single person boast that he was a member of this great movement. I know several people whose eyes brighten at the words "social revolution," but none who become exalted at "coöperative republic." And never have I overheard anyone anywhere pointing to an exceptionally beautiful car, or a fine bicycle, or tasting tea or coffee or butter, or noting a lovely dress stuff or a wonderful costume, or admiring the decoration of a fine public building, say: "That is *our* stuff, coöperative stuff. Those others cannot produce stuff like ours." But then I belong to the south of England, and the north, I am told, feels very differently. There such popular music-hall stars as Gracie Fields sing songs in favour of the Coöps which are received with enthusiasm, and the Glasgow housewife would never "go past the Coöp." But even in Glasgow, would a man feel proud to be told that he looked as if he had been rigged out at a Coöp?

Enthusiasm and distinction may increase. The European coöperatives supply good honest goods at honest prices but they do not lead in the production of better and novel goods. They do not supply *interesting* goods. The privately owned shop can beat them at that. They may evoke partisan excitement, but they do not evoke pride. They have grown to great things in a hundred years, but they have to grow still more rapidly in this age of new bigness if they dream of leading the world. Or as Mr. Redfern puts it: "Whether the movement can lead a stubborn world decisively along this coöperative road, probably will depend more and more, not only on its numbers but also on its power to enlist intelligence, and develop in all ranks a leadership capable both of creating enthusiasm and producing everyday conviction amongst the masses of mankind."

Which is not to say that the coöperative movement will be so much defeated and disappear as be overtaken—as it has already been overtaken in Russia and Italy—and incorporated in bolder and wider enterprises with a more explicit plan and a deeper emotional drive.

§ 10. *The Public or Private Direction of Big Industries and General Services*

What do we find playing the rôle of a head to the greater number of businesses and services, of economic coöperations, that is to say, in the modern community? It is sometimes a proprietor, but not so frequently as it was a century ago. It is more often a partnership. Most businesses and services confess to a founder, to a single man who, either alone or in congenial partnership, made the concern in the first place. But most typically, nowadays, the business or service has become a company, and the headship vests in a board of directors on which the original organizer or his heirs sit dwindling in relative importance. The company has created a body of shareholders who in their annual meeting exercise certain limited powers of criticism and of changing the directors. And the directors in council deal with the managers and so forth who run the operations of the concern.

But side by side with businesses and services directed in this way we now find others run by managers and officials appointed by the elected representatives of city, county, country or other governmental constituencies. Except for the final bookkeeping of the concern, these publicly owned services and industrial plants bear the closest resemblance to their privately owned and organized parallels. The criticism of the shareholders' meeting is replaced by the criticism of the voters. There is no distribution of profits: that is the essential difference. The profits, if any, go to reduce charges or relieve taxation. The tendency is to keep profits down and give better and cheaper services or products to the general public. Sometimes, where there are no profits but losses, the loss is justified on the grounds of the common convenience. These public enterprises have increased in proportion to the private profit-making concerns during the last half century, and their development and substitution for the latter is one practical outcome of socialist thought and propaganda.

A vast, voluminous literature has been devoted to the rights and wrongs and the relative efficiency and vigour of initiative of these two forms of economic process. The two classes of enterprise are connected in practice by many intervening forms. There is no hard-and-fast boundary. At one end of the series you have concerns run on privately owned premises and working entirely with privately acquired material. But few businesses attain to considerable proportions without trenching on roads and waterways and the like, requiring concessions from public bodies and access to material in the public domain. They then—like the railways—expose themselves to public responsibility and a measure of public control. If a public body will not take over such businesses, it must still inspect and restrain them to the best of its ability. If it does not provide directors, it provides controllers and inspectors. And if the publicly owned service has no shareholders, it has had to begin more or less with a capital outlay, and that has had to be provided by an issue of bonds secured on the rates and taxes of the community. Few people can tell a privately owned from a publicly owned omnibus, or a company glass of water from a municipal glass of water. Comparatively few Londoners, for example, know whether the water they drink has yielded a profit to anyone or not.

It is alleged in the controversies between Individualism and Socialism, controversies still garrulous in their decay, that the search for profit has an enormously stimulating effect upon the energy, enterprise and responsiveness of a concern. The profit motive plus competition is regarded as the perfect method of adjusting supply to need; the consumer is supposed to have unlimited leisure to pick and choose and go from one firm to another. In practice various forms of rationalization are destroying competition, and few of us have the leisure to hover over and judge most of our purchases. The critics of Socialism assert, moreover, that a profound moral difference exists between those who work under the direction of proprietors seeking profit and those who work under the direction of elected persons. The former are understood to be kept up to the mark by the balance sheet; they are alert, enterprising, energetic, economical; they have been chosen for their profit-making fitness, and they must continue to display that fitness, for upon it they depend for their positions. But transfer these men to a publicly owned concern, and at once they change in character; they become slack, extravagant, careless, they feel themselves above criticism and irremovable. The same manager who will work with disinterested zeal for a company and choose his subordinates with an acute regard for their suitability and loyalty will, so soon as he becomes a manager under a public body, evoke a vast crowd of relations and dependents to whom he will distribute places with an utter disregard for their suitability. Moreover, the public business is amenable to the politician, and the politician, they say, will be swayed by the votes of the workers more than by the votes of the public he serves, and he will sacrifice the interests of the business to his private ends and the exigencies of his party—while no private owner would ever dream of sacrificing the quality of a product or service to the exigencies of finance.

Most of this we would dismiss at once as preposterous nonsense if it were not for the fact that it is a quite fair summary of much that is said and written as anti-socialist argument.

We are dealing here with a limitless chaos of accusations and excuses through which we might blunder interminably, sinking now into morasses of twaddle and now entangling ourselves in libel actions. The plain facts of the case seem to be that as businesses grow beyond the scale of one-man concerns, they become impersonal in character, and that by the time they have reached the dimensions of a railway system, a modern catering organization, an urban water or milk supply, the differences between public and private ownership cease to be matters of structure, organization, or working efficiency, and remain only differences in the spirit of the direction.

Publicly conducted business may be in many cases unenterprising because of the ordinary politician's habit of following, rather than leading, public opinion and his dread of popular hostility to changes, but privately owned business may more easily develop conspiracies to monopolize markets or raw material, and so restrain innovation. Private-profit, coöperative, municipal, and State directorates all tend to develop characteristic faults; none are perfect. All work better in the light of intelligent criticism, for the responsible official is by the nature of his training more responsive to good repute than to gain. But criticism must be intelligent and fair and open. Adequate criticism is the preservative of all human affairs, and while public concerns may suppress criticism by governmental action, private businesses have shown themselves extremely able and energetic in controlling the press—which is their medium for advertisement—for the anticipation and strangulation of adverse comment. (Newspapers are very chary of publishing the names of advertising firms convicted for adulteration, for example.) The public authorities of a region at a low level of social organization and general education are incapable of conducting even quite limited businesses; but public authorities and government departments administering large areas, scientifically organized and sustained by an intelligent community, may be able to direct production and service with an efficiency far exceeding that possible under a profit-seeking group. It is a question of scale and of quality.

It would be easy to cite local authorities, state governments, small sovereign powers, which have fallen more or less completely under the sway of great business organizations altogether too powerful and efficient for them. The great trading companies of the seventeenth and eighteenth centuries, the East

India Company, for example, exceeded and subdued governments and became themselves quasi-states. The armament industry, as we shall tell later (Chapter XII, § 9), played the rôle of a super-state in Europe. Gangs of politicians can seize control of the State and sell the State's authority to private entrepreneurs. That flat opposition in thought, of private control versus public control, is therefore a misleading one. It throws a false simplicity over the vast and intricate variety of ways in which human coördination can be arranged and worked.

Later on (in Chapter X), in certain studies we shall make of particular instances of wealth aggregation, we shall note the way in which the private ownership of great economic utilities lends itself to the purposes of the financial adventurer. Publicly owned utilities are not subject to such mischief because the rapid and violent changes in control due to the forced or panic selling of their stocks and shares, cannot occur.

§ 11. *Grades of Social Organization*

What has gone before makes it very plain that for every sort of collective enterprise there must be grades of organization whose practicability and applicability depend on the interplay of a number of mutually interacting variables.

For example, there is the state of the general intelligence and of the public understanding of, and acquiescence in, the enterprise. The telegraph has been hampered in its extension through some parts of tropical Africa by the artistic preference of the natives for bracelets and anklets of copper wire and their lack of sympathy for unguarded property. The early development of letter boxes in several European countries was delayed by the temptations offered to the facetious young. Large-scale agriculture in Russia has had to struggle against the love of the peasant for taking machinery to pieces and his lassitude in the phase of reassembly. The willing coöperation of the public is essential to the spread of every new invention and the working of almost every public service. At every level of intelligence and public spirit there is a type of organization which will prove most successful with the public—and there will also be types above and types below its requirements.

Similarly, for every factory there is a relationship between the work and the available personnel. Women and men cannot work together unless a certain minimum of restraint and decency has been attained. You must drop all sorts of methods if your workers cannot read. There must be certain standards of honour in effective operation. A sanitary service in French North Africa attempted to restrain the eye disease so prevalent there by distributing lotions for the eyes of the children affected. It was necessary to entrust the distribution to native agents, who, forthwith, put a price on the stuff, set up as quack practitioners and largely defeated the end for which they were employed. The honesty of the staff in any retailing concern is not simply a matter of discipline and supervision; it is also a matter of the general social tone of the employees. All sorts of modern trading operations become impossible with a filching staff or a filching clientèle. The old Phœnician traders bought and sold with arms in their hands. The abolition of haggling in retail trade released vast possibilities of distributive organization that did not exist before prices became fixed. In the West End of London anyone with a banker's reference can have goods sent to his home on approval, and one may confidently buy goods without even asking the price until the bill comes home.

The extension of the idea of function to the trader and manufacturer and the increasing confidence of the buyer open wider and wider possibilities to trade and manufacture. Every step towards general honesty in regard to metal, coins, notes and cheques diminishes friction and enlarges the vigour and scope of economic operations. In ordinary life every one of us knows the difference in speed and precision of dealing, between the fair dealer with a conception of a legitimate due and the fellow who watches for a chance of a smart turn on us, and who seems unhappy in his trading unless he leaves resentment in his wake.

We may ascend the scale to the financial and economic advantages of government enterprises. What can be done in comprehensive production by public ownership where there is a conception of public duty and an intelligent public alert to enforce it, is altogether beyond what can be attempted in a society where political success is regarded as a legitimate opportunity for unrestricted gain.

But we will not multiply instances to show how dependent our economic development is upon these matters of atmosphere, on the grade and quality of popular education and the existence of an effective public opinion. All we wish to establish here is that for every level of education and public morale there is a limit to the size and complexity of businesses possible. What would be unwieldy at one stage becomes practicable and easy in another. The obvious course for the great city would be fantastic absurdity in a kraal. These considerations lead us on to what is the very quintessence of this work, to the truth that with every grade and type of human social, economic and political association, there should go a certain definite philosophical foundation of a certain sort and a certain quality of educational training. The educational and practical factors should interlock, each sustaining the other. Educational revolutions must accompany economic and political revolutions. All economic enlargements, all economic progress, demand an adequate corresponding modification of teaching in the schools. They are ideas in action. They fail or they prevail by the ideas they encounter.

To the relationship between the ideas in a man's head and the part he will play in social and economic life we will therefore direct our attention in the next chapter.

CHAPTER THE EIGHTH

WHY PEOPLE WORK

CHAPTER THE EIGHTH

WHY PEOPLE WORK

§ 1. *The Persona and Conduct*

AND now we open up the fourth, the final and most important, section of our examination of human activities, the portion devoted to Will and the organization of Will. We have to enquire what forces within mankind keep all this great economic system going.

We have thrown a picture on the screen, so to speak, showing our contemporary world ant-hill at work and being fed, clothed, housed and induced to buy this, that and the other necessity or luxury, and in this picture, thus far, the men and women who work and buy and sell have been represented for the most part as moving about like neat little toy men and women in a working model. For all we have said hitherto, the participants in most of the operations might be wooden dolls wired to move and play their parts in the general scheme. Well-disposed dolls. No word have we said yet of those deep discontents that lie at the root of strikes and labour troubles generally, nor of disloyalty to the general task of production.

But now we have to get inside these puppets and make them come alive. We have to ask why they work and buy and sell. Why do they carry on at all? Why do they do it? Why do they stand it? How do they feel about it? We have to redeem the promise of our opening and explore the psychology of work and wealth.

At the outset we made it clear how large a part suppression played in the socialization of man. We have reiterated the essential difference of man's social life from that of any other social creature's. While the social life of the insect world is essentially instinctive, and the various workers, soldiers, queens and what not, are moved by simple inherent impulses to play their part in the biological and economic whole, *Homo sapiens* has undergone no such adaptation and specialization. He plays his individual part through a balance of motives. He is *educated* to his rôle. It is rare that he is completely fitted to his job. Generally he does what he has to do with a very considerable amount of internal conflict and external friction. At bottom he is still a highly individualized animal, resentful of subordination, competitive and exclusive, demanding freedom and the world for himself.

But he is also amenable to fear and affection and capable of self-restraint and reservation. In the *Science of Life* we have traced the growth of the human community through the establishment of the primary taboos, and we have shown how ideas of superiority and inferiority, of leadership and obedience, were established in youth and sustained, imposed, upon the unwilling mind of adult man. From his very dawn into the world *Homo sapiens* is a creature at war within himself; he has a moral conflict; he controls his impulses, he does things that he dislikes, and in particular he toils to escape other possibilities that he fears will be even less agreeable. This internal conflict is essential to the nature of man. He can never escape from it; never return to the simple internal unanimity, the "state of innocence," the direct unencumbered reactions, of lower animal types. But he will not be content with a bare recognition of the restraints upon him. He will shrink from the unpleasant fact of his own unwillingness. He will always be seeking consciously and subconsciously a personal adjustment of this conflict; he will always be trying to group his motives about as agreeable a conception of himself, within the range of his possibilities, as he can contrive.

A man's guiding and satisfying idea of himself is what Jung calls his *"persona."* It is a very well chosen term. The original meaning of *persona* was the mask worn by an actor in the Greek and Roman drama. It gave his "character," it was what he thought he was. In his hand he carried his *rotulus,* his little roll on which was written the part he had to play in the story, his *rôle*. It was what he had to do. From the very beginnings of the human adventure and throughout the whole world to-day every human being is steering a cherished persona through the allurements, buffetings and frustrations of life. That is "conduct." Every one of these busy puppets we have seen making and buying and selling in the great economic spectacle we have displayed has a persona, an idea of himself, either more or less harmonized to and accepting the rôle he has to play, or more or less in rebellion against that rôle. The continued, progressive working of this continually more complicated and continually more centralized economic society of mankind is dependent upon the sustained harmony between its operations and the hundreds of millions of personas involved in them. Beneath the material processes of economics lies the social idea; its driving force is will. The clearer the idea, the better organized the will in the personas of our species, the more hopeful and successful the working of the human ant-hill.*

§ 2. *The First Class of Persona: The Peasant Persona and Types Mainly Derived from It*

The earlier subjugations of man to toil were comparatively crude. Fear of the stronger individuals, the chief and leading men within the tribe, was sublimated as a sense of obligation, and the disposition to accept their rule was sustained by the greater fear of wandering from the tribe into the wilderness. The retention of immature characters has been a frequently

---

*The reader will find much that is said here in terms derived from Jung put in quite another terminology in, for example, Chapter XVII (Wages) of Henry Clay's excellent *Economics for the General Reader*. His is the more orthodox phrasing. There the willingness to work is studied in relation to what is called the "standard of life" of the worker. A man's standard of life, his conception, that is, of what is due to him and his proper scale and quality of living, is not, of course, his whole persona as we have here defined it, but it is, from the economic point of view, a very important factor in his persona. But the persona brings in a vast motivating complex over and above the standard of life; it brings in his sense of obligation, of what it is graceful and becoming to do, his pride, what is honourable or insulting for him; and we believe that for the purposes of social and political as well as economic analysis, the wider mode of approach adopted here is altogether more comprehensive and effective.

recurring event in animal evolution. The common man, as he grew up, escaped less and less from the natural subordination of childhood. As life grew more secure and productive and laborious, toil came to him as part of that subjugation.

In those obscure ages during which human society developed, in that phase of the taming of the human animal to subordinated associations into which the archæologist, the psychoanalyst and the student of primitive expression now probe, there were built up traditional systems of personas, or, if you prefer the phrase, "ideals of rôles," to which we find men adapted, as writing and record develop and their mental lives become accessible to us. We find them subdued to the conception of the classes to which they belong. We find them all saying to themselves, "This is what I am. This is what is becoming for me to do. This is what I will not endure." It is manifestly necessary, if we are to carry this survey into the field of mental reactions, that we should attempt here some sort of classification of the primitive types of persona. Man, as history in the narrower sense, history in human record, dawns, has ceased to be a spontaneous wild man, he has brought himself into a community through this self-reference to an ideal of a rôle.

What, then, are the chief forms of these operative rôles?

Here we shall have to break at times into what is almost untouched ground. Into it we must go with humility, apologies and the firmest resolution to explore it as thoroughly as we can. Social psychology has hardly begun. It is extraordinary that it was not begun long ago. Economic science, in all its schools, has been accustomed and content to work upon the crudest assumptions about motive, that it is possible to make. The Marxist indeed makes some pretensions to psychology with his phrases about a "class-conscious proletariat" and a "bourgeois mentality" and the like. He shows at least an awareness of differences of persona. But under the stresses of political and social combat such phrases have long since degenerated into mere weapons, aspirations and terms of abuse. So discredited and warped are they that they will be of no use to us here.

The basal mentality of that traditional social order from

which we are now emerging seems to be that of the types for which we have used the general name of peasant. The distinctive character of the peasant type of persona is its complete acceptance of the idea that toil is virtue, and its close, intense adhesion to property and the acquisition of property. All over the world and continually peasants murder for property. Wherever there is a peasant countryside the newspapers rarely go for many weeks without an account of such a murder. Murders of passion characterize towns and the middle and upper classes. The peasant lusts and breeds, but without any pride or romantic play. He trains his young to toil at an early age, to getting and to avarice.

His suppressions make him prone to envy. His soul is equalitarian. His hostility to exceptional display imposes a standard costume and decorum upon any countryside where his is the dominant ideology. Housing and furniture too are standardized there, and the slightest departures from the rigidities of usage provoke a bitter resentment and moral condemnation. Everywhere in Europe and Asia where the peasant persona rules, sentimentalists delight to prate of its lovely local costumes and customs, its music and art. Everywhere, except for differences due to conditions of climate and natural resources, these costumes and art are practically the same, the industriously made lace, the bright buttons, the white linen, the red and black colourings, the tedious repetitive carving, the traditional music, the staid dancing, the plaintive and tragic song. It is essentially and visibly the same from Biscay and Brittany to China.

The peasant's persona is subdued to a life of hard monotonies and stereotyped pleasures. He is always under the observation of his neighbours. He is much worried about his character and personal prestige; he exists because of his reputation—for this or that—for his good thatching or his skilful pruning of the vines. When he is sober he is afraid. He is afraid of his lord, afraid of the opinion of those about him, afraid of lawyers with "bits of writing," and of priests with mysterious powers over the gates of heaven and hell. Drink releases a fund of suppressed brutality and self-assertion. With pestilence or bad seasons the subjugated imagination escapes very readily into superstitious observances. The puzzled and distressed peasant is never very remote from the ancient blood sacrifice. His religion is primordial, it is unsophisticated superstition, entirely unspiritual.

All these realities must, by a psychological necessity, be made to appear in the peasant's consciousness of himself in the most pleasing light possible—interwoven with a palatable presentation of any individual idiosyncrasy he may possess. He asks no why nor wherefore to explain his work and his property. There they are. What else could you have? But about himself, against any lurking doubts he must be sturdily reassured. He sees himself therefore as a good honest fellow, the friend of that friend of his, the local god or the Good God, as the case may be. That god also is as possessive and jealous and as hostile to strange ways and displays as his Maker. The peasant's God and the peasant stand upon their "rights" and do what they like with their own. The peasant is free from affectations and fal-lals, and none can better him at a bargain. Let anyone who would do him an injury beware. But nothing "stuck-up" or arrogant enters into his composition. He can be shrewd as well as worthy. He "knows his way about" and is far too wise to make enemies of the rich and great. A certain humour helps him to swallow and ignore any humiliation that may come to him. He will laugh and, later on, get the better of them. The mills of the peasant, he flatters himself, grind slowly, but they grind exceeding small. On such terms with himself he finds his rôle in life endurable. It is a great consolation to reflect that many are (deservedly) worse off than himself.

Derived very directly from this fundamental type of human persona is that of the mediocre town dweller who has drifted in from the countryside. The normal townsman is indeed a transplanted peasant. This peasant-minded townsman is under the same necessity to reconcile his egoism to a laborious and inferior rôle, and he displays the same consequent exaltation of toil as a virtue, the same self-congratulation upon simplicity, sardonic humour and sagacity, and the same disposition to

avarice and a tenacious adherence to a residuum of "rights."
He is brought into closer contact with a greater number of
people, and that gives him a greater mental quickness. He
needs a livelier sense of the instability and ultimate humiliation
of those of better estate than himself, because their better
fortune presses upon him more closely.

In most forms of popular religion throughout the world, the
theory of compensations hereafter has been a useful help to
equanimity. The priest, amidst the closer population of the
town, has always been less of a medicine man and more of a
consoler than upon the more superstitious countryside. He has
played a helpful part in the reconciliation of man to his destiny
during the ages of toil. In the end he still assures us, Lazarus
will corner the water supply of Dives. And the affections and
relationships of family life have afforded the peasant type
throughout the world, the consolations of authority and self-
esteem which it has had to relinquish so largely in its outward
social rôle. He clings to his family, therefore, as he clings to
his scrap of property, and resists any infringement of his
absolute ownership of either. They constitute his inner freedom,
his private assurance, his self-respect. To lose them is to become
a lost soul, a wanderer or a slave. He may have to submit, as
peasants in Russia and central Europe submitted until quite
recently, to such little infringements as the *"droit du seigneur."*
But after all that was soon over and he was left master in his
own hovel, free to beat and compel. It was just another tax in
kind which you evaded if you could and yielded if you had to.

Arising out of this great and world-wide system of tradition
and interpretation, which gives us the peasant type of persona
—the prevalent type of human persona still—are others,
essentially of the same nature, but liberated or disturbed by
certain broad modifications of condition. In the town and in the
countryside individuals may prosper exceptionally. They may
get enough property to give employment to their less successful
fellows or to lend them money and entangle them in debt. The
acquisitive and competitive sides of the peasant mentality may
lead them to a position in which they may even come to defy

their original traditions so far as to indulge in display and open arrogance. The rich townsman, the moneylender and middleman, the big peasant and farmer of mediævalism, all arise out of the main mass of peasant-minded society in a logical development of its ideas.

Nearly all the early pioneers of the modern large-scale industries arose in this way, and brought with them into the developing new conditions the grasping conceptions and domestic severities of their origins. The social history of Lancashire cotton or Birmingham metal goods would illuminate this very plainly. Even to-day, the persona of the big business man remains fundamentally a peasant persona. What the Communists call the "petty" and "big" bourgeoisie are in reality only the primordial peasant writ urban or writ large. They are "kulaks" one stage further on. One peculiar value of the "Five Towns" novels of Mr. Arnold Bennett lies in the clear, convincing, intimate, and yet almost unpremeditated way in which he shows the industrialized peasant mentality of the employing class in a typical industrialized region, the Black Country, waking up to art and refinement, to ampler personality and new ideas.

But while on its upper face the main peasant-souled mass of the human community throws up this prosperous minority, this crop of "well-off" families, on the lower side it produces, through excessive breeding, through selective competition—once in small quantities, and now, through changes in the scale of production, in abundance—a number of "expropriated" individuals to whom the Communist, with his infallible inexactitude of nomenclature and his ineradicable passion for sham erudition, has applied the term "proletariat." The typical modern proletarian is generally without children, that is to say without "proles"; he has lost his grip upon any property and is unable to sustain and control a family. He is a quite landless and homeless man denied the normal consolations of his kind. He may fall into this condition from the peasant and town tradesman level, or, as happens nowadays with increasing abundance, he may be born to these conditions. In the former case the persona to which he squares his conduct and consolations may be a very rough adaptation of the fundamental peasant persona; in the latter, it may be something much more distinctive.

Now the psychological make-up and disposition of these expropriated people, these proletarians—for we have to accept that word now—is of very great importance to our present study. As small ways of trading, cultivation and manufacture give place to larger ways of doing these things, great numbers from the old peasant-townsman stratum will be forced down towards the proletarian level, while a small proportion will clamber upward to ownership and direction in the new giant concerns. Those forced down will be obliged, in sheer defense of their self-esteem, to deprecate family and property. An element of adventure, defiance, and sentimental brotherhood will be required for a satisfactory persona. All are either unemployed or threatened by intermittence of unemployment, and that too gives a chronic uneasiness. The proletarian wants change of general conditions, therefore, and is not afraid of change. In that he differs absolutely from the peasant who is still holding on to property.

Our Western business community has neglected altogether to study the new type of persona—our Western business community seems indeed to neglect the study of everything that does not make obviously for immediate profit—but the Communist has made some plausible generalizations about it. One considerable error seems to me to be his exaggeration of the power and sincerity of the proletarian sentiment of brotherhood. He has developed this alleged disposition to fraternity into an inspiring but misleading cant. And also he mistakes a craving for change due to uneasiness, a desire to upset the uncomfortable arrangement of things for a creative desire.

Here we are under no compulsion to idealize the proletarian. Generally speaking, he is a poor creature, and in the mass he may disgorge great accumulations of envy and be dangerous, destructive and cruel.

It is also a grave error in the communist ideology to confuse the true proletarian persona with that of organized labour in

Britain, France, Germany and elsewhere. A large part of such labour is not and never has been truly propertyless and proletarian; it has never parted company with the simple domestic industrious saving ideals of the peasant types. It has generally savings to its credit. In America it has almost always savings to its credit. And its trade-union and political leaders are essentially like any other members of the peasant-townsman class who have "got on." They have personas closely akin to those of rising business men.

A much more fundamental error on the part of the Communist is his assumption that the types and classes we have dealt with thus far, the acquisitive people growing rich and the working people growing poor, constitute the whole of contemporary society. They do indeed constitute its greater mass and impose their characteristic types of persona upon the great majority of human beings, but they are no more the whole of the human community than flesh and bones, viscera and blood vessels are the whole of a human body. The nerves and brain and the endocrinal glands may seem out of all proportion less, but until the activity of these controlling systems is reckoned with, our account of human physiology is very incomplete and altogether misleading.

It is only fair to admit that Communism began its career with a realization of the need of a psychological analysis of human society, but for various obscure reasons that movement has been continually the victim of its own phrases, and it early fell into slavery to "the materialistic conception of history." This phrase, however carefully it may have been qualified originally, has had the effect of insisting upon the *entire* supremacy of economic considerations in human life. Naturally, therefore, every type and class of human being that did not fall into simple economic categories was ignored. But man was man long before he became an economic animal.

For strategic purposes Communism has now become entirely dogmatic. That has given it enormous revolutionary effectiveness at the price of any scientific development of its ideas. Perhaps we of the Atlantic world are too disposed to be ungrateful to the vast experiments Communism has made and to underrate its achievement. But there can be no doubt that its dogmatism sets a very definite term to its usefulness in the world, and that ultimately it may become like every other rigid motivating system that has preceded it, a mass of mental encumbrance to human thought.

THE FISHERMAN, THE PEASANT OF THE WATERS

We may note here the variations of the peasant type that appear where fertile rivers flow and where land meets sea. There appears fishing. The fisherman is a water cultivator. Fishing has produced its own distinctive types of habitation in pile dwellings which still survive in the Celebes to-day, and which, because of the facile preservation of their remains, figure so largely in the archæology of the Neolithic period. The Swiss lake dwellings, the Glastonbury finds, mark important points in the history of our knowledge of this science. Fishing probably crept down the rivers to the sea and mingled with the casual life of the long-shore prowler looking for shell fish and edible seaweed and leaving his "kitchen middens" of shells for posterity. Probably fishing clung to the shore and rarely went out of sight of land until the Middle Ages. Inland people ate river fish or none at all, and oysters brought from Britain were, as everyone knows, a Roman luxury, but sea fishing as an industry and a regular food supply is of recent origin.

The fisherman in our study of personas has to be distinguished quite sharply from the seagoing man. Maybe the latter learnt the first tricks of navigation from the river and longshore folk, but from the very beginnings of history we find him trader, slaver and pirate, and he falls under the second broad class of personas we shall next consider. The first real sailors linked the seaways with the desert routes, but the villages of the fishermen spread along the rivers, dotted lagoons and sheltered in coves and inlets away from any ports or cities.

The expansion and industrialization of fishing came only with the general expansion and industrialization of enterprise in the fifteenth and sixteenth centuries. Its most picturesque and romantic extension was whaling. Since the beginnings of human association men have no doubt attacked stranded whales or whales in shallow water. Since palæolithic man did not hesitate to attack an embarrassed mammoth in a swampy place and even trap the monster in a pit, he would certainly have set about a whale had he got the slightest chance to do so. The Esquimaux have killed whales among the ice from time immemorial, and wherever there were fishing boats we may be sure that men would find the presence of whales offshore provocative and exciting. But the arts of shipbuilding and navigation had to precede any attempt to push the assault further. It was only after the sixteenth century that the systematic extermination of whales became a business enterprise, and the same period saw the invasion of fishing by larger ships and apparatus and the methods of capitalism. In the broad issues that concern us here, the psychology of the industrialization of the seas and ocean does not differ materially from the industrialization of the land.

§ 3. *The Second Class of Persona: The Typical Nomad's Persona and Its Variations*

Let us now bring in certain other strains of tradition to this account of human motivation. Our general problem of why people carry on in, and submit to, social and industrial life, and how the progressive organization of human life is to be sustained, will then take on quite a new and different appearance.

And first there is a very considerable range of ideas that come into modern life from the mentality of the aggressive nomad. We write "aggressive nomad" and not simply "nomad." Our introductory history has followed the Bible in its recognition of the early schism between Cain and Abel, between the cultivator and the herdsman. This was a regional climatic difference between arable and periodic pasture lands. In the one, cattle were accessory; in the other, cultivation was incidental. Normally the nomad led a life almost as inaggressive as the cultivator, but his mobility made him more easily a thief, a robber, a raider, a merchant, and at times a cultivator. Cattle was naturally his money of account. Outside the arable levels of recently deposited soil, "the great alluvial valleys" in particular, he wandered into ore-bearing districts and became the first metallurgist. The gipsy tinker, with his distinctive morals and traditions and pots and pans, is the last decaying survival of the nomadic life in western Europe.

But at times, as we have told in the *Outline of History,* the herdsman gathered in strength and raided "for keeps." Then he founded kingdoms and autocracies and ruled the men with the peasant personas. He had, and has to this day where he still maintains his freedom in the Asiatic midlands, an entirely more robust and swaggering tradition than the peasant. Fundamentally he despises work. His spirit towards property is "easy come and easy go." Not to get easily and give freely reflects upon his force and vigour. His love is fierce, romantic, personal and not nearly so prolific as that of the cultivator in constant need of "hands" for the soil. He gambles, and he does it with pride and elegance. Waste is a glory to him. He is, and in his persona he knows himself to be, a fine, reckless, desperate fellow.

Such have been the quality and disposition of kings, aristocrats, soldiers and ruling classes since the social world began. From them by snobbery and imitation, through romantic poetry, literature, art and example, this tradition has soaked into the general imagination of mankind. It introduces an element of conflict and fluctuation now into most personas in the world. Even the young peasant sits in the village cinema theatre to-day watching the familiar situations of romance unfold, and imbibes new notions altogether of what it is to be a man.

And upon the ideology of the nomad and the sword the incessant search and fight for territory and ascendency, the essential forms of our political life are framed. It seems perfectly natural to us to see a king with spurs and sword; we should never dream of seeing him with a hammer or a spade. These are the implements of the robbed and subjugated. It was only in the nineteenth century and under the menace of the peasant-minded moralist that kings began to flaunt their virtues and imitate the bourgeoisie. As indeed it was only in the same period that the acquisitive classes won their way to spur and coronet. The onset of great-scale production was altering all the values of the old dispensation.

The Communist confuses this predatory tradition of the robber nomad with the tradition of the acquisitive peasant type, growing rich. In modern life the two mingle extraordinarily, but that does not make them the same. They are and remain different threads. They make indeed the personas and conduct of people in dominant positions muddled and confused, but mixture and confusion do not mean assimilation. The strands are fundamentally different and essentially separable. The present solidarity of the rich with the royal and "noble," based on mutual accommodations and common fears, is an apparent solidarity that will probably fail to stand any great social or economic strain. The aristocratic woman sells herself and her pride of caste in marriage for money, and her family finds a compensation in the snobbish imitativeness of the newly rich. She feels herself that she has not so much sold herself as captured money. But recent revolutions have greatly cheapened "nobility," and its prestige declines as the social confidence of the plutocracy increases.

I do not know how far we may be able to establish and demonstrate the ideological confusion and indecisiveness of collective initiative, this mélange of the rich boor and the proud baron has produced in the directive classes of the modern European community. Presently some shrewd student of social psychology will gather and focus the light of letters, memoirs, well informed novels and plays and reports of divorce proceedings upon this clash of cultures.*

§ 4. *The Third Class of Persona: the Priestly or Educated Persona and Its Derivatives*

But now we must consider a third great system of tradition, a third great system of personas and self-esteems. This in the early stages of society was represented by the priest. From the beginning the priest represents a type of persona more or less

---

*Sombart's *Moderne Kapitalismus* is illuminating here.

detached on the one hand from the family idea and the obsession with property of the peasant, and on the other from the personal assertion and lordship of the aristocrat. It would be extraordinarily interesting to work out the evolution and ramifications of the priestly type of persona. In that we should find a mass of indications of the utmost value in our final estimate of the need and destinies of our planetary ant-hill.

It is a biologically important fact that generally speaking the priest has been as often as not unreproductive. The characteristics of the priestly persona are not therefore inherited; they are the outcome of a particular training, a particular system of suggestions, and not of any selective process. It is not necessary to breed an educated intellectual class. The Brahmin caste in India, which we may regard as an experiment to that end, shows no distinctive mental superiority. Priests over a large part of the world are drawn from every section of the community. Throughout Christendom for example, noble, trader, peasant have all contributed their quota to the priestly stratum.

I write "priest" here. But I intend much more than the specialized religious officiator in the modern scheme of things. "Cleric" might have been a better word, but then there is risk of confusion with the modern "clerk." Originally the priests constituted the entire learned class; the priesthood was all the learned professions. The Egyptian priest was doctor, lawyer, teacher and financier. His order supplied the only writers and poets. He was architect and artist. He stood at the side of the ruler as secretary and minister. The temple was bank, treasury and museum. This original monopolization of education by the religious organization is written plain over the history of those mediæval and Renascence European communities from which the contemporary world derives the bulk of its tradition. If there was any collateral development of writing and reading in ancient times it was probably in relation to the account keeping of nomadic and seagoing traders. The estate clerk and the court scribe may also have been laymen from very early times—but they must have been educated by men in the priestly tradition.

Until the Protestant Reformation universities were monastic in spirit and organization; the great statesmen were church dignitaries, and there was scarcely any intellectual life at all outside the priestly organizations. From this identification of intellectual activity with the clerical tradition arises a fact that is too often overlooked in progressive discussion. Liberalism is too apt to denounce "priestcraft" as altogether evil. Yet the progressive and revolutionary initiatives of the past have been almost entirely of priestly origin. True that in theory the priest has been the inflexible guardian of tradition, but in fact it has been priests and learned clerks who have led almost every breakaway from tradition that has ever occurred. Roger Bacon, that morning star of modernity, was a Franciscan. Huss, Wycliffe, Luther, Calvin, Knox were all priests, dissentient priests. Mendel, the founder of genetics, was a priest. And it is interesting to note how many of the pioneers of that most revolutionary of all sciences, anthropology, were priests. Even Karl Marx was a university product, a doctor of distinction.

Through the scholastic clerical tradition nearly all the intellectual growth of humanity has come. The contribution to human initiatives of the vast peasant-souled majority is small by comparison. A few starry men of genius break through, a Shakespeare, a Burns, but even these are expressive rather than critics and innovators. The aristocrat gave more, but not so very much more, his principal gift that pride which tells the truth, and even his loyalty and chivalry have a quality of plagiarism from the priestly conceptions of devotion. It was the Church that saved learning throughout the Dark Ages. From priestly sources all learning had to come, and only in learned circles could the flame of criticism and discussion be kept alive. At times the protection afforded that flame may have impeded the access of air, but it was better for us on the whole that it should sometimes have been in need of blowing up than that it should ever have been altogether blown out.

And now let us look a little more closely into the type of persona produced by the priestly tradition. Under this heading we shall have to deal not only with priests and ministers of religion, but with a vast world of quasi-disinterested effort, with teachers of every class, with writers and creative artists, with scribes and journalists, with doctors, surgeons and the associated professions, with judges and lawyers generally, with administrators, and particularly that excellent type the permanent official, with technical experts, and finally, most hopeful, various and interesting of all, with the modern scientific worker. All these types of persona have characteristics in common that mark them off quite definitely from either the proliferation of the varieties of acquisitive peasant townsman soul, or from the royalties, aristocrats, robbers and genteel social parasites, who constitute the predatory classes. In the modern professional soldier we have perhaps a type intermediate between the predatory and priestly group and deriving more and more from the latter tradition, and in the modern barrister the pretensions of an aristocratic protector of a client subdued to the exigencies of a hireling bravo, and mingled too often with the unredeemed greed of the peasant. (So that it is with dire public lamentations that he "gives up" a practice "worth" so much for some honourable promotion that is not so heavily feed.)

The first distinctive element in this third and most important class of persona, the educated persona, is the conception of self-abnegation, of devotion. The individual is not supposed to work directly either for his own enrichment or for his own honour and glory. He belongs, he has made himself over, to an order consecrated to ends transcending any such personal considerations.

That is the essence of priesthood, of professionalism, and of all artistic and literary pretensions. The robber type has its devotions to king and chieftain, intensely personal and sentimental, often to the sexual pitch, but the devotion of the learned-priestly type is to a God or to a divine overruling idea. This idea runs through almost all the endless developments and variations of the learned-priestly type we find in the world to-day. The doctor, the solicitor, the teacher, the artist all have their professional standards and repudiate "mere commercialism." Neither the barrister nor the physician works for definite fees. There is a tradition of gratuitous service both in law and medicine, and in Great Britain a quack can sue for his fee while a registered practitioner is restrained from doing so by his professional organization. Even the undisciplined writers have their unwritten code, and when three prominent authors, Mr. G. B. Shaw, Mr. Arnold Bennett, and another, were invited by a great London general store to write matter for its advertisements for some enormous fee—with full liberty to say what they liked, praising or blaming as they saw fit—they all declined the proposal as an infringement of their priestly function, as an imputation upon that complete disinterestedness and spontaneity which is to a self-respecting writer the most vital quality of his persona.

The element of devotion in this learned-priestly tradition is absolutely essential to the processes of civilization. One cannot imagine the economic social machine running at all, without the services of this now very various class, these definitive or constructive public servants, these judges, doctors, teachers, writers, officials, more or less honest and trustworthy. And they are practically trustworthy and efficient because they have all been brought up to and educated in this type of persona. That is a point to note. These types are more "made" than the peasant, townsman, money-earning types, who for the most part take up the tradition in which they find themselves without much scrutiny, or than the robber, aristocrat, military types;—though the military at least develop now an increasing distinctive moral training. This third great class of persona is moulded and its qualities are evoked out of germs of purpose which remain latent in all the less educated elements of the social mélange. That is the key-fact to the study of social psychology.

Again we approach the culminating topic of our survey, education. But from that we will diverge for the present to discuss the secular change in mental attitude which the priestly-learned factor in human development is undergoing. In the traditional past, education has been the preserver and transmitter of tradition. The mass of the priestly-learned class was essentially conservative. It learnt, it repeated, it handed on. So it remains in bulk. But there has been an increasing development of critical and reconstructive qualities in that mass. The priestly-learned class has never been blindly obedient and disciplined. Because, behind his teacher, the novice has always been aware of the overriding idea, the Truth, the Deity, or the spirit of the order or profession he was entering. The bolder ones have always found confidence and strength in that. They would derive courage from it to question the authority of their immediate teachers. In the past almost all the great changes in teaching have been proposed as returns to the original orthodoxy, as rebellions against recent corruptions. "Reformations" have been due not to a defect but to an exaggeration of loyalty. It was clerics, not Jew nor Moslim nor pagan, who broke the Catholic unity of Christendom.

And though such dissentients might seek support in other quarters for their novelties, it is in *the ineradicable idea of disinterested integrity* which this priestly-learned class alone has fostered that the future of humanity resides. The innovating spirits of the closing eighteenth century pitted the expansive urge of the new industrial and financial bourgeoisie against aristocracy, and so created Liberalism. It was not the newcomers who produced Liberalism. They took to it very readily, but that is another matter. The socialist thinkers of the following decades sought for driving power in the discontent and resentments of the multiplying proletariat. But in either instance the "idea" came from the class that alone breeds ideas. A great mind-dominating organization like the Roman Catholic Church is for ever searching its own body for the infection of original thought and revolt, because it knows that the deadliest antagonists to its current procedure are the men who most intimately possess its tradition. It fears the good it has engendered.

All complex reforms of method and spirit come from within. It is lawyers who must simplify law and harmonize it with social biology and psychology; it is medical men who can alone readjust medical practice properly to modern ideas. The schools are the ultimate citadel which must be won, if the general character of human thought is to be changed. It does not matter whether most doctors, most lawyers and most schoolmasters and spiritual teachers are formal and reactionary or not. It is within the training of these professions that the redeeming impulse is to be found. Liberalism and Marxism, whether they are right or wrong, are mere phases in that great conflict for orderly creation to which the gathering liberation and gathering courage of the priestly-learned mind have brought humanity. They are not really insurrectionary impulses from below.

§ 5. *The Civilization of the Entrepreneur**

Out of the interplay of a vast multitude of variations and distortions of these three primary types of persona, the peasant, the aristocrat-soldier-robber, and the priestly-learned man, arose the mental life, the tolerances, acquiescences, concessions and usurpations of the old traditional life from which we are now emerging. Out of the development of these, out of their steady modification by circumstance and their deliberate remoulding by a new directive education, must come the mental life of this new phase of scientific purposive organization towards which our species is at present moving.

And here perhaps is the place for a preliminary look upon certain types which we may lump together roughly under the name of entrepreneur. The mentality of the industrial and financial entrepreneur who has thus far been the immediate agent in carrying mankind over from localized and petty to large-scale and mondial production and trade, is best understood if we realize that he comes mainly from the urban variation of the peasant type, for whom property, money, and visible triumph over one's neighbour are the criteria of success. The first exploitation of the gifts of invention and science was very largely an instinctive, unintelligent exploitation. And to this day the typical face of the big industrialist and the big financier has a boorish quality.

But there is no innate necessity for this. As the organization of business increases in complexity, the importance and freedom of the individual owner may be dwarfed more and more by the necessity for directive assistants who will be trained and special-

*See R. H. Gretton's *The English Middle Class.*

ized men, essentially of the new innovating variety of the priestly-learned intellectual type, and with its inseparable inspiration of disinterestedness.

Here is an interesting field for some student of the social aspects of economics. It is a piece of work that has to be done. It will be profoundly interesting to explore novels, memoirs, interviews and reported utterances of all sorts to trace the progressive civilization of the entrepreneur during the last hundred years. Our investigator may even collect opinions directly from some of the more original outstanding industrial leaders of our time. The big business man as a powerful and irresponsible savage is probably quite a transitory phenomenon in the development of the new world-wide civilization. The rationalization movement is essentially the organized expression of his entry upon a new phase. The chaos of competition becomes the oligarchy of production and distribution; the erstwhile plunderer of profits becomes a ruling and responsible economic aristocrat.

With, of course, exceptions.

§ 6. *The Idea of Property**

The three main types of human persona differ most widely in their attitude to property. The first type is acquisitive, tenacious and preservative; the second is rapacious and consumes; the third professes to be more or less aloof from possession and gain, and to carry on the service of the community for satisfaction of a quite different type. Let us now look a little into this idea of property which is manifestly a very primary idea in binding man to man in a common effort and a mutual servitude.

We live and breathe in a world of property, just as we live and breathe in air, and yet that idea is as little analyzed as air was three hundred years ago. We—the generality—have as little ordered and explicit knowledge of its elements and pressures.

It is, for example, interesting to turn to the index of the latest edition of the Encyclopædia Britannica, that compendium of

---

*See Professor Laski's *Grammar of Politics,* chapter on "Property," and Tawney's *Acquisitive Society,* for a good classification of types of property.

general knowledge and the current mentality, and note how far we are as yet from any understanding of the need for such an analysis. One finds a reference to certain legal articles thus:

Property: see Compensation, Conveyancing, Personal Property, Real Property.
Property, Devolution of: see Intestacy, Legitim, Will.
Property, Law of: see Real Property and Conveyancing.

And finally one little article, a column and a third long, on Primitive Property, in which alone is any realization of the fundamental significance of property ideas apparent. This is in a work which gives seventy-four columns of letterpress and forty-one page plates to Pottery and Porcelain!

The article upon Primitive Property is compressed, but does recognize something of the subtlety and variety underlying the apparent simplicity of this fundamental concept of social ideology. Rivers, Laveleye, Malinowski and other explorers of this neglected territory are mentioned. Indeed, in spite of the silences of the Encyclopædia Britannica, there is already available a considerable amount of work which converges upon the problem we are suggesting. But it is dispersed in all sorts of books and publications. For example, we have the work of such a writer as Lowie (*Primitive Society*), the material gathered for us by Malinowski, piquant suggestions from that psychological genius Jung, and the Yerkes' focussing of simian behaviour, a mass of such work indeed, all ready to be assembled in a larger synthesis. That assembling waits to be done by some competent and industrious student, but we may, with a certain confidence, throw out some general anticipations of its conclusions.

The idea of "mine" seems to be of much earlier origin than the idea of "me." Some birds, many predatory animals and gorillas, for example, seem to have very definite territorial ideas. Possessive jealousy is manifestly interwoven into the very substance of many mammals. Man, as he began to discover himself, discovered himself an owner. The linkage between himself and certain objects, places and persons must have appeared as something obvious and necessary to him. And not only was there a "mine" in his awakening and clarifying consciousness to keep him snarling warnings at his brothers and sisters, but also there was an "ours",—all sorts of other larger things that rallied the pack to a common defensive.

These primitive appropriations were already becoming definite and recognized in the very earliest societies to which our knowledge or imagination extends. The establishment of taboos, on which, as we have shown, human social life rests, concerned not merely sexual ownership but many other forms of ownership, *varying with the nature and use of the thing owned*. The ownership of weapons and adornments must have always been very personal and thorough. The ownership of a strip of meat still on the body of the tribe's last kill was not nearly so well defined. Many sorts of ownership, and particularly the ownership of one's own body and life, were very precarious and may have been largely dependent on the will of the tribal chief.

People write and talk of "primitive communism" and "primitive individualism." But both communism and individualism are highly abstract ideas, too abstract for my taste altogether, and with a little mental slovenliness either can be applied to savage conditions. Dr. Frith, in the Encyclopædia article I have cited, very properly dismisses both these "labels." The statement I have italicized above and to which I return as the cardinal proposition in the matter, is that originally the significance of ownership was dependent altogether upon the nature and use of the object under consideration. In the development of savage ideas, as in the development of language, the particular came before the general. "My" meant what I have now or what I mean to monopolize: woman, axe, bead, sunny corner or cave. Certain things I might covet but dared not touch because they were taboo to the headman or to someone else. And, as the common use of language testifies, "my" went beyond the idea of property altogether when one talked of my master or my enemy.

From such indefinite beginnings, which indeed signified hardly more than that a thing could focus on "me," the intensification of "mine" progressed. The idea of "mine" tended to generalize.

But the generalization of property was never perfect. From the beginning there seem to have been these plain divisions between, first, the crude absolute property of a man in his nose-ring or beads; secondly, claims on services and particularly sexual property with certain customary reciprocities and limitations; and, thirdly, property in which there was manifestly a communal interest, such as hunting rights and collective cultivation.

Sexual property we will not discuss at this point. It does not concern this review of human activities very greatly, and the points where it does come in may be conveniently deferred for a special chapter on woman. The progressive emancipation of women and the social protection of children, seem likely, as we shall see, to relegate it, at no very distant date, to the world of private feeling altogether.

But with regard to the other two categories of property there have always been in the human make-up two conflicting dispositions: the first, the disposition of the primitive ego-centred human animal to make "mine" as absolute and extensive as possible, and the second, the more or less lucid realization of the frequent incompatibility of absolute property with the general welfare. The craving for absolute property is perhaps the most vigorous survival of the primitive savage in modern life. His lust, for example, is far more under control. He even wants to own his property when he is dead, and resents any interference with his freedom of bequest.

Confronting this excess of primordial egotism is the law. The lawyer is the property-tamer. It is time the lawyer came into our picture. He defines property. Let us consider at what point he comes in. He is a specialization from the clerical type. Lawyer and judge are essentially men of the literate and devoted tradition. With an element of authoritative aristocracy. No class has been so bitterly satirized and reviled, but the very bitterness of the abuse reveals a recognition that from this class it is natural and reasonable to demand a conscientiousness and self-suppression beyond the normal limits. The peasant who curses the lawyer for selling justice and making all he can by it sells his own produce without compunction and makes all he can by it though other people starve. When every iniquity of the lawyers of the past has been admitted, we still find that there were abundant gentlemen of the long robe, haunted, even if they were not inspired and pervaded, by the spirit of righteousness. The illumination they shed may not always have been a beacon, but at any rate the wick never ceased altogether to glow, and down the centuries we see a succession of these unloved men boring away in their tedious frowsty courts, really struggling in that dim mediæval light to import some semblance of justice, some thought for the commonweal, into the limitless greed of robber barons, the unqualified imperatives of feudal chiefs and the grasping cunning of the baser sort. And they are still working to-day towards the satisfaction of this permanent social need— the exact definition of proprietary rights.

There has been, as we have just remarked, an age-long recognition of at least two varieties of property; that economic property in which the family, tribe, or other community had an intervening interest, and particularly land, *real property;* and that other more intimate type of possession, absolute property, *personality,* the bead, the spear, the dog, that was part of a man and was often made to "die" and be buried with him. These two main divisions still rule. But it is manifest they are not comprehensive. Copyright and patent rights are instances of a third variety of property, an expiring property of a peculiarly intimate character. Nor is either division, real or personal, more than a miscellany. There are in practice a great number of kinds of property which develop species and subspecies as the complexity of society increases, and every species and variety has its particular limitations of hold, disposition and use.

The law does in theory recognize at least two sorts of personal property, though the distinction has disappeared from the thought of the average man. To a lawyer a chattel, which may be owned absolutely, differs from a "chose in action," such as a copyright, in respect of which one merely has rights. Even in regard to saleable property, an owner may have more or less power. Before property in human beings disappeared it was gradually modified until, from the right to kill and torture slaves, we arrived at the present position, when a man may not grossly injure even his own children, but controls them only for their benefit. Our property in animals has been limited quite recently by humanitarian legislation.

According to the law of England, all land is the property of the king, and its "owners" are his tenants. They have succeeded in establishing absolute rights against the spirit of the law, but the idea that land is held on trust is not deeply buried. During the privations of the last war public opinion supported public interference with owners who neglected to get all the food they could out of their land, and if similar action of this sort were proposed to-day it would be attacked not so much by lawyers as an infringement of elementary rights as by allegations that it would not work.

Indeed, against the whole range of individual rights, both in property and conduct, the law holds up the notion of public policy—a man may not act in a manner contrary to the public good. And the operation of this idea is not limited or governed by precedent, but varies freely with the moral and economic ideas of the age. On grounds of public policy judges have recently upset decisions relating to cruelty to wives, freedom of bequest and the doctrine that agreements to fix prices are illegal conspiracies. In the days of reverence for "economic laws" price-fixing was condemned because it checked their operation. With the passing of the school of economists who held this opinion the decision has been reversed. This attrition and modification of property is always going on. The lawyer knows it is going on, and his conception of property is of a very modified and graded ownership.

But in the thinking of the ordinary man—which is what concerns us most here—this is not clearly and habitually recognized. There is a discord between the existing legal realities of property and popular thought which still holds that "a man may do what he likes with his own."

Just as, long after Dalton and the discovery of the elements, my education began at the "fire-air-earth-and-water" stage of chemistry because of the lag of popular education, so in spite

of current legal thought the ideology of the ordinary man begins
with the idea of absolute property. And generally speaking it
stays there. For the ordinary school teaches nothing about sorts
of property. And the normal teacher knows very little of any
property whatever. The ordinary man therefore is continually
acting upon the idea that what he owns he owns absolutely, and
he is continually being pulled up by restrictions and limitations
which are discordant with this crude ideology.

Perhaps the nearest approach to absolute ownership—the
complete power to do what one likes with one's own—lies in the
change a man carries in his pockets and (provided it is not an
heirloom) the ornamental ring he wears upon his finger. Next
comes the money he has within reach or within call. The shadow
of debt may lie on that, but otherwise his ownership is very
complete. Beyond the range of such immediate property, his
ownership could very well be treated as nonexistent, and his
relationship to its object,—whatever it was,—home, land, stock
or share,—treated as a personal claim or right to do merely this,
that and the other definable thing with the object in question.
It would work out to practically the same results. But it would
work through a rather different mental process in the mind of
the owner.

When we have grasped this fact, which is in the habitual
thought of every lawyer, that property is a limited, definable,
alterable claim, varying with the object concerned, a claim either
upon a passive object or a debt or other claim for service upon
a person or persons, we are in a position to measure the reality
of such phrases as the "abolition of property" and the "abolition of private property" which played so large a part in the
socialist and communist movements of the late nineteenth and
early twentieth centuries. At what were these phrases really
aimed, if it is true that we are always changing, abolishing and
sometimes even extending property rights? Because, as we are
showing, we might "abolish" property almost altogether and
still leave things working very much as they do now.

We could quite easily call the owner of anything, "the person
in charge," the official responsible for it. This would be a change

of terminology, but it would not be a social revolution. It would be like the League of Nations device of calling tropical possessions "mandatory territories." We should by a verbal substitution turn owners into mandatories. We should "abolish property" in theory while retaining it as a working method of dealing with things and people until—if ever—a better way could be devised. By so doing we should open the mental door to a scientific revision of legal controls that would in the end reconcile all that is reasonable in socialist and communist theory with the utmost personal freedom that is socially permissible, and that is all we should do. The governments of the world might "abolish" all private property to-morrow by a series of declarations, and until they had devised that better way, those declarations would have about as much effect upon the everyday business of life, as the Kellogg Pacts have had upon the naval and military establishments of the world.

Let us make this clearer. The reality of property is this, that an individual called the owner, possesses rights of enjoyment, use and disposal over a thing owned, or he possesses certain claims for service or supply upon a debtor. Now the abolition, the destruction, of such rights and claims, as distinguished from their transfer to some other ownership, can mean only that the thing owned or the service claimed, if it is at all desirable, is flung out to be scrambled for, and that in the end someone else or something else will be found in possession, which, as Euclid says, "is absurd" because plainly you have not abolished anything if it reappears.

But if you cannot abolish property altogether, you can abolish the property of this man or that—on condition. The condition, the only way in which the property of any individual or class can be abolished, is that there exist a *competent receiver* for the property in question. This has always been the weak point in communist proposals, that they do not clearly indicate a competent receiver. And they do not indicate a competent receiver because in relation to most types and varieties of property there is no competent receiver. They are the first to denounce the national State as a competent receiver, or the parliamentary politician as a proper administrator of the confiscated spoils. A large part of the constructive task before mankind consists in the invention and creation of a competent receiver which will embody the commonweal. The Socialists' and the Communists' criticism of the working of private ownership in our economic life is often sound and very penetrating, but from that their transition to impossibly premature receivers is entirely too rapid. They mistake their statements of guiding principles for practicable working plans.

At the beginning of this section we asserted that we live and breathe in a world of property as we live and breathe in air, but, as we have shown throughout this chapter, the way in which the property motive works varies very widely. You may be induced to work in order to get and hold; you may get and spend without working, or you may work without wanting to get. Now this third alternative we have stressed, and to it we shall return again. We have shown that throughout the ages the proper conduct of human affairs has been very largely due to the continued existence of the educated devoted type of persona, in which the property motive is secondary or suppressed. To this type we must look for the organization and control of a competent receiver whenever we consider the removal of any sort of social activity from the spontaneous direction of private owners. And what the Socialist or the Communist is really after when he uses such phrases as the "abolition of property" is, in fact, the abolition of the property motive in economic life; that is to say, the abolition of the two most fundamental social types in favour of the third, the trained and educated type. The world has to become a world of men and women working to serve and not to own. To that possibility we shall return later. Here let it suffice to point out that the socialist idea is really the idea of a universal education for service, and that if it does not mean that, it means nothing at all of the slightest practical value.

At present an entirely educated world is no more than a speculative possibility. At present this world is a world of getting. The ordinary man works for himself primarily, and he works for others only in so far as he wants and needs to get from them.

§ 7. *The Education of the Lawyer*

The lawyer, we have said, is the property-tamer, and here, if we were being fully encyclopædic, we should give a lengthy description of the legal organization of the world. We should take the reader into law courts from China to Peru, discuss the legal procedure of the Moslim world, and the reason why the British barrister wears a wig, while his French confrère is adorned with a peculiarly shaped hat. We should glance back to the courts of Greece and Rome. But here again our convenient fiction of the *Science of Work and Wealth* must relieve us. It would be all there, and if it was there, the really interested reader would merely glance at it and then return to the main discussion. Here we will consider the legal organization only in the most general terms and think of it mainly in the forms it has assumed in the Atlantic civilizations.

What is the rôle of the legal organization in the social complex? In many respects the legal profession is one of the most antiquated types of activity in the world. It was one of the earliest to be detached from the primary priestly calling. It is still of very great importance indeed, though that importance is diminishing with the diminution of the traditional element in law and the establishment of codes. With the growth of civilization it will probably continue to diminish relatively to other fields of activity.

In his greater past, when law was a compromise between the will of rulers and the customs of a tribe or people, the lawyer was the sole repository of the law. At his best he upheld the rights of the common man against the encroachments of chiefs and kings. And his record is not a bad one. If his "bit of parchment" terrified the peasant, it often baffled the lord. He alone could state with authority what a man's rights were; it was his tradition to defend them; indeed, he had no *raison d'être* if he supported absolute power; and his skill subdued the hearts of rulers towards the current conceptions of mercy and justice. In those days, if the courts abandoned a man he was lost indeed.

Nobody is now in that position of dependence. We can read,

we can write and argue to the point. Printing, popular education, representative assemblies and newspapers have made knowledge of the law accessible, and they have provided anyone who can attract attention with powerful if capricious defenders. The Public Trustee sets a standard for solicitors, judges may complain from time to time of the encroachments of, say, Civil Service regulations, but the battle thus started is no longer fought out in the courts of law but in Parliament. The lawyers have not so much to expound a common law known only to themselves as to administer word for word the statutes handed to them. Perhaps nine-tenths of the cases which come before the courts now are matters of statute law.

This is a limitation of the lawyer's function, and on the whole it is a change for the better. There is no such room in the administration of justice for individual beliefs and difference of culture as there used to be. An enlightened man, free to adjust the law to his own conceptions, would do more harm than good. For in most spheres of legal action what matters (within limits) to the members of a community is not so much how rights and obligations are parcelled out between them as that their rights shall be the same in this court as in that, next month as last month, and that they shall be enforced without fear, favour or distinction between persons. This is not so true of criminal law, but criminal law is only the sensational relief of the calling.

The lawyer, then, must know and follow precedent, and to this is doubtless due the wholly irrational scheme of his own professional arrangements. The modernization of the legal organization lags behind that of the medical services, lags behind the reform of the educational system. This is disastrously true of legal education. The barrister is a specialist. He influences the common life at few points; his general education, unless he becomes a judge, is of value chiefly to himself. Fortunately, for social reasons, it is the custom to give him what is considered the best education the country can offer. Solicitors, on the other hand, wield enormous influence. Now that clerical advice is less often sought than it was, we call on our solicitors to advise us at all those moments of crisis—death, marriage, disaster—when momentous personal decisions have to be made. The flow of inherited wealth, the employment of savings, our practical handling of all the vexed social questions, lie largely in the hands of our solicitors. No body of men stands so much in need of the widest and most generous equipment of ideas. And yet it is the custom to take them from school at the age when the mind should expand most rapidly and confine them to routine work in traditionally dusty offices, as though we were anxious to secure for our intimate counsellors men of stunted and dingy mental growth. Happily most of us are able to find men in the profession who have transcended these limitations. A day may come when the Incorporated Law Society will insist upon a modicum of social biology, psychology and modern economics for the professional qualification of a solicitor. It may even demand some elements of literary culture. Until that day arrives the adjustment of legal and social practice to modern knowledge will remain imperfect at many points.

§ 8. *"Scientific" Property*

We may recall here that brief history of human mental development we traced in the opening sections of Chapter II. We have shown how recent are abstractions, generalizations, and directed thinking in the development of society. We have reminded the reader how children and untrained minds are disposed to personify and to ascribe everything to agents and doers and deal with everything as a personal matter. They think not only of powers and inanimate objects as persons, but they think of tribes and communities as persons. They abstract with difficulty. We shall see presently (in Chapter X) into what difficulties human affairs have been brought by the inability of people to think of money except in terms of gold-bartering. Here we have to consider how recent and under-developed is the idea of common property, of any property, that is, not private and personal.

In the old civilizations two great personifications owned all the property that we should now consider collective, the God (administering through the temple priesthood) and the king. When tribal gods gave place to a universal God, he owned the earth and the fullness thereof. That conception of personal ownership came down to quite modern times. The road eighteenth-century Englishmen travelled on was the king's highway, the ships that defended them were the king's navy, anything otherwise ownerless, like treasure trove or an intestate's estate, was the king's. There was no difficulty then in proposing to expropriate an owner or a class of owners. God and the king were thought of as receivers of unlimited competence. And whatever restriction there was upon a man "doing what he liked with his own" was imposed in the name of the super-owner. "For everything a personal owner," has been almost a necessary principle of human thought, until the spread of socialist and communist views. Outside human interests, of course, were the things of the wild, wild beasts and birds and fish and the like, but they could only come into human affairs by being annexed and owned. They were owned so soon as they mattered. The feudal king owned the forests. Not even the seas were masterless; the Carthaginians warned the Romans off the western Mediterranean and, as Britons sang, Britannia ruled the waves.

But after a century of socialist discussion, after a century of thinking over such declarations as Proudhon's that property is robbery, we find ourselves released to take quite another view of property. We find it possible to start from a point absolutely opposite to that from which our grandfathers started. Instead of assuming the need for an owner for each individual thing, we can begin now with an absolute communist proposition, that everything belongs to all mankind, and try what result we can get by asking: To what persons or groups of people would it be best to assign the responsibility for protecting, controlling, exploiting or enjoying this, that, and the other division of everything? We can work downward from the conception of one human commonweal instead of upward from the basis of nineteen hundred million individual appropriations. We can do so now because the shock of that phrase "the abolition of property," reverberating for a hundred years, has released our minds. We can do now, with all the freedom of a scientific enquiry, what the lawyers through the centuries have been doing with an industrious elaboration, by instinct and rule of thumb, and attempt a really scientific treatment of the apportionment of duty, control and consumption over ownerable things.

It was pointed out at the end of § 6 that it would be possible to "abolish property" to-morrow without any hindrance to our present occupations. But having done so we should then be in a position to ask each and every holder of property in the world to show reason why he should continue to administer that property, enquiring further whether his administration was the best possible for the human commonweal, and if not, by what means it could be transferred, with as little social disturbance as possible, to a better administration.

As a matter of fact, and with certain obscurities and indirectnesses, that is what is being asked in the world now, in a great variety of forms and phrases. What in any particular instance is the better administration? The first people indeed to imply this question by running into the arena with an answer to it were Herbert Spencer's Individualists, of whom Sir Ernest Benn is the most living British representative. They broke out in the middle of the nineteenth century replying, to an unspoken challenge, that the best social results, the greatest wealth, the greatest happiness, would result in leaving private property as it now exists, and as free, as untaxed, as uncontrolled as possible. Half of Herbert Spencer's writings were an indictment—a fairly sound one—of the contemporary State as a competent receiver. But by defending personal property as an institution they admitted that the institution of personal property could be called to account, and prepared the way for the world-wide discriminating and exhaustive enquiry that is now proceeding. They did good work in showing how incomplete, to the pitch of futility, was the socialist project until competent receivers could be indicated, but they satisfied no one by these instances of State stupidity that competent receivers were generally impossible.

Very much of this present work is, at its level, a contribution to the scientific conception of property. From first to last, indeed, it is a treatise on the management of the human estate, a balance sheet and report on current business, an account of the working of the world as a going concern. In this chapter upon motives we are concerned with property mainly because its acquisition is a social motive. The insistence of the Individualist upon the beneficent effect of a competitive struggle for acquisition, with private personal ownership as full, free and wild as possible, has to be taken into account. He tells us that men have a land hunger, a planning and management hunger, a passion for "founding a family." In a manner which he never fully explains, these base orientations of the egotistic drive, will, he assumes, work together for good, provided they are not thwarted and restrained.

But are any of these dispositions instinctive and ineradicable in the human animal? The social analysis we have made regards their domination over conduct as entirely the outcome of educational circumstances; they are great and powerful in the peasant and least so in the priest. The ideal "economic man" of the Individualist is simply the peasant, bathed and in control of a business. The Individualist approaches this complex question of human incentive too exclusively from the point of view of the prosperous nineteenth-century protestant business man. Mr. John Galsworthy has devoted a large part of his career as a novelist to the meticulous study of the motives of a family of this type, the Forsyte family, and more particularly to the life history of Soames Forsyte, the *Man of Property*, and even nowadays, while practically a contemporary, the reader is left wondering whether any real human beings were ever so rigid and impenetrable as this constellation of meanly discreet and discreetly respectable beings who figure in the Forsyte Saga.

The thesis of this chapter is that both the peasant's craving for land and tangible property generally, and the motive that made Soames Forsyte want to own pictures, estate, wife, and everything else that was seemly, is not a fundamental motive. The human animal wants a feeling of security, and it wants freedom and the feeling of power. Those wants are truly fundamental. The ideology into which the peasant and business man and other developments of the peasant have been born, has moulded these natural, fundamental and ineradicable motives into the form of tangible property, which carries with it to them the assurance of satisfaction for these essential desires. Their persona is that of the struggling or successful owner, and they can see themselves comfortably in no other rôle. But the experience of the "educated" series of types shows that the satisfaction of these desires (security, freedom and the desire for power) can be guaranteed in quite other forms. And just so far as it is guaranteed in other forms, so does the desire to possess tangible property evaporate as a social motive.

This is well shown in the preference so many people display for irresponsible property, the preference for being creditors rather than owners. We shall study the genesis of the "investing public" in Chapter X, and the characteristics of the modern rich in Chapter XI, and then it will become manifest how profoundly and extensively the idea of property is being changed from an array of material possessions to entries in a bank account. The Individualist's picture of the modern rich man as a property owner, owning, cherishing, increasing, extending his estate and possessions, is already a dream of past conditions. Soames Forsyte was behind his own times. Even the French peasant now, instead of hoarding, cleaning and counting his precious coins, sends his money to the bank and buys "*bons*." The disposition to disencumber oneself of property so soon as the human values it stands for, security, freedom and the sense of power can be got in some other way, seems to be well-nigh universal. "Do it *for* me," says the modern successful man, working away at his own special task, and is only too careless of the competence of the receiver to whom he hands his gains.

The objective of any theory of Scientific Property must be just this release of successful people from their present obligation to own irrelevant property they do not want to administer or watch over, and conversely to release property from the absentee owner and the hands of those who do not want to administer it to the best advantage for the community.

We have said that the sub-man began the accumulation of

wealth when he kept and carried a stone in his hand, and that our species tied itself to locality when it had accumulated more gear than it could conveniently carry all the time. There are many ways of viewing history, but from one angle it is to be seen as the piling up of more and more encumbering stuff. At last man is seen tied to the fields he has ploughed, the trees he has planted and the house he has built. We have written of his enslavement to toil and his present hopes of release. His personal release from his maximum encumbrance with property has also been going on—with intermissions—for a considerable time. He has gradually been freeing himself from tangible burthensome ownership by a process of monetary abstraction. To understand how that has come about we must begin with some elementary considerations about money.

§ 9. *The Complexities and Mutations of the Money Idea*

We will begin our exploration of this process of the "dematerialization," shall we call it? of property by a sketchy and generalized consideration of Money, of the money idea and suggestion, which becomes in abnormal cases the money passion. We are dealing here with a variable intricate complex. "Money" means in a thousand minds a thousand subtly different, roughly similar, systems of images, associations, suggestions and impulses. And this variety is disregarded in almost all our discussion of monetary questions. The general disposition is to treat it as something simple—if a little difficult to define.

Two convenient ways of discussing money present themselves. The first, the traditional, is to treat money as the development of a particular type of portable property and trace its progressive specialization as an intermediary in barter. The second is to consider money as the medium through which the general economic life of mankind is now being conducted and to criticize the laws and conventions determining its use from the point of view of the racial welfare. The convergence of the two methods brings tradition to the test of the creative idea.

A large amount of the literature of finance fails to distinguish clearly between these two different ways of approach or to realize that there are still imperfectly explored gaps between the current conclusions attained by one process and those reached by the other. In these still unmapped gaps lie the psychological processes by which money has achieved its present cardinal importance in economic life.

In our historical introduction we have glanced already at the onset of money. A sort of money of account seems to have preceded real money. A shield was worth so many head of cattle, and so on; the need for a numerical standard by which to envisage barter was early recognized. It is quite possible that debts were remembered in terms of such "proto-money," as soon as, or even sooner than, the time when metals—weighed at first and later stamped—began to be used as a convenient intermediary in trade. The tally conception of money, that is to say, may be older than the precious, portable, hoardable commodity conception. Gold and silver, copper and iron, became first the most convenient and habitual and then the standard materials for meeting the demand of the tally. With coinage they became the realized tally. But quite early in the story we hear of the Carthaginians using "leather" money, tokens or parchment bills; that is to say, the valuable metals were not handed about but set down somewhere in security, while the tally element of the money circulated by itself.

In a preceding section we pointed out that the idea of property is a *simplified* idea, that primitive man, with no general terms and no habits of generalization, thought of each thing and variety of thing according to its uses and conditions and had no general concept of material property at all. We noted that down to the present the law has always struggled with an apprehension that property is classifiable and should be classified. But the effect of money, even of money of account, was to help man very far towards an unsound simplification of the property notion. He was able to get out of sight of its variety by abstracting it as a monetary value. He began to think of everything as vendible, interchangeable and divisible. How far that extravagant extension of this idea of vendibility has been carried in human thought can be measured by the fact that such things as the crown (king-ship) of Poland, wives, the command of regiments, the cure of souls, the caliphate, have on occasion been reduced to monetary values and sold and purchased.

And this simplification of property favoured also the extension of the idea of absolute ownership to all things. What you could buy and sell you could surely give, change or destroy. You could buy a slave—and break him. You could buy a picture by Holbein and burn it.

Further, crude conception of money undermined the feeling of joint and collective ownership and responsibility. It was easy to step from the idea that a collective property could be esti-mated in monetary terms to the authentic division of the total into the vendible shares. So that in both the ages of money, that is to say, under the Roman republic and empire and from the Middle Ages down to the present time, money ideology, by the facilities and enhancement it has afforded absolute individual ownership, has been potent in breaking up communal and collec-tive systems and detaching customary owners from contact with and responsibility to the soil. In both the First (the Roman) and the Second (the Modern) Money Age there have been parallel changes that did not occur in any preceding phase of civilization. Debt was less restrained, it was incurred with great ease, usury assumed fantastic dimensions, and taxation developed to an un-precedented degree. The "poor" appear in the denunciations of the prophets; the proletarians take their place in the Roman constitution. For the first time "estates" arise from the selling up of dispossessed men. The accumulation of capital and the concentration of production in large enterprises become pos-sible. The Roman process was already in its dégringolade before partnership developed into shareholding. Joint-stock enterprise and power-driven mechanism are two essential differences between the First and the Second Money Age.

We turn from the historical study of money, as the develop-ment of a system of conventions, simplifications and disregards, to its second aspect, to its study as a method of carrying on the work of the world. And that means beginning not with money

368 The Work, Wealth and Happiness of Mankind

as the measure of property, but with money as wages, conferring "purchasing power." At the outset of this second enquiry we must ask what is required of money. Just as man takes the horse and without much discussion of how that animal reduced its toes to one and what its life on the steppes and prairies of pre-historic times was like, castrates it and sets it to dragging carts, so those who approach the money idea from the second point of view seek to reduce this growth of conventions and acceptances, to the service of our economic life with as few concessions as possible. And just as the horse, because it is not a simple *ad hoc* machine but the product of a long organic evolution, has to be taken at times to the veterinary surgeon, driven with caution, fed with care, and sometimes put out to grass, so the money complex, which has never been a simple *ad hoc* contrivance, needs wari-ness and watchfulness in its economic use, or it may fail and fall or bolt with or overset the machine. Essentially both horse and money complex were evolved without human premeditation and are only partially subjugated to their functions.

Primarily money was a tally for property; it arose out of the needs of barter, but for the purposes of this second discussion money can be considered as primarily wages and salary; as the sure and reasonable reward of labour, the cheque for so much purchasing power. How far it can be, and how far it really is that, we must enquire. Here, at any rate, we can say that it is at present sufficiently that to keep the great world machine of pro-duction going. Because of their confidence in this cheque, the workers pour into the shops, mines, fields and factories we have surveyed in our earlier chapters. Destroy that confidence ab-solutely, and the machinery will stop dead.

Our generation has seen in two big human communities the practical loss of that confidence, and has some measure of the effect. I wish I could give statistics and photographs of scenes in Berlin during the final slump of the mark in 1922. Berlin was a terrible city then; never had I been before in a city where nearly every human being was visibly dismayed and broken-hearted— except in Petrograd in 1920. The German collapse was due to very complex causes; the Russian state of affairs was mainly due to a frank and deliberate attempt to abolish money. It was to be made utterly worthless by the unlimited printing of paper money, and then it was to be replaced by cards with tear-off coupons like the rationing cards issued in Great Britain during the Great War. Every citizen was to receive a card periodically, with tear-off coupon for milk, meat, wine, clothing, transport, fuel, books, furniture, theatre, all his needs, and these coupons he was to exchange for these necessities at the communal stores. It was an entirely needless and clumsy experiment to make upon a population already sorely distressed. One insurmountable obstacle was that there were practically no goods worth talking about in the stores. There was a shortage even of flour. It had been quite impossible to improvise the organization of supply and distribution upon the new lines, and everyone was attempting evasions of the law against old-fashioned buying and selling. When I was in Russia at that time I found money still had value: ten thousand roubles was considered rather a better tip than a hard-boiled egg—I had provided myself with both forms of money—and there were still individuals who were not in urgent need of an egg, who did not want it to decay on their hands, and preferred the reserve purchasing power of money even though it might be difficult to exercise. Furtive trading was going on in the north in spite of an iron régime of suppression, and in Moscow and at wayside railway stations there was open selling. The distinctive quality of money is the freedom of choice it gives its possessors, and this those tickets destroyed altogether. A certain peddling of coupons presently arose between people anxious for more of one thing and less of another, and after a time the complexity of supplying goods to meet coupon demands became so great that the whole experiment was abandoned. What the worker needs, if you would keep him working, is plainly a cheque for "anything money can buy" in return for his services rendered.

Our modern economic organization, our whole modern human society, has grown up on the assumption, the colourable pretense at least, that the money distributed in wages does give that, and I cannot conceive of it carrying on now in any other fashion without becoming almost unrecognizably different. Our civilization can as little give up the use of money now, as our bodies can the use of blood. The practical problem is to ensure the best blood possible—to keep out poisons and contagions and avoid anæmia.

To these matters we will return in greater detail in Chapter X. Within the limits of this present chapter we consider money only in so far as it is a motivating idea.

§ 10. *A Résumé of the Coördinating Motives in a Modern Community*

Let us now recapitulate this chapter and state in general terms the psychological essentials of modern economic and social coöperation. In the first place, as we have pointed out, it is, at bottom, coöperation against the grain. The human being, when fully adult, is still fundamentally a highly individualized and ego-centred animal, and his social life is based on subjugation and education. In the past subjugation and the retardation of the fiercer adult qualities, have been the prevailing factors in the process.

Compared with the male gorilla, *Homo sapiens* never really grows up. We have already pointed this out in § 5 of Chapter I. In every man a war is continually going on between the gregarious instincts he has retained from immaturity, his innate desire to conform to the opinion about him, to be liked and respected by his fellows, on the one hand, and on the other his egoism, his desire to do the best for himself, to express himself fully and to dominate and prevail over others. This conflict is not so apparent in many of the savage communities, as it is in contemporary life. It reveals itself with the development of privacy and private property and with opportunities for individual enrichment. Civilized social life is based on the fact that the second, the egoistic system of ideas, can be mastered and modified by and subordinated to the first. Where the community accepts an ethic those individuals who disregard it can be forced to conform. The ethic itself can be changed by education. There has been an immense amount of mere subjugation in the past. In the future, we are going to suggest, education may largely replace subjugation. We may replace the broken and retarded individuality by a directed and self-disciplined individuality.

As we have seen, three main strands of tradition mingle in the process of breaking-in man to society. There is the peasant tradition with its exaltation of toil and its desperate clutch upon property, its fear, its political submissiveness, and its great power of passive resistance. There is the nomad tradition with its rapacity and handsome spending. There is the priestly tradition, the tradition of the trained and educated man with its repudiation of mercenariness, its conceptions of service and disinterestedness. How these strands interwove and interacted to constitute mediæval society is a matter of history. The civilized aristocrat touched thought and learning with a quality of enterprise, and the clash of cultures, of Latin Christendom with Arabic-Greek knowledge, released the scepticisms and enquiries that opened the way to the modern world. All these traditions still mingle in us and about us. Out of them we build our personas, our conceit of ourselves, our conception of our rôles and of what becomes us. But the proportionate influence of these three factors changes.

As we have seen, the new world-wide economic system that has been coming into existence in the last century and a half is rapidly superseding the independent small cultivator and the independent town trader and town artisan, by large enterprises employing wages—workers, foremen, managers and directors. With the diminution of that peasant-small-townsman stratum which was until recently the bulk of human society, goes the disappearance of the peasant-small-townsman type of persona. It is replaced by a complex of new ideals. Similarly the advance of social discipline has turned the aristocratic predatory type, partly in an instinctive effort for its self-preservation, to militarism and the maintenance of nationalist and monarchist institutions, and partly to a mercenary social mixture with the inflated entrepreneurs who have arisen from the peasant-townsman mass. The struggle for the new civilization with nationalist militarism is all about us—and is still indecisive. And meanwhile there has been an immense extension of education, *with all the strands of disinterestedness it brings with it*. The modern population is rapidly becoming a wholly literate one. The mentality of the learned clerk penetrates everywhere. Popular education has been recognized as necessary even by business entrepreneurs frankly anxious to keep the worker under. A machine civilization has no use for an illiterate citizen. The tradition-based mind is too inflexible for its varying and progressive needs.

The priestly-intellectual tradition has never set any value upon either the accumulation or the violent acquisition of property. Its disposition is to secure a position, through salary, savings or what not, in which it can operate freely, and then to take no more thought of money, but rather to get the work or service done. The satisfaction of good achievement is greater than the satisfaction of possessions. Our teachers arise out of this tradition and bring with them the same repudiation of accumulation and mercenary motives, which they instil into a larger and larger proportion of the population. The modern wages worker and that extending class, the salariat, do not even think of ever being wealthy; they are not in that competition; they want to be safe, comfortable and pleasant in their lives, free from anxiety, free from excessive labour, free to do their individual task well. For these ends they will be acquisitive of money. They do not want money for its own sake, and they do not want money for power. They want it to spend, they want it in the background for emergencies. They cannot do without it. When they come into the modern economic-social organization, this is the material end they have in view. This is the chief motive our developing modern economic organization has to reckon with. This search for security, comfort and liberty, is, as we bring consciousness into our review of human activities, the ruling motive which keeps the marionettes busy in our model industrial machine.

People say that modern life turns wholly on getting money. But the getting of money either by trading or other forms of "making money," or as wages, salary, rent and interest is now only in a small minority of cases an end in itself. The satisfaction of the demands of the persona constitutes, now as ever, the guiding principle of human conduct, and the value of the money system in the machinery is to be judged entirely by its ability to satisfy those demands. By that criterion we shall go in our subsequent examination of the currency system and its conceivable developments. Suffice it here to repeat that the modern persona is being steadily modified by education in the direction of substituting service of some type, and generally now coöperative service, for the pure acquisitiveness and desire for dominance of the traditional social scheme.

Compared with the localized economic systems of the past, the new order which is developing about us, which makes a larger and larger part of the human population, employees, workers, officials and specialists seems at the first glance to be abolishing freedom and making more and more people subordinated to a single world economic machine. But that is due to a common confusion between independence and freedom. Independence is no doubt being abolished by the synthetic forces at work, in the case of individuals just as in the case of sovereign states, but independence is not freedom. An "independent" peasant or small tradesman is tied, with scarcely a day's holiday, to his cultivation or his shop; he is the slave of local custom, and he must toil without surcease to the end of his days. An employee under generous modern conditions—dictated, be it noted, not by sentiment but by considerations of maximum efficiency—has daily leisure, holidays and an altogether greater meed of personal freedom.

Large-scale production and distribution release human beings to self-respect and initiative at every point in its organization. Domestic service in the past was practically personal slavery; the servant was at the beck and call of the employer from morning to night. Where mediævalism still prevails, as Lady Simon's admirable book on China has recently reminded us, domestic servants are still slaves. They are bought and sold. They are struck and beaten. In such backward countries as Italy servants are still beaten; I have seen a chambermaid beaten by the manageress of a hotel. But under collective housekeeping and in any large establishment servants become a "staff" with clear rights and definite limits to their duties. A great deal of nagging, bullying and oppression may still occur in any staff where the housekeeper, the head waiter or house steward is under-educated and evilly disposed; the new age is not the immediate coming of the kingdom of heaven; but in a well organized concern there are powers above the tyrant and modes of resistance against tyranny. It is possible to appeal against ill-treatment, and in the closely observed business of the ultra-modern type, friction will be perceptible in the lowered quantity and quality of the work and will be made the subject of enquiry.

PERSONAL SERVICE

At many points in the economic social machine there is still and probably there will always have to be direct personal service. There is the valet or courier to a busy man; there are the devils, amanuenses and secretaries, who eke out the powers of some person of exceptional initiative; there are the "companions" of the old and isolated. But a society which is replacing conceptions of advantage and dominance by the idea of disinterested effort will change such relationships very substantially even when it does not abolish them. The old way was for the principal person to behave towards his seconders as a lord towards inferiors. He was their substitute for motive; theirs not to reason why he commanded this or that. But in the atmosphere of an educated community he will be recognized not as a lord but as a specialist, and his claim for assistance will be based not on his highmightiness but upon his insufficiency. The valet or courier does things for him because, having regard for his preoccupations and limitations, he is totally unable to do them himself; the secretary supplements, extends, clarifies and checks his efforts. The secretary or valet is a protector of his principal from petty distresses and details generally. The relationship rises therefore from the level of subjugation towards the level of sympathetic aid and friendship. Exceptional ability can be recognized on either hand, and respect can be mutual and complementary. Occasionally to the end of time, the secondary person will have to show loyalty to the principal. Loyalty one may define as personal obedience to the initiatives of another even when those initiatives are not understood or seem to be wrong, obedience because, on the whole, the secondary person believes in the general rightness of the initiator, and in some distinctive unpredictable and inestimable quality that gives him or her the right to indisputable initiative.

CHAPTER THE NINTH

How Work Is Paid for and Wealth Accumulated

CHAPTER THE NINTH

How Mankind Is Paid and Wealth Accumulated

§ 1. *The Counting House Comes into the Picture*

IN THE preceding chapter one or two fundamental things about money have been stated. It was at first a commodity like any other commodity. And there were various standards of value: cattle, land, for example, by which the relative values of things could be appraised. Metals were only one sort of standard by which things were valued. But in a slow, complex way money has become something more than a commodity. And now it is becoming something which is not a commodity at all. There is now, as we have pointed out, another way of looking at money, that is to say, as a guarantee of "purchasing power."

That was as far as Chapter VIII went with the discussion of money. It passed on to other aspects of human motive, for motive was its essential subject.

In this chapter this matter of money and monetary property is to be studied more closely. We are, as the heading of this section intimates, going to bring the Counting House into the picture.

But first let us step back for a moment and consider the whole plan of this work. The earlier chapters were designed to show the purely material development of the human community. We showed substances being subdued and handled; extraneous power brought into the service of man; food being made, treated and distributed, clothing, housing, roads, and ever increasing means of transport being provided, and at first there was hardly a human being, except for a few scientific workers and a customer here and there, in the spectacle. It was the mechanism of human life we dealt with and nothing more. Then, having prepared the scene and the stage, we brought in the workers and managers and set them to work.

But the way in which everyone was toiling remained unexplained. Why did they do it? We tried to get inside the heads of these workers, to make an analysis of their mental operations. We introduced the idea of the guiding "persona" in the mind. We showed how money came into human life to liquidate what would otherwise be an impossibly complex system of services and exchanges.

The design of those earlier chapters was to suggest a panorama of great productive and distributing plants, wide cultivations, housing, hotels, transport systems, research laboratories, and the like, but in all these presentations, certain oblong areas remained blank and no attention was given them. These blanks were the counting house and the board room. But now, after our study of motives, we are in a position to deal profitably with these necessary organs in the industrial body. We can now take into our purview the going to and from the bank, the question of prices and profits that underlie the more grossly material processes of the workshop and mine. Particulars about pay envelopes, tills, cash registers, estimating costs and determination of prices, are secondary and technical matters upon which we will not enlarge, but the going to and from the bank, the declaration of a dividend, are broad essential things to which we have to give our very best attention.

Why does the factory now increase its output and take on more hands? Why does it now slack off and slow down? Why does it raise or lower the wages it pays? What is happening? It is making profits or it is making a loss. The board room and counting house are getting or losing money. Through all the machinery of production and distribution runs money. Money is the blood of this monstrous economic organism we are studying, and finance is its circulatory system.

In the *Science of Life,* there is a chapter called The Living Body. There is an account first of the blood, then of the way in which it circulates about the body, then of the organs in which it is made, refreshed, cleansed, and finally of its working and control. This is not a bad plan to follow now with the blood of the great economic body of mankind. Only we have to bear in mind that while the blood and circulation of a human body have been perfected by millions of ancestral trials, successes and failures, the economic body of mankind is a new and unprecedented and untried organism that is struggling into being, a body experimental to the extremest degree and begotten not of like parents but by the flowing together of a number of smaller economic systems, themselves experimental and not tried out, but suddenly by the development of communications brought into our present larger synthesis of work and effort.

§ 2. *What Currency Has to Do and What It Is**

Now here our limitless museum of economic activities becomes extremely useful. Let us admit the enormous possibilities of curious and almost useless knowledge about money, and let us put it all in a great wing of that museum, and leave it there. (There is perhaps hardly a reader of this book who has not at some time stood on the threshold of a room devoted to numismatics—and turned away from that awful vista of yards and yards of idealized royal profiles and symbolized pretensions.) And further, in that remote wing we will imagine a most instructive exposition of old and new methods of gold-winning, and that there it is possible to trace every stage from the mine to the mint; learn about the finding of gold, the method of distributing the minted money and the immobilization of large quantities of it in reserves and hoards. That collection would also display the various types of paper and token money. Mints, assaying and the special nature and precautions of paper money printing would have their place. There would have to be a picturesque section devoted to the activities of the forger and the sweater of coin, a footnote section, so to speak, a museum exhibit of false money in the smasher's depot. All that history and detail we may take for granted here and pass on.

---

*A good and lively book not too long for the general reader is Professor Edwin Cannan's *Modern Currency and the Regulation of Its Value*. 1931.

Moreover, if that display was to be at all comprehensive, it would have to include all the material for a précis of the varieties of monetary method, some of them still very primitive, operative or recently operative in the different sovereign states of the world. Laborious and tedious it would be, and yet discursively interesting, to trace how the widely dispersed right to mint money in the Middle Ages was gradually concentrated by the development of the modern national State, and how the steadily intensified obsession of the human mind by the idea of independent sovereignty since the Treaty of Westphalia has stood in the way of any international issues. The money of every country has been subjected to the advertisement of national symbols. Almost always, when a monarchy existed, one side of the current coin, at least, has been given over to the advertisement of the reigning prince. It is more than a little absurd that the gold sovereign which is now used by the British only for foreign trade should carry such advertisement matter, but the association dates from the remotest use of money, and few people seem to realize its present irrelevance. It is the visible reminder that a matter of world-wide importance is still controlled by a patchwork of authorities all working for their own self-preservation, and none realizing fully or admitting frankly the functions money has to perform in a world-wide economic community. It is a picturesque survival from the quaint romantic past through which our ancestors worked their way darkly to our present use of money.

"It is surprising," said Sir Robert Hadfield in a recent address, "to realize how comparatively small in weight is the total quantity of this metal which holds such sway over our affairs. The production and stocks of gold are measured in ounces, whereas the metallurgist working in iron and steel reckons in tons.

"Recently I came across a most interesting and ably written pamphlet, 'Summarized Data of Gold Production,' by Mr. Robert H. Ridgway and the Staff of the Common Metals Division of the United States Department of Commerce, which throws much light on the part which gold has played in the history of the world during the past six hundred years. From a careful study of available records, it is concluded that the world's production of gold since the discovery of America, from the year 1493 to 1927 inclusive, amounted to 1,004 million fine ounces, including 1 per cent. for unrecorded or under-estimated output.

"Expressed in ounces, this sounds to be an immense quantity, yet in dead solid weight it amounts to about 30,720 tons, occupying a volume of slightly more than 56,000 cubic feet, or if we consider the whole of the gold produced in the world since the time of the discovery of America, this would go into a 38-foot cube. Not a very impressive block as regards size or weight to have ruled men's passions and destinies for more than half a thousand years! I wonder if its magic power is destined to continue. . . .

"The value of the actual and latest annual output, that is, for the year 1927, amounted to £83,000,000. From the weight point of view of a ferrous metallurgist this represents the miserable figure of only about 600 tons, or a 10-foot cube!" . . .

But we must turn away from that obscure and glittering miscellany of curious facts about gold. Our business with money is its functional value in the world organism; we are concerned not with what it has been (except in so far as this throws light upon its working now) but with what it is and what is now required of it.

We have dealt already (in Chapter VIII) with the psychological rôle of the money complex and shown how the bulk of the ordinary man's activities is based, however insecurely, on a belief in the practical trustworthiness of money. The money complex keeps the wheels of the modern economic world turning. That is the point of maximum importance about money, that *it works the worker*. Its relation to the worker is closely parallel to that of the blood in our bodies to the individual cell. It brings him alimentation and stimulus; it carries off his products.

Money guarantees, or to put it more truthfully, if the social machine is to work it should guarantee, to every worker who receives it as wages or salary, a certain definite purchasing power, and to every producer of a desired commodity, a reward in general purchasing power commensurate with the general need for his product. Then the worker or producer "knows what he is about." Work is done, services are rendered and goods produced under the most harmonious conditions. Money, then, from the point of view of the living, coöperating individual, has to be a trustworthy counter on which everyone can rely without further scrutiny. It must stand, steadily, for so much goods. On that basis everyone can deal. If a worker—in a world of steadfast money—is not content with what he gets he demands a rise in wages; similarly the producer raises or lowers the price of his commodity, and things adjust themselves by haggling and bargaining; the money throughout remaining a trustworthy and unchallenged counter of what is going on.

That is the ideal. That is money as it should be, seen from both the point of view of the general healthy activity of the community and from the point of view of the ordinary working individual. That is what almost everyone tries to believe money is—a sure thing—and something that will keep good. A worker who earns money wants to feel and should feel that to-morrow, or next month, or if he wants to save up for something, next year, the purchasing power of that money will be practically the same. Or, putting the phrase "purchasing power" into an equivalent expression, he wants to live in a world of stable prices. "Stabilized prices" is only another expression for trustworthy money.

But now, where are we to find the guarantees that the money we receive and pay is such a stable, trustworthy counter? Where and what is the guarantee that goods will be forthcoming and that prices are to "stay put"? The issuing authority, which is, under existing conditions, the State, the sovereign government (in the United States the federal government to which the states in that contract of federation, the Constitution, delegated the right of issue), or a controlled central bank working in more or less close coöperation with the State, makes or rather seems and tries to make, this guarantee. But it does so under rather difficult conditions. It is not itself in the position to supply the goods its money should guarantee and which the normal worker believes it will guarantee. Except in Soviet Russia the responsible State is not the prime producer of goods nor the distributor

of goods. It is not in very close or effective control of the production and distribution of goods. It has no direct and exact
means of preventing shortages or gluts. Its guarantee therefore is at most the expression of its faith and belief that, through
channels outside its immediate jurisdiction, the necessary goods
will be forthcoming. It implies that it will do its utmost to keep
the money it issues in a stable relation to the supply of goods,
and the confidence and security of the general working community rest in the prevalent belief in its ability and good faith.

This, let us repeat, is the ideal money seen from the point of
view of the active individual and the point of view of the commonweal. We are not writing here of the actual money in our
pockets, nor of the current state of affairs. We shall come to
that later. We are discussing the money that ought to be in our
pockets. And clearly this ideal money of which we are writing,
can only serve its end of giving a fixed and definite purchasing
power, if it is issued in strict relation to the volume of goods
available. In other words, a satisfactory money must be a "regulated" money. The circulation must be, as Keynes terms it, a
"managed" circulation. It must be barometric. If prices tend to
rise, the issue of money should in some manner be restricted; if
they tend to fall, the issue of money should be increased. For in
no other way can the worker be sure of his due reward in satis-
factions and consumable goods.

We are writing here of money from the point of view of its
function of working the worker—of providing an incentive to
toil. But that is a modern criterion. The idea of money represented *commodities in general* and controlled to that end is entirely modern. In the ruder past, money represented or actually
consisted of one single commodity which experience had found
convenient and reasonably stable for trading purposes, and the
worker was much more frequently satisfied by payments in kind
in lieu of or in addition to monetary wages. He did not live so
entirely on his wages as the modern worker does—and he did
not save to the same extent. His interest in commodity prices
was less vital.

Nowadays statisticians give us "index numbers" to show the

fluctuations in the prices of commodities. They will give an index number for any particular year to show the general state of prices for all the staple goods consumed by the community in that year. The determination of such an index number is a highly technical matter.* It is an approximation which can never become precise. But then every quantitative matter in life is approximate. The nature of the indications of the index number will vary with the importance attached to this, that and the other particular commodity. And manifestly our ideas of what is desirable in life, our ideas of what the normal citizen's life should be, will play an important part in the value given to this or that commodity. Social politics cannot be kept out of the index number. But under criticism and acute examination, index numbers can be worked out which will be more and more precisely indicative of the value of money in terms of material welfare—as it is judged by contemporary standards. A managed circulation of money would maintain such an index number at a constant level. The issuing authorities would watch the principal factors in general price movements, such as bank credit, money rates and the prices of raw materials; they would check their deductions by any increases or decreases in the production of goods and the figures of unemployment, and would then make up their minds whether the all important price index was likely to move. If they anticipated too great a rise in prices they would make money dear and restrict bank credit. If prices seemed about to fall they would counteract this by making money cheap and credit plentiful.

All this so far is fairly simple—until we come to working it out in practical detail. The principles are simple. They follow naturally upon our previous consideration of the rôle of money in human motivation. And if we were offering this explanation to one of Mr. Shaw's young men just hatched out of the egg, to whom we referred in § 1 of our Introduction, it would be quite natural for him to say: "Then what is all this bother about money? All this is quite straightforward. Your statistical de-

---

*A good book for the general reader is Irving Fisher's *The Making of Index Numbers.*

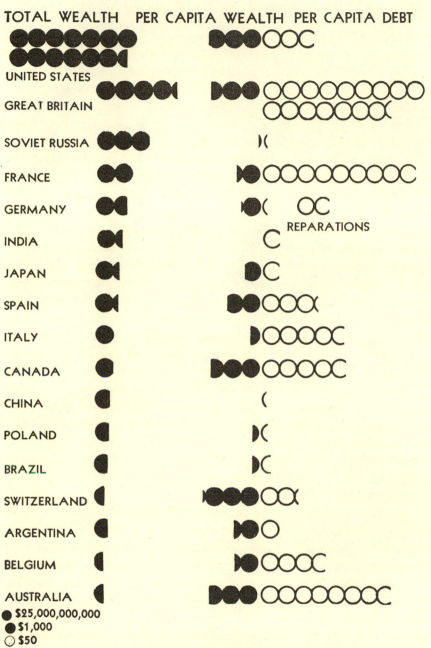

TOTAL WEALTH   PER CAPITA WEALTH PER CAPITA DEBT

UNITED STATES

GREAT BRITAIN

SOVIET RUSSIA

FRANCE

GERMANY

INDIA

JAPAN

SPAIN

ITALY

CANADA

CHINA

POLAND

BRAZIL

SWITZERLAND

ARGENTINA

BELGIUM

AUSTRALIA

REPARATIONS

● $25,000,000,000
● $1,000
○ $50

INHERITANCE OF WEALTH AND DEBT

Post-war estimates of national wealth and debt, showing the inequalities of the debt burthen under which children are born in various countries.

partment tells you—with ever increasing exactitude—how much money you need to have in circulation for the type and standard of life you desire, and you issue it and increase or restrict it accordingly." And if we told him that that was not at all what we were doing at the present time, he would be very much astonished.

When we told him that the issue of money in most of our communities was directly related to the amount of gold stored in certain national banks and treasuries, he would ask us why we chose to introduce this complication into a relatively simple matter. Why drag in the gold at all? What has gold to do with it? Why take this particular commodity of all commodities and pin your monetary issue to that? Why pin money to any single commodity when it has to deal with all commodities?

We should have to answer this, and the first thing we should have to explain to him would be that this complication with gold has not been introduced into a simple business, but that the complication has always been there and that it is only now we are attempting to simplify it away. We should have to tell him that this institution of currency has grown age by age; that it has not been invented suddenly to serve its present ends; and that he must carry his mind back to a past when there was no such thing as currency at all. In fact, we should have to take him to those museum galleries we have already glanced down in the earlier part of this section and tell him the old, old story, how first all trade was barter, how the precious metals were found to be a most convenient intermediary in bartering—you bartered goods for them and afterwards bartered them for other goods—and so how it has come about that to this day the idea of barter, bartering gold, hampers our minds at every turn when we try to work the money invention. We want—to put the thing compactly—to give our ordinary working citizen a certain definite amount of purchasing power; that is the modern idea; but what we do in reality is to give him a bit of gold (or a bill or cheque representing—or purporting to represent—gold) which he then has to trade for what he wants. Our money is not yet actual functional money at all. It is a privileged commodity in disguise. We have built up our modern economic life on the wages system very rapidly and uncritically, and it is only now that we are beginning to see clearly and feel the consequences of the difference in nature between the functional money, the worker's cheque, we now require, and the metallic commodity that has hitherto met our requirements.

"But it would be perfectly easy now to cut the gold out of the story, would it not?", our young man out of the egg would ask.

We should have to embark upon further explanations to show why that is not so easy. To these explanations we shall now proceed. And first it may be advisable to show our egg-born enquirer some of the things that may happen to money when it is liberated from its dependence on gold, and not, as yet, securely tethered to a statistically satisfactory index number. Then he would realize why the world puts its trust not indeed in a golden calf but in a cube of gold measuring rather less than forty feet each way, and why it clings to that block in spite of the greatest strain and hardship, for fear lest worse betide if its grip relax.

§ 3. The Inflation, Deflation and Devalorization of Currencies

Let us tell that story as simply as we can and with as little use of technicalities as possible.

From the middle of the nineteenth century until the bills came in for that orgy of waste and slaughter, the World War of 1914–18, the progress of the world in wealth and prosperity had been unexampled and continuous. Indeed, for three hundred years after the break-up of Christendom that progress had gone on. Much of that advance was due no doubt to invention and geographical discovery, but the realization of the possibilities opened up by science and invention, was greatly facilitated by the stimulation brought about by an increasing supply of the precious metals, and—in particular since 1849—of gold. Before 1849 the stimulant was silver rather than gold—silver from the discovery of America onward with gold in the second place. And then gold.

Just how much that enhanced supply of metal for currency was necessary to the modernization of the world; whether the world could have been modernized without an abundance of money is a speculation into which we will not enter. The stimulation is undeniable. Upon successive floods first of silver and then of gold the world was carried from the toil civilization of the past to the power civilization of to-day.

In 1849, gold in great quantities was found in California; in 1851, Australian gold poured in abundantly, and then Canada joined the producers and, richest source of all, South Africa (from the eighties on). Eighty-five per cent of the gold raised in the world has been added to our monetary resources during the past eighty years, and well over half in the present century. This influx of gold provided the world for a time with a world currency, an informal world currency. No one foresaw, no one planned the sudden liquidation of world trade which resulted from this gold flood. It came. And reinforcing it was a steady development of banking and a use of cheques that were, in effect, an addition to currency. But of that reinforcement we will speak later. This increase in the amount and speed of currency, by a happy coincidence, did to all intents and purposes what an intelligent economic world control would have done deliberately. It met the increased productivity of the new railway, steamship, metallurgical era, with just the thing that was needed to prevent a great fall in prices, an arrest of production and unemployment; that is to say, it *increased the volume of available means of payment.* Money was more abundant, credit had increased, and it was easy to repay debts and launch out upon new enterprises. There were fluctuations and crises, but no break-down; there were sixty years of advance and prosperity. For that period of maximum progress which ended in the war, all the chief countries of the world had currencies based on gold, currencies that underwent no very great fluctuations in regard to one another, and which increased in volume so as to keep pace generally with the ever increasing production and trade of the age. There were undulations in the process, and more particularly between 1873 and 1896, but no catastrophic fall. Mankind paid off the past and faced the future with confidence.

If our young enquirer, just out of the egg, had hatched out in 1910, let us say, we should have told him of the unparalleled merits of this great gift of Providence, the gold standard; we should have expressed no doubts of its permanence; we should have explained how it combined cosmopolitan economics with national integrity, and unless he had the shrewdness to ask certain penetrating questions we should have left it at that.

The war arrested and ultimately broke up this unpremeditated monetary cosmopolitanism. Following upon the outbreak of the war the belligerent governments withdrew gold from internal circulation and resorted to the printing press to replace it. Each in its own measure overprinted. At the close of the war the practical monetary solidarity of the world had disappeared, and the overprinting of paper money continued. Without any concerted action. The exchanges between the various national currencies were fluctuating in a manner that would have been incredible in the tranquil decades before 1914. Each sovereign power was struggling with its own monetary problems, and there was no world-wide realization of the need for an economic conference and board of control to deal with the world's economic situation as a whole. No one saw it as a whole. Providence had kept money working very well for sixty years—and people felt that the benevolent work would surely go on again as soon as things settled down. The Conference of Versailles, a gathering of politicians obsessed by the romantic nationalism of their school books, concentrated chiefly upon the elaboration of good rankling boundary disputes for posterity and upon punitive reparation arrangements that recalled the end of the second Punic War. And each power tried to get the better of the others. The sentimental generosities of the 1914 alliances were all forgotten. Every belligerent country was wounded, damaged, overstrained, irritated, greedy, afraid and in a state of inflamed patriotism. Each victor was resolved to get *something* for the victory. Each, therefore, presently set about the readjustment of its evidently very shaky money arrangements in its own fashion.

For the better part of a century finance had been cosmopolitan and had centred upon London. No one had planned that: it had happened. Finance now became national. A new spirit came into monetary affairs. As long as England had been the world's banker, the Germans, Jews, Italians and so forth, who had controlled the City naturally did not seek any undue advantages for Great Britain. They worked the gold standard by rule of thumb, taking only economic factors into account. Banking was an international service, centring in London. It had concentrated about the London nucleus, quite independently of English national quality. Financially London had never been a national centre, it had been a cosmopolitan focus. The City, throughout its gold-standard free-trading period, had existed not for Britain but for the world. All this was now changed. With the utmost ease the world forgot a monetary unification it had never fully realized.

Nearly every country in the world had been issuing more paper or token money for internal use than its resources justified. That is, there were more tickets for goods than could be honoured at the existing price level. So prices rose to restore the balance between tickets and goods. But in order to meet the interest on their debts, and to pay for war materials, swollen war salary lists, costs of demobilization, reparations, etc., etc., the separate sovereign powers (each in its own fashion) continued to increase the supply of these tickets. That is to say, independently and separately, they *inflated* the currency already in circulation. And with every increase of the volume of issued money, prices rose higher and higher.

Inflated money favours the worker and the active producers against the creditor, because one need not do so much or produce so much to earn a particular sum of money as one would have to do were the circulation not inflated. It is easier to pay off debts, to pay fixed rents, debentures, interest on loans, in a phase of inflation. Also the holders of the national securities, while receiving the monetary interest they had bargained for, get in effect nothing like the original purchasing power of their money. The community as a whole therefore is able to carry its debts more easily. It is true that higher money wages will be eaten into or even eaten up by higher prices, but these in their turn are made up for by increased employment. It is the family wage and not the individual wage which determines the level of working-class prosperity. Every belligerent government was heavily in debt for war expenditure to the creditor sorts of people, and inflation was a very convenient equivalent of bankruptcy. All the world was burthened with debt, and it would probably have eased the world situation immensely if there could have been a concerted simultaneous equivalent inflation of all currencies, if, for example—and disregarding various local adjustments and complications—an ounce of gold had been given three or four times its pre-war monetary value.

Gold at that time was actually cheap, but that was because it was not being used as a standard. It was cheap because it was in abeyance. So soon as there was an attempt to refer money back to gold, it appreciated, and the reality of the situation became apparent.

When an individual goes bankrupt he pays his creditors a fraction, a "dividend" of so much in the pound, to settle his debts. Money is, in effect, the acknowledgment of a debt from the community in general to the individual, and for a community the equivalent of bankruptcy is for it deliberately to pay only a fraction, a dividend, of the purchasing power its money originally represented. That is to say that monetary inflation is for a country what bankruptcy is for an individual. A concerted general inflation was indicated. Such a world bankruptcy would have relieved the situation altogether, and the general economic life, released and refreshed, could have been resumed at a new monetary level in much the same manner as before.

But nothing of the sort was possible in the feverish post-war atmosphere. Impossible reparation payments in gold had been imposed upon the protesting Germans, and the United States had been figuring out and building great hopes upon the debts (reckoned in gold) owing to her by her allies for munitions supplied them for the common effort. America returned to the gold standard in 1919. She returned to the pre-war weight of gold represented by the dollar. Any increase in the monetary value of gold would have enabled the defeated Germans and the debtor countries of Europe to pay with smaller amounts of it. But the more prices were brought down, the more onerous was the repayment of debt.

It is doubtful if this was done with any idea of increasing the burthen of the debt on the debtor countries. It is more probable that the American deflation was carried out in simple obedience to banking routine—because the Federal Reserve Bank of New York was losing gold—and without regard for the effect that it would have on millions of human lives. At all events, the value of gold was raised in terms of goods—the dollar rose 75 per cent in a year relative to commodity prices. Great Britain took the same course of supporting gold, partly because she did not like to allow the pound to fall too far below the dollar, and was already anxious to get back to the pre-war parity of 4.8. Partly, too, the great rise in prices which had taken place during the war—they had risen over three times from 1913 figures— had inflicted a sense of loss on the debt-owning classes, and British finance is in the hands of just those classes. To them any rise in prices savours of dishonesty, even though it may be accompanied by general prosperity, while falls in prices which create millions of unemployed and bring trade to a standstill nevertheless seem mysteriously "sound."

On the continent of Europe the reverse was going on. The French government, for instance, was seeing the franc fall and making no real effort to stop it because it was realized by the business world in France that this was building up French industry and clearing the country of debt. The other European currencies were fluctuating wildly, but the sum of their movements was always in the direction of inflation.

The monetary situation about May, 1920, was one of immense local inequalities. America was back at the gold standard. But there had been a great interruption of economic life and a great diversion of productive energy to supply munitions to the whole of the allies. There had been a lowered production of goods and an inflow of gold, and goods generally were relatively scarcer in comparison with gold than they had been before the war. Prices rose. There was a rise in prices, although there was no deterioration of the currency by the measure of gold. Prices in the U. S. A. in 1920 were, all over, $2\frac{1}{2}$ times as high as they had been in 1913; $\frac{247}{100}$ to be exact. In Britain the gold standard was still in suspense; Britain was using paper money; prices as compared with 1913 were $\frac{324}{100}$ and the pound note was at that level of inferiority, $\frac{247}{324}$ to the gold dollar. Instead of being at its gold parity, which is nearly five dollars to a pound (4.8), it was under four. Many other European countries were much further away from any gold equivalence. They had so increased their uses of paper and token money that prices were soaring to levels hardly measurable by index numbers. In France the rise in prices was slower. French prices took some time before they doubled the British figures. Denmark, Norway, Sweden, Holland fluctuated within still narrower limits.

Each country pursued its own course with a sublime indifference to the common weal of mankind. In America, there was a steady fall in prices. There was also a drastic restriction of credit. By the end of 1920 prices in America were $42\frac{1}{2}$ per cent what they had been in May of that year, and at that level they remained fairly stable until 1929, when a new fall brought them down to the pre-war figure.

Meanwhile the British authorities set themselves to deflate their currency. The issue of money was restricted, credit was restricted; in two years prices were forced down to 50 per cent of the May, 1920, figure, and the process was continued until in a little over four years, parity with the dollar was attained. This involved a tremendous restraint upon business enterprise and a gigantic transfer of wealth from the producing to the creditor classes. People who had bought War Loan with pounds signifying so much purchasing power found themselves receiving interest in pounds of more than double that purchasing value. They were the lucky ones, and the general community paid for their luck.

The rest of the world did not sink so complacently under the yoke of the creditor. Many states did their utmost not merely

OWED	OWES

UNITED STATES

OWED — GREAT BRITAIN / FRANCE / GERMANY / OTHERS

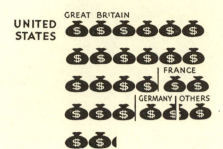

OWES — NONE

GREAT BRITAIN

OWED — GERMANY / FRANCE / OTHERS

OWES — UNITED STATES

FRANCE

OWED — GERMANY / OTHERS

OWES — UNITED STATES / GREAT BRITAIN

GERMANY

OWED — NONE

OWES — FRANCE / GREAT BRITAIN / U.S. / OTHERS

THE STATE OF THE GAME OF INTERNATIONAL DEBTS

WITH units of $10,000,000 indicated by a single sack of gold, this chart shows the annual payments which should normally pass between the principal debtor and creditor nations for the fiscal year ending June 30, 1932.

to shake him off, but to destroy him. A number of governments inflated chaotically. Soviet Russia deliberately inflated the rouble currency to nothing and so pulverized every scrap of savings and abolished its entire creditor class completely. Germany, Austria, Poland and Hungary were all forced to follow the same path. They paid off their internal creditors with rubbish money. No other country went quite so far as these extreme inflationists. But everywhere prices reeled and leapt and staggered. Innumerable modest life schemes were wrecked, and every kind of business was disorganized. Everyone was forced to become something of a speculator; you lent your money, and you did not know whether it would be worth more or less when the time came for repayment; you fixed a price for a transaction, and when the paying time came you were ruined. The varying exchange values of these moneys as they rose or fell in regard to one another produced convulsive movements of goods from one country to another, and there was a vast amount of absolute prohibition of exports and imports, and later a great raising and elaboration of tariff walls, to keep home products at home or to save home industries from avalanches of imports.

The next stage after this phase of chaotic independent inflations was an attempt to return to the monetary cosmopolitanism of pre-war days by a *stabilization* of currencies, that is to say, by restoring the dependence of issues upon gold, either at the old equivalence or at a new equivalence. The American dollar had been put back to its former gold value, the pound sterling had been inflated but, as we have seen, a successful attempt had been made by restricting the issue to "deflate" it up to parity with the dollar; while France, after an alarming plunge towards inflation, frankly accepted the new order of things by *devalorizing* the franc, which had been worth nominally about one fifth of a gold dollar, to a fixed equivalence of about one twenty-fifth. Italy also devalorized. Most of the other debtor countries devalorized.

So in the course of seven or eight years the world was brought back to something formally resembling its previous monetary conditions. Every country except the United States was still saddled with big external debts for war expenditure, payable in gold, and the United States was carrying a big internal gold debt on the same account. Soviet Russia had repudiated its external debts—at a grave injury to its foreign credit and trade—and abolished its internal debts, and most other European countries except Great Britain had had a more or less complete massacre and clearance of their internal obligations. But the workers and producers of Great Britain with its deflated currency, carried an undiminished weight of internal as well as of external debt. Indeed, as we have already pointed out, it was an increased weight so far as the internal debt was concerned, because Great Britain had borrowed enormously when the pound was at an inflation value, and was now paying back at a deflation value. Before, however, we can carry this question of reconstructing a world currency further, it will be necessary to take up certain other contributing issues that enter into the problem.

It will be convenient to return for a moment to our egg-born enquirer. He wanted to know why we did not cut out the gold altogether from our monetary methods, and by way of a partial answer we have informed him of these, the main facts, about the post-war inflations, deflations, and devalorizations. We had to break it to him that the world is not yet an economic unity. The world has not one monetary authority but many, and that is the sort of thing that happens when individually and separately states attempt to get away from gold. The countries of the world are economically interdependent and politically and financially they are independent. Thus far they have been totally unable to get together for any concerted monetary control. That is the gist of the trouble. Until they are able to get together effectively, any modernized world monetary system, released more or less completely from the gold tie and based on a steadily more accurate and trustworthy index figure, is impossible. It may be the plain common sense of the world situation, but it cannot be done. We cannot make money what it surely can be made, a due and trustworthy cheque for social services to the world commonweal. We shall remain at our present stage of comminuted barter. And everywhere money must continue to have uncertain purchasing power dependent upon the available gold supply, and be an unsatisfactory link in the economic machine.*

§ 4. *The Gold Standard*

After their various experiments in the inflation and deflation of their currencies most sovereign governments of the world had struggled back in a cowed state to the gold standard, that is to say, to barter, through the intermediate bartering of gold or gold notes, which worked so admirably in the great period of human expansion after 1850. But it was not working so admirably this time, for reasons that we will now very briefly examine.

One reason why the gold standard cannot work indefinitely is the inevitable drying up of the gold supply. The amount available from known sources is calculable, and its limits are in sight, and geologists are more than doubtful of the existence of any new gold-fields at present undeveloped. By 1950 competent authorities estimate that new gold production will have shrunken to a fifth of its present volume.† Consequently, while in the pre-war period reliance on the gold standard had the effect of a steady, stimulating inflation, gently dissolving away the relative purchasing power of the creditor, raising wages and encouraging the producer with rising prices, a new period of a restored gold standard is likely to have exactly the opposite effect. Adherence to the gold standard means a progressive deflation of the currency. It will never again have the effect it once had of a regularly and progressively inflated currency. It will tend now to make the patient inactive hoarders of gold the lords of the earth. Public debts under the new conditions

---

*A short but clear and stimulating little book which the beginner in these matters will find interesting to read side by side with this and the following sections is J. S. Wardlaw Milne's *The A. B. C. of £. S. D.*

†Lord Brabourne (January, 1931), at the annual meeting of the Consolidated Gold Fields of South Africa, said that in ten years' time the world's production of gold would fall from £85,000,000 to about £55,000,000, and that in a further five years South Africa, which is now responsible for half the world's output, would be giving no more than £10,000,000. From 1910 to 1919 the world produced £900,000,000 of gold; from 1920 to 1929 only £771,000,000.

will become more and more difficult to meet. Concerns with obligations towards debenture holders and the like will find their overhead charges becoming more and more onerous until bankruptcy supervenes. There will be, therefore, a strangulation of industrial activity and, from this cause alone, (there are several others) a secular progressive fall in employment. All this follows necessarily if the gold standard is maintained indefinitely.

It is absurd that the general economic prosperity of the world should be at the mercy of an unknown probability, the probability whether fresh auriferous deposits will or will not be discovered, but that is how things are while we are ruled by gold.

On the other hand, let us note that the solution, which is quite possible and probable, of the problem of converting baser metal into gold upon paying lines, may also, at any time, if we are to hold to the logic of the gold standard, impoverish or altogether wipe out the *rentier* class and stimulate or overstimulate all the activities of the work and wealth of the world to an incalculable extent. To trust to gold is to put the economic life of the world at the mercy of the unforeseen. It is to rob the world of any pretence to economic justice.

But this approaching exhaustion of the gold supply is not the immediate factor in the unsatisfactoriness of gold as a monetary standard. In the pre-war period the most remarkable merits were ascribed to this metal. It was pointed out that it is almost incorruptible chemically; it could not be forged or fabricated, it has a magnificent stupid honesty. The quantity of gold in the world could be increased only by new production. It remained available even if it was used in the arts, as jewelry and the like. In a fluctuating world it was the symbol of stability. This was all very well in the pre-war period, when the monetary centre of the world was the cosmopolitan, unpatriotic City of London. Then, except for a regular and so not very disturbing amount of hoarding in Asia, all the gold in the world was forthcoming as coin or as a coinable or pawnable metal, and the instinctive unpremeditated cosmopolitan benevolence of the City was ascribed to it. But in this new post-war era of competitive nationalist finance this has ceased to be the case. The United States, which collects debts in gold and wants to sell without buying, has been taking gold out of circulation to an enormous extent. "America," said Lord d'Abernon in an interesting little book, *The Economic Crisis, Its Causes and Its Cure* (November, 1930), "has now the equivalent of 800 millions of pounds sterling in her Central Treasury; France has the equivalent of 414 millions compared with 160 millions five years ago; we" (Great Britain) "have only 150 millions, the same amount as in 1925. Therefore we are not responsible for the *maldistribution or corner in* gold."

This was published a year before the date of printing of this book. By September, 1931, the American accumulation had passed 1,000 millions and the French 500 millions and the British reserve was down to 130 millions.

This cornering of gold was a quite new thing in world economics. It was a breach with all the traditions of the City and all the usages of the expansion period. And it had been one of the chief factors in producing the present world-wide inability of everyone to pay debts or buy or go on producing.

"Since the time of Midas," says Lord d'Abernon, "there has not been a more paradoxical position than that in which America finds herself; for the central reserve vaults are bulging with gold, while in New York and other shipping points warehouses are overcrowded with wheat, with cotton, with copper; all unsaleable except below the cost of production."

In 1931 mankind was getting gold out of mines in South Africa and elsewhere in order to bury it again in treasuries— and to no other perceptible end. It seems a pity to spend all the labour of mining and transport on such an operation. "Ten countries," says the Interim Report of the Gold Delegation of the Financial Committee of the League of Nations, "acquired 1,055 millions of gold dollars during the three years ending December 31st, 1928, a sum equal to nearly 90 per cent of the total amount of new gold mined during this period." In 1929

France and the United States together took 538 millions of gold dollars or probably over two years' supply of new gold. To immobilize it.

National hoarding of gold had taken place before—notably when Germany went on to the gold standard—but it was on nothing like so large a scale. It was an artificial anticipation of the exhaustion of the gold supply, and it had the inevitable effects of discouragement and arrest of business (and human unhappiness) a fall in prices invariably entails. Gold which we had always supposed to be an honest incessant worker, incorruptible if stupid, had been led off unprotestingly from its appointed task to sleep in the national treasuries and work no more.

The Gold Standard had culminated in this Gold Scramble and it was plain that as a cosmopolitan currency it had failed altogether. The world staggered along with it for a time because of the impossibility of immediately imposing another. Exhortation like that of Lord d'Abernon, financial diplomacy, might induce the two great hoarders among the nations to release some or all of the stores of economic alimentation they had amassed, and there might be a helpful resort, as the League of Nations' Report suggested, to an extended use of cheques, credit transfers, and clearing-house, but these were obviously emergency reliefs, palliatives. Before the world, if economic progress was to go on, lay, it was evident, a vaster, more heroic task than any such temporary adjustments—namely, the establishment of a world money organized primarily to give the worker or entrepreneur his sure reward and divested of the last trace of barter. It was due to a conspiracy of favourable accidents that gold money, or money that consisted of tokens or tickets for gold, worked so well during the age of expansion. That age has taught the world what money can be, and sooner or later the human intelligence will see to it that what money can be, money shall be. Meanwhile an educational period of economic stresses and widespread discomfort and misery has come upon mankind. The dominant fact now in the world's affairs is the reconstruction of money.

§ 5. *Currency Schemes*

The experiences of the past century should have taught the whole world quite convincingly that it needs a currency, that is to say, money, purely as a counter, a cheque, between services and commodities. Such a money is, as we have shown, possible in the measure that trustworthy index numbers can be established. To keep the maximum of people at work, content and hopeful, the issue of currency needs to rather more than keep pace with the increase in the production of commodities. A continuous moderate inflation will be continually easing off the accumulation of debt. And this currency must be a world-wide currency; it can no longer remain under a divided control. All this seems to follow from the present facts of the world situation, when they are viewed broadly and dispassionately from the point of view of social interaction.

Circumstances have recently stirred up the general intelligence to the main factors of the currency situation. It has never hitherto been a very attractive subject. People have avoided it if they could, because it made them feel slightly uncomfortable and had an air of being highly technical and inconclusive—it was at once as intimate and as unconvincing as talk about one's liver—and general discussion has been further burked by dubbing anyone who raised the question, a "Currency Crank." Still, there may come a time when a man will be obliged to look his doctors in the face and consider the state of his liver, and the time has certainly come for mankind at large to consider the working of its monetary organization.

In the preceding sections we have done all we can to show that the elementary consideration of money need be neither obscure nor cranky. The broad lines of the matter become plain enough when we approach them from the study of social motive. It is only when the business is discussed in smart-looking, unsound technicalities and obscured by undefined terms and secondary implications that it becomes difficult. Here we have stuck to fundamental elementary considerations, and the conclusions to be drawn seem as plain as they are sound. It may appear to many that it would be a Herculean, an impossible, a "Utopian" task to bring about any world control of currency. But since plainly the alternative is disaster, that is no reason why the task should not be discussed and attempted.

For some years as the world's monetary situation has been unfolding and becoming demonstrative, there has been an increasing ferment of ideas and a great output of books on this subject. We cannot attempt any detailed examination of that literature, most of which is already out of date, but still it may be advisable here to summarize in the most general terms the nature of the proposals made.

This literature of monetary reform has some very distinctive characteristics. For the most part it has been extraordinarily superficial. Very few of those who have dealt with money have made any attempt at all to go down to its roots in psychology and material necessity. Currency reformers, as we have insisted already, have a way of beginning in the air, high in the air, even more detachedly and arbitrarily than did the old political economists. They assume international competition for prosperity and all sorts of secondary, questionable and transitory complications as though they are essentials in the matter. Few of them approach their subject from the point of view of world interests. And also, few of them are content simply to establish a working generalization. Usually they produce some Scheme or Plan for national, imperial, or (more rarely) universal adoption. They advance it with polemical vehemence. Few of them, except for a passing execration, take notice of the others, much less do they attempt any consideration, analysis or criticisms of previous and competing Plans, Remedies and New Models. Yet since many of them are active, bright-minded people, there is surely a wealth of half truths in this enormous accumulation of suggestions and proposals. Whether that wealth is in paying quantities is less certain. There ought to be an exhaustive classification and analysis of this chaos, and whoever attempts it may count with certainty upon a special circle of enemies of exceptional pamphleteering and epistolatory power for the rest of his life. Here we can only note in the most general terms the

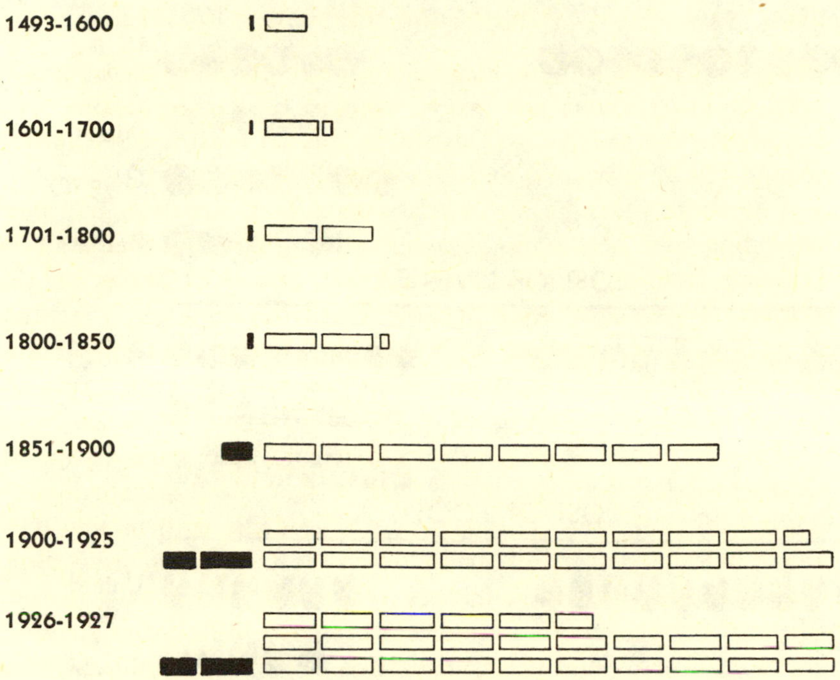

1493-1600

1601-1700

1701-1800

1800-1850

1851-1900

1900-1925

1926-1927

FOUR HUNDRED YEARS
OF GOLD AND SILVER PRODUCTION

ONE of the problems of economists has been the vastly disproportionate
increase in the production of silver over the production of gold. This
chart, in which each red ingot represents the production of ten million fine
ounces of gold a year, and each white ingot the production of ten million
fine ounces of silver, shows the average annual production of these metals
since 1493.

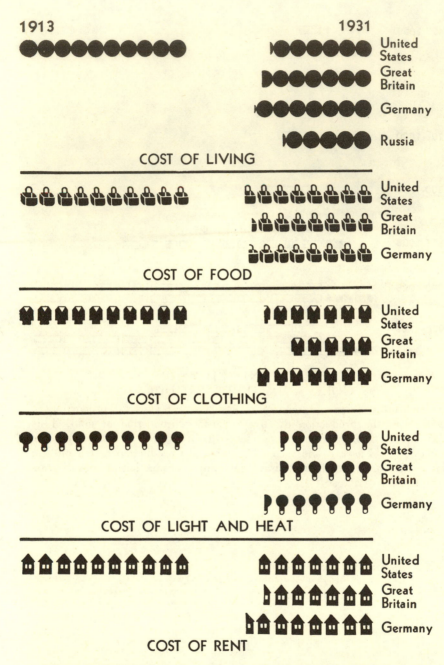

1913   **1931**

United States
Great Britain
Germany
Russia

COST OF LIVING

United States
Great Britain
Germany

COST OF FOOD

United States
Great Britain
Germany

COST OF CLOTHING

United States
Great Britain
Germany

COST OF LIGHT AND HEAT

United States
Great Britain
Germany

COST OF RENT

THE INCREASED MONETARY COST OF LIVING

THIS chart shows how the cost of living has increased since pre-war days. The 1913 unit of currency in each country is taken as standard; the symbols on the left represent the proportion of various commodities which the same unit will purchase to-day.

leading types of project in order to illustrate our present attitude.

The first broad classification of monetary reformers is divided into two sections: (1) those who still cling to the barter core, who insist that some commodity be made the standard of value by the substitution of other commodities for all or some of the gold in use, and (2) those who have already turned the matter about from the point of view of the money manipulated to consider it from the point of view of the worker, and who have realized that money can be detached altogether from standard commodities. We might put together all that former class of projectors as the Old Money School and this latter the New Money School. An outstanding name among the exponents of the New Money ideas is Mr. J. M. Keynes,* whose common-sense suggestions are rapidly spreading into and saturating contemporary monetary thought. The conception of a barometric

---

*A Tract on Monetary Reform, 1923: A Treatise on Money, 1931. But let us not forget that long before the war Arthur Kitson and Silvio Gesell were writing of managed currencies, though they did not use that term, or at any rate of elastic currencies entirely freed from commodity standards, and Major Douglas was active with his "scheme" before 1920. See Douglas's Economic Democracy and Credit Power and Democracy. Arthur Kitson's Scientific Solution of the Money Question was published as early as 1894, and his Money Problem, in 1903. Professor Irving Fisher of Yale was discussing money from the new point of view a quarter of a century ago and when the story of these ideas comes to be written, his influence will probably be found to bulk very large in their development. (The Nature of Capital and Income, 1906, The Purchasing Power of Money, 1911, e.g.) The history of the origin and interaction of ideas is the most obscure and difficult form of history and priority is rarely to be determined with any exactitude. In no field is this more true than in the one of currency discussion. Gesell will probably be a quite cardinal name in that story when it is unravelled. Most of his Natural Economic Order (Die Naturliche Wirtshaftsordnung) was published in Switzerland in 1906. The ideology of Silvio Gesell and his followers differs widely from that of this book. His doctrines are in agreement with the present work upon the necessity of increasing the amount of purchasing power in the world with increased production, but he would do so by giving the increased purchasing power to the individual producer. And while we would modify or thrust aside individual ownership of natural resources and productive organizations in favour of highly organized collective controls, he would modify or thrust aside the monopolistic and unproductive ownership of natural resources and productive organization in order to give individuals free access to them. From our point of view his projects are projects for chaotic production; from his, the conception of the organized world state we are unfolding here looks no doubt like a collectivist tyranny. Our whole enterprise involves a criticism and repudiation of the uncontrolled individualism of Gesell. We show that the socialization, education and civilization of Homo sapiens is essentially the restriction of individual impulse.

currency based on an index number is set forth very clearly in that work.

The difficulty that prevents the Old Money School from assimilating the newer views, is the difficulty of escaping from the desire for intrinsic worth in money itself. Whatever token or note is circulated, they seem to think, somehow, somewhere it must be "presented" and something of value, a piece of metal or the like, handed over. That is the haunting idea that encumbers their minds. They will accept, as we shall see, the most remote and shadowy refinement of this presentation and payment, but they will not part with it altogether. They have a profound dislike, based on the horrid memories of the post-war currency convulsions, of any money that cannot be brought to the test in this fashion. "Sad experiences suffered by many countries," says Professor Cannan, for example, "have convinced the world that a currency . . . must be made to conform with some outside standard"—and he argues no more about it.

At bottom theirs is a mistrust of the probity and intelligence of their fellow creatures, of even their official and responsible fellow creatures. They believe that index numbers would surely be faked, falsified and manipulated. In the world of a managed currency they ask, they continue to ask, where are you to take your note and present it? The New Money School answers that it can be presented in any shop where you want to buy something. That, for the old school, is not enough. There is something, they feel, disingenuous in such a reply. Any commodity does not suffice them; they want a particular commodity.

Both classes of monetary reformers, the Old Money School and the New, can be divided into two main sub-classes; those who focus their attention upon national or imperial welfare, and those who take a wider view. The former subdivision of each class has hitherto been the more considerable, but the trend of events during the past few years is bringing more and more minds to the realization that nothing effective can be achieved in monetary and financial affairs, except upon a scale that transcends existing political boundaries altogether—upon, in fact, a planetary scale. As this realization becomes general, the projects of both the Old Money School and the New become cosmopolitan.

A considerable body of opinion in the Old Money School has turned towards silver, very naturally, for it is not so very long ago since silver stood in the place of gold as the chief precious metal. The history of silver as a standard of value is a long and very illuminating story, and it may help our exposition here to note one or two salient points. Before this present age of economic confluence began, people lived so "locally" (cp. Fosdick's New England farmer in our Chapter IV, § 4) that international payments were quite a minor interest in public affairs. International trade hardly affected the staple commodities of life. Countries could have quite different standards without serious inconvenience.

At the beginning of the nineteenth century (1819), England had its currency on a gold basis and most other European countries used silver as their standard. It was believed then that silver had a fairly steady value in regard to gold; 1 oz. of gold was supposed to equal 15½ ozs. of silver, and France (in 1803) on that supposition adopted a double standard of value, that is to say bimetallism; and for a time it worked. The ox of gold pulled the plough of industry amiably side by side with the ox of silver. The ratio in value between the metals in their uncoined state had not changed very strikingly for a long time. J. F. Darling (who makes proposals for the remonetization of silver through an Imperial bimetallic standard of value to be called "Rex"* combined with a restraint upon the export of gold beyond the Imperial frontiers) asserts that it held good for two and a half centuries. Bimetallic arrangements seem to be based on the belief that that ratio holds good eternally. Even that statement of Mr. Darling's is extremely "loose in its handle." There were considerable undulations in the ratio throughout this period. Under William III the ratio was close upon 1 to 16. In 1717, when Sir Isaac Newton was Master of the Mint, it was 1 to 15¼, and the value of the golden guinea was in consequence changed from 22 to 21 silver shillings. In 1760

*J. F. Darling, C.B.E.: *The "Rex": a New Money to Unify the Empire.*

the rate of exchange between uncoined gold and silver was 1 to 14.14 while the Mint was still maintaining gold and silver on the 1 to 15¼ ratio. How did it manage to do this? It was only coining gold. It had not coined any more silver, says Professor Cannan, after 1717, and it did not do so again until 1816. For a hundred years the English people made their old silver coins, for the most part very worn and reduced in weight, serve their needs. And after 1816 when new silver coins were issued, they were token coins of a less value intrinsically than monetarily, and the ratio did not matter.

Under the fourth dynasty in Egypt silver was more precious than gold. In the days of the Roman Empire the bullion ratio of silver to gold varied about 10 or 11 to 1. In recent years silver, demonetized, has fallen steadily in value; the bullion ratio has descended to 1 to 20, to 30, to 40, 50, 60, and still it tends to sink. On May 23, 1931, the price per oz. was $12\frac{5}{16}$d., while fine gold remained at its fixed value of £4. 5. od. per oz. and standard gold about £3. 18. od. per oz. Greater ease of separation from gold, lead, copper, zinc and other metals, is one of the factors in this cheapening of silver. The production of any of those metals involves the production of silver also. No fall in the price of silver can check this "by-product" supply. It has to be separated, anyhow. If the "gold mines" of the world were closed, there would be no more gold, but if all the "silver mines" in the world were shut down, there would still be millions of ounces of silver forthcoming.

In America at the beginning of the nineteenth century, the ratio adopted was 1 to 16, and this did not work, because then it overrated gold. It paid on those terms to change gold coins for silver ones in order to sell the silver abroad or for industrial use at home. The great gold discoveries, from 1848 onward, led for a time to a relative cheapening of gold. Silver began to be driven out of circulation even at the French rate. A fairly obvious fact then dawned upon the world, that there was no divinely fixed ratio of the two precious metals, and that whenever the relative production of one of them increased, the other went out of circulation (this principle is what is commonly called "Gresham's Law"). No system of bimetallism which is not based upon a comprehensive international agreement can overcome this difficulty. It is a difficulty which is bound to arise sooner or later whenever more than one substance is used as a standard.

Professor Henry Clay in his *Economics for the General Reader* points out that bimetallism, the joint use of gold and silver, would be a much more practicable method if all the mints in the world acted in concert to *fix* a price between gold and silver. They would then become a world combine, a world co-operative of precious metal buyers. The chief use of both gold and silver is for coinage; the mints are the chief buyers of both metals, and if they presented a united front to producers, instead of competing against each other for the gold output, production would have to adjust itself to the ratio they determined. The question of the ratio of bullion values would lose its importance. If either metal became more abundant, it would supply the bulk or all of new currency, and the output of its companion would be checked. This would not matter in the least to the general economic process if all the mints of the world were acting together. The rarer metal could not be driven abroad in accordance with Gresham's Law, because there would be no abroad to drive it to. And that nightmare of the exhaustion of the gold supply would be lifted from our minds at once. Such a combine of mints might prove a very helpful preliminary to a world currency control. But that we must consider later on when we take up the question of sovereignty. Let us return to our history of the gold-standard age which is now coming to an end.

In the 'sixties, with gold getting rapidly more abundant, the trend was all against the further use of silver, and in the 'seventies Germany and the United States adopted the gold standard. But (in the 'seventies) the gold output declined for a time, a fall in prices and commercial depression ensued, and the discovery of rich silver mines in America restored more than the former cheapness and abundance of silver. Wherever that metal was still acceptable for coinage it began to push out gold. There was an attempt to get along with a strictly limited amount of silver coin used as well as gold. Gold was to be coined without limit but silver only to a defined amount. This arrangement, the "limping standard," was adopted by France and a group of associated countries. Coined silver by this adjustment became more precious than uncoined silver; coined silver was silver that had been ennobled, so to speak; and forgery became almost an honest trade. All that the forger had to do was to buy silver and make coins exactly like the government ones.

Meanwhile the shrinking of the gold output, the shrinking that is of currency in the gold-standard countries, and particularly in America and Germany, was producing the inevitable consequence of deflation, that is to say, a fall in prices and a phase of world-wide depression (1885–86). These were the great days of the bimetallist agitation. Let silver be rehabilitated, and the required inflation would be achieved. In the United States the struggle for the free coinage of silver side by side with the free coinage of gold went on into the 'nineties; silver became the symbol of release for mortgagors and for every form of debtor, and in 1896 William Jennings Bryan made his great speech about "humanity," debtor humanity, and particularly the mortgaged Western farmer, being "crucified upon a cross of gold."

Then abruptly the Transvaal reefs came into play and the mines of South Africa began to pour so much gold into the world that, although the output of silver also increased in even greater proportion, the monetary tension was released without its intervention, and for a quarter of a century little more was heard of bimetallism. South Africa had pumped new life into the declining gold standard.

Now, in a fresh phase of falling prices, projects for the rehabilitation of silver are reappearing—still with no real solution whatever of the problem of fluctuating relative value that every attempt at a multiple standard must raise. The nearest approach to a reconciliation between the two metals, so that currency can be inflated by the addition of silver without Gresham's Law operating, is the proposal known as Symmetallism, in which a gold-silver alloy is suggested as the single monetary standard. That is really the most thinly disguised inflation imaginable. Exactly the same effect could be got by diminishing the gold value of a pound note and not bothering at all about the silver, because since silver is the cheaper metal it would merely be a diluent of the gold. . . .

Such are the primary facts which account for the present widespread disposition to replace the existing control of currency issues through the commodity gold, by more complicated controls bringing other metallic commodities to the aid of gold. The end sought is inflation. Or at least the end sought is a reversal of the process of destructive deflation that has been going on under the Gold Standard. Always the end sought is a local or general distribution of more purchasing power to producers and increased ease of debt payment.

We will not expand this section further by a more detailed examination of particular currency projects. They are all provisional projects. The broad issue is simple, and it is practically beyond dispute. The arguments that a managed currency, free of entanglement with any standard commodity, under a world board of control, is the best possible currency, are so overwhelming that any other scheme, plan, or project can only be regarded as a compromise, a political expedient, a way of getting round the supposedly invincible opposition of national policy, popular prejudice, and powerful interests, or of carrying on until that opposition can be overcome. In this work we do not admit that opposition is invincible. We believe that *Homo sapiens* is fundamentally sane—if sometimes disastrously slow and inattentive to his proper interests.

The question of carrying on is on an altogether different footing from the broad final necessities of the matter. One must distinguish sharply between the two sets of issues. The world's business must be carried on from day to day. That is a primary political principle. The release of the captive gold in the United States and France or a return to some form of bimetallism through the concerted action of the world's mints may do much for a time to relieve the strangulation of economic life that has been going on. A grave dislocation of the world's economic life,

Professor J. W. Scott alleges, has been caused by the demone-
tization of silver, which has changed over India and China from
purchasing communities to communities unable to buy and driven
therefore to the worst forms of sweated production. Sir Arthur
Salter cites figures which qualify this assertion very considerably.
But the conviction is widespread that some manipulation of the
standards in favour of silver may restore this lost balance. It is
less questionable that the credit boycott of Russia has also driven
that country to ferocious exportation at cut prices.

But we must not be lured into questions of current politics
and current expediency. Our objects here are descriptive and
scientific, not legislative nor administrative. Our business has
been to show as plainly as possible what money really is and the
nature of the difficulties the world is encountering in its use,
and there our part ends. It is for the reader to apply these facts
to the problems of every day. The final settlement to be sought
is the world organization of a New Money based on an index
number, but a score of expedients may be necessary to avert
disaster and gain time for the propaganda and establishment of
the scientific method.

Let us in conclusion recapitulate the essential facts about the
New Money idea. Barometric money, "managed currency" is
paper money of which the issue and withdrawal are planned to
secure stability of purchasing power in general. An index price
of staple commodities has to be maintained. If it falls, issue is
increased; if it rises, issue is restricted. So the primary end of
a sure real value in wages is attained.

But a managed currency would have to be controlled by other
factors as well as current prices. In certain circumstances, whenever, for instance, employment and production are increasing
rapidly, an anticipatory increase of issue may be needed to keep
pace with the general enlargement of economic operations.
Where populations are increasing, more money will be needed
to provide purchasing power for the additional human beings
unless the general standard of living is to be forced down. As
a special case of this we may note that as invention progresses
and industrial plant becomes more elaborate and expensive,

more capital is required to equip each worker in an efficient and modernized industry with the power, tools, machines, etc., which he will use in his task. The Federation of British Industries has estimated that this item has risen in England from under £1,000 before the war to over £3,000 in 1927. The new workers and the new machines are of course a potential source of greater wealth, but unless money is provided to balance this increased potentiality it will only tend to lower prices and dislocate trade. The whole literature of currency we have already noted is permeated by the feeling that the amount of purchasing power in the hands of the public should be subject to a continued slight increase. This is sometimes referred to as "inflation," but as long as it is only desired to *stabilize* prices there is no true inflation. Inflation occurs when prices are made to rise, and this too is often advocated as a method of devaluing money and thus gradually lessening the world burden of debt.

Were this policy adopted, in course of time each unit of currency would cheapen down out of common use and give place to a successor, as in France the double sou is giving place to the franc, and the franc to the five-franc note.

It is evident that the efficiency of barometric money depends very largely on the soundness of the index prices used. At present index prices are often very debatable. To make them quite trustworthy there is need for a trustworthy world-wide system of economic reports. That great and neglected pioneer, David Lubin, almost succeeded in creating a world bureau for the registration of production in Rome, but the war crippled that development for some time. We shall have more to say about his Institute of Agriculture later (Chapter XII, § 7). Slowly but surely it seems that the science of statistics will overtake and resume his fine ambitious effort. We shall become more and more able to anticipate shortages and abundances and the gross and relative values of commodities.

The science of statistics is still only in its infancy—a vigorous infancy. Every year the possibility of "figuring out" quantities in the human outlook increases and the problems of money and credit change. They change in the direction of managed currency and credit scientifically controlled. The rate of that change is dependent largely on the amount of knowledge and understanding available. To this idea we must return after we have directed the reader's attention to the speculative element in all contemporary business enterprises.

§ 6. *The Bank*

From an examination of these remarkable monetary counters by which our unconsolidated, fragmentary world civilization is still so painfully, so distressfully, endeavouring to compute its affairs, we must pass to the elementary phenomena of credit. We come back to the counting house and board room. We have to ask how the entrepreneur carries on, between the beginnings of his enterprise and the payment for the goods his enterprise has produced. We have seen him first paying out and later on receiving money again. Who hands him the money in the first instance, and why does he send his takings to the bank?

The history of banking is a comparatively simple one. It is easy to trace and understand its development from the time when it was a mere expedient for storing valuables and minimizing the dangerous transport of money by means of bills of exchange.

At first banking and usury had very little to do with each other. One was an affair of safe-keeping and the other was an affair of safe-lending. I suppose the earliest usury, the usury of the ancient world, was practised because cultivation had to carry on until harvest, or after a bad harvest, and the loan was material sustenance for which the cultivator pledged his future produce. Or else it was sustenance of the merchant until the ship or the caravan came home. Or it was supplied to the monarch embarking upon a raid or conquest that promised to be remunerative. In the ancient world, the temple was the primitive treasure-house, pawnshop and loan-office of the community, and some god the nominal lender. The priest was the first financial expert.

I do not know how far the financial expedients of the ancient world were carried over into the reviving economic life of mediæval Europe. What is desirable—I do not know if it is at present practicable—is a study of the evolution of ideas about credit loans and usury in the ancient world, an account of the financial methods prevalent under the Roman and Byzantine Empires and the way in which these ideas and methods emerged again, modified or not, after centuries of social and political collapse in western Europe, as social security was restored. There may have been a practical continuity. There may have been fresh initiatives. Ordinary history helps but little here. Scholars have always been disposed to condemn account books. What we want is a History of the Counting House. Few historians of the old school escaped sufficiently from the blinkers of language and national traditions to attempt anything of that kind. But a competent history of finance would have to flit from Constantinople to Venice, from South Germany to the Hansa Towns, and wherever credit was showing itself and new devices were working.

However wide and diverse that preliminary survey, the broad treatment of modern banking conditions would begin with the returning abundance of trade and money in the sixteenth century and the extension of arrangements for its deposit. The goldsmiths, who were developing into bankers, took care of money and issued signed receipts; the receipts were made payable to bearer and the bank note was evolved. It was an age of religious dissension, and the Christian temple never recovered the financial prestige and advantages of its Semitic and Egyptian predecessors. It kept the primary religious domination over marriage and burial and education, but the new economic developments remained outside its influence. It restrained the believer from usury, so that before the Protestant reformation produced a new Christian business persona, the Jews were given something like a monopoly of money-lending.

It was soon realized that the deposit and issuing bankers who were appearing could lend out part of their money in hand, so long as they had the confidence of the public and there was no danger of a run upon them. They were thus able to attract deposits by paying interest in the place of charging for their services, as they did at first. From these beginnings the banking organization grew rapidly. A long history of legislative control, the definition of banking activities, and the creation of national and central banks, would have to be given to display this growth with any completeness. But here again that capacious and inclusive *Science of Work and Wealth* of ours may very conveniently relieve these pages. The broad effects of the growth of banking were these. It utilized and vitalized savings. Under mediæval conditions, which held good almost up to the present time in India and China, savings were either hoarded as treasure or spent upon display, palaces, gold plate and jewels. Nowadays everyone has a paying use for savings, and they are all turned back, practically, for the animation of industry. Even the European peasant's stocking has unravelled and released its hoard. The bangles of the Indian women will follow the bank-ward movement. Business which in pre-banking days would have had to keep a treasure chest out of which to pay wages, buy material, finance particular operations, now goes to the bank for a short-term loan.

Unexpected consequences of banking convenience have appeared. The idea of the cheque was a very obvious and simple one, and yet its working out leads us towards results of a quite remarkable kind. The opening nineteenth century saw the rise of the cheque to an importance far exceeding that of the restrained and regulated bank note. Even allowing for the increasing production of gold, it is doubtful if the great economic expansion of that period could have occurred without the cheque. It let out the financial clothing of the growing economic giant who might otherwise have been strangled. If cheques were forbidden to-morrow, all the money in the country, even if no one held any for more than a day, would scarce suffice for half the needs of the very slackest working of our economic life. An enormous amount of the business of the English-speaking communities is now transacted by cheque without the shifting of a bank note or the movement of a coin. The clearing-house has become an organ of primary importance in economic life.

The use of the cheque is by no means equally developed throughout the world, and its handling varies in different countries. French business, for example, is much more realistic than English, and for transactions of a few thousand or a few score thousand francs a larger proportion of at least paper money passes from hand to hand. But the experience of a century is making it clear that, except for the convenience of paper or coins for small immediate transactions, it would be possible now to dispense with actual concrete money altogether; it would be possible to sustain the general working of an entire economic system by clearing-house bookkeeping, by the continual transfer of money of account, of crude "purchasing power" that is, from one account to another.

This consideration alone opens out a very interesting prospect of the future of banking. If it is possible to get away from money to this extent, it may be possible to get away from it to a very much greater extent. There must be many imaginative and scientific minded bankers and statisticians who have already glimpsed something of a phase in economic development to which these facts may be pointing. If it has already become possible to carry on a voluminous tangle of productive and distributive activities with all the monetary side simplified down to cheque sorting and bookkeeping, may it not be possible, ultimately, to carry on the whole productive and distributory system of mankind on a basis of debit and credit entries of purchasing power to the account of this or that community or association or individual?

It is difficult to discover any inherent impossibility in such a suggestion. One can think, of course, of a jungle of manifest obstacles, at present trackless, but I should imagine that any banker who is not the mere creature and slave of routine, must apprehend to some extent this conception of a world system of current accounts and cheques, comprehensively embracing all his particular activities and providing a medium for the final adjustment of the main economic discords of our present world.

§ 7. *The Contemporary Evolution of Banking*

It is by the criterion of this possibility, the possibility of the banking system of the world becoming a complete guiding record of "purchasing power" from day to day, that we must appraise contemporary banking organization and usage. Banking falls far short of that possibility, but it is not at an immeasurable distance from it. The story of the *record of purchasing power*, the story of modern banking, that is, runs on lines closely parallel to the story of modern industrial development. We shall have to note the same rapid progress in a century or so from small completely independent personal enterprises enormously various in their character and trustworthiness, to vigorously competing companies, and so on to grouping, associated working and amalgamation.

But here the factor of State intervention, regulation and participation, is from the outset more important. In the United States, for example, there are legal restraints upon the opening of branch offices by banks. Consequently, small independent local banking concerns, of very unequal stability, take the place there of the local branches of the great amalgamations that one finds everywhere in Britain or France. The tradition of international malevolence also plays an even more important rôle in hampering the extension of banking systems beyond national boundaries than it does in restraining the production and distribution of commodities.

A full, illustrative and descriptive history of human credit methods would include an account of the earlier, more adventurous days of banking and of typical "runs," stoppages of payment and failures. Much material for this lies buried in the newspaper files of the nineteenth century. Those were the days of "romantic" banking. In America, for the reason just stated, local banks remain romantic. As the story approached contemporary conditions it would carry an increasing quantity of pictures of the typical buildings and other tangible property of banking concerns and give glimpses of strong-rooms, safe-deposits, and the like. Half the prominent street corners of London witness now architecturally to the great wealth of the modern banking corporations, and in Professor Soddy's *Money Versus Man* the reader will find a bitter protest against the extraordinary privileges that have favoured this accumulation.

The State gives banks the privilege of issuing money and then borrows money at interest from the banks. That, on the face of it, seems more than a trifle absurd. But we shall give a reason for that absurdity a few pages further on. The State, we shall find, is too afraid of its own temperamental fluctuations to issue money and reap the profit of the issue itself.

Our next exhibit, so to speak, in the banking section of our survey, will show the entrepreneur in conference with the bank manager. The rôle of the latter varies between that of the mere self-protective and acquisitive money-lender and that of the sympathetic (and even encouraging and stimulating) associate. But there is always a risk that sympathetic participation may pass into interference and control, and a mind directed mainly to security and profit may see a business organization from a widely different angle than the point of view of the creative entrepreneur. In all great industrial organizations there must be a constant risk of conflict between material and financial considerations, and especially, when monopolies are created either by natural conditions, patent rights or tariff protection, is there the danger of holding back improvements in method while profits are still being made upon obsolescent lines.

The whole trend of the mass of description and narrative our imaginary encyclopædia would assemble, would be to show how far we are as yet from that unified, simplified exchange of purchasing power which is the ideal bank. Things have progressed far enough to render that ideal conceivable and credible, but they are still at an incalculable distance from its effective realization. It is as yet only in his moments of exaltation and lucidity that the banker is able to think of himself as the guardian of the measure for human interaction; for ordinary everyday purposes he is still under the sway of a long tradition of profit-seeking. In the latter phase, if his practice is less satisfactory to his higher nature, it is certainly more grossly sure and gratifying. Only a change, not merely in his own ideology, but in the standards by which people judge and esteem him, can alter that.

Such a change is certainly going on at the present time. A time may come when profit-seeking banking will not be tolerated and all banking operations will be recognized as vital public services. That does not mean that banks will be "nationalized." They tend through the natural development of financial affairs to become quasi-public organizations side by side with the politician's governments. Already "profit-seeking" is a rather excessive phrase for most great banks. There is much legal limitation upon their capital, and upon the dividends they may pay their shareholders. They may have maximum and minimum dividends fixed for them.

What are called central banks, about which we have more to say, are in several countries partly or entirely the property of the State as the chief or only shareholder. There is a great variety of such restraining arrangements, summarized very clearly in Kisch and Elkin's *Central Banks*. There is more or less legal restraint upon all banking businesses. The modern banker arose out of the townsman-trader tradition, but he is rapidly assimilating the educated ideology. His manner nowadays mingles the reserve of the confessional with the alertness of a responsible controller. The vast amalgamations of Joint Stock Banks, banks of enterprise, that have occurred in recent years, tend to transfer the direction of banking more and more from bank "owners" to scientifically trained functionaries, who look not to profits but to promotion as the result of their work, and whose pride is rather in honour and prestige than in super-abundant riches.

The possible and probable development of the world's banking system towards a central exchange, a world clearing-house of purchasing power, becomes still more evident when we turn our attention to the way in which currency control is passing out of the hands of governments into the hands of a system of central banks. At first (in the eighteenth century, e. g.) bank notes were simply the promissory notes of banks to pay definite sums of cash at sight, and governments everywhere were the sole money-issuing authorities. Then in the interests of the public the banks were obliged legally to hold more or less adequate reserves of money to cover their notes. There was more and more restriction upon the right to issue notes, as the notes became more and more manifestly an accessory currency. Then from being accessory currency bank notes became the main currency. They are ousting metallic currency everywhere, except small-change metallic tokens. The period of monetary confusion that followed the Great War created a strong disposition to transfer currency issue from the direct control of politicians to expert management. Kisch and Elkin quote a declaration of the Irish Free State Banking Commission that is very significant:

"Mindful as it is of the disasters of past years in all countries where currency was issued by the Government, and recognizing the hazards which come from changes of Government, from the development of budget deficits and other evils from which no country has found itself immune, the Commission is definitely of the opinion that the management of the legal tender note issue should be placed in the hands of a non-political and independent body, which shall control the conditions of issue and shall have full control and custody of the securities it holds."

These are the ideas that have ruled the post-war development of Central Banks throughout the world. With comparative rapidity a network of these organizations has been created either by special modifications of the constitutions of preëxisting national banks, or by the creation of new ones, and from them it is, and not from the State directly, that the money now used by the ordinary citizen comes. This banking nexus, working with a considerable and increasing detachment from politicians, diplomatists and the press, is a comparatively new and most interesting organization in the economic life of the world. Its full possibilities are still largely unexplored.

We shall note in Chapter XI, § 10, and in Chapter XII, § 13, certain new broad strands that have come into existence since 1929 to make this banking nexus still more effectively cosmopolitan. These strands are still too new for judgment; they are the Bank of International Settlements at Basle and its projected associates the International Trust and the International Mortgage Bank.

Here, because of the living interest of the subject, instead of motioning our reader towards museum galleries vanishing into imaginary perspectives and nonexistent encyclopædias, we will name a few recent books that he will find informative and stimulating if he wants to expand what is given here. There is no really comprehensive history and description of banking in existence, but the interested reader may be referred to *A History of Modern Banks of Issue* by C. A. Conant (6th edition, 1927), which is thoroughly good within its scope, and *Currency and Credit* by R. G. Hawtrey (1928), which deals very soundly with the general theory of money and the theory of banking. His Part II, "Historical Illustrations," describes most of the great banking crises from the Middle Ages onward. There is as yet no outstanding history of Central Banks or Central Banking. The history of cosmopolitan banking is being made but it is not yet being written. Kisch and Elkin (1930) give the constitutions of various Central Banks and the statutes governing them. *The History of the Bank of England*, by Andreades (translated from the Greek), is also well worth reading by the student.

These books will give methods of dealing and figures, but to make this part of our picture of human activities concrete and vivid something more is needed. How can we conjure up the visible manifestations of this banking network that now binds the vast complex of work and wealth together? At prominent corners, in busy streets, wherever there are towns and cities, rises the stout and handsome architecture of the banks. Within are the familiar bank desks and counters with their brass rails and guichets; altogether there must be miles and miles, hundreds of miles, thousands of miles of desks and counters; and clerks, clerks now by the hundred thousand, by the million, busy, intent, entering up billions and billions of transfers of purchasing power, sorting cheques, adding, subtracting, balancing.

Already the world's clearing-house for purchasing power,

which may ultimately supersede the use of all money but small change, is half evolved.

This also we add now to the panorama of mines, plantations, factories, warehouses, docks, shipping, railroads, habitations, villages, towns, cities we have evoked, culminating in those gold-mines where, with the use of the most skilful organization, the most efficient apparatus, the most beautiful applications of modern science and the toil of many thousands of workers, gold is released from the quartz rock in which it was disseminated countless ages ago, to start forth on its long, indirect and solemnly idiotic journey to be sterilized in the vaults of the hoarding powers.

§ 8. *The Modern Fragmentation of Ownership*

So far it has been simple and convenient to speak of the entrepreneur as though he were a single person, a man of the peasant-townsman type touched by imagination and larger ideas. That is what he was. But the fruitful device of joint-stock enterprise, fruitful of evil as well as of good, has long since made the entrepreneur no longer the organizing owner of an enterprise, but simply the organizer of its ownership. A very large and miscellaneous body of prosperous people, "the investing public," now exists whose wealth consists partly or wholly of the shares or obligations of enterprises over which they exercise no control, or of loans made to governments or public bodies equally outside their range of personal activity.

The expenditure arrangements of this comparatively novel class of people are fairly uniform. They carry about with them a small amount of ready money, which they constantly renew from the current account they have open at the bank. This current account, according to the fortunes of its owner, credits him with a few score or a few hundred pounds. Any more purchasing power than that, waits in a deposit account bearing interest, from which usually it can be withdrawn at short notice, either to be brought forward into the current account for actual spending, or invested. Behind the current and deposit accounts come the "securities" which constitute some or all of the investor's possessions. These may be stored for the investor in the bank's strong-room, or in the investor's solicitor's bank, or in a strong-box, and normally they can be converted into cash (at variable prices), in a few days. They are from the owner's point of view a sort of money, a slightly congealed purchasing power, which may be liquidated with reasonable facility and which has the advantage of yielding higher interest than the deposit account and possibly increasing in value, but which also carries grave risks of deterioration.

Such is the typical investor's position; he is essentially a concentration, small or great, of irresponsible purchasing power. To borrow a term from biology, the body politic has *secreted* him as an oyster secretes a pearl. But his reaction on the social body is much more considerable than the reaction of the pearl upon the oyster.

The existence of this stratum of people, wholly or partly supported by investments in businesses over which they exercise no control, or in the loans made to governments and public bodies, at home and abroad, is one of the most important differences between the social structure of the modern community and any previous state of society. In every preceding phase where there has been a concentration of wealth it has been far less easily converted into kinetic purchasing power and far more burthensome upon its owners. Securities are an abstraction of purchasing power hardly less mobile and irresponsible than a cash balance. That causes a great complication of the currency question. In the preceding sections we have talked of monetary inflation sending up prices and deflation sending them down. But easy credit and a rapid movement of cheques are in their effect indistinguishable from inflation. And so also is a general rise in the prices of securities during a boom period. A phase of hopefulness among security owners and buyers—to all intents and purposes *inflates*.

It would be an intricate task to disentangle the statistics that conceal the relative importance of the income earner (individually and collectively) and the investor, as spenders. I am inclined to think we shall find the investing public is now quite dominant in the exercise of purchasing power so soon as we consider any but the broad staple necessities. The investing public calls the tune for the rest of production. Its demands and its refusals determine the forms and quantities of all that production. It is the decisive customer in the world of work, the free buyer.

There is no great freedom in buying below a certain level of individual prosperity. It is a delusion that individual buying gives the freedom to get what you want. You get what the shops will let you have. Unless you are very wealthy and will take the trouble to order and have exactly what you want made, your buying is only a few degrees more free than if a socialist autocrat gave you what he thought good for you. You may buy model A or model B or model C. That is the limit of your freedom of choice. You are served out your necessities wholesale, and live by a definite standard. Your spending, at the middle class or any lower level, is dictated for you almost as much as your work. You *must* have this, you *must* have that, and by the time you have got this, that, and the other thing you cannot do without, your money has gone.

But as the individual earner's income rises above the demands of his standard of life, as he begins to "make money," he enters either partially into the investor class by purchasing securities, or he expends his money as his fancy dictates upon pleasures and an increased consumption of perishable goods, or he acquires material property for exploitation or enjoyment. The prevailing practice is probably, in the first phase, investment. The first impulse is to "put something by." The prospering money-maker does not immediately expend his surplus, but puts it out to earn interest or dividend and so supplement his own earning power. He withdraws this sum from the to-and-fro dealing of consumer and producer to increase the capital wealth of the country, and then he sits down to wait for the interest or dividend to come to him. Then, feeling safer, he readjusts his purchasing activities to his new scale. He launches out upon that new scale. He begins to signify now to the advertiser. Will he have a new automobile or a better automobile? Will he en-

large or refit his house? Or his wardrobe? Will he travel and see
the world? Or will he reinvest and grow still richer? He has
become one of those people who—in the measure of their freedom of initiative—command the world. The producer considers
his wishes.

Let us ask how this investing and spending public, this most
characteristic and influential stratum in the existing social order,
achieved its present importance. It is not very ancient history.
We shall need only to glance back to the sixteenth century to
see a social system in which none but the actual holders of very
real property, or people with money in pocket or strong-box,
had any purchasing power at all. To own anything was a task.
Rents, tithes and taxes formed the wealth of the rich and powerful, and they needed constant watching, collecting and administration. A mediæval strong-box, with its mighty locks and its
key that had to be hidden, was a dreadful monster in comparison
with a cheque book. The borrowing power of governments was
slight. Partnerships were active and very personal, and only a
few chartered trading companies had transferable stock. The
free-spending investor was unknown.

It was not until towards the end of the seventeenth century
that business corporations and trading and industrial companies
appeared in any abundance in the world. They were simply
partnerships with transferable shares and undefined liability.
The great speculative storm of 1720 in France and England, the
Mississippi scheme and the South Sea Bubble, marked the appearance of the investor as a serious factor in the world's affairs.
Probably few of those who were ruined in these crashes were
independent investors, people who had "made money" and were
seeking a use for it; they were landowners, merchants, farmers
and sinecure holders in a wild fever to grow much richer. They
were people who sold their concrete property in order to invest;
they brought their skins into the business. The mass of the modern "investing public" is not doing that.

There was a steady development of this new form of mobile
wealth in stock and share, and a concurrent expansion of national
debts, through the eighteenth and early nineteenth centuries,

leading to the epoch of larger business organizations, of gas companies, railways, ship canals and town building, that followed the recovery from the Napoleonic Wars and the spread of invention and imaginative enterprise. We have traced already how this larger handling of affairs became mechanically possible, and now here we have to note how it became financially possible. The entrepreneur had insufficient credit for these enlarged undertakings, and so he had to call upon the credit of others. He had to form companies to share and realize his hopes. Company promoting became an art and a profession, businesses were merged, vast new adventures were contemplated, and the proportion of the economic apparatus in the country owned by company shareholders increased rapidly. This development was enormously facilitated by the device of limited liability, which with due legislative precautions gave a long-needed reassurance to the hesitating investor.

Within a few decades there was a great increase of the productivity of the world; a considerable expansion of population followed, and the rate of its increase rose to a maximum and declined; individual wages rose with relative slowness, but the numbers of the earning class multiplied greatly, and there was in particular an immense proliferation of the investing public and of the organization of investment. A new and growing system of purchasing power was arising, not in equivalence to, but in association with, and dependent upon, increased production, and it was diverting a large amount of the increased product both from the active earner and the genuine economic entrepreneur on the one hand, and, on the other, from the landowner, the rent receiver, into the pocket of the investor.

The contrast between the economic life of four centuries ago and life under the new conditions can be easily stated. The social-economic process of the sixteenth century distributed the power to acquire its product, that is to say, purchasing power, as wages, as profits of manufacture or trade, as rent, as interest upon incidental loans, and as taxes in support of the still very undeveloped State and such other public organizations as then existed. By the middle of the nineteenth century the same process had become much vaster and more highly organized, and in addition to the former recipients of purchasing power, workers, traders, landlords, usurers, tax-gatherers, there was now added this great and growing body of inert investors, receiving interest or dividends, and constituting a vast expansion of those formerly rare and minor items, the money-lender and the sleeping partner. The State and public bodies were now not only functioning in new and elaborate and expensive ways, but they were also carrying a great and growing burthen of debt, so that the share of purchasing power over the general product which was assigned to taxes was rising steadily, to be returned in part to the community in services, and in part paid to the State's creditors, the investing classes. The old social classifications had changed both in their proportion and in their nature because of the great expansion of this practically new class of investors.

That change continues. The war preparation of the opening years of the twentieth century, the Great War and its legacy of unsettlement, have enormously increased the public debts of the world, and the pressure to buy War Loan has, in America particularly, extended downward the disposition to invest to classes hitherto innocent of aught but petty hoarding. Beneath the body of investors who live mainly or entirely on their investments, comes a stratum, a multitude now, of earners, who may be, as regards a quarter, or a tenth or a hundredth part of their spending incomes, investors. The investor's income is taxed heavily, but so far as his money is directly or indirectly in public securities, a sufficient part of it returns to him to leave him now the dominant purchaser, albeit not the chief consumer of common needs, in the world's markets to-day.

In Socialist and Communist literature, that ill-defined term, the Capitalist System, is abundantly used. Because of its confusing implications I have preferred not to use it here. What these thinkers of the Left have in mind when they say "Capitalism" is just this predominant presence of the investing public, the creditor public, in the social organism. But they seem to think the investing public exists through some inherent malignity of its own; they do not realize that it is an inevitable and necessary part in the confused evolution of a world economic system. There is a continual production for profits and a continual withdrawal of a proportion of these profits from consumption to investment and the creation of further capital demanding further dividends. The creditor mass, the debt burthen, increases steadily therefore until bankruptcy, inflation or—the Communist would add—revolutionary repudiation, relieves the economic body.

§ 9. *Contemporary Investment Practice*

The voluminous pages of that non-existent encyclopædia of Work and Wealth, would afford space for a detailed account of the current methods of company promotion and the flotation of public loans. It would explain the varieties of investment, in ordinary and preference shares, in debentures, in public loans. It would give a conspectus of the variations in company and corporation law in different countries, and the methods of subscription and sale. The reader would be taken in imagination to some of the world's stock exchanges with their supplementary outer markets, and be shown something of the manners and graces of these vortices in the modern economic process.

At these centres, from which financial stimulus or restraint radiates out to the material processes of world production, there is an incessant uncertainty and fluctuation of values, and a whole world of human activities concerned primarily with these fluctuations. An immense amount of human intelligence is being directed to the safety and "yield" of every item in the list of quotable and buyable securities, and beyond the acute professional practitioner, selling and buying to achieve a maximum of income and safety, is this whole vast "investing public" of ours, never altogether indifferent to the falling and rising prices and payments upon which it counts for its sustained purchasing power, and very prone to moods when better returns seem imperative, or when distrust chills the heart and panic impends. Climatic vagaries, bad crops and excessive crops, sudden revelations of mineral resources, new methods of production and unexpected inventions, fire, flood and political stresses, are all reflected in the plus and minus entries of the price list of stocks and shares.

But the stock and share market is not merely a barometer to register the unpredictable weather changes of the economic life of the world outside. It has also moods and pressures and storms of its own, originating within itself and having also heavy repercussions on the general life of the community. A study of company promotion reveals how great are the temptations to overestimate the price and prospects of any undertaking that is offered to the investing public. There is a natural disposition to "overcapitalize" undertakings and to exaggerate the permanence of profitable returns. There is so much hopefulness in man that, according to Mr. Mellon of the United States Treasury, as much as 1,000,000,000 dollars is lost annually in the too sanguine investments of American citizens. Much of this may be due to honest miscalculation, but a considerable proportion, it would seem, goes to support an interesting industry of deliberate investor exploiters, who deal systematically in unsound and bogus securities. There exists a very complete organization for this exploitation; there are even registers of "suckers" who may be trusted to subscribe to almost any rotten project that is put before them with sufficient attractiveness. A special study of the methods by which these trash dealers acquire their thousands of millions of purchasing power would make an entertaining and instructive section in our encyclopædia. There must be thousands of them and their families, rich but, one imagines, a little indisposed to "talk shop." If you are prosperous enough you may have sat beside some of these browsers upon the investment public last night at the theatre, or travelled very pleasantly with them in the train de luxe. Our sons and theirs may become great friends at college.

Hopefulness is a recurrent epidemic in America, and, as we shall show by a study of the 1929–31 boom and slump, it is possible to have a whole community overcredulous of values and prospects. While the mood lasts, everyone seems to be making a fortune, and purchasing power is used to stimulate industry to the utmost. The prices of securities rise—and bull speculators (buying for the rise) push them up still further. As we have pointed out already, this works almost exactly in the fashion of currency inflation. When a phase of disillusionment arrives, buying ceases, and workers are thrown out of employment by the hundred thousand and bereft suddenly of purchasing power. Their slackened demands further intensify the slump, and so the slump continues.

From these phenomena our encyclopædia of human activities would pass to the various methods of operating upon the exchanges. It would tell of bull and bear operations; of the way in which bear sellers of stock may be "caught short" and "skinned" and so forth. The fine question of how far a man may sell what he has still to buy cuts down to the roots of incessantly recurring financial situations. The foundation of considerable fortunes has been this dubious expedient of anticipatory selling. Some able but practically impecunious salesman has induced a seller or sellers to quote a price to him, or has secured an option to buy, and has then found either a purchaser at an advanced price or a bank willing to support him until he could put his proposition to the investing public. Such intervention, with a great range of variations, constitutes indeed a conspicuous part of contemporary "business." If the adventurer can keep his credit throughout the transaction he "gets away with it"; he becomes one of the New Rich, a Power in the financial world. If bankers become unfriendly, if they decide to call in his credit and he can find no friend to help him, he must unload what he carries, at disastrous prices. He is "skinned." There may be bankruptcy and suicide or effacement. Here too we find a system of inexactitudes and uncertainties that do not merely admit, but invite and provoke, the speculator and the cornerer, the seeker of wealth without work, the bold and brilliant parasite upon the sap and vitality of the economic body.

All the matter sketched out in this section will be so familiar in a fragmentary form to most readers that few will find it anything but natural and inevitable. It is, however, if we measure it either by former social conditions or by utopian standards, a very extraordinary state of affairs in which we are living. The modern world of work and wealth, with all its industries, cultivations and distributive organizations, has been evolved *pari passu* with the development of the investing and speculative public, as the desert camel was evolved with its hump, or the elk with its antlers; it has been all part of one evolution; and no one has ever yet speculated what changes of the environment, great or small, legal, political or "natural," might have developed the creature in a different form, with a smaller hump or a lighter burthen of bone and horn. Nor have we any measure yet of the extent to which, or the rapidity with which, this hump may not under changing conditions be reabsorbed into active nerve and muscle. Or whether the whole organism is so tied to its hump that it will perish rather than lose it.

§ 10. *Is the Investing Public More than a Transitory Excrescence upon Economic Development?*

A very natural enquiry arises here. This is the question: how far uncertainty is inevitable in economic processes, and how far a more scientific handling of the quantitative, distributive machinery of mankind may not eliminate most of the weaknesses of the system that renders this fungoid growth of large speculative fortunes, and the still larger growth of speculative fortune-seekers, possible.

After all, we have to remember that the present state of affairs is recent and novel. Our world has not always suffered from the superposition of a great creditor class "living on debt." Our civilization has been floundering about with experiments in partnership and joint-stock enterprise for only a brief century or so; limited liability dates from 1855. We have been realizing as yet only the crude possibilities of invention and science, and it is altogether too much to assume that the first adaptations of the old property-money-credit ideas to these new powers and their new range were anything but provisional.

Behind the adventurer, the speculator, comes that scavenger of adventurers, the statistician. He ends adventure and cleans up the mess. The method of trial and error will surely give place to analysis and the plan. Enterprise will then cease to look for support to the casual investments of ill-informed amateurs. Industrial projects will become more and more exactly calculable. *Pari passu,* the company promoter, will be brought under more effective control; there will be a more critical supervision of his acts and a readier jail for his delinquencies. And the "investing public" will gradually be helped and persuaded to avoid spasmodic investment, and its search for a safe return turned into new and less adventurous directions.

Perhaps it would not be a bad thing for the world's work if this swarm of amateur distributors of purchasing power were restricted altogether from direct investment in business enterprises. At present there is a very remarkable development of "investment trusts" which spread their clients' little capital over hundreds of securities. The small investors merge in one big investor, the Trust. This development, this pooling of small investors, may go on. It may be found possible, in the future, to confine individual investments absolutely to semi-public properly audited Investment Trusts.

At present the Investment Trust is in its early phase, and in making this suggestion we conceive of the Investment Trust evolving and rising to its possibilities and opportunities. It may seem an extreme suggestion that the freedom of the individual to throw away his savings should disappear. But it is at any rate worth while investigating how much of that 1,000,000,000 dollars per year, of Mr. Mellon's estimate, might not be embanked back by some such restriction from sustaining a horde of rogues and unproductive financiers, and directed into economically fruitful channels.

Dividends would, of course, fall as this was achieved, but the capital would be secured. High dividends are the reward of risk taking. High dividends are due to the uncertain profit of an exploitation, and where the exploitable value of anything can be calculated with certainty there is no need to pay unduly for the use of money. The enterprise can obtain its capital at the minimum rate of interest that is ruling at the time. In a perfectly safe, perfectly calculated social and economic system, the various directive and employing boards would do their book-keeping with one another, and individuals would neither hoard nor lend their money; they would have no reason for doing so, and they would spend it. Consumption would equal production. Money then would have simplified out to its ultimate use as a check, giving purchasing power against a claim established or services rendered. Stock and share and all such interest-bearing quasi-money would have disappeared. A world economic control, evolved perhaps from the banking organization of to-day, would apportion purchasing power to the various world services, to experiment and research generally, and to bodies engaged in localized development. The existence of this investing public of ours would then become unnecessary. It would become an interesting past phase in the economic history of mankind.

There is nothing fantastic, and so far there is nothing Utopian, in these intimations of a world that will be largely released from the inconvenience of uncertain and fluctuating values. It is no imaginary "No-where," it is here on this planet that such an exact and unencumbered economic life is possible. Possible, in the sense that no absolute obstacle can be defined. People will be disposed to object that such completeness of organization is "incredible"; they will rake up the old vague rubbish about "human nature" being in the way, meaning ignorance and bad habits of mind; and they will attempt to substitute a confused vision of romantic incoherence, a distorted and foreshortened continuation of the past two thousand years of human life, for this plain prospect of a world with an adequate system of bookkeeping. But the movement of the last hundred years is all in favour of the statistician.

It is no good saying nowadays that "man has always been so and so and always will be so and so," meaning that he must remain forever an ignorant, limited, pitiful, disastrous fudger. Human biology knows better. We can trace our escape from dreams to ordered thinking. We can trace the spreading subjugation of life to ordered thinking. We see all about us the struggle of the human mind to escape from Realist delusions to

Nominalist methods of thought. Science spreads into all human concerns, changing spirit as well as method. What science, with quite small resources, has done in a century or so in establishing a progressive order throughout a large part of the field of possible knowledge, all mankind in a century or so can do for all the affairs of earth.

This prospect of a proper accounting in human affairs presupposes certain things. It presupposes a vigorous extension of scientific enquiry into the field of business, the development of a powerful body of scientific workers in the social and economic field that such institutions as the London School of Economics foreshadow; it presupposes also an increasing honesty and broadening intellectual interest among business men, and a wide diffusion of the ideas and conclusions this gathering cloud of work and thought will produce. Further, it presupposes a correlated change in the business atmosphere where greed, rapacity, cunning and secrecy have played so freely hitherto. Every step that is won in ousting that tradition of hidden methods which is dear to the mediæval peasant and trader, and that other tradition of rapacious adventurousness which comes to us from the mediæval brigand-noble, in favour of the modernized intellectual tradition—the mentality, that is to say, of the self-devoted coöperative *educated* man—brings this prospect of a clear accounting in economic life nearer.

At bottom the dire economic stresses of our present world, its injustices and its vileness and the tantalizing uncertainty and irregularity of its progress, are due to the defective or pernicious education, mental and moral, of the vast majority of energetic people. It is not that they are bad at heart, but that they do not think sanely; they have no idea of what is needed, no image of conduct necessary to run the great machine of the world properly.

In Chapter VII, §11, we discussed grades of organization and their relation to the moral and intellectual level of the community. To that idea we now recur.

As that scientific devoted persona, which must be the guiding object of modern education, is built up in more and more of the minds of active men and women, the face of our world will change. Things that are now impossible will become practicable, easy and "natural," and this dark and wasteful tangle, muddle, and obscurity in the counting house of humanity, this vast leakage of purchasing power, will no longer hamper the development of our racial life.

There is no essential reason why a world-controlled monetary system should not be continually draining away indebtedness by a steady gentle continual monetary inflation; why it should be necessary to upset the balance of production and consumption by "savings"; why the creation of new productive capital should be possible only by the evocation of debts. The economic mechanism of mankind groans under a vast burthen of debt now, by habit and custom, and not by necessity. Debt prevents plenty, it is a restraint and a subtraction, but debt is no more essential to economic life than was human sacrifice to the building of a bridge or the raising of wheat. Yet for ages men were unable to disentangle the one thing from the other.

§ 11. *The Elements of the World Depression of 1929–31**

We have now put before the reader, in an orderly fashion, the main facts about the payment for, and financing of, human work at the present time. We have pointed out some manifest looseness in the machinery and some conspicuous weaknesses, defects and dangers. And lest this should seem to be mere carping at human and tolerable characteristics of the monetary and financial organization of mankind, let us now make a compact study of the machinery in a phase of bad results. This is a simple, unbiassed report upon the way in which the machinery has been grinding and stalling in the past three years. It recapitulates very conveniently many points already raised in this chapter.

Never has the industrial and commercial intelligence of man-

---

*The elements of the story are to be found also in the Report presented to the Assembly of the League of Nations, 1931, *The Course and Phases of the World Economic Depression*.

kind shown to such complete disadvantage as at the present time. Sum up the position calmly, and it remains unbelievable. All over the world are exceptionally large stores of the raw materials required for every type of manufacture. There are in the industrial areas more factories, better equipped and organized, than ever before. The knowledge and skill of workers, directors and inventors have never been greater. Our treasure of gold has reached the highest known level and is being steadily increased. The banks are choked with money which they cannot put to profitable use. There is no war to speak of anywhere—communications are safer and speedier than at any time in history. Wholesale prices are back at pre-war level, and millions of decent, industrious people would be glad to obtain more food, clothing, houses, furniture and other goods which it would be well for them to have. And yet the League of Nations has just announced that twenty millions of the world's workers are unemployed; machinery stands idle everywhere; whole towns are stagnant and desolate; the manufacturer, unless he has already sold his product, hesitates to manufacture, and those who can afford it hesitate to buy. In the United States alone—a country which is drawing tribute from all the principal nations of the earth—eight or nine million men and women, who were in productive employment a couple of years ago, can find no work and many of them are in urgent need of food. At the same time and within a few hours by train from these starving people, enormous stocks of wheat are held up unsaleable in the elevators, while something like £1,000,000,000 worth of gold is lying in cellars, most of it performing no work at all, beneath the banks of Washington and New York. We have arrived at a deadlock.

Let us recall the main features of the story to the reader. We can begin most dramatically on October 24, 1929.

No one doubts that the proximate cause of this economic desolation is the crash which occurred on the New York Stock Exchange on that date. It is possible to put a finger on the calendar and show the exact moment on which the avalanche began to slide. But that was only the proximate cause—the

Americans have speculated before without involving the whole world in industrial disaster. Their smash, bad as it was, merely widened and accelerated a downward movement which had been going on already for three years, worsening the position in countries which were already depressed, and laying open to the infection those, like France and the United States, which had so far escaped it. It is that downward movement which must first be examined if the great slump is to teach us anything worth learning.

One dominating influence can be indicated in a sentence: in an industrial world both trade and money seek to be international in their movements, while at the same time we have no international machinery, either physical or mental, for dealing with them. If our vast contemporary populations living in completely different climates are to be fed and maintained in reasonable comfort, goods must move to and fro across the earth, and gold, or its equivalent, must to some extent go out to meet them. And at present mankind is trying not so much to encourage or guide this process as to interfere with it from a dozen independent and hostile centres and on as many different principles. Some of the ideas now shaping economic policy date from the Middle Ages, some from the Roman Empire, some from before the dawn of history. Nowhere do we see conceptions based upon actual world conditions in operation. There is no authority to-day trying to promote world trade, or empowered to enquire whether the maximum quantity of desirable goods is produced and consumed. There are only partial governments trying to secure for their own nationals some opportunity, not of enjoying goods, but of making a profit which might otherwise have fallen to the citizens of a different country, whether or not this adds to, or subtracts from, the volume of their trade as a whole, or even contributes to the real comfort and welfare of the nationals concerned.

This state of affairs shows no tendency towards improvement —on the contrary it seems probable that there is less harmony to-day than there has been since the rise of modern industry. Before the war the financial side of international trade was in practice, as we have pointed out, controlled very largely from London, and the difficulties of the post-war period have been greatly increased because that no longer happens. It may be possible to produce all the goods the world needs and to distribute them in a rational manner while London, Paris, New York, Berlin, Calcutta and Shanghai are all in their greater or lesser degree empowered to take their own line, issue their orders that money is to be made scarce here or to accumulate there, that goods are to be refused admittance at one frontier or heavily taxed at another. But an examination of the policies and actions which led to our present stagnation does not encourage one to think so. If we are to avoid a recurrence of this slump, and if these separate powers are to be retained, they will have to be used in a very different way. The tragedy of the years 1929–31, in the last analysis, must be traced to suspicion and ignorance, to a flat refusal to use the accumulated knowledge of economic science, or to understand that even a nation cannot ruin its customers without suffering itself.

To illustrate this contention in detail would be a very complicated business and would take far more space than can be given it here. But it should be possible to make the main features clear and to indicate their importance and their interrelations. They will be found in the first instance to be rooted in economic nationalism. Whether such disasters can be avoided in the future while that background remains unaltered is for the reader to judge.

Economic nationalism, we say, is at the root of this, the greatest slump the world has ever known. But we do not mean that it is the only operating cause. Were all the world one, we should still have to face the distresses created by an ever-increasing efficiency in production, whereby output increases while employment and the general purchasing power under our present system of distribution diminish. But that problem, as we shall see later, would be altogether less formidable if the world were economically unified.

Plainly a chief cause of the trade depression which preceded the great slump was scarce and dear money. When the crash came there had been in the majority of countries and for several years a dearth of money for ordinary buying and the purposes of trade. Money is an artificial thing; its amount can be artificially increased or lessened, and it is as a result of monetary policies that consumers have been short of power to buy, while producers have been unable to afford the money they wanted either to reëquip their existing businesses or to establish new ones. To rebuild the world after the war, cheap money in adequate quantity was vital. And yet almost every step taken anywhere to influence its supply has been taken in the direction —and with the result—of making it dear and scarce. Each central banking authority has had its reasons for this—they have not restricted the supply for the sake of restriction—but the result has been that up to the day of the New York crash interest rates remained at a high level. The price of loans frightened off ordinary trade borrowers. And at the same time national incomes, instead of being increased to allow for the increases which have taken place in populations, have either been prevented from growing fast enough or have been actually contracted.

As Mr. J. M. Keynes has pointed out* there have been two main sources of pressure on the supply of money and credit. The first has been the financial distress of governments, aggravated in some cases by reparations payments. Unable to balance their budgets, states have been compelled to borrow, no matter what rate of interest they might be charged. If the money-lenders have made a good thing of it, the blame for that must go to the politicians. The other main cause is almost certainly the return to the gold standard on the part of Great Britain and the other important industrial countries. For one thing this meant that huge sums in gold had to be removed from active use in order that they might be stored away as cover to currencies—a policy which has brought about a wholly unnecessary scarcity of gold. By 1928 nearly two thirds of the world's monetary gold—almost £1,250,000,000—had already been locked away to perform a function which can better

*A Treatise on Money, Vol. 2, pp. 378 et seq.

be filled by interest-bearing securities. Secondly, the various currency acts passed during the period of return have imposed upon central banks the statutory duty of protecting most of this gold, and thus forced them to check every sort of movement which might have led to the metal leaving the country. In England, where the Currency Act is elastic, the Bank of England refused steadily to make use of this elasticity and part with gold. The blame for the consequences which have flowed from this can hardly be escaped by Great Britain, for she, with her dominant financial prestige, not only took the lead in returning to gold, but urged and encouraged other nations to follow her example.

In a little book, *Stabilization,* by E. M. H. Lloyd, published in 1923, the reader will find how clearly the evils of deflation were foreseen at that time, and how plainly the British and American authorities were warned by such experts as Maynard Keynes, McKenna and Professor Cassel of the mischief they were doing the world. To these warnings, the British bankers, speaking in the person of Sir Felix Schuster, replied:

"Countries which had departed from their pre-war gold standard must aim at deflating their currencies gradually so as to inflict the least injury, but with one object in view, a return as soon as possible to the pre-war gold standard. That would be the policy of the Bankers of the United Kingdom, and until that object was attained he thought they must adhere to a policy of gradual deflation—certainly in this country."

Looking back now, it is evident that the history of the decline began with this return. Before the gold standard could be restored, it was necessary for her financial authorities to raise English money rates and check supply in order to force the pound up to a pre-war parity with the American dollar, and so the Bank of England found itself committed to a régime of dear money and restricted credit, a régime which has led straight to the present débâcle. Owing to the extent of the British Empire and to the position of London as the centre of international finance, money rates and conditions in London still govern those prevailing in lesser centres, and the dominant factor making for world-wide depression has been the policy pursued in London. In 1925 the Bank of England's discount rate was put up first to 4½ per cent and then to 5 per cent, and these steps were accompanied by a serious contraction in credit.

Choosing a different aspect of the same facts, we may say that the pound was forced up in terms of other currencies and of goods, so that prices fell. British exports were reduced by £9,000,000 in nine months and the national output fell by £100,000,000 a year. Britain was unable to import so much or to pay so highly for what she did import, and there followed a depression in Germany, the United States and the British Dominions. France escaped by taking the opposite course— allowing the franc to fall in value and thus stimulating her exports and throwing the burden onto her rentiers and fixed salary-earners.

From then onward the economic vitality of Britain declined, and the diminished purchasing power of this great consumer of raw materials acted as a steady downward drag on world prices. The English bank rate may be taken as the mercury which registers monetary conditions, and until the present slump made money unusable it never fell below 4½ per cent, while at times it rose to 6½ per cent. As a corollary, during all this time credit was restricted whenever a demand for it arose. A progressive strangulation of business was inevitable under the conditions thus created.

The fundamental idea of the gold standard is that in certain financial centres, and particularly London, there shall be a free gold market, and the essential feature of that arrangement is that anyone who wishes to do so may buy gold from the central bank at a fixed price. The Banking and Currency Act of 1928 left the Bank of England provided with a very narrow margin of exportable gold, and there has been continual pressure upon that margin. The provision in the Act which allows the bank to relieve this position it refused to use. The position was that since the bank could not refuse to sell it was forced to prevent its customers from wanting to buy. This it is able to do, but only by the roundabout method of so decreasing the amount of money in the pockets of the public that everybody was obliged to buy less of everything.

There are three main reasons why individual purchasers require gold for export, and all of them in turn, during the period under review, exercised pressure upon the London rates. In the first place gold may be wanted to pay for imports. Where, as in the case of Great Britain, imports of commodities normally exceed commodity exports by large amounts, there is always a possibility that gold may have to be sent abroad to pay for imported goods. Other countries deal with this difficulty by duties which discourage their people from importing, but the central bank of a free trade country is fully exposed to the hazards of demand. And since it cannot prevent people from buying imports in particular, it must take the course of checking confidence and diminishing credit, and so discourage them from buying not only imports but anything at all.

A second and possibly a much more important influence during these years, is the traditional disposition of English investors to send their money abroad. Before the war Great Britain, in receipt of immense revenues from foreign investments, was virtually obliged to keep on relending the interest abroad, in order that other countries might continue to purchase her goods. Since the war the amounts coming in have been smaller, and they have been set off in part by a larger adverse balance of imports, yet the country has continued to lend abroad in excess of its real power to do so. Custom plays a considerable part in these arrangements, and the machinery for foreign lending in London is planned on a large scale, and, so to speak, draws in its own supplies. Borrowers are accustomed to come to London, and London is accustomed to lend. From a world point of view that function should now be shared by Paris and New York, the money centres of the two other great creditor countries. But the French fared so badly over their pre-war Russian investments and the Americans show such a preference for investing in their own industries, that large though the loans from the United States have been in particular years, neither of these countries has in fact played the part which international trade now demands of it. Even had the French wished to invest they would have met with legal difficulties for France, in her inveterate nationalism, taxes both issues of foreign loans and dividends received from them by as much in some cases as 25 per cent. As for the private investor in England, his motive was the reverse of his American brother's; he wanted to get his money out of the depressed industries of his own country. The worse conditions became at home, the more reasonable it seemed to him that he should seek his profit abroad. Political fears have accentuated this tendency, and it has been further increased by the discovery on the part of wealthy citizens that there are ways of placing money abroad which enable them to escape income tax and surtax.

These were influences which affected long-term investments. Another cause of the drain on the British gold supply was the movement about the world of what is called short-term money—funds which are lent for days, weeks or months on money markets and stock exchanges. Money of this sort is very mobile; it follows high rates of interest from one great financial centre to another, and there is always a danger that when it comes in paper it may be taken away again in gold. To prevent those persons who are accustomed to lend money in this way from dislocating monetary conditions, money rates in the various centres have to be kept in step, and the country which is in need of cheap money must forego it whenever a leading foreign central bank thinks well to raise its rates. Thus as long as countries consider it necessary to maintain large reserves in gold while selling gold freely at a fixed price, the mobility of this form of capital is a continual reason for keeping money dear, and again and again during the period with which we are dealing it had this effect.

Further, both these factors combined to aggravate a third —that storing away of money in central banks to which reference has already been made. Both France and America in one way and another were receiving more gold than they could use. During 1930 alone they added to their already swollen reserves more than twice the annual output of the mines. France, as we have already noted, held over £500,000,000 in 1931, and the United States nearly £1,000,000,000. As against this the whole British Empire possessed only £250,000,000, of which something like £150,000,000 was held in the Bank of England. And since these two great hoards had been accumulated faster than new gold had been produced, all other countries were in constant fear of losing their own reserves, and Britain especially tried continually to tempt money to London or to keep it there by the offer of exceptional rates.

All these modes of human behaviour, the buying of what in the circumstances were too many foreign goods, the desire to invest abroad, the wish—expressed through central banks but reflecting a profound instinct in peoples—to amass as much gold as possible and part with as little, helped to make the British system unworkable except at a monstrous cost to its industry. Taken by themselves alone they would have formed an adequate explanation of bad trade and unemployment. No country could have flourished under the monetary conditions which have been considered here. But in all their badness they were aggravated by another influence, that of the high tariff walls erected by both France and the United States. It is argued on behalf of the gold standard that if gold flows into a country, goods will flow in after it and bring the gold back again. That is how things ought to work. Under a system of free trade, if France and America had used their gold either directly to increase the money in circulation, or as a basis for fresh credit, or both, demand would have increased, prices would have risen, and goods would have been sent from all over the world to take advantage of the higher prices. In this way prosperity would have spread from the centres where trade was brisk to other producing countries. Purchasing power would have risen there in response to the intelligent exercise of purchasing power by these creditor countries. But by means of higher and higher tariffs foreign goods were in fact shut out from these two prosperous areas, so that nations buying from them, unable to pay their debts in goods, found themselves obliged to remit

yet more gold to markets already gorged with it. Great
Britain especially, unwilling to prevent her own nationals from
buying from France and America, suffered by being refused
a market for her own merchandise. From a world point of view
the countries which should have admitted goods freely were
the most determined to shut them out, and the nation which
could perhaps least afford to do so—having regard to its
monetary system—bought too much from abroad.

To these main factors of the world's distresses—dear money
during a period when cheap money was most urgently required,
faulty working of the international loan machinery and mal-
adjustment of tariffs—other causes of adversity must unfortunately be added. The war-debt arrangements increased the
flow of gold to the United States, which did not need it, from
Europe, which needed it very badly indeed. The position of
Russia, with her depreciated currency and inadequate foreign
credit, was another source of weakness. She had ceased to be a
customer on an adequate scale, and in order to buy even the
equipment vital to the success of her Five Year Plan, she was
forced to be a constructive seller, throwing wheat, furs and timber into the market for what they would fetch, and dislocating
the trade of the countries which took advantage of her necessity.

Lastly, all over the world a series of plentiful harvests occurred, and agricultural countries made unprecedented efforts to
recover prosperity by increasing and improving their production.
Had world trade been good, these additions to real wealth would
have been absorbed and added to human well-being, but coming
at a time when prices were already being forced down by monetary influences—when less and less money was available for
buying—they caused the prices of raw materials to fall yet further and increased the distress they would otherwise have alle-
viated.

These are the fundamental causes which had been operating
to prepare ruin in the midst of potential plenty. The last touches
were added to the picture by greed, folly and mismanagement.
In 1926 one effort was made to stop the decline. When the
Federal Reserve Board of the United States found that Great

Britain's return to the gold standard was preventing the sale of American harvests and producing a depression, it took the wise step of releasing money and keeping its rates of interest low. This enabled trade to recover, and a period of prosperity in America ensued. It even led to a certain amount of gold being withdrawn from New York in order to take advantage of the high money rates in Europe. Had this been followed by a lowering of tariffs so that some of the fresh money could have gone abroad in payment for goods, prosperity might have spread across the Atlantic and the balance been restored. There was a potential world recovery in the 1926 situation. So much sanity was still too much to expect from the current American ideology. Moreover, the spectacle of European indigence side by side with American plenty led the American investing public to tip the scales still further by decreasing their purchases of foreign loans and using their money at home. And so we come to the American boom of 1928, when it still seemed to the ordinary man in America that his favoured continent was to be exempted from the malaise of the rest of the world and that an era of abundance opened before him. Everyone was to buy hopefully. Prosperity was assured.

The prices of stocks soon answered to this feeling, and as they rose the gambling instinct of that great adventurous people awoke; the plentiful bank credit which had been created in order to help agriculture, was lent to provide money for speculation, and there followed one of the worst Stock Exchange booms in history. America went through a phase of violent inflation— not currency inflation but inflation of security values. A man's bank balance remained the same but the negotiable securities, which formed his next line, mounted to astonishing levels. America passed into this phase of inflation by security values, while the world at large was in a process of steady currency and credit deflation. Prices of commodities did not rise in America, but they did not fall as they were doing elsewhere. But ,an immense rise in production and profit was *anticipated*. There was consequently a fantastic exaggeration of the value of all but fixed-interest-bearing securities. There was a boom in hope.

People became giddy with this rise. You bought, you sold again; you got out with your profit as the rise went on. You were sorry you had not stayed in—just a little longer. So you went back to it. Attention focussed on the Stock Exchange. People did not spend their profits at once; they reinvested. No such expansion of trade occurred to justify the mounting prices of industrial shares. Nothing real was responding to all this hopefulness.

All America rang with a new gospel, the gospel of wealth by consumption. It seemed possible to evoke prosperity through a mere imaginative effort. "Every day, in every way," said the American investor, following the Coué formula, "we grow richer and richer."

By the middle of 1928 the Federal Reserve Board began to feel alarm. It had already been fiercely attacked in the Hearst papers for its policy in allowing gold to leave the country, and it now decided, as Mr. R. G. Hawtrey has put it, "to stop speculation by stopping prosperity." During 1928 the rediscount rate was raised by steps from 3½ per cent to 5 per cent, securities were sold by the banks in the open market, and other action was taken to reduce the supply of money. Trade began to suffer at once, but nobody was paying any attention to trade. The upward gamble continued. The results were that the rates for call money in New York rose to extraordinary heights—in March, 1929, they touched 20 per cent.

It takes time to stop a gambling fever; people will pay whatever they are asked to pay for loans so long as they imagine that they can make a profit with the borrowed money, and money was, of course, rushed in large amounts from Europe to earn this preposterous interest, in spite of the fact that European banks had raised their own rates to check such adventures. In August the New York Federal Reserve rate was put up to 6 per cent, in September the London rate went to 6½ per cent. These figures foreshadowed a crash, and doubtless operators of sufficient intelligence recognized this and got out of things.

On October 24th the crash which we have made the starting date of the world slump came, and on the 31st of that month the bank rates began to go down. But instead of attempting to offset the inevitable wave of depression by a decided policy of cheap and plentiful money, the Bank of England brought its rate down slowly and reluctantly and did nothing whatever to expand credit. This was probably due to nervousness engendered by the behaviour of the French, who were characteristically engaged in turning everything they could lay hands on into gold or notes and hoarding it away. A currency shortage in France could only be avoided by the issue of notes to replace those hoarded, and the Banque de France, under its charter, is obliged to cover in gold every such fresh issue whether its gold stock is already too great or not. In any case it was May, 1930, before the London rate fell to 3 per cent, and by that time the effect of widespread losses, combined with that of the Hatry scandals (a forgery of securities on a large scale), had conspired to establish an atmosphere of dismay and hopelessness.

§ 12. *The Suspension of the Gold Standard by Great Britain in 1931 and the Situation thus Created*

During the year that followed nothing was done to relieve the gathering stresses. Wholesale prices fell almost week by week; gold continued to flow into France and the United States to be sterilized by their central banks. Economists were at one in pointing out that this could not continue without dislocating the finance of the whole world, but as the debtor countries did not wish to default, only the two great world creditors could take any steps to arrest the process, and neither in France nor America was public opinion thought to be ready for a change in policy.

Attempts were made here and there by producers to hold up this or that particular commodity in order to check the fall, but the knowledge that accumulated stocks were overhanging the market if not actually on it served only to depress the price still further. Moreover, it was known that Russia was enormously increasing her acreage of cotton and wheat and everything else that she could grow. Most of these projects to restrict sales ended in disaster, and by the summer of 1931 producers were planning actually to destroy crops, throw them into the sea, burn them or hoe them in. The problem of wheat prices was considered so pressing that a series of international conferences was held to devise some means of getting rid of the stored-up American wheat and checking new production, but all these conferences failed. The interests of Russia and the older producing countries were completely antagonistic, and there was no supernational authority to force an agreement, no representative even of the world interests which should have been paramount. Those were left to the consciences of the delegates. By the summer of 1931 Brazil and the United States were actually bartering wheat for coffee because of the difficulty of monetary payments.

The complete failure of concerted international action, left each country faced with its own problems. There were two solutions of the riddle conceivable: either to make a resolute attempt to check the fall in prices by spending money on some programme of development, or else so to cut costs that production would become profitable once more at the lower level of prices. The first involved State action, for private enterprise cannot in the nature of things be expected to incur heavy expenditure without even a reasonable expectation of paying its way, much less of profit. And State action meant either additional borrowing or further taxation—at a time when people were already crushed by taxation. Moreover any single nation which adopted this course while its competitors were taking the alternative path of cutting costs, placed itself at a disadvantage in the world market, while to cut costs itself seemed to offer some hope of undercutting its competitors, even though such a course meant sending down world prices still further and depressing its own standard of living.

It was to the competitive expedient that the continental nations turned. Wages fell everywhere—sometimes by as much as 30 per cent. This drove prices lower and increased both the burden of the external debt and the proportion of wealth automatically received by the *rentier* classes. In Italy the Dictatorship was able to ease the adjustment by enacting—and securing—that retail prices should fall *pari passu* with a 10 per cent drop in wages. In other countries this was not done and the poor were left to manage as best they could. In Great Britain alone wages did not fall, because they were buttressed by her system of unemployment insurance (the dole). But unemployment increased as her export trades found themselves less and less able to hold their own in the world market, owing to their disproportionate bills for wages. And though Great Britain's exports fell, her imports rose in amount—a fact masked by the continual fall in prices—because her masses still had purchasing power because of the dole.

In February, 1931, Mr. Snowden, her Labour Chancellor, warned the country that it could no longer hope to maintain the existing level of public expenditure, and an "Economy Committee" (the May Committee, named after its chairman, Sir George May) was set up inspired by the idea of economizing in every possible direction.

By June, Austria was unable to bear the gathering strain of the situation any longer, and banking failures occurred there which dragged some important German banks down with them. Germany since the war has been obliged to carry on her economic life by means of loans, and in particular she has been forced to borrow the money for her reparations payments.* According to the Midland Bank Review for June–July 1931 her debts by the end of 1930 amounted to nearly £400,000,000 on long-term and £300,000,000 on short-term account. The American crash abruptly dried up the chief source of these loans, and as they ceased and the true situation became clearer to the mass of the German people, a political party, the Nazis or Hitlerites, came into being, pledged to repudiate reparations payments. At the General Elections in September, 1930, the Nazis gained enough votes to weaken the confidence of foreign investors. Loans except for very short periods really did become very difficult to obtain, a new "flight from the mark" began, and the Ger-

*A brilliant analysis of the German position and the position of debtor countries generally under our existing financial system will be found in Chapter IX of the Macmillan Report—Report of Committee on Finance and Industry. Command Paper 3897, 1931.

man government was forced to confess that it could no longer maintain its foreign payments.

At this point the United States, whose citizens held over half the German loans, came forward with a constructive offer in the interests of German solvency. President Hoover, acting on the advice of the leading American bankers, announced that if all the other creditor countries would agree to follow her example America would for a year excuse her debtors from the payment of their war debts. It is said that he had intended, had this offer been accepted immediately, to make the improved situation so created, the occasion for an attempt to release money from the United States hoard and so send up commodity prices.

Great Britain accepted, so did all the other creditors of Germany, with the vitally important exception of France. France, alas! has still to disentangle finance from foreign policy. She held out, on the grounds that Germany's position was due to her own extravagance, that she was still finding enough money to build ships of war and that France owed it to herself not to give up her just rights. It is unnecessary to recount here the hasty meetings, the goings to and fro, the haggling, the marvellous diplomacies which followed. An arrangement was finally patched up, but not before Germany had had to close her banks while she set up machinery to ration imports and prevent the export of currency and gold. Under this arrangement she was relieved for the moment from repayment of her foreign debts, and it was immediately clear that this must have serious effects in England. The City of London found itself with £70,000,000 locked up in Germany, much of which had unfortunately been borrowed on short-term account from France. At a time when every economist was explaining the imperative need for the richer countries to lend freely to the poorer, it is perhaps unfair to blame the City for carrying on business in this way, but use was certainly made of the fact to carry on anti-British propaganda in France, and the heavy French deposits in London began to be withdrawn in gold. We have pointed out already that these short-term French deposits have been a grave nuisance to world finance throughout the whole post-war period. Whenever the English bank rate went up they flowed to London; whenever it fell, the bank was under the threat that if the short-term lenders chose to withdraw, London would be pulled off the sacred gold standard. So long as London was obsessed by the gold standard it became possible to provoke a rise in the bank rate by withdrawing a due amount of short-term money, thus enhancing the interest on what remained. For a certain type of big operator abroad this had an irresistible appeal. But now the end of this process seemed to be in sight and the successful operators began to take away their gold and their gains for good.

The outward movement began on July 13, 1931, and proceeded so fast, that to protect its gold the distressed Bank of England arranged credits of £50,000,000 in Paris and New York. And at this most inopportune moment the May Economy Committee which had been appointed in the spring presented its report. This document informed an already uneasy Europe that there would be a British budgetary deficit in the current financial year of £70,000,000 and a further deficit of £120,000,000 in 1932–33, and proposed to meet these deficits by drastic retrenchment on education, housing and the salaries of all State employees, whatever the nature of their contracts, and by reducing the amount of unemployment benefit. Military preparations were left practically unchallenged by this mischievous report, nor was any suggestion made for scaling-off from the *rentier* the advantages which had accrued to him through the fall in prices.

The report was seized upon in the usual way by persons and parties opposed to the government, regardless—or perhaps not altogether regardless—of the effect their propaganda must have upon opinion abroad. For party ends the Labour government was denounced as insanely spendthrift. These denunciations lost nothing by translation in the continental press. The foreign panic intensified and the drain of gold increased—one alarmist article in a leading London journal is said to have been directly responsible for the withdrawal of £11½ millions in one day—and by the middle of August the £50,000,000 credits were exhausted. The Bank of England informed the government that it must raise further credits and that these were obtainable to the amount of £80,000,000, but only under certain conditions. These conditions, as laid down by the New York bankers, were firstly that the budget must be balanced, and secondly that a cut must be made in the rate of unemployment insurance benefit. Such conditions may seem peculiar, coming as they did to one of the greatest "sovereign" countries in the world from a group of private bankers, more particularly when it is borne in mind that Washington displayed no intention of balancing its own budget, though faced with a very much larger deficit. But Great Britain had apparently always made it a condition of loans that the state receiving them should balance its budget and the Americans obviously had this precedent in mind.

The Labour Cabinet agreed to balance the budget but could not agree to reductions in the rate of unemployment benefit. It resigned, and at the personal request of the King a "National" Government was formed on August 25, 1931, composed of the two opposition parties, the Conservatives and the Liberals, plus the Labour Prime Minister, his Chancellor and a dozen of their followers. It proceeded without delay to carry out its pledges—that is, to reduce the national income, pile fresh burdens upon industry, check consumption and thrust prices down still further. The *rentier,* like everyone else, was to submit to a 10 per cent increase in his income- and sur-tax, but he was not specifically taxed as a *rentier,* nor was any attempt made to relieve the burden of internal debt, lest he should take his money out of the country if this were done.

The British public under the guidance of its press and politicians, rallied to this programme. An heroic struggle to save the gold standard was staged, a struggle which lasted exactly twenty-six days. The British people had come through a previous crisis, the war, by going without, in order to provide goods and money for the army and munitions, and it was apparently prepared to accept the suggestion that it was right to tackle this new problem of a world impoverished in the middle of unconsumed wealth, in precisely the same manner. The Labour party adopted this view as well as the other parties—and quarrelled merely over the details of its application. There was much enthusiasm for economy in the correspondence columns of the *Times*. The King made an exemplary reduction of his civil list by £50,000, and many people sent voluntary offerings to the Treasury.

But the run on gold, though checked for a day or two, increased again. Britain was still paying—heroically—and there was a scramble for its final outpour of gold. Holland and Switzerland were now drawing on London as well as the United States and France. Both the Federal Reserve Bank and the Banque de France did what they could, now that it was too late, to staunch the flow. The Americans left their funds in London and the French stated that they would follow the American example. By September 20th the Bank of England had lost £200,000,000 in ten weeks, and gold was still going at the rate of over £10,000,000 a day. Then it was that the Bank advised the government that England must go off the gold standard, which it had been constituted to defend. Still in the heroic manner, the British National Government turned round to the new direction.

At this point there began to be a general feeling that it would be as well to call the leading nations together and hold a conference on the gold situation. When this was put to the Chancellor of the Exchequer he explained that tentatives in that direction had already been made but that "certain nations" had refused to participate. Apparently that was the limit of effort for himself and his colleagues.

As this book goes to press the pound is, it seems, being left to find its natural level relative to other currencies. An offer by the French of a loan of Fr. 4,000,000,000 to "peg" the exchange has been refused. There seems no reason why the pound should sink very far; for the steps taken to prevent British nationals from exporting their money seem to suffice, and by the time that the embargo is removed it may be hoped that exports will have been stimulated and imports checked and the balance of trade restored. Unemployment should fall, some of the deposits lying in the banks should be made available for industry and Great Britain enabled to compete again upon equal terms with her competitors. But while that may alleviate the situation for the British it is no solution of the general world problem. Great Britain going off the gold standard is an excellent thing, but a permanent benefit only if it leads on to saner methods of regulating consumption throughout the world. Of itself it will not end the world depression. On the contrary though it will help the producers in those countries which like Sweden, Norway and Denmark have decided to link their currencies not to gold but to sterling, it will cause an actual fall in prices in countries where this is not done. Unless the gross amount of purchasing power in the entire world is increased, the getting of a larger share by Great Britain and her associates, will only mean that some other populations will have less. In spite of the suspension of war-debt payments—payments which it now seems clear will never be resumed—France and America still remain great absorbers of gold, and are still apparently unable to use their swelling hoards even to mitigate the deepening distresses of their own peoples. The poor nations are still growing poorer, becoming less and less eligible as borrowers as the need to redistribute money grows more and more urgent. They are sinking deeper into discontent, until it only needs a demonstrable rise in the Russian standard of living to make communism a vivid issue in half the cities of Europe. An immense amount of misery is being produced during these slow blunderings towards adjustment—if indeed they are towards adjustment—and it is still an open question whether the world conferences needed for the restoration of the ebbing economic life of mankind, can now be assembled and made effective, before the intolerable vexations and sufferings of the generality produce a world-wide series of social catastrophes. What Mr. W. Wylie King has called a "Grand Audit" of the world's affairs is an unavoidable preliminary to world action, and such an audit would take time. Yet concerted devaluation of money by America, Britain and France with a stringent repression of speculation and (as we shall show later) a vigorous policy of public employment, may still give the existing order of things a new lease of life.